THE MIND AND ART OF
JONATHAN SWIFT

THE MIND AND ART

of

JONATHAN SWIFT

BY

RICARDO QUINTANA

OXFORD UNIVERSITY PRESS

LONDON   *NEW YORK*

1953

First published in 1936
Reprinted with additional Notes and Bibliography in 1953

PRINTED IN GREAT BRITAIN BY
BUTLER AND TANNER LTD., FROME AND LONDON

TO
MY MOTHER

PREFACE

WHEN the great dean of St. Patrick's died in 1745 he had already ceased to be understood by the eighteenth century. Disregarded he could not be; his satires, misinterpreted, vexed the more, and his imperious personality took on an almost diabolic aspect. No English writer of corresponding stature has been repudiated so persistently and so fiercely by immediately succeeding generations, but this repudiation had in it a strange kind of excitement which was instantly communicated, so that one did not avoid the fearful object but sought it out in fascinated horror. Thus later critics—the Jeffreys and the Thackerays—found a Swift mythos ready to hand, waiting only for forcible restatement and amplification. Thackeray exercised all his superb art to paint a portrait which would revolt honest men for all time. Yet who, having looked at the portrait, could refrain from going straight to *A Modest Proposal?* Through the immoderate hostility of his critics Swift's fame was assured: he was a man of unclean mind, a blackguard, a faithless priest, but he was represented as having been all of these things to an unnatural degree; to find him, one must perforce venture into a region where the commonly understood laws of moral being no longer hold control. He was irresistibly evil.

To correct this absurdly false view was the object of the great Victorian biographers of Swift,—Forster, Craik, Stephen, and Collins,—who in varying degrees perceived the true genius and character of the great satirist. They worked manfully to break down the traditional prejudices in order that truth might at last show forth, but so well had the Jeffreys and the Thackerays done their work that the English-speaking world continued to regard Swift as a monstrous genius. In fact, it is only within the past twenty years or so that everyday readers have shown anything like a marked tendency to accord to the dean the sane consideration which other great English writers have always enjoyed.

In the meantime—let us say since the appearance of Forster's unfinished biography in 1875—Swift's life has been minutely explored, his works and correspondence have been edited anew, and all the resources of modern scholarship have been brought to bear upon the significant aspects of his work. Furthermore, the age in which Swift lived has been brought steadily closer to us by the manifold researches of political, ideological, and literary historians. There is no longer any excuse for the savage misinterpretation of Swift, nor for the failure to judge him in the light of the period into which he was born. The purpose of the present study is to present what is now known of Swift the writer, and by projecting him against the background of his age to estimate the qualities of his mind and art.

A word concerning the canon of Swift, regarding which I do not presume to have the assured sense of one who has made long and detailed studies in this field. So far as I know, I have included among Swift's works no piece which recent scholarship has called in question—not at least without due warning—but vexing problems of authorship I have not gone into.

My friend and colleague, Professor Ruth C. Wallerstein, of the University of Wisconsin, read my book in manuscript form, and for her encouragement and acute criticism I am deeply grateful. Professor Louis I. Bredvold of the University of Michigan and Professor George Sherburn of the University of Chicago I must thank for information which they gave in answer to several queries on my part. I am also indebted to Professors Paul Knaplund and John Gaus of the University of Wisconsin and Dr. Mark Schorer of Dartmouth College for their helpful suggestions. And lastly, I should add that the research committee of the Graduate School of the University of Wisconsin, by granting me a half-year's leave of absence from academic duties, made it possible for me to complete this study much sooner than I could otherwise have done.

RICARDO QUINTANA

Madison, Wisconsin
June 1936

PREFACE TO 1953 REPRINT

DURING the sixteen-year period lying between the first publication of this study of mine and its reappearance in the present reprinted form a good deal has taken place in the way of editorial, scholarly, and critical work concerned with Swift. Sir Harold Williams's editions of the *Poems* and the *Journal to Stella* have appeared, Mr. Herbert Davis has thus far issued eight of the fourteen projected volumes in his Shakespeare Head edition of the *Prose Works*, and there have been several full-length treatments of the Dean and at least ten important monographs. These, along with certain other items of recent scholarship, are given in the Additional Bibliography to be found on pp. 378-80, which, it should be noted, is highly selective — a complete listing of every item of Swift scholarship which has appeared since 1936 has not only been out of the question but is probably unnecessary in view of all the bibliographical aids within easy reach of most students to-day.

For *The Mind and Art of Jonathan Swift* I cannot claim the hundred beauties though I willingly yield the hundred faults that Goldsmith once spoke of. The re-reading of one's own work after a long interval does not afford pleasure. There is much that I still hope to say about Swift and his contemporaries and the entire age, but with a somewhat different tone and emphasis in keeping with certain shifts in perception. Since revision, however extensive, I should find impossible to undertake, it seems better to let my sixteen-year-old statement stand in its own right. The notes appearing immediately hereafter will serve to bring into accord with the presentations of Sir Harold Williams and Mr. Herbert Davis those of my original statements which, bearing on the canon of Swift's prose and verse, stand in need of correction or modification. Of the many running observations — not *all* of them adverse — which, if time permitted, I should be only too glad to make upon my own work, I allow myself the bare minimum. What I have said about Swift's 'æsthetic principles' (pp. 62 ff.) certainly calls for some rephrasing ; as it stands it is not so much misleading as obscure, chiefly by reason of my failure

to distinguish sharply enough between various concepts carried
by that troublesomely protean word *imagination*.   The precise
place which Swift occupies as a writer whose rhetorical-æsthetic
principles reflect both the accident of time and his own
insistent and fully contrived choices has not yet, so far as I
know, been satisfactorily defined by anyone who has undertaken the task, but there is not a little in recent criticism that
suggests increasing awareness of this central problem.   A quite
different matter concerns the relation of the *Memoirs of
Martinus Scriblerus* to *Gulliver's Travels* (pp. 206-8, 289-90),
which has been discussed in great detail and with admirable
clarity by Mr. Charles Kerby-Miller in his edition of the
Memoirs of Scriblerus (New Haven, Conn., 1950).   In this
connexion attention should also be called to the interesting
discussion of the entire Scriblerus group provided by Mrs.
Edna L. Steeves in her recent edition of the *Art of Sinking in
Poetry* (New York, 1952).   Finally, the study by the late
Arthur Case, *Four Essays on Gulliver's Travels* (Princeton,
1945), challenges some of the theories concerning the composition of *Gulliver's Travels* which were standard when I summed
them up (pp. 289-91), and goes on in the striking third essay —
'Personal and Political Satire in *Gulliver's Travels*' — to set
forth a partially new and on the whole convincing interpretation of the political allegory embodied in the *Travels*.   Some
of his conclusions regarding textual matters have been questioned by Williams and Davis (see particularly the former's
discussion in *RES*, xxiii [1947], 367-69, and his monograph,
The Text of 'Gulliver's Travels', now announced for publication), and I think Case goes too far and falls headlong into
the so-called intentional fallacy in suggesting that Swift's
central purpose in the *Travels* was to devise a 'politico-
sociological treatise', but his book has made several notable
contributions to our understanding of the greatest of all the
Satiric *Utopias*.

R. Q.

Madison, Wisconsin
June 1952

NOTES BEARING ON THE CANON OF SWIFT'S PROSE AND VERSE

These notes are arranged in the order in which I make initial reference to the work in question. *The Poems of Jonathan Swift*, edited by Sir Harold Williams (3 vols. ; Oxford, 1937), is sometimes cited as *P*, sometimes as Williams. *The Prose Works of Jonathan Swift*, edited by Herbert Davis (Oxford ; by mid-1952 there have appeared, out of fourteen vols., vols. I, II, III, VI, VII, IX, X, XI), is variously cited as *W* and Davis.

p. 30, *Ode to King William on his Successes in Ireland* : Williams gives the text of this (*P*, pp. 11-13), but also gives another piece, *Ode to the King. On his Irish Expedition* (*P*, pp. 6-10), which he believes is really the poem Swift wrote.

p. 47, 152, 'Down come the lofty roofs, the cedar burns' : the piece in question, *On the Burning of Whitehall*, Williams regards as a questionable attribution (*P*, p. 1069).

p. 64, 65, 66, 234, 273-76, 283, *A Letter of Advice to a Young Poet* : the *Letter* was printed in 1721, but when it was written is not known ; and Davis, who can find no proof that Swift wrote it, removes it to an appendix in his edition (*W*, IX, xxvi-xxvii, 323-45).

p. 67, 130, 273, *A Letter to a Young Gentleman, lately enter'd into Holy Orders* : it was printed in 1720 (Davis, IX, xxii).

p. 107, 153, *The Problem* : this does not refer to Berkeley but to Henry Sidney, earl of Romney (Williams, p. 64).

pp. 123, 130, 145-46, 147, 186, *An Argument against Abolishing Christianity* : it was first published in the *Miscellanies*, 1711 (Davis, II, 277).

pp. 123, 129, 136-41, 186, *The Sentiments of a Church of England Man* : its first appearance was in the *Miscellanies*, 1711 (Davis, II, 275).

pp. 126, 129-30, 141, 143, 170, 349, *A Letter to a Member of Parliament, in Ireland, upon the choosing a New Speaker there* : according to Davis, it was probably written in 1710, though it is 'unlikely that it was published then, as no printed copy is known' (*W*, II, xxxii).

p. 130, *Sermons* : on the dating of the *Sermons*, see Davis, IX, 133 (discussion by Louis Landa).

p. 152, 155, *A Meditation upon a Broomstick* : Davis inclines to 1702 as the date of composition (*W*, I, xxxiii-xxxiv).

p. 158, *The History of Vanbrugh's House* : the date would seem to be 1706 (Williams, p. 86).

p. 166, *Squire Bickerstaff Detected* : Swift was not one of the authors (Davis, II, xiv).

p. 167, 214, *Tatler* : on the entire subject of Swift's contributions to the *Tatler*, see Davis, II, xxv-xxxv.

pp. 186-87, 214, 218, Harrison's *Tatler* : Davis admits only Nos. 5 (27 Jan. 1710) and 20 (6 March 1710) to the Swift canon, but shows that there is evidence of Swift's help in Nos. 1, 2, 8, and 28 (*W*, II, xxxv).

p. 187, 219, *A Town Eclogue* : given by Williams, who nevertheless regards Swift's part as a distinct possibility, under attributed poems (*P*, pp. 1087-89).

p. 203, *The Fable of the Widow and his Cat* : Williams gives the text hesitantly, though he feels the evidence for Swift's participation is strong (*P*, 151-54).

p. 233, *Ode to Archbishop King* : the proper title is *Part of the 9th Ode of the 4th Book of Horace, address'd to Doctor William King, late Lord Arch-Bishop of Dublin*.

p. 234, 283, *The Progress of Beauty* : the date is 1719 (Williams, p. 225).

p. 239, *Cadenus and Vanessa* : Williams finds no foundation for the story that in her will Vanessa left directions for the publication of this poem, nor does he attribute its appearance in print in 1726 to Marshall (*P*, p. 685).

p. 243, 284, *A Love Poem from a Physician to His Mistress* : Williams finds no clear evidence for Swift's authorship (*P*, p. 1152).

pp. 253-4, *The Present Miserable State of Ireland* : excluded from the canon by Davis ('The Canon of Swift' in *English Institute Annual, 1942*, pp. 119-36), and shown by Williams to have appeared as a Dublin half-sheet dated 1721 (*P*, 844).

p. 259, *The Speech of The P[rovo]st of T[rinit]y C[olle]ge to his Royall Highness George Prince of Wales* : Williams find the style unlike Swift's (*P*, p. 1099).

p. 265, *Ireland's Warning, Being an Excellent New Song, upon Woods's Base Half-pence* : Williams finds it 'difficult to credit Swift's authorship' (*P*, p. 1110).

p. 269, *An Excellent New Song upon the Late Grand-Jury* : the ascription to Swift is dubious (Williams, p. 1110).

p. 269, *Will. Wood's Petition to the People of Ireland, being an excellent New Song* : Williams regards this as a doubtful attribution (*P*, p. 1115).

p. 270, *On Wisdom's Defeat in a Learned Debate* : Williams finds a clear possibility that this may be Swift's, but prints under attributed poems (*P*, p. 1117-18).

p. 271, *The Duke's Answer* : the proper title is *His Grace's Answer to Jonathan*.

p. 271, *A Letter from D.S—t to D.S—y* : to be dated 1725 (Williams, p. 369).

p. 271, *On Rover* and *A Christmas Box for Namby Pamby* : whether Swift took any part in these is impossible to determine (Williams, p. 1125).

p. 276, *A Wicked Treasonable Libel* : though in Swift's ironic manner, Williams finds that its authority 'must remain in question' (*P*, pp. 1105-06).

pp. 282-83, *Phyllis, or the Progress of Love* : Williams gives under 1719 (*P*, p. 221).

p. 333, *A Pastoral Dialogue* : that is, *A Pastoral Dialogue Between Richmond-Lodge and Marble-Hill* (1727), to be distinguished from Swift's poem of 1729 entitled merely *A Pastoral Dialogue*. In my index (p. 396) the two are dealt with as though they were one and the same poem.

p. 334, *A Character of Sir Robert Walpole* : to be dated not 1727 but 1731 (Williams, pp. 539-40).

p. 341, *A Pastoral Dialogue* : to be dated 1729 ; and see note above for p. 333.

pp. 347-48, *Epistle to Mr. Gay* : the precise title is *To Mr. Gay on his being Steward to the Duke of Queensberry*.

p. 348, *An Excellent New Poem on the Bishops* : that is, *On the Irish Bishops*.

pp. 359-60, *Death and Daphne* : refers, not to Mrs. Pilkington, but to Lady Acheson (Williams, pp. 902-03).

ACKNOWLEDGEMENTS

1. Swift's Prose

All quotations from *A Tale of a Tub, The Battle of the Books,*
and *The Mechanical Operation of the Spirit* are from
A Tale of a Tub, etc., ed. A. C. Guthkelch and D. Nichol
Smith (Oxford : Oxford University Press, 1920).— By permission of the publishers.

The Journal to Stella is quoted from
Journal to Stella, newly deciphered and edited by J. K.
Moorhead (New York : E. P. Dutton & Co. ; London : J. M.
Dent & Sons, Ltd., [1925]. 'Everyman's Library').— By per-
mission of Messrs. E. P. Dutton & Co. and J. M. Dent &
Sons, Ltd.

Gulliver's Travels is quoted from
*Swift : Gulliver's Travels and Selected Writings in Prose and
Verse,* ed. John Hayward (New York : Random House ;
London : The Nonesuch Press, 1934).— By permission of
Random House and The Nonesuch Press.

The Drapier's Letters are quoted from
The Drapier's Letters to the People of Ireland, ed. Herbert
Davis (Oxford : Oxford University Press, 1935).— By per-
mission of the publishers.

All other prose is quoted from
The Prose Works of Jonathan Swift, ed. Temple Scott (12
vols. ; London : George Bell & Sons, Ltd., 1897-1908. 'Bohn's
Standard Library').— By arrangement with Messrs. George
Bell & Sons, Ltd.

2. Swift's Verse

Swift's verse is quoted from
The Poems of Jonathan Swift, ed. W. E. Browning (2 vols. ;
London : George Bell & Sons, Ltd., 1910. 'Bohn's Standard
Library').— By arrangement with Messrs. George Bell & Sons,
Ltd.

One piece — on the burning of Whitehall — six lines of which I
quote in my third chapter — is taken from
F. Elrington Ball, *Swift's Verse : An Essay* (London : John
Murray, 1929).

3. Swift's Correspondence

The correspondence between Swift and Vanessa is quoted from
Vanessa and Her Correspondence with Jonathan Swift, ed.

A. M. Freeman (London : Selwyn & Blount, Ltd., 1921).—
By permission of Mr. A. Martin Freeman.
Several letters from Swift to Ford — indicated in my notes — are
quoted from
> The Letters of Jonathan Swift to Charles Ford, ed. D. Nichol
> Smith (Oxford : Oxford University Press, 1935).— By per-
> mission of the publishers.
All other correspondence of Swift is quoted from
> The Correspondence of Jonathan Swift, ed. F. Elrington
> Ball (6 vols. ; London : G. Bell & Sons, Ltd., 1910-14).— By
> arrangement with Messrs. G. Bell & Sons, Ltd.

4. *Other Quotations*

In Book I, chap. i, footnote 6, the quotation from Lady Giffard's
Life of Sir Wm. Temple is from, and in Book I, chap. ii, quota-
tions from Lady Giffard's *The Character of Sir Wm. Temple*
are from
> The Early Essays and Romances of Sir William Temple, ed.
> G. C. Moore Smith (Oxford : Oxford University Press,
> 1930).— By permission of the publishers.
On p. 25 the two lines from the Duchess of Somerset's letter to
Lady Giffard are from
> Martha, Lady Giffard, Her Life and Correspondence, ed.
> Julia G. Longe (London : G. Allen & Sons, 1911).— By per-
> mission of Messrs. George Allen & Unwin, Ltd.
The Addresses of the Irish commons and lords, quoted in Book
IV, chap. ii, are from
> The Drapier's Letters, ed. Herbert Davis (Oxford : Oxford
> University Press, 1935).— By permission of the publishers.
I wish to thank all the publishers above named, and with them I
must include Mr. A. Martin Freeman, for granting me permis-
sion to use these materials.

R. Q.

CONTENTS

Book I

1667–1699

Book II

1699–1710

Book III

1710–1714

Book IV

1714–1726

Book V

Gulliver's Travels

Book VI

1727–1745

BOOK I
1667-1699

BIOGRAPHICAL SYNOPSIS
1667-1699

30 Nov. 1667 :	Born Dublin, a posthumous child, son of English parents who had settled in Ireland :

The Rev. Thomas Swift (1595-1658) : married———————Elizabeth Dryden : vicar of Goodrich, in Hereford-shire ; a stout resister of the roundheads during the Civil Wars. | probably a first cousin of the father of Dryden the poet.

Many children by this marriage, among them :

Jonathan Swift : married———————Abigail (H)Errick, born ca. 1640 ; to Ireland ca. of Leicestershire : 1661 ; admitted a solicitor in died 1710. Dublin 1666 ; appointed steward of the King's Inns there ; died April 1667.

Jane Swift :———————Jonathan Swift : born 1666. born 30 Nov. 1667, eight months after his father's death.

1673 — 1682 :	At Kilkenny School.
24 April 1682 :	Entered Trinity College, Dublin, as a pensioner.
Feb. 1686 :	Graduated B.A. *speciali gratiâ*.
Feb. 1686 — early 1689 :	In residence at Trinity College, studying for the master of arts degree, until the outbreak of the troubles in Ireland early in 1689.
Early 1689 :	To England, visiting his mother, who had previously returned to Leicester.
Spring of 1689:	Entered the household of Sir William Temple as a secretary ; by autumn Sir William Temple, Swift accompanying him, had re-established himself at Moor Park, Surrey.
Summer of 1690 :	Returned to Ireland.
Autumn of 1691 :	In England again, first at Leicester with his mother, then at Oxford with his cousin Thomas, and, before 1692, at Moor Park, again acting as secretary to Sir William and serving as such until 1694.
5 July 1692 :	Received the master of arts degree at Oxford — Swift took no or very perfunctory examinations, having all but qualified for the degree at Trinity College, Dublin, in 1689.
May 1694 :	Left Sir William Temple, returning shortly to Ireland.
5 Oct. 1694 :	Ordained a deacon in the established church.
13 Jan. 1695 :	Ordained a priest ; appointed to the prebend of Kilroot, and took up residence in the parish of Kilroot, a few miles north of Belfast.
May 1696 :	Left Kilroot, returning to Sir William Temple at Moor Park, resigning the prebend of Kilroot Jan. 1698.
27 Jan. 1699 :	Sir William Temple died, and Swift was left 'unprovided both of friend and living.'

CHAPTER I

FROM IRELAND TO MOOR PARK

1

EARLY in the year 1689 a young man, just twenty-one and unmistakably of English blood, was making a winter passage across the Irish Sea from Dublin to England. His dark hair and his very blue eyes were in striking contrast. One noticed the eyes particularly; they were 'quite azure as the heavens,' we are told, with a 'very uncommon archness' in them.[1] His features were large but firmly modelled. Humour, restrained to something like insolence, was expressed in the curve of the sensitive, almost pouting, lips.[2] His thoughts we can only guess, but it is safe to say that discouragement, impatience with present events, and an eagerness for the future awaiting him in England were all churning round in his turbulent mind.

Jonathan Swift was, in effect, fleeing from a land and a city at this moment unsafe for Englishmen. Whereas the Revolution of 1688 had in England been effected quickly, surely, and in the face of only the feeblest opposition, events in Ireland were taking quite another turn. When James II fled from London to be shortly superseded on the throne by William III and Mary, the English breathed a great sigh of relief and settled down to enjoy an order and security which James's presence had been rendering increasingly impossible during the previous four years. But in Ireland matters stood on a different footing. Here a comparatively small group of English settlers, their centre in Dublin, ruled by virtue of conquest and spoliation over a catholic people. Violently protestant, confirmed in the arrogant code necessary and inevitable under such conditions, their chief wealth in Irish land to which their titles were only as strong as protestant ascendancy in England, these Englishmen in Ireland did not underestimate the danger to their lives and property when the Irish rallied to James's banner. Swift

3

was but one of many who that winter crossed to England.

Of the life of this dark-haired, blue-eyed young man up to the moment of his departure from Dublin there is not a great deal to be said. He came of good English stock. Outstanding in the recent annals of the family was his grandfather, the Reverend Thomas Swift (1595-1658), vicar of Goodrich in Herefordshire, who endeared himself to his great descendant by his rugged resistance to the roundheads during the Civil Wars. Six of the Reverend Thomas Swift's ten sons had gone to Ireland early in the sixties to make their fortunes, one as a merchant, one as a barrister, the others as solicitors. Of these Godwin Swift, the barrister, had by good luck and perhaps by superior ability risen to eminent prosperity. His younger brother Jonathan died before establishing himself securely, leaving his wife, daughter, and unborn son to the care of his brothers.

Jonathan Swift the younger had not fared badly at the hands of his uncles. Godwin had sent him first to Kilkenny School, the Eton of Ireland, and then to Trinity College, Dublin, which he entered as a pensioner in 1682 and from which he was graduated B.A. *speciali gratiâ* early in 1686. Much has been made of this special dispensation under which his degree was granted, and Swift himself dwelt upon it morosely, writing in his autobiographical fragment (*ca.* 1727) that 'he was stopped of his degree for dulness and insufficiency' and at last 'hardly admitted in a manner, little to his credit, which is called . . . *speciali gratiâ.*' However, later investigations have shown beyond any doubt that his undergraduate record, if not a brilliant one, was by no means disgraceful and that the special dispensation implied nothing particularly discreditable.[3] With the intention of proceeding to the master's degree Swift stayed on at Trinity College for three more years. During this period his increasing restiveness under college discipline appears to have driven him to minor revolt; twice he was admonished for misconduct, but it should be added that his companions in disgrace were sons of eminently respectable families.[4] Swift did not stay to complete his candidate-master's course. For one thing, his uncle Godwin, on whose generosity he was dependent, was sinking rapidly into a sea of financial troubles. Then, at the close of 1688, the political storm burst over Ireland, and Trinity College, stronghold of English and protestant sentiment, was marked for attack. His student days thus unexpectedly terminated by family misfortune and political violence, he set out to try his fortune in England.

If at twenty-one Swift had little reason to regard himself as highly favoured of the gods, his life thus far had been scarred by no gross indignities. Those who had contributed to his support had seen to it that he enjoyed the best education that Ireland afforded. True, they may at the same time have withheld the sympathy which their nephew's proud spirit demanded, but one does not know. And it would be unfair to blame them for not providing what fate unkindly withheld—those early years of home life, deprived of which Swift was rendered uncomprehending and hard where another retains always some measure of understanding tenderness. At Trinity College—there is nothing to show whether as a student he gave any promise of future literary power—one seems to detect a growing bitterness. The uncertainty of the future, the dread of poverty and dependence undoubtedly contributed. But chiefly it arose from his intense aversion to the pedantic and narrowly scholastic atmosphere which in his time lay heavily about Trinity College, still insulated against the new world born of the Renaissance and established in the course of the seventeenth century. For years the new philosophy and the new science had been stirring at Oxford and Cambridge; Trinity College proceeded as of old, enforcing the study of the Greek and Latin classics, but placing chief emphasis upon the mastery of the scholastic philosophy.[5] Starved genius would take its revenge; the satiric impulse had already been implanted. It would be a grave error, however, to conclude that bitterness had gained ascendency over young Jonathan Swift. The humour that twisted at the lips belied that. His contempt was an energetic, life-breathing thing. And there was eagerness everywhere about him, for the world was to conquer.

2

For once luck was with him. Sir William Temple, the great whig diplomat and statesman, now retired, had at one time resided in Ireland and had known the Swifts there. Thanks to this acquaintance Swift gained an introduction and was offered by Sir William a position as secretary in his household. Early in 1689, after a visit to his mother in Leicester — she was a native of Leicestershire and had apparently returned there from Ireland a few years after her husband's death — Swift took up the post which he was to fill off and on for the next nine and a half years. That autumn the Temples moved back to their former residence at Moor Park, Surrey, from which it had seemed prudent to withdraw during the disturbances of the previous year, and the young secretary accompanied them.[6]

Swift's residence at Moor Park extended, with two interruptions, from 1689 to Temple's death in January 1699. Its importance it would be difficult to exaggerate. Here life really began for him, here he attained full intellectual and artistic maturity. Further, because Moor Park supplied precisely what Trinity College had lacked — an atmosphere of worldly culture and sophistication, a relationship between life and letters — it must be regarded as having to a certain degree affected the tone and character of his maturing genius.

The Moor Park residence, however, was not of a piece. It fell into three periods separated by two intervals during which Swift was again in Ireland. The background remained the same throughout, but as his powers developed, Swift's attitude towards it underwent such changes that the three periods are clearly distinguishable.

The first lasted a year and was terminated about May 1690 when he was advised to return to Ireland to regain his health. His illness, however trifling — 'a giddiness and coldness of stomach' caused, he believed, by a surfeit of fruit[7] — was in fact the first warning; some obscure structural defect in the semi-circular canals of the ears lay in wait, eventually to strike with full force and to produce torturing periods of giddiness, deafness, and emotional despondency which in his latter years extended their sway until there was little remission. Of Swift's first year at Temple's practically nothing is known. He was probably none too happy. The world he had been so eager to encounter was all about him here at Moor Park, but the position of a humble secretary was at its remotest edge. When he departed in the spring of 1690 for Ireland he was, one imagines, a sombre, lonely figure, discouraged, awkward, and still conscious of provincialisms of speech and manner.

The end of 1691 found him again at Moor Park and marks the beginning of the second period. His spirits were picking up. He began to move with assurance, no longer paralysed by awkwardness and diffidence. As Temple's aloofness thawed, Swift came to perceive in him not a cold and distant employer but a man admirable for many things : for a high sense of honour, for a wide knowledge of the world and of books, for distinction as a writer, above all for the cultivated and informed perceptions which set him apart alike from the pedantry of the schools and the vulgarity of the mob. It was Temple's presence which confirmed Swift in his hatred of scholasticism and all forms of intellectual aridity and established in his mind a hitherto vague ideal — that of taste, a possession of the cultivated few, to be defended against all the conspiring forces of malice and ignorance. Soon he was writing verse : the *Ode to the Hon. Sir William Temple,* the *Ode to the Athenian Society,* the *Ode to Doctor William Sancroft,* a translation of Virgil, and later two more pieces, *To Mr. Congreve* and *Occasioned by Sir William Temple's late Illness and Recovery.*[8] These verses — they can be called poetry only by courtesy — should not be dismissed lightly. Execrably bad in every literary sense, they have, nevertheless, a peculiar interest and significance by reason of the fact that they afford us our first glimpse into Swift's mind. When he wrote them he had not yet found his true medium, which was prose satire, but the enormous intellectual energy which marks the work of his maturity was already astir in these turgid stanzas. In May 1694 the second period closes. There was a quarrel or a misunderstanding between Swift and Sir William, whereupon Swift again returned to Ireland.

Some two years previously, Swift had mentioned in a letter that he had thoughts of entering the church, and in another letter (29 November 1692) he had announced that he was not to take orders till King William — who sometimes visited Temple and who, if an oft-repeated story is true, had condescended to converse with the young secretary — gave him a prebend. Such a mark of distinction was not forthcoming, but in Ireland Swift at length took the step which he had been debating. He was ordained a deacon on 25 October 1694, and on 13 January 1695 a priest. Fifteen days later he was appointed by the lord deputy, Lord Capell, to the prebend of Kilroot, in the north of Ireland, worth about £100 a year. How Swift passed his days at Kilroot one does not know. A particularly foul rumour, intended to account for his return to England, tells of gross misconduct at this period, but does not deserve notice. The sole record of unimpeachable authority is a letter which he wrote on 29 April 1696, just before his departure. It was addressed to a Miss Jane Waring, the daughter of the late archdeacon of Dromore, and contained a proposal of marriage. When Jane refused him or temporized — her reply has not been preserved — Swift was apparently in no way downcast. He accepted Temple's invitation to return to his old post, and once again crossed to England.

The third and final period at Moor Park began, and Swift entered upon two and a half years of the best work he was ever to do. He was experiencing complete freedom for the first time. He had taken holy orders and could always, if the worst came, be sure of a modest living, though he cherished the hope that Temple's influence would one day gain him preferment of some distinction. So secure did he feel that in January 1698 he resigned Kilroot in favour of his friend, the Reverend John Winder. Thanks to Jane Waring's coyness he had escaped matrimonial captivity. He slipped back into his familiar place at Moor Park with contentment — there was nothing like an Ulster parish to make one appreciate the complete civilization of an English country-house. And Temple had capitulated: both men of taste, they now recognized each other as equals. Happily, too, Swift had failed in his first attempt at poetry, and acceptance of defeat had relieved a tension; the humourless earnestness had vanished, adventurous paths appeared everywhere. He paused exultantly, insolently. Then he plunged into *The Battle of the Books* and *A Tale of a Tub*, the latter by common consent one of the greatest of all prose satires. In no later work did Swift surpass the artistic brilliance of this great piece, and while he had still to amplify his ideas in new fields, particularly in political theory, it can be said that hereafter nothing essentially new was added to his thought. His genius was fixed. Henceforth it was to be largely a matter of chance in what direction this genius found expression.

CHAPTER II

MOOR PARK AND SIR WILLIAM TEMPLE

1

CONCERNING Sir William Temple neither contemporary nor later estimates agree very closely. To his future brother-in-law he was one who considered neither religion nor honour but 'would take any engagement, serve in any employment, or do anything to advance himself.' Bishop Burnet hated him : an epicurean in principle and practice, who corrupted all who came near him. Macaulay found the key to his character to be a mean caution. Recently he has been described as a pompous gentleman who, failing at the political game, sought in retirement to restore his shattered ego. Born in 1628, he had been drawn into diplomatic affairs in 1665, when King Charles and Lord Arlington, then secretary of state, had sent him to the continent to negotiate a treaty with the bishop of Munster. Temple acquitted himself well, was created a baronet, and appointed resident at the vice-regal court at Brussels. In 1668 he achieved lasting fame for his display of diplomatic skill during the negotiations which led up to the Triple Alliance. Afterwards he proceeded to The Hague as English ambassador, but his career as a statesman, begun so brilliantly, went to pieces on the rocks of Stuart intrigue. The Triple Alliance fell before Charles's secret Treaty of Dover. Temple was recalled, and war broke out between England and the States General. In 1674, the war at an end, he again accepted the embassy at The Hague, where he and Lady Temple were received graciously by the prince of Orange, whose marriage in 1677 to Princess Mary was forwarded by Temple's offices. But despite his commanding position and the general confidence which he enjoyed both at home and on the continent, his powers for good were limited — how severely Temple knew only too well — by the sordid interests of the king and his councillors. In 1677 Charles summoned him home to London and urged on him

the office of secretary of state.   Temple refused the offer.
Again in 1679, at a time of crisis, he was recalled, again he
was urged to take office, and again he refused.   Shortly thereafter he withdrew to the country to cultivate his garden
and take up his writing.   From this retirement none of the
ensuing events of Charles's reign or James's could draw
him.   Not even the arrival of William and Mary, whose
trust he enjoyed and by whom he was urged to re-enter
public life, altered his resolution.

It is not surprising, in view of his career in the world, that
Temple should strike the historian as a bit contemptible.
Was he not over-cautious?   Was he not essentially selfish
in his steadfast refusal to place himself in any position likely
to entail danger?   These questions are perhaps partially
answered by reference to *The Character of Sir William
Temple*, written by his sister, Lady Giffard.   It is a vivid
portrait, the sharp, certain strokes revealing to the modern
eye a seventeenth-century gentleman of spotless character in
whom were mingled the graces of the Caroline period and
the wider interests which were gaining during the second
half of the century.   He was naturally, we are told, of
warm and quick passions, but over these he had complete
mastery.   Because he lost his temper in disputes, he avoided
them.   He loved exercise, music, pictures, sculpture, gardens, and conversation, in which he 'was easy and familiar
with all people, from the greatest Princes to the meanest
servant, to children whose imperfect language & natural &
innocent way of talking he was fond off . . .'   His great delight was in the happiness of those about him.   He was
ordinarily gay in humour, but he suffered periodic fits of depression—'of spleen and melancholy.'   These were brought
on sometimes by bad weather

but most from the cross & surpriseing turns in his business, &
cruel disapointments he met with soe often in (what nobody ever
had more at heart) the contributing to the honnour & service of
his country ; wch he thought himselfe two or three times so near
compassing he could not thinke with patience of what had hin-
dred it, nor of those that he thought had bin the occasion of it.[1]

The truth is that Temple was an anomalous figure in the court of Charles II. He was untouched by that indifference to everyday morality so general about Whitehall, and he carried his integrity into his political life. Intellectually, in his theory of government, he was equally at odds with most of the men then in power, for his mind had accepted naturally the principle, emergent in England from the conflicts of this century, that 'the ground, upon which all government stands, is the consent of the people, or the greatest or strongest part of them. . .' (*An Essay upon the Original and Nature of Government.*) For Europe peace, for England a harmonious government in which should be recognized this broad base of authority — these appear to be the ends he worked for. But everywhere he was checked. A man of tougher fibre might have fought back. Temple withdrew to the country. He did so, one suspects, not solely out of fear of danger or aversion from conflict or because he knew the pleasures waiting in library and garden; his political sense must have borne in on him the futility of resisting the eddies of the moment, while his insight into the temper of the age may well have convinced him that it was only a matter of time before the new spirit of reasonableness would sweep away all opposition. But his mind sometimes moved back over scenes at The Hague and in the council room at London, the delights of country air and fresh gardens were forgotten, and a black mood seized him as he considered the two or three times he had been so near compassing his ends and those who had ruined his plans.

2

IT is doubtful whether Temple, now declining in years, brooding much upon the past and otherwise absorbed in the composition of his *Essays,* ever became genuinely interested in the mind of his young secretary. Certainly he gave no indication, early or late, that he recognized the presence of genius. It would be wrong, however, to imagine that Temple interposed between himself and Swift an impenetrable barrier of frigid pride. It was rather that he was old and often weary and separated from humble youth by a distinction of position which humble youth doubtless exaggerated. He was not unkind; merely, in this instance, unaware. That he steadfastly disregarded Swift the human being is disproved by his repeated acts of kindness, and it is evident that with the passing years he came to lean increasingly upon his secretary for literary assistance. On Swift's side there was respect, even admiration. Of their intellectual relations this may be said : if Temple played no active part in forwarding Swift's development, the latter was never denied access to a mind of some originality, stored with experience, subtilized by an exquisite taste. The influence thus indirectly brought to bear is not, save once or twice, of a clear and traceable kind. Together, Moor Park and Temple were an enveloping atmosphere.

Moor Park with its gardens, its library, astir sometimes with excitement during a visit of the king, and always alive with the news of books and the turn of events in London, was in itself the liberal education which Oxford or Cambridge might have given Swift but not the Trinity College of his time. Here at Moor Park, where the interests of the world all seemed to converge, it was only natural that the pedantry from which he had recently escaped should seem doubly futile and mean; and while the revelation of the good life was still a new and inciting experience Swift turned to fashion — clumsily, indeed — satiric bolts wherewith to blast this pedantry. Later, when familiarity and ease had conquered Moor Park and made of it a normal scene for civilized existence, he attacked again — but with a difference. Pedantry had ceased to be a specific malady; it had become the spirit of malevolent nonsense that everywhere dethroned reason; the elect few, the men of taste, were alone immune from the virus. The depth and extent of the satire had increased immeasurably; the tone had lightened. It was not only that Swift had contrived a new satiric medium; he had achieved a new attitude. *A Tale of a Tub* is the philosophy of taste, of urbanity, of civilization, expounded with breath-taking originality by a conjured spirit refined to easy insolence by the bland air of Moor Park.

A further point concerning Swift's liberal education at Moor Park should not be lost sight of, as repeatedly it has been. Swift's character had many facets. On different occasions he exhibited the moralist, the humorist, the satirist. He was also, in a special sense, the polished gentleman, which we are apt to forget. Gossip and anecdote show us the dean pinching poor Lætitia Pilkington black and blue ; *Gulliver's Travels* reveals to the sentimentalist an intolerable misanthrope. But the Swift of daily intercourse in London and Dublin, the Swift from whom one received letters of raillery and again of condolence, was a man of the world, unfailing in social perceptions, never at a loss for the right act or the right word. Nor is this air of refinement wholly lacking from his writings. Oftenest it appears in his letters, several of which it is not exaggeration to say are marked by a restrained preciosity. Swift was no boor when he came to Moor Park, and if he had never come he would have found another way of making himself a gentleman of the world. But for all that Moor Park left its sign upon him.

Finally, there was Temple's library and the leisure to use it. Swift read ten hours a day, we are told, and we can well believe it, for the wealth of allusion in *A Tale of a Tub* is not its least astonishing feature. But, as has often been pointed out, Swift was never overwhelmed by his reading. Of all his works *Gulliver's Travels* has been studied with greatest persistency, yet the 'sources' which have here been disclosed are chiefly of interest for showing with what transforming originality Swift handled his borrowings. He was never a more voracious reader than during his third residence at Moor Park, and at the same time never so charged with intellectual energy and independence. A full list of the books which he read at this period would be interesting ; whether it would cast much new light upon these first exultant years of awakened genius is doubtful. A great deal must have been deposited in his mind as well as in his commonplace-books, but it was his originality and energy, sustained and heightened, to be sure, in the library, that chiefly counted.

3

BUT to come to Temple himself.   To begin with, he gave
a living form to the spirit of Moor Park.   He was, *par excellence*, the man of taste,[2] widely travelled, widely read, dis-
criminating.   In him literature and life were seen, probably for the first time on the part of Swift, in a close and
natural relationship.   Aside, however, from an influence of
such a general nature, are any imprints of the older upon
the younger mind apparent?   Very few.

It would seem that Temple's direct influence if it is anywhere in evidence should be found in *The Battle of the
Looks* and *A Tale of a Tub*, the latter indirectly and the
first immediately concerned with the defence of an essay
by Temple round which a storm of controversy had gathered.   Of the details, more in due course.   It is sufficient
at this point to observe that Swift's defence, though it follows the episodes of the controversy with some care and is
in effect a satiric sermon on taste, in behalf of which it appeared to him that Temple had made war, brings to the
affair a spirit and a turn of thought equally foreign to the
elder writer.   It seems, in fact, that Temple regretted such
a defence.   Furthermore, Swift disregarded the theoretical
grounds on which Temple had based his argument; either
they seemed an encumbrance or, more likely, they had not
struck home.   In defending his patron Swift used a weapon
all his own; it was forged at Moor Park but the pattern
was not Temple's.

If as an ally of Temple, Swift was incapable of sinking
his originality, it is not surprising that in other matters he
was never profoundly touched by Temple's thought.   This
is a subject, however, which must be pursued a bit further.
It was once customary to dismiss the *Essays* of Temple with
a polite word or two of praise for their style and an assurance
that in content they are nugatory.   Today they are more
highly regarded.   Temple was not a profoundly acute
thinker, but it is now apparent that he was closely in touch
with his times.   His observations are not devoid of origi-

nality; their real interest lies, however, in their reflection of
the intellectual problems of the seventeenth century. Since
the older commentaries on Swift antedate this recognition of
Temple's importance as a writer, the treatment which they
afford of the possible influence of essayist upon satirist is
more casual than our present knowledge will allow.

Temple was both a moralist and a historian. As a moralist he studied the problems confronting individual man, and
the chief of these centred in the conflicting claims of reason
and the passions. As historian he dealt with the laws of
civilization : was the course of history one of progress, of
degeneration, or of recurrent periods of efflorescence and
decay? The moral problems he treated most directly in
his essay *Upon the Gardens of Epicurus* (*Miscellanea* II,
1690). In man, reason generates passion; hence arises a
conflict the solution of which is the problem of moral philosophy. Now, most men proceed in life by diverting rather
than conquering their passions; that is, they more or less
unwittingly harness their passions to everyday affairs, some
in accumulating wealth, a few exceptional ones in grasping
power. Wiser men, however, try 'to subdue, or at least to
temper their passions, and reduce their appetites to what
nature seems only to ask and to need.' Temple declares
for a mild epicureanism : instead of the complete denial of
the passions taught by the Stoics, he advocates the epicurean
control thereof, which produces a 'tranquillity of mind and
indolence of body.' Temple's conclusion in favour of a life
in which reason has its part but in which the passions are
recognized and given play is remarkable. Was it this
which Bishop Burnet had in mind when he called him an
epicurean in principle and practice, who corrupted all who
came near him? Temple, as has recently been shown, was
in fact a seventeenth-century *libertin*,[3] of all the English
essayists of the time the most thorough-going in his espousal
of an epicurean acceptance of the passions. The bishop was
shocked. That Temple appeared to the two succeeding centuries as merely the urbane gentleman is to say that his
libertinism was in practice but a high gusto for the good life
and a recognition of certain of its principles.

Such was the fascination which these ethical problems held for him, that in comparison with moral philosophy the sciences — natural philosophy he termed them — seemed trivial. The proper concern of man was man, not the external world of nature:

. . . as to that part of philosophy which is called natural, I know no end it can have, but that of either busying a man's brain to no purpose, or satisfying the vanity so natural to most men of distinguishing themselves . . .; and whether this distinction be made by wealth or power, or appearance of knowledge, which gains esteem and applause in the world, is all a case. More than this I know no advantage mankind has gained by the progress of natural philosophy, during so many ages it has had vogue in the world, excepting always, and very justly, what we owe to the mathematics. . .

To us who look back upon the seventeenth century as the period during which the foundations of the modern sciences were being laid with such magnificent energy Temple's dismissal of natural philosophy may seem naïve and a bit contemptible. It was not. Socrates had affirmed much the same belief as Temple's, and with the awakening of scientific interest at the Renaissance the claims of moral philosophy to an importance superior to any which the investigations of nature could show were again advanced, to be maintained by many throughout the seventeenth century. Temple's ignorance of scientific progress appears unforgiveable to us because in this respect we have all the advantage of historical perspective. As a matter of fact there were in Temple's day keen and widely informed minds still holding to the point of view which he expressed.

Temple's theory of civilization is to be found in the following essays: *Upon the Original and Nature of Government, Of Heroic Virtue, Of Poetry, Of Ancient and Modern Learning*, and *Some Thoughts upon Reviewing The Essay of Ancient and Modern Learning*. This theory is an extension into the historical field of a principle revealed through the ethical study of the individual: man is essentially the same at all times. There is, then, no great upward or downward curve of civilization, no law of progress or degeneration. But from this it does not follow that civilization rests

3

at the same level. Man is fundamentally the same always, but the conditions under which he lives are never uniform. Differences of climate seemed to Temple all-important, in that they produced in men 'by a different mixture of the humours, and operations of the air, a different and unequal course of imaginations and passions, and consequently of discourses and actions' (*Upon the Original and Nature of Government*). In accordance with such varying conditions, civilization rises and falls; its law is one of cyclic movement — 'science and arts have run their circles, and had their periods in the several parts of the world' (*Of Ancient and Modern Learning*). It may be asked whether culture is not, despite recurrent periods of declination, accumulative; whether, for instance, the moderns are not at an advantage because of their classical heritage, albeit enjoying conditions far less favourable to creative genius than the ancients of Greece and Rome. Temple answered that culture is not accumulative, that it is native genius which counts, that one's heritage is so much débris stifling originality. The pre-eminence of the ancients in poetry, oratory, painting, sculpture, and architecture is granted, wrote Temple, even by those maintaining the superiority of the modern age. It is in the sciences that modern advocates rest their case, but an examination of these sciences — as made by Temple — fails to reveal the boasted progress. Thus, to Temple the claims that the modern age excels past epochs seemed fallacious in that the cyclic law of history had been misconstrued into a law of inevitable progress. He could only look upon enthusiastic confidence in the present and the future as the blind pride of ignorance.

Temple's conclusions were in denial of the modern spirit. Paradoxically, they were arrived at in a manner wholly modern, for like Montaigne he rifled history for the facts wherewith to support his theories and drew freely upon modern books of travel for what we should call sociological information. In so far as modern knowledge could render it so, his mind was liberated from Western European prejudices. Only, the farther his vision was extended, the clearer did it appear that man had always been substantially the same;

progress was an illusion of the ill-informed. Equally in the spirit of the times did he speculate concerning theories of government and the origin of authority in the state. In European commonwealths, he maintained, there is a distinction between authority and ultimate power : authority resides in those who govern, but the seat of ultimate power remains in the governed. What is the source of this governing authority? Temple questioned the theory which held that authority had arisen at a remote time when in the interests of self-preservation men had surrendered to a central power their anarchic liberties. This contract theory, of wide appeal during this century, had been given consummate expression in England in the writings of Hobbes. It was the highly theoretical character of this concept which Temple challenged. Things do not happen this way. He sought an explanation which should accord with normal behaviour, and found it in the authority which comes naturally to preside within families : 'these seem to have been the natural and original governments of the world, springing from a tacit deference of many to the authority of one single person' (*An Essay upon the Original and Nature of Government*).

4

THE question now to be considered is the degree to which these leading ideas of Temple's found a place in Swift's thought — necessarily one must pass for the moment to the mature thought of Swift's last years at Moor Park and of succeeding periods. To a much greater degree than Temple, Swift was a moralist, and as such profoundly concerned with the war of the passions against reason. The ethical psychology, however, which represents man's life as a battleground swept with the never-ending conflict of reason and passion is not only as old as the human race but in the seventeenth century came, for many reasons, to play a major rôle in ethics and literature. It is the seventeenth century that speaks in Swift the moralist, not any single teacher. Least of all did Temple bend Swift's mind to the epicureanism of the *Essays,* the most original aspect of these moral observations. Swift's was an austere philosophy: the passions were repudiated; only through severe rational control did one rise above folly. There was no place here for Temple's epicurean 'tranquillity of mind and indolence of body.'

On the other hand, Temple's repudiation of natural philosophy may very well have established in Swift his lifelong prejudice against the sciences, though here again the pressure of the century must not be forgotten. Swift's steady hatred of science and scientists has often been a cause of wonder. It is to be explained on the same grounds as Temple's contempt. Both were moralists to whom the study of natural phenomena seemed of no importance beside the study of man.

The theory that man is the same at all times is implied throughout the thought of Swift, but it did not come from Temple. In Temple the theory is a specialized one applied to the history of civilization. Swift, in contrast, is merely affirming a general doctrine characteristic of the entire age. The difference as thus stated may seem nugatory, but a real difference there is, as will become apparent in later chapters. It may appear that Swift's advocacy of the ancients and his vicious satire of the moderns in *The Battle of the Books* should somehow be in relation to Temple's cyclic theory of civilization, but this is not the case. Swift was ever a confirmed anti-intellectualist: all speculation, that is, which attempts to reach beyond what is immediately obvious to enlightened, everyday reason is wasted energy. In *The Battle of the Books* Temple's honour is defended, but nothing is said of the laws of civilization. The doctrine of taste suffices the satirist : the cultivated man is everywhere at home among the best ; for him, ignorant pride no matter where or when it asserts itself will never pass for superiority.

Temple's wide reading in history and in travel literature and his observations on government and the source of authority were probably the channels through which the most telling influences passed into Swift. Swift's first political pamphlet (*Contests and Dissensions in Athens and Rome,* 1701) has a historical sweep and is full of parallels between ancient and modern times which not only suggest

long hours in the library at Moor Park but bear the stamp
of Temple's method. As for the books of travel to which
Swift was introduced, their influence was to appear much
later. Lastly, there is the matter of Temple's remarks on
government. How he maintained that the ultimate source
of power remains in the body of the governed and how he
objected to the contract theory as an explanation of the rise
of authority because this theory seems not to reckon with
the actualities of human behaviour we have already seen.
In respect of both points Swift's thought, as expressed in his
political writings, is at one with Temple's. Again, one must
not be led into the error of assuming an exclusive influence
from Temple. The spirit of the age is the most important
influence. But such was Temple's prestige as a statesman
and an observer of foreign governments that when he wrote
and spoke of things which lay within his special province
he must have done so with an authority recognized even by
so independent a person as Swift.

For this reason it is difficult to believe that the first principles of Swift's own philosophy of state and government
were not implanted by Temple. To such a belief the fact
that Temple was a great whig constitutes no bar. True,
Swift came to stand pre-eminent among the tories of his age,
but even as a tory he was steadfastly guided by fundamental
axioms identical with Temple's. Swift's political tenets, like
all his convictions, are marked by clarity because they are
grounded in the fewest possible axioms, by depth because
the implications are developed with superb analysis and
brought everywhere into relation with human experience :
the absolute, unlimited power in a state rests always in the
hands of the many ; the administration or executive power
should reside in as few hands as possible, but the exercise
thereof cannot abrogate the absolute power of a people ;
neither in origin nor in practice is government remotely
theoretical — it is a historically developing institution, an
aspect of human conduct, existent only through the laws
of human nature. This insistence upon experience and the
laws of human nature there revealed lies at the heart of
Swift's later toryism.[4] Now, it must be remembered that

pre-Revolution toryism and the toryism which was emerging
in the days of Queen Anne and was to be gradually trans-
muted into the conservatism of the mid-nineteenth century
were not one and the same thing. If the new toryism was
reinterpretation after the fact — the events of 1688 and the
consequences thereof rendered much that had lain behind
the old attitude untenable — there was still need of definition
and emphasis, and it was here that Swift employed the commanding authority of a style and voice unmatched in political journalism. It was he as much as anyone who endowed
the new toryism with the spirit by which it was to survive —
insistence on the actualities of experience and human nature.
There was fierce partisanship in his writings, but deeper than
the prejudice and hatred there will always be found a wisdom untouched by party spirit. Nor were Swift's theories
of man's relation to the state called forth by his sudden rise
in 1710 to a commanding position as chief of the tory
pamphleteers. In preceding years and while yet unmoved
by any deep party loyalties he had already formulated and
expressed them. There is every reason to believe that he
came by them through Temple.

The preceding paragraphs are not to be taken as a summary of Temple's influence. There is too little, and that
too vague, to be reckoned up in any precise sense, for Temple was not a dominating force in Swift's life — merely the
central figure at Moor Park. The degree to which he was
more than a negligible factor in Swift's development can
be perceived by one conversant with Swift's thought, but
even then the final impression is of two minds uncongenial
in temper, and when incited to the same end moving upon
it by different ways.

5

IF it appears that we have been travelling a long course only
to arrive at a dull conclusion, that is because the entire
significance of the conclusion is not at once clear. Temple's
Essays, it has already been said, are now regarded as more
than polite discourses; the observations on moral philosophy
and the history of civilization with which they are packed

give expression to much that was foremost in the minds of
the time.   It is consequently worth the effort to estimate
with some precision their effect on the secretary who edited
many of them.

But our conclusion embraces another and a more important point.   It was at Moor Park and in the presence of
Temple that Swift's genius took shape.   That the highly
idiosyncratic character of this genius and its satiric manner
of expression were in any way owing to rebellion against
an oppressive environment and an unsympathetic master is
flatly to be denied.   It was from Moor Park, as we have
seen, that Swift drew his liberal education.   If Temple
himself was of less importance than this atmosphere of an
English country-house, that is because Swift was not constituted to receive a deep imprint from any single mind.
At least during his third residence he was altogether at ease,
with perfect freedom of access to all about him, and growing
daily in the assurance of his powers.

The myth which represents the years from 1689 to 1699
as a period of servitude and suppressed rage we find in its
most highly embellished form in Thackeray:

His youth was bitter, as that of a great genius bound down by
ignoble ties, and powerless in a mean dependence. . . It was at
Shene and at Moor Park, with a salary of twenty pounds and a
dinner at the upper servants' table, that this great and lonely
Swift passed a ten years' apprenticeship — wore a cassock that was
only not a livery — bent down a knee as proud as Lucifer's to
supplicate my Lady's good graces, or run on his honour's er-
rands. . . When Sir William has the gout or scolds it must be
hard work at the second table; the Irish secretary owned as much
afterwards; and when he came to dinner, how he must have
lashed and growled and torn the household with his gibes and
scorn! [5]

This is the height of romantic misinterpretation.   Thackeray, however, was but repeating with stunning emphasis
what others had said before.   We can trace the myth back
through Macaulay to Samuel Richardson, who only seven
years after Swift's death retailed to Lady Bradshaigh what
he had heard from Sir William's nephew: '. . . Sir William never favoured [Swift] with his conversation, because

of his ill qualities, nor allowed him to sit down at table
with him.' ⁶ It must indeed be confessed that Swift himself
lent some semblance of truth to such gossip, for his references to Temple in *The Journal to Stella* are barbed with
asperity. What had really happened is this : in 1709, less
than a year before the *Journal* was begun, a bitter quarrel
between Swift and Temple's sister, Lady Giffard, had arisen
out of Swift's publication in that year of Sir William's
Memoirs, Part III, and from this time forth Swift's animosity
was extended ungenerously enough even unto the dead.
Previously he had expressed his true feelings ; to John Temple — Richardson's informer — he had written in 1706, 'I am
extremely obliged by your kind invitation to Moor Park,
which no time will make me forget and love less.'

The vitality which kept this myth so long alive was derived, however, not primarily from love of gossip but from
a misreading of Swift's character and genius, and not so
much the disproof of the gossip as a truer conception of
Swift has revealed the falsity of the romantic picture of
Swift's bitter servitude. There have been those incapable
by temperament of estimating sanely any satiric writer, not
to mention the author of *A Modest Proposal* and *Gulliver's
Travels,* and for such the assumption that Swift was from
his very youth contorted by hatred and rage has produced
its own evidence. The innumerable and specific abuses
against which Swift's satire is aimed, the exhaustless energy,
the sustaining art and rationale — these have gone unob-
served or have been perversely misconstrued. But as the
temper of our own day takes on something of the hardness
of the age which produced Swift — by hardness is not meant
inverted sentimentality — the injustice of such a view is seen
increasingly. The romantic misconception of Swift's life
at Temple's was the inevitable outgrowth of a misreading
of his character and art.

6

SOMETHING should be said, while we are still on the subject
of Moor Park, about several other residents there whose
lives crossed Swift's.

Two unusual women shared Temple's life, Lady Temple and his sister, Lady Giffard.   The latter, years before the time of which we write, had been left a widow thirteen days after her marriage, and from that day until her brother's death lived constantly in his family.   The esteem in which she held her brother shows clearly in her *Life of Sir William Temple* (1690) and the shorter *Character* supplementing it. It would appear that from the beginning Lady Giffard entertained no very high opinion of her brother's secretary, but the source of the ill feeling is not recorded.[7]   Whatever it was between them, Swift's publication of her brother's *Memoirs,* Part III, in 1709 — Temple left him, Swift wrote in the autobiographical fragment, 'the care, and trust, and advantage of publishing his posthumous writings' — gave her an opening.   She inserted in the newspapers an advertisement declaring the *Memoirs* an unfaithful copy — a public chastisement of Swift, the acknowledged editor.   There was little that Swift could do but remonstrate in a letter to her (10 November 1709).   How much more harm Lady Giffard had actually accomplished than appeared from her advertisement Swift perhaps never realized.   Lady Giffard numbered among her friends the duchess of Somerset, in whom she found an ally in this affair of the *Memoirs.*   Swift's act, the duchess wrote to Lady Giffard, is unpardonable 'and will confirm me in the opinion I had before of him that he is a man of noe principle either of honour or religion.'[8]   She uttered no advertisement against Swift.   But time placed in her hands a far more deadly weapon.

Lady Temple, so far as is known, entered not at all into Swift's life, but it would be ungracious to hurry by the author of the *Letters of Dorothy Osborne to William Temple* without a word.   Her marriage to Temple in 1654 had been preceded by a long romance begun in 1648 when they chanced to meet on the Isle of Wight.   The trials which beset them during the ensuing six years only served to unite them in spirit.   Temple was abroad much of the time, while Dorothy, caring for her invalid father at Chicksands in Bedfordshire, must hold siege against a succession of suitors urged upon her by her family, to whom Temple, then undistinguished by wealth or social position, was quite unacceptable. But by degrees the steadfastness of the lovers broke down all obstacles. Their marriage was finally arranged. At this moment Dorothy contracted smallpox, from which she soon recovered, but at the loss of her beauty. Soon afterwards they were married. It was during the two preceding years, when their situation seemed more hopeless than ever, that she wrote the letters for which she is chiefly remembered, letters notable not only for their charm but for their historical importance, for they are deeply revealing of the manners of a royalist family during the puritan regime and more especially of the character and outlook of a cultivated woman of the seventeenth century. Dorothy is a constant reader — of prose romances, of books of travel — but no bluestocking; she knows the world, she understands completely her family's objections to Temple, but she is never cynical; she is tender, but never in the remotest way sentimental. She had more charm, one feels, than Lady Giffard, but both women were unusually cultivated and both possessed that sense of realism which their age provided naturally. Together, they must have given much to the dominant tone at Moor Park.

And lastly there was Stella. Hester Johnson — it was only after he became dean that Swift conferred the immortal sobriquet — was a girl of eight when he first came to Moor Park. Her father was then dead, her mother some manner of domestic in the Temple establishment. What more natural than that the forlorn secretary should have turned for companionship, during his first months at Moor Park, to this girl with the raven-black hair? Later, when his diffidence had quite vanished and he was perfectly at ease with the entire household, he claimed her as his special property, taking her education in hand and directing what books she should read. By the time that Temple died there had already been established between Jonathan Swift and Hester Johnson an indissoluble bond of friendship and sympathetic understanding.

Whether Swift and Stella were ever married is a question which the critic, if he pleases, may dodge with a better grace than becomes the biographer. This is not to say that the present critic has arrived at no conclusion regarding this long-debated matter. He has, and he here gives it as his settled belief that Swift and Stella were never man and wife. It seems to him that the evidence adduced by those who have sought to prove that there was a marriage is quite unconvincing — this, it may be said, is more and more the conclusion of modern students of Swift. But it is the character of the man and the quality of his mind as revealed through his art which with the present writer weigh most heavily against a marriage. In the pages that follow no attempt will be made to assay the mass of conflicting evidence that has accumulated in the course of the long controversy, but the view that Swift's patterns of thought, emotion, and behaviour reduce the marriage theory to nonsense will be enforced as occasion arises.

At this point, in lieu of the discussion which has just been avoided, we may notice briefly the rumour which reflected upon Hester's birth : Mrs. Johnson, so it was whispered, was Temple's mistress ; Hester, Temple's natural child. It seems extremely doubtful whether any mystery would have settled over Stella's parentage had there not been the greater mystery of her relations with Swift. At least the only direct evidence of her illegitimacy which has to date been cited is, to say the least, unimpressive. It is first, that she was said to resemble Sir William strikingly ; and secondly, that Sir William willed her £1500 in Irish land, this being a much larger bequest than that to anyone else outside his recognized family.[9] How, then, did the story get abroad? The first clear reference to it that is known occurs in a letter written in July 1723 by Dr. Evans, bishop of Meath, to Archbishop Wake. On 2 June of that year Vanessa had died. Her passion for Swift was already the subject of conversation and there was much speculation about the exact circumstances of her death. Evans, then Swift's bitterest enemy in the church, lost no time in picking up every particle of the scandal and forwarding it to his correspondent. 'In April last,' he wrote, '[Vanessa] discovered the D. was married to Mrs Johnson (a nll. daughter of Sir. W. Temple, a very good woman) . . .'[10] But however it began, the rumour persisted and served well those of Swift's earlier biographers who had the wit to put two and two together. Granted that Stella was the natural daughter of Sir William, could anyone prove that Swift was not his natural son? In 1752 we find Lord Orrery in his *Remarks on the Life and Writings of Dr. Jonathan Swift* quite seriously denying illegitimacy in either case 'although the general voice of fame was willing to make them both the natural children of Sir William Temple.' But Delany, Swift's next biographer, so far from sharing Lord Orrery's opinion approached the matter vaguely in his *Observations* (1754), and is reported actually to have believed the most improbable of all the versions of this story,[11] according to which the real tragedy of the marriage of Swift and Stella was their discovery immediately after the ceremony that they were half-brother and sister. In 1757 an article in the *Gentleman's Magazine* signed C.M.P.G.N.S.T.N.S. gave specious authority to much the same version : all Stella's features resembled Sir William's so closely that their relationship was universally recognized and she was informed of it by Temple himself; years later in Ireland when the dean proposed marriage it became necessary 'for that person, who alone knew the secret history of the parties concerned' to reveal the entire truth; thus, separated by an everlasting barrier, they sublimated their affection to 'a true *Platonic* love, if not something yet more exalted. . .'

Such the evolution, such the astonishing convolutions of this bit of gossip, which is here offered as a fair sample of the kind of thing which grew up about Swift and the woman whose life, beginning with the days at Moor Park, was so closely associated with his.

CHAPTER III

THE EARLY VERSE

1

WHEN Swift returned to Moor Park late in 1691 it was with the ambition of rising to literary prominence as a poet. With such energy did he set to work that in February of the year following he could report to a friend 'that in these seven weeks I have been here, I have writ, and burnt and writ again, upon almost all manner of subjects, more perhaps than any man in England.' Of the products of this huge activity but five have been preserved: three Pindaric odes in the manner of Cowley and two compositions in heroic couplets.[1]

This early verse has seldom called forth from Swift's commentators other than derision. Nor will the casual reader, if he has the pertinacity to get through the five pieces, ever be tempted to return to them. Yet despite their badness they are so much a part of the record that the critic must deal with them fully.

Be it said in mitigation that as a matter of literary history Swift's three Pindaric odes are by no means the worst of their kind — Cowley had been imitated with results far more distressing. Furthermore, Swift's unsuccessful struggle with the Muse was not protracted to the length sometimes imagined, for its beginning can be dated at Swift's return to Moor Park in the last days of 1691 and it ended with the close of the year 1693. Even a genius may be allowed two years of floundering.

But here there is no intention of defending the early verses or of discovering therein unrecognized virtues. In a study of Swift's mind and art their function is clear: through them and through nothing else are we enabled to view the writer's mind before it attained that assurance displayed in every line of *A Tale of a Tub*; while on the score of art Swift's incapacity in these first efforts is commentary of remarkable significance on his later mastery.

The first verses of Swift which have been preserved ante-date the period of the second residence at Moor Park, of which we have been speaking, for it appears that the *Ode to King William on his Successes in Ireland* was the work of late 1690 or early 1691. Written in heroic quatrains, of which there are an even dozen, it is a piece undistinguished either for excellence or marked inferiority. William is the greater for not being hereditary king of England; he has saved Britannia from the jaws of the monster France; amazed, we follow his action at the Boyne:

> The brave attempt does all our foes disarm;
>   You need but now give orders and command,
> Your name shall the remaining work perform,
>   And spare the labour of your conquering hand.

Swift's enthusiasm for King William and the Revolution lends the ode an interest out of proportion to its otherwise colourless character. But it should be remarked that these stanzas are perfectly clear in expression and technically correct enough — proof that upon his return to Moor Park in 1691 he had achieved control of a sort over one of the conventional verse forms of the day.

But at this point something happened. Re-established at Moor Park, he set to work at new verses designed to bring him distinction in England; the result was the *Ode to the Athenian Society* (February 1692) and the contemporary *Ode to the Hon. Sir William Temple*. Dryden, seeing one of these productions, is reported to have said to Swift, whose grandmother was a Dryden, 'Cousin Jonathan, you will never be a poet.' And the worst of it was that although Dryden's remark, as prophecy, was in time to prove false, the two odes would have made any other judgment cruelly misleading flattery. Nevertheless, the astonishing clumsiness and turgidity of these two pieces were really not signs of a hopeless incapacity for verse but of an intellectual energy out of control at the moment. Had Swift remained content with the artistic possibilities of heroic couplet and quatrain, had he been willing to check his thought in favour of graceful articulation, had he, in a

word, been satisfied to go on turning out more *Odes to
King William,* he would have done well enough.   At least he
would never have brought forth these monstrosities.   But
his mind was like a conjured spirit, and scornfully he rejected the easy manner and the slight subject.   For the
development of ideas he demanded a freedom of movement
impossible in couplet and quatrain, and accordingly he
turned to the Pindaric ode ; yet even this metrical form
proved insufficiently flexible.

The *Ode to Temple* and the *Ode to the Athenian Society*
are closely packed discourses the weight of which only prose
could carry.   The verse, having obstructed the thought
often to the verge of unintelligibility, sinks under the load.
The *Ode to Temple* is made up of several successive themes,
the dominant and recurrent one being eulogy of a man
too eminent in virtue to come off successfully in the world.
In the opening stanza Temple is called upon to discover and
conquer the Terra Incognita of Virtue, a clumsy way of saying that Temple is a model of taste, his mind untouched
by academic dry-rot, perceptions sharpened by worldly experience, the ethical sense alive to realities.   Then, in the
immediately following stanzas, the poet turns from praise
of his patron to exposure of his own erstwhile companions
in Academe — his revenge on the pedantic impostures of
Trinity College :

II

We have too long been led astray ;
Too long have our misguided souls been taught
With rules from musty morals brought,
'Tis you must put us in the way ;
Let us (for shame !) no more be fed
With antique relics of the dead,
The gleanings of philosophy ;
Philosophy, the lumber of the schools,
The roguery of alchymy ;
And we, the bubbled fools,
Spend all our present life, in hopes of golden rules.

III

But what does our proud ignorance Learning call ?
We oddly Plato's paradox make good,

Our knowledge is but mere remembrance all ;
Remembrance is our treasure and our food ;
Nature's fair table-book, our tender souls,
We scrawl all o'er with old and empty rules,
    Stale memorandums of the schools :
    For learning's mighty treasures look
      Into that deep grave, a book ;
  Think that she there does all her treasures hide,
And that her troubled ghost still haunts there since
    she died ;
Confines her walks to colleges and schools :
    Her priests, her train, and followers, show
    As if they all were spectres too !
    They purchase knowledge at th' expense
    Of common breeding, common sense,
    And grow at once scholars and fools ;
    Affect ill-manner'd pedantry,
Rudeness, ill-nature, incivility,
    And, sick with dregs and knowledge grown,
    Which greedily they swallow down,
Still cast it up, and nauseate company.

More of this, after which a new theme is introduced, and
Temple's diplomatic work in behalf of peace is celebrated,
war is denounced, and Temple's exposure — in his *Memoirs,*
one assumes — of the trickery behind the scenes of state is
discussed at length.   As the contrast emerges between the
imposing exterior and the meanness concealed behind, the
verse again becomes satirical :

    Great God ! (said I) what have I seen !
      On what poor engines move
The thoughts of monarchs and designs of states !
    What petty motives rule their fates !
How the mouse makes the mighty mountains shake !
The mighty mountain labours with its birth,
    Away the frighten'd peasants fly,
    Scared at the unheard-of prodigy,
Expect some great gigantic son of earth ;
      Lo ! it appears !
    See how they tremble ! how they quake !
Out starts the little beast, and mocks their idle fears.

The rest of the ode is chiefly in praise of Temple, save
where the poet laments his hard fate, tied to the Muse's
galleys, where

In vain I strive to cross the spacious main,
    In vain I tug and pull the oar;
    And when I almost reach the shore,
Straight the Muse turns the helm, and I
        launch out again. . .

On 14 February 1692 Swift addressed a letter to the
Athenian Society and enclosed therein the ode which he
had written in their honour, requesting them to print his
verses in their next publication. When he first heard of
the Society — so he wrote — he fancied it some new folly
of the age, but since coming to England he has met with
their four volumes at Oxford and Moor Park and the
perusal of these 'has produced what you find enclosed.' The
volumes in question were the first four numbers of the
Athenian Mercury, an anonymous publication, wherein John
Dunton, with assistance, undertook to supply universal information to all inquirers. In *A Tale of a Tub* Swift was
not only to satirize John Dunton — by that time revealed
as the prime mover of the *Mercury* — as a Grub-Street writer,
but was to hold up to immortal ridicule all those 'boulters
of Learning' who compiled compendiums of useless information precisely calculated to the corrupt taste of the age.
But in 1692 he was perfectly genuine in his enthusiasm
and his praise. A hatred of pedantry and everything suggesting the academic atmosphere dominated his mind.
It enabled him to penetrate Temple's character accurately, whereas in the case of the *Athenian Mercury* it misled him completely.[2]

The *Ode to the Athenian Society* — with the exception
of the remarkable lines at the close — is unquestionably
the worst thing Swift ever wrote. The opening stanzas,
in which Swift is describing the end of the late war, his
recent arrival in England, and his joy upon discovering
the Society, are so contorted in syntax and crossed with
inconsistent imagery that only a free translation could reduce them to sense. The precarious position of the 'great
unknown, and far-exalted men' who compose the Society
is then described and enlarged upon. They will be set
upon by that part of mankind that makes obloquy a trade.

They will be censured by all the wits spawned by events since the war :

> The wits, I mean the atheists of the age,
> Who fain would rule the pulpit, as they do the stage,
> Wondrous refiners of philosophy,
>   Of morals and divinity,
> By the new modish system of reducing all to sense,
>   Against all logic, and concluding laws,
>   Do own th' effects of Providence,
>   And yet deny the cause.

But true Fame, which is far above all reward, is in this age only known in these far-exalted men. Proteus-like, they assume all shapes in answering the questions directed to them. They have restored to Philosophy her charms, obscured by the doubts, impertinence, and niceties which she has borrowed from every age through which she has passed. Yet since there is a noontide and a night in all our lives, these men 'may fall at last to interest, folly, and abuse.' In the closing stanza the satirist foretells the ruin that will mark the final, triumphant progress of pedantry through the land :

> And thus undoubtedly 'twill fare
> With what unhappy men shall dare
> To be successors to these great unknown,
> On learning's high-establish'd throne.
> Censure, and Pedantry, and Pride
> Numberless nations, stretching far and wide,
> Shall (I foresee it) soon with Gothic swarms come
>   forth
> From Ignorance's universal North,
> And with blind rage break all this peaceful govern-
>   ment :
> Yet shall the traces of your wit remain,
>   Like a just map, to tell the vast extent
> Of conquest in your short and happy reign :
>   And to all future mankind shew
>   How strange a paradox is true,
> That men who lived and died without a name
> Are the chief heroes in the sacred lists of fame.

For once, the satiric intensity has enforced direct statement and firm rhythm. It is Swift's first passage in any way to be touched by the power which he was later to command at will.

On 3 May 1692 Swift wrote his cousin Thomas, whom he had visited at Oxford in the previous year. The greater part of his letter is concerned with his problems as a poet, which Swift discusses with a rather self-conscious air. He envies the ease with which Thomas writes verse; for his part he can compose nothing of a sudden, nor write anything easy to be understood. Two hours in the morning, 'the flower of the whole day,' he gives over to poetry, but ordinarily he requires an entire week for two stanzas of a Pindaric ode, and when all is done he must alter them a hundred times. He is, he confesses, overfond of his own writings and can reread them a hundred times with pleasure. But he finds it equally difficult to criticize severely the writings of his friends, for he discovers beauties in their work in proportion to the love he bears them: 'I never read [Temple's] writings but I prefer him to all others at present in England, which I suppose is all but a piece of self-love, and the likeness of humours makes one fond of them as if they were one's own.'

In discussing his poetry with Thomas, Swift mentions three pieces, the *Ode to the Athenian Society,* the *Ode to Doctor William Sancroft,* and a translation of Virgil. In regard to the first of these, he writes with a show of triumph that not only was it composed in little more than a week but that it has been printed by the Society and quoted 'very honourably' by the author of the *History of the Athenian Society.* The *Ode to Doctor William Sancroft* is here mentioned for the first time: he has been at work on it for five months, but has written only nine stanzas and finds it difficult to finish, and this despite his respect for the 'excellent person' addressed in the ode. As for the translation of Virgil — which has not been preserved — it sticks plaguily on his hands, although Sir William Temple and Lady Giffard like the sample they have seen 'as I would have them.'

The *Ode to Doctor William Sancroft* Swift managed to extend from nine stanzas to twelve, but finish it he never could. And yet, of the three surviving Pindaric odes, it is

decidedly the best.[3] It is not poetry or even good verse, but
Swift has come upon a theme which matters immensely and
his passionate reasoning burns away much of the involved
rhetoric fatal to the earlier compositions and almost bends
the recalcitrant verse into a serviceable medium. Again
eulogy is made the point of departure for satire. It is in
the satiric passages that the greatest advance is observed.
Previously, his satiric impulse had been aroused by the
pedantry and ill manners of the schools, the centre from
which the attacks radiated being the positive concept of
taste. The *Ode to Sancroft* discloses a broadening of the
positive concept. There are two realms, one of Eternal
Truth, one of mundane affairs. Such is the distance separating them that in this inferior world of ours the image
of Truth shows but dimly. But within our world a second
dualism is exhibited : on the one hand is the small company of rational men like Sancroft, who alone cause Truth
to appear this side the Eternal realm ; in contrast are the
vast numbers of mistaken idiots, for ever deprived of light,
led blindly by opinion. This essentially is the central concept of the ode, though part of it is expressed vaguely and
part by implication alone.

The Platonic element — the contrast between our world
and a realm of perfect Truth — never again appeared in
Swift's thought. It was utterly foreign to his mind, and
its momentary appearance in the ode is evidence of an
odd sort that he was yet uncertain of his intellectual base.
On the other hand, the dualism distinguishing two levels
of human society, the rational and the vulgar, became one
of the informing ideas underlying his mature work. The
theory and the attitude behind it are imbued with intellectual scorn. But there is an all-important distinction to
be made : that between intellectual scorn and egoism. The
repeated failure to perceive this distinction has led to an
interpretation of Swift which cannot be reconciled with
Swift the man's man, the companion of Pope, Gay, and
Arbuthnot ; with Swift the friend ; with Swift the benefactor.
Only by positing a split in personality or by sophisticating
every action of his life to provide an impure motive can

all sides of the man be explained in reference to the egoism which is sometimes thought to have consumed him. Now, it would be false to hold that the kind of intellectual scornfulness illustrated in Swift leaves no mark upon a man's character. It did upon Swift's, in the form of an increasing indignation which made peace impossible. But the indignation was not that of an egoist. It was theoretical and essentially disinterested.

The *Ode to Sancroft* was Swift's first religious treatise. When he wrote it he was already, we know, entertaining the thought of taking holy orders. Did he feel a sincere desire to enter the church, or did he regard orders in a spirit of pure opportunism? If the ode fails to supply an answer, it does show beyond any doubt the exalted position which from the very first Swift conceived the church as occupying. William Sancroft was the non-juring archbishop of Canterbury, deprived of office in 1690 for his passive resistance to the theories implicit in the Revolution: that an anointed king could be deposed by a people; that the church could be subordinated to and controlled by the state. Sancroft's refusal to recognize William as king *de jure* or *de facto* Swift, at this time a thorough whig, passes over in silence. It is Sancroft's position regarding the independence of the church which he praises. Why, he asks, is the church 'still led blindfold by the state?,' and he proceeds to castigate the 'wild reforms' responsible for this threat to the church's independence:

> Say what this senseless malice meant,
> To tear religion's lovely face:
> Strip her of every ornament and grace;
> In striving to wash off th' imaginary paint?　　(Stanza xii)

Here, be it noted, is the theme later enlarged upon in the story of the three brothers in *A Tale of a Tub*.

The multitude, misled by opinion, cannot appreciate Sancroft,

> the brightest pattern earth can show
> Of heaven-born Truth below. . .　　(Stanza iii)

The satirist turns upon the multitude:

In vain then would the Muse the multitude advise,
  Whose peevish knowledge thus perversely lies
    In gath'ring follies from the wise ;
  Rather put on thy anger and thy spite,
    And some kind power for once dispense
  Through the dark mass, the dawn of so much
    sense,
To make them understand, and feel me when I
    write ;
  The muse and I no more revenge desire,
Each line shall stab, shall blast, like daggers and
    like fire ;
  Ah, Britain, land of angels ! which of all thy sins,
    (Say, hapless isle, although
    It is a bloody list we know,)
Has given thee up a dwelling-place to fiends ?   (Stanza v)

Without a guide from Heaven, without a Sancroft, every
wandering fool will miss the way :

  I mean the way which leads to Christ :
Mistaken idiots ! see how giddily they run,
  Led blindly on by avarice and pride,
    What mighty numbers follow them ;
    Each fond of erring with his guide :
  Some whom ambition drives, seek Heaven's high
    Son
  In Caesar's court, or in Jerusalem :
    Others, ignorantly wise,
Among proud doctors and disputing Pharisees. . .
                         (Stanza viii)

Swift, it has been said repeatedly, was lacking in spirituality.
This is true, but not in the vague sense usually taken, as the
passage just quoted will show.   Here Christ is not a symbol
of emotional experience but of practical reason ; the way
that leads to Him is not one of spiritual discipline but of
unperverted judgment — the reference is entirely to a world
of law and order revealed to the few of superior intelligence,
concealed from the dupes of opinion.   It is not to be
doubted that in the secrecy of his inmost thought Swift
was sometimes shaken by sickening glimpses from the corner
of his eye of a realm beyond man's reason to comprehend.
But in his case this psychological vertigo was never the
occasion of religious experience ; rather, it threw him back

upon the world of law and order with his trust in practical
reason and his scornfulness of vulgar error intensified, his
hatred of all speculation not confined within the limits of
common sense deepened. The Christian religion presented
two aspects. One — mysterious, sanctioned by revelation,
and as such to be accepted without curiosity — concerned
belief. The other engaged the body of individual and
social morality recognized by practical intelligence. This
severance of faith and reason, and all that it carried with
it of philosophical and emotional attitudes is the source
of the scornfulness in Swift. For 'scornfulness' may be
read 'lack of true spirituality,' and thus the constant charge
brought against him substantiated. But to Swift himself,
as to any number of his contemporaries, this charge would
have been incomprehensible, and if we on our part fail
to understand his position we show ourselves sadly lacking
in historical perspective. It is not that Swift wavered in
belief, nor that in conduct he failed to be guided by it.
In all these matters he was rigorously consistent, rigorously
in accord with his theoretical premises. It is the premises
which we may question, but remembering always that they
were given by his age.

2

THE three Pindaric odes were the work of 1692, presumably
of the first six months. During the remainder of this year
and the greater part of 1693 we may imagine Swift still
courting the Muse with undiminished violence, but of the
verse of this entire period nothing has been preserved. We
must come down to November 1693. In this month Swift
wrote his lines *To Mr. Congreve,* in the following month
the lines *Occasioned by Sir William Temple's late Illness
and Recovery.*

The occasion of the first of these pieces is explained in
Swift's letter of 6 December to his cousin Thomas, who is
requested to say how Congreve's new play, *The Double
Dealer,* has been received in London ; Swift intends to send
his verses to the dramatist to be printed along with the

play. Had Swift had the faintest spark of envy in him, Congreve's rising fortunes would have fanned it to raging fire. Congreve had been at school and college with Swift, and was besides the younger man, yet already his plays were being produced. To date, Swift had seen in print one Pindaric ode. One of Swift's finest characteristics, evidenced throughout his life, was an utter lack of any sense of rivalry with his literary fellows.

To Mr. Congreve Swift describes to Thomas as consisting of 'almost two hundred and fifty lines not Pindaric.' There is, perhaps, a certain grim emphasis on the 'not Pindaric'—as much as to say that he has finally come to his senses and does not intend to be misled longer by Cowley's Muse. At any rate, he has now discarded the Pindaric ode in favour of the heroic couplet. But it is one thing to adopt a new artistic form, another to change one's manner and tone. Unfortunately the bad habits confirmed during a year's desperate struggles with the Pindaric ode still ride him hard : ungainly from start to finish, he is perversely obscure through entire paragraphs ; he hammers his ideas home with a rhythm out of all relation to the movement of the verse ; he refuses to relieve the intensity with the barest touch of humour or irony.

Yet, because it marks a development of the satiric mood, *To Mr. Congreve* deserves careful reading. Swift's attention is turned by Congreve's dramatic work away from the previous objects of his scorn — college pedants and vulgar idiots — and towards the corrupters of taste who overrun London : the mean wits who would imitate Congreve ; the carping critics who crowd the pit ; and their associates in impertinence, the virtuosos. It is his mission to lash such as these, which he proceeds to do in the manner of the Latin satirists. His attack is direct, his tone one of quivering moral indignation, his satire — so he explicitly declares — a Heaven-decreed instrument of chastisement. Because Swift was soon to drop this satiric directness for implication and ironic statement, a fundamental and persistent likeness between him and the great Latin satirists — Juvenal and Persius rather than Horace — has been lost sight of.

Whether thou choose Cervantes' serious air,
Or laugh and shake in Rab'lais' easy chair. . .

Pope's famous lines are bad criticism, for Swift's humour —
consistently underestimated — is of an entirely different order
from Rabelais's, being sub-acid and starkly intellectual, while
his 'serious air' is irony without a trace of Cervantes's pathos.
But there is in Swift a seriousness of another kind which
Pope is overlooking here and which too few of the later
commentators have sufficiently emphasized — the moral earnestness, that is, of one who regards himself as a censor of
the follies and depravities of his age.   In this Swift resembles
the Latin satirists.   The similarity, however, extends farther, for like them Swift is never capricious but directs his
attacks from a position definitely marked out and fortified
by reason and psychological theory.   Because so much of
his later work is in prose and is imbued with an irony
which is all his own one forgets how close in spirit he was
to the great Roman satirists.   His early verse serves to
remind us of this kinship.

It is well, the satirist proceeds, after a very involved introduction, that praise of Congreve has come to soften the
thunder of his Muse; the godlike force 'of my young Congreve's bays' has been sent

> to assist an old unvanquish'd pride
> That looks with scorn on half mankind beside;
> A pride that well suspends poor mortals' fate,
> Gets between them and my resentment's weight,
> Stands in the gap 'twixt me and wretched men,
> T' avert th' impending judgments of my pen.

Having expressed the wish that Congreve may reform the
stage, the satirist turns upon the vile pretenders who counterfeit true wit and upon envious critics, and for a second
time — the first in the *Ode to the Athenian Society* — he
introduces the theme of a Progress of Dulness:

> What northern hive pour'd out these foes to wit?
> Whence came these Goths to overrun the pit?
> How would you blush the shameful birth to hear
> Of those you so ignobly stoop to fear;

> For, ill to them, long have I travell'd since,
> Round all the circles of impertinence,
> Search'd in the nest where every worm did lie
> Before it grew a city butterfly;
> I'm sure I found them other kind of things
> Than those with backs of silk and golden wings;
> A search, no doubt, as curious and as wise
> As virtuosoes' in dissecting flies. . .

The word *virtuoso* as used in England at this time bore a sense different from its original Italian one; it now meant a man interested in natural philosophy, particularly a member of the famous Royal Society. Since the Restoration scientific enthusiasm had been the object of all kinds of jibes from playwrights and satirists, who, since they had ordinarily no understanding of the immense significance of what was taking place, assumed that these scientists had fallen victims to some new 'humour.' In them, it seemed, the balance of common sense had been upset; a flaw had split their judgment from end to end. How else could be explained their trivial passion for natural curiosities and their nasty habit of dissecting animals dead and alive? Now, Swift was among the most relentless enemies of the new science; to him the virtuosos symbolized modern madness in one of its acutest forms. But his opposition, as we have already seen, was something more than instinctive prejudice; it was the considered judgment of one for whom natural philosophy was altogether overshadowed by the philosophy of human conduct. To his contempt for the sciences Swift was not to give full satiric expression until he wrote the third book of *Gulliver's Travels,* but he was irrevocably committed to this point of view as early as 1693.

The most effective passage in the poem occurs about midway in the piece. It concerns a lad recently at school in Farnham, the village near Moor Park:

> Last year, a lad hence by his parents sent
> With other cattle to the city went;
> Where having cast his coat, and well pursued
> The methods most in fashion to be lewd,
> Return'd a finish'd spark this summer down,
> Stock'd with the freshest gibberish of the town;

A jargon form'd from the lost language, wit,
Confounded in that Babel of the pit ;
Form'd by diseased conceptions, weak and wild,
Sick lust of souls, and an abortive child ;
Born between whores and fops, by lewd compacts,
Before the play, or else between the acts ;
Nor wonder, if from such polluted minds
Should spring such short and transitory kinds,
Or crazy rules to make us wits by rote,
Last just as long as every cuckoo's note :
What bungling, rusty tools are used by fate !
'Twas in an evil hour to urge my hate,
My hate, whose lash just Heaven has long decreed
Shall on a day make sin and folly bleed :
When man's ill genius to my presence sent
This wretch, to rouse my wrath, for ruin meant. . .

One more passage before dismissing the verses to Congreve.
In the second paragraph from the last the satirist's Muse
is set upon by a school of rallying critics. The Muse,

> who on shady banks has joy'd to sleep
> Near better animals, her father's sheep,
> Shamed and amazed, beholds the chattering throng,
> To think what cattle she is got among ;
> But with the odious smell and sight annoy'd,
> In haste she does th' offensive herd avoid.

In these lines, as elsewhere in the poem, there enters what
M. Pons has happily named *le mythe animal,* a satiric theme
revolving about the comparison of man to animal. As Swift
here employs it, it is only a degree removed from the
device dear to children and exhibited in story-telling from
earliest times. But as he perfected its use, it became in the
last book of *Gulliver's Travels* and in *A Modest Proposal*
perhaps the most devastating weapon ever used by a satirist.
  To Mr. Congreve is dated November 1693. Swift's first
adventure with the Muse is nearly at an end. In the following month he writes *Occasioned by Sir William Temple's
late Illness and Recovery* — also in the heroic couplet — and
in this he berates his Muse and dismisses her. The language is unfortunately so cryptic that the precise reasons
for the discouragement which is voiced throughout the piece
are not apparent. The Muse and poet meet by the stream

running through the estate at Moor Park. The Muse bids him put off his melancholy air now that the cause of his sadness, Temple's illness, has happily been removed. The poet, however, is unable to share the joy felt by the others at Moor Park — the Muse herself is the occasion of his woes. Time, who 'o'er the happy takes so swift a flight,' tramples with heavy pace over the afflicted; in the havoc of the poet's looks appear a 'tyrant's trophies of a year.' It is all the Muse's fault:

> To thee I owe that fatal bent of mind,
> Still to unhappy restless thoughts inclined;
> To thee, what oft I vainly strive to hide,
> That scorn of fools, by fools mistook for pride;
> From thee whatever virtue takes its rise,
> Grows a misfortune, or becomes a vice. . .

Her recipe for poetical greatness he has followed long enough; his few ill-presented graces only seem to breed contempt where he has hoped for esteem; he is always cheated, never pleased:

> There thy enchantment broke, and from this hour
> I here renounce thy visionary power;
> And since thy essence on my breath depends
> Thus with a puff the whole delusion ends.

It is perfectly clear that he is depressed not by lack of consideration at Moor Park but by his failure at poetry. But what exactly are the signs of this failure? His critical sense prevailing over his pride in the Pindaric odes? Harsh judgments of others upon his talent? Rebuffs brought on by his satirical temper? The references to 'that scorn of fools, by fools mistook for pride,' to contempt where he has hoped for esteem, and to a year of discouragements suggest strongly some episode during 1693 that we know nothing of.

But with the capacity of genius for retreating in order after a major disaster and planning an attack in an entirely new direction, Swift dismisses from his mind his fond hopes of achieving distinction through poetry and looks elsewhere.

3

It is probably safe to date the beginning of Swift's extraordinary transformation from the moment late in 1693 when with a puff the whole delusion ended. Shortly thereafter he is on his way back to Dublin, he takes orders, and for a year and more at Kilroot tastes life in an Ulster parish. When he returns to Moor Park it is not to write clumsy verse but to fashion prose satire which speaks to Folly's children in a tone unheard since the days of Erasmus.

His transformation was brought about, however, not by any renunciation of the themes and ideas which he had been striving to develop in the early verse, but by a rich elaboration of these and a sudden discovery of a new medium of expression. It is this fact which bestows importance on the verse and which justifies our taking a final conspectus of it before leaving it for things more exciting.

One aspect of these early compositions to which no explicit reference has yet been made is this : they bear out the view previously taken of Swift's position at Moor Park and his attitude towards Temple. It will not do to say of the *Ode to Temple* and of *Sir William's late Illness and Recovery* that forced and empty compliments alone are expressed. The entire five pieces must be taken together, and when they are it is clear to what degree Swift is conscious of his spiritual independence. More than that, he is responsive to the new environment and comes to centre his concept of taste in Temple.

By far the most interesting disclosure is the tone which runs throughout the verses. As always, it is this which can least accurately be suggested through excerpts and comment. In the present instance the dominant note is often muffled through entire passages by mere rhetorical sound, but sooner or later it is sure to emerge. It is the tone of intense moral indignation. The satiric impulse was in Swift neither a sadistic nor a cynical one. The sadist flays for the acute pleasure, the cynic for amusement, but the great satirist is moved by indignation. But in its pure form

indignation is more than likely to defeat itself, for the undisguised fury of the moralist does not always make the wicked
tremble. It is in this case that Swift's first satires in verse
stand: there is a too eager earnestness. His subsequent
transformation is more than anything else the discovery of indirection, a sublimation of wrath through irony and wit and
civilized insolence. How dear a price Swift paid for his
satiric artistry is understood when one listens to the abuse
which hostile critics from the duchess of Somerset and Archbishop Sharpe down through Thackeray have poured on
him. Yet, a moralist in his first compositions, a moralist he
never ceased to be in his own eyes. And no other interpretation of Swift is possible to-day.

Regarding the thematic material which is developed in
the verses, little need be added to what has already been
said. The central concept is that of taste — i.e., the attitude
of the well-bred, attained through worldly experience, common sense, civilized good will, and reason. Opposed to it
is pedantry, the corruption of all taste. This fundamental
contrast is expressed in another and broader way as a dualism which cleaves society into the rational minority and
the vulgar crowd.

It may be said that in respect both of moral attitude and
of specific ideas Swift's early verse of Moor Park is generically
akin to his prose satire. But in these respects alone. Between the *Odes* and *A Tale of a Tub* the distance seems
enormous and almost inexplicable, to be accounted for
neither by increased intellectual grasp nor by greater erudition, the fruits of maturity. It is not a problem of development but of discontinuity: a new element appears; there
is a shift in level.

The nearest approach to a solution of the problem presented here lies through analysis of Swift's art. At the start
he was hopelessly incapacitated by the medium of verse,
which committed him to a grimness unrelieved by humour
or irony and to a formality of statement which checked
any experiments in satiric technique. When he did hit
upon *le mythe animal* he was unable to develop it. It was
the new medium of prose which released his energies. Im-

plication took the place of formal statement; insolent assurance supplanted the grave airs; irony, sober-countenanced,
indulged at will in preposterous sport.   Were it not for his
unsuccessful experiments in verse satire, it would be natural
to assume that Swift came by the Swiftian manner without
a struggle.   To show how far off the truth such an assumption lies is one of the purposes of this chapter.

And now a final word, not about the very early verses,
but about two metrical compositions which date from Swift's
last year at Moor Park.   Dryden's prophecy—'You will
never be a poet'—was to prove false in time, we have already
said.   (In order to avoid controversy this statement should
perhaps be modified.   Those who are committed to 'high
seriousness' as a touchstone will deny that Swift ever wrote
so much as a line of true poetry, and for the benefit of
such the word *verse* will continue to be used in the present
study rather than *poetry*.   It does not matter what term
one uses so long as one arrives at a clear perception of the
artistic properties which are exhibited.   Swift, after his
transformation, never aspired to exalted verse.   He preferred to develop his true vein, which was occasional verse
now complimentary and again satiric, *vers de société*, and
Horatian imitations.   With those who lack the true taste
for eighteenth-century verse, which is perhaps an acquired
one, it will be useless to join issue over the merits of Swift's
metrical compositions.)   Early in 1698 the palace at Whitehall burnt.   Swift's commentary on this event, a commentary extremely whiggish in sentiment, was written in heroic
couplets that flow with unimpeded ease.   In his description
of the burning building he achieves intensity with no unnatural straining:

> Down come the lofty roofs, the cedar burns,
> The blended metal to a torrent turns;
> The carvings crackle and the marble rive,
> The paintings shrink, vainly the Henrys strive,
> Propt by great Holbein's pencil, down they fall;
> The fiery deluge sweeps and swallows all.[4]

His new manner in verse appears more startlingly, however, in the piece entitled *Written in a Lady's Ivory Table-*

Book (1698; probably revised 1706). The octosyllabic couplet, the familiar style, the intensity with which the subject is developed, the social satire — these characteristics of his greatest verse all appear here.

> Peruse my leaves thro' ev'ry part,
> And think thou seest my owner's heart,
> Scrawl'd o'er with trifles thus, and quite
> As hard, as senseless, and as light;
> Expos'd to ev'ry coxcomb's eyes,
> But hid with caution from the wise.
> Here you may read, 'Dear charming saint;'
> Beneath, 'A new receipt for paint:'
> Here, in beau-spelling, 'Tru tel deth;'
> There, in her own, 'For an el breth:'
> Here, 'Lovely nymph, pronounce my doom!'
> There, 'A safe way to use perfume:'
> Here, a page fill'd with billets-doux;
> On t'other side, 'Laid out for shoes'—
> 'Madam, I die without your grace'—
> 'Item, for half a yard of lace.'
> Who that had wit would place it here,
> For ev'ry peeping fop to jeer?
> To think that your brains' issue is
> Exposed to th' excrement of his,
> In pow'r of spittle and a clout,
> Whene'er he please, to blot it out;
> And then, to heighten the disgrace,
> Clap his own nonsense in the place.
> Whoe'er expects to hold his part
> In such a book, and such a heart,
> If he be wealthy, and a fool,
> Is in all points the fittest tool;
> Of whom it may be justly said,
> He's a gold pencil tipp'd with lead.

CHAPTER IV
CONTROLLING IDEAS

1

THE continuity of our critical study of Swift would be preserved were we now to proceed to the crowning work of the Moor Park period, *The Battle of the Books* and *A Tale of a Tub*. It seems the wiser course, however, to sacrifice continuity in the interest of a full understanding of the controlling ideas which, beginning with these two great satires, were the bone and sinew of everything that Swift wrote.

There is little in the present chapter which will not, it is believed, cast direct light upon *A Tale of a Tub* — upon the *Battle* also, though the latter calls for considerably less. It is not to be expected, however, that the references to Swift's work will be confined to *A Tale of a Tub*, for as befits one who entertained the doctrine of uniformity — of which more shortly — Swift's mature work is ideologically of an astonishing sameness. Sometime between the end of 1693 and his return to Temple in 1696 he reached intellectual maturity at a single bound, with the result that the first pages of the *Tale* conduct us straight into the country wherein Swift was henceforth to abide. With most great figures of literature there are preliminary episodes to engage our attention; our interest is properly accelerated as the lights go on one by one. But with Swift the full current is thrown on instantly, without warning. The initial difficulty thus imposed on those seeking to give and to find insight into his mind is great. It is next to impossible to adhere to the chronology of his writings. One must weave back and forth, drawing where necessary on the work of his early, middle, and late genius.

2

SWIFT'S writings, from end to end, are a magnificently firm and insistent exposition of a complex of ideas and attitudes given by the period of European culture into which he was born. These ideas and attitudes underlie his moral theories, his æsthetic and literary principles, his social, political, and historical views, and the conception of religion which he entertained. They are expressed in one fashion or another in every pamphlet which came from his pen, while in his satiric writings they are pointed at men's souls. It will not do to say that Swift was a confirmed rationalist and let it go at that, for there are countless attitudes to which the term rationalistic may be applied exactly or loosely. If we desire to understand his intellectual outlook in more than a vague way, we must put aside sweeping generalities.

The mind of the youthful versifier we have already explored. The emotion which dominated Swift upon his departure from Trinity College was a hatred of pedantry, a hatred which under the influence of the Moor Park scene and of Temple's personality was quickly rationalized into the positive doctrine of taste, according to which the civilized attitude is the possession of a small group of refined men who by virtue of inborn qualities and of good breeding and education are to be distinguished from the throng of blind and ill-natured pedants. Then, as the composition of further Pindaric odes led Swift's thoughts away from the academic scene and towards the world at large, he was shortly insisting that the whole of society exhibits a dualistic character, the men of reason at the higher level, the vulgar mob at the lower. Finally, throughout his early metrical compositions he consistently displayed the temper of the moral satirist. We may say that the prevailing mood of the early verses is intellectual scornfulness. It seems scarcely necessary to add that to the end this mood appears both in Swift's behaviour and in his writings. Though the scornfulness comes to be mixed with other elements, some of which at certain times almost neutralize the basic acidity, it is always present, a nettle behind his words and actions.

Beginning, then, with the Swift who speaks in the Pindaric odes, our task is to discover the concepts and assumptions which he took over before his emergence as a great prose satirist. Now, it is much easier to isolate the different

elements which went to make up his system of controlling
ideas than it is to describe the living force which was the
mind and personality of Jonathan Swift. It is possible, that
is, to analyse his controlling ideas with some accuracy, and
yet to miss entirely that quality of the man which sets him
apart from all of his contemporaries. There is in Swift a
Dantesque intensity of apprehension which has little to do
with his formal thought. The world, he insisted, presents
a deceptively fair exterior; reality, which is not fair but
simply real, exists only beneath the surface. It is not as
you think — look! Not until we have felt what we shall
call Swift's moral realism should we venture to explore
Swift's formal ideas, which enforced the emotional intensity
and canalized it but did not generate it.

Swift's thought, a unified whole as entertained by him,
presents from the point of view of the history of ideas two
different sides. In a number of respects we may say that
he embodied the characteristic rationalism of the Enlightenment, and it is this rationalism which we shall discuss first.
Here the leading concept is that of the uniformity of reason
and nature, from which concept stem (1) the neo-classical
hatred of 'enthusiasm,' (2) a kind of equalitarianism, (3)
anti-intellectualism, and (4) a negative philosophy of history.
The central concept as well as the derivatives just mentioned
are all present in Swift's thought. On the other hand, we
find in him an ethical doctrine which, though of the seventeenth century, is not 'rationalistic' in the same sense as are
the concepts referred to above. In Swift's ethical doctrine
'reason,' it is true, plays a major rôle, but the context of this
'reason' is that of neo-Stoicism rather than of characteristic
neo-classicism, and there is in his doctrine, furthermore, a
large admixture of what may be called anti-rationalism — the
insistence, that is, upon man's fundamental irrationality.

3

To proceed now to that side of Swift which displays the
characteristic rationalism of the Enlightenment.[1]

The doctrine of uniformity entertained by Swift and his

contemporaries arose from the interpretation given to the terms *reason* and *nature*. There were involved here two concepts from which what is individual and particular had been banished. [Reason, it was held, was the same in all men. When, therefore, one's life was in accord with reason it would conform in all respects to the principles given by the general sense of mankind; from the norm established by uniform reason there should be no departure, for divergencies, rather than marks of distinction for which in another period they have sometimes been taken, were proof of error.] Cognate to *reason* was the term *nature,* and this too enforced the idea of conformity to unvarying and universal standards, for *nature* indicated not that 'nature' external to man which romantic poetry celebrates but a cosmos exhibiting a uniformity of law revealed through reason. 'Life according to nature' and 'life according to reason' were the same thing.

All this, to Swift and his fellows, was far more than philosophy; it was not only a clearly defined set of propositions — it was the system which engaged their instinctive belief, which determined their countless assumptions, which patterned their emotions. This we must remember when observing the energy which Swift at all times displayed in enforcing conformity to what he believed to be the normal and the natural — a characteristic feature not only of his æsthetics but of his moral views. Many readers feel an aversion from Swift's Houyhnhnms, who are not so much animals as exemplars of the perfect life of reason — they 'thought, Nature and Reason were sufficient Guides for a reasonable Animal . . . in shewing us what we ought to do, and what to avoid' (*Gulliver's Travels,* Book IV, chap. v). They are — so the modern criticism goes — humourless creatures at best, but on further acquaintance they become thoroughly repellent because of their undiverting adherence to the precepts of a colourless wisdom. In such a statement speaks all the deep-rooted antipathy of a later age to the uniformitarianism of Swift's period. But misinterpretation is worse than antipathy. It has been suggested, for instance, that Swift wrote *A Project for the Advancement of Religion and the Reforma-*

tion of Manners (ca. 1708; ptd. 1709), which for moral inflexibility outdoes almost any other reforming tract that one
can think of, with his tongue in his cheek; that he was
ironic instead of earnest in his plea for stringent uniformity of moral conduct. Not so. If there is irony in the
Project it is peripheral — as though to say, if men only could !
Similarly, there is no *arriere-pensée* in the account of the
uniformitarian educational theories of the Lilliputians (*Gulliver's Travels,* Book I, chap. vi) or of the life of the
Houyhnhnms (*G. T.,* IV, viii). Difficult as it may be for us
to understand, the rationalist in Swift, turned moralist, was
a thorough-going uniformitarian, to whom divergencies from
the standard pattern of conduct seemed unnatural aberra-
tions. It is true that Swift the moralist was more than a
uniformitarian. He was in addition one who entertained
a stringent ethical doctrine the background of which is not
the characteristic rationalism of the Enlightenment, and it
is this ethical doctrine which is involved in his terrible castigation of corrupt man. But the uniformitarian can almost
always be detected.

As used by the neo-classicist the term *enthusiasm* covered
any and all pretensions on the part of individuals to special
and direct insight, while in its more restricted usage it had
specific reference to fancied religious inspiration. Since
reason was universal, since the general sense of men was in
all things an adequate guide, originality was naturally suspect. In matters affecting society, in the arts, in religion,
the true course was given by the general sense. It was these
assumptions which rendered the neo-classicist so eager to put
down enthusiasm, and which gave to the satirists of the
period a norm whereby to detect and estimate the ridiculous.
Of all the satirists of the age none surpassed Swift in the
violence with which he fell upon enthusiasts. Much of his
animosity, it is true, was fed from sources other than the
ones which we have just been defining, and for this reason
we shall postpone our analysis of it to the following section
of this chapter. But because he shared so fully in the characteristic rationalism of the Enlightenment Swift would in
any case have been alive to the dangers of unbridled enthu-

siasm, and the satire which he directed against it is in part but an expression of one who insisted upon the adequacy of the general sense.

As the hatred of enthusiasm follows from the neo-classical concept of reason and nature, so too does a kind of equalitarianism. Even the neo-classicist of the most aristocratic instincts was of necessity checked in his scornful attitude by the consideration that reason is the possession of all men. The extent to which Swift's intellectual pride was tempered in this manner has not been sufficiently emphasized, though it shows unmistakably in those of his writings which deal with political theory. As a political thinker Swift was in no sense original, his sole contribution being the intellectual energy with which he took up contemporary theory, extended its applications, and gave it a statement irresistibly forcible because of its superb clarity: Common sense is reason applied to homely things, and like reason is a possession of all men. Therefore society at large may be trusted to keep the state upon a true course. Political storms arise not from the body of the people but from the cunning individuals who for their own discreditable interests would pervert the common sense which governs average men. In the ensuing disorders political and social stability is destroyed, and though in due time there will emerge from the chaos a new authority, it will be the authority not of society as a whole but of the single tyrant. In a commonwealth, therefore, the fundamental power must be preserved in the hands of the entire people, and this calls for unremitting exposure of unscrupulous agitators. Common sense must flow unobstructed and unpolluted through the commonwealth — therein lies the assurance of political freedom and the protection against tyranny. 'God hath given the bulk of mankind a capacity to understand reason when it is fairly offered; and by reason they would easily be governed, if it were left to their choice' (Some Free Thoughts upon the Present State of Affairs, 1714). The satirist whose representation of human nature has been called sacrilegious was nevertheless, in his pamphlets on government, one of the most reasonable of all writers, insisting upon the healthy character of the people as a whole.

Still another characteristic attitude of neo-classicism is to be seen in the anti-intellectualism of the period. The general sense of mankind is in all matters a sufficient guide. Speculation which aims to penetrate those regions unmapped by the general sense is presumptuous; almost certainly it will lead not to truth but to error. Indulgence in intellectual subtleties is the pastime of the fool. The mark of wisdom is not fine-spun theorizing but the firm application to man and society of the universal truths revealed by reason. This doctrine, central in the thought of Swift, is implied or given explicit statement time and again in the prose works: it is present in his political and religious theories; it puts teeth into his satire of the corruptions of learning; it forms the basis of his supreme contempt for science. The art of government is not a mysterious one:

God hath given the bulk of mankind a capacity to understand reason when it is fairly offered; and by reason they would easily be governed, if it were left to their choice. Those princes in all ages who were most distinguished for their mysterious skill in government, found by the event, that they had ill consulted their own quiet, or the ease and happiness of their people. . . (*Some Free Thoughts upon the Present State of Affairs.*)

The Christian religion bids us accept certain mysteries, into which we may not inquire; but outside these it offers nothing which reason cannot instantly assent to:

I believe that thousands of men would be orthodox enough in certain points, if divines had not been too curious, or too narrow, in reducing orthodoxy within the compass of subtleties, niceties, and distinctions, with little warrant from Scripture and less from reason or good policy. (*Thoughs on Religion,* undated.)

As for the anti-intellectualistic criticism of science, let Gulliver, who is describing what reason meant to the Houyhnhnms, speak:

. . . *Reason* among [the Houyhnhnms] is [not] a Point problematical as with us, where Men can argue with Plausibility on both Sides of a Question; but strikes you with immediate Con-

viction ; as it must needs do where it is not mingled, obscured,
or discoloured by Passion and Interest. . . When I used to explain to [my master] our several Systems of *Natural Philosophy*,
he would laugh that a Creature pretending to *Reason*, should
value itself upon the Knowledge of other Peoples Conjectures,
and in Things, where that Knowledge, if it were certain, could
be of no Use.   Wherein he agreed entirely with the Sentiments
of *Socrates*, as *Plato* delivers them ; which I mention as the highest Honour I can do that Prince of Philosophers. (*G. T.*, iv, viii.)

The neo-classical philosophy of history was a negative one
in the sense that it did not embrace the idea of progress.
If we desire to insinuate ourselves into Swift's mind, if we
desire to view the universe as he viewed it, we must at once
discard our own prejudice in favour of progress as the law
of history.   The outlook typical of his day was determined
not by faith in the inevitable melioration of society through
constant advance from a less to a more perfect develop-
mental stage but by the conviction that all change must be
for the worse.   The uniformity of reason and nature defined culture as the expression of the general and unvarying
sense of mankind.   Conditions may be now favourable and
again inimical to its full expression, but by the laws of the
universe the high level has been fixed by an unalterable
bench-mark.   The time sense of one like Swift gave to past,
present, and future an identical colouring.   Quite without
the concept of historical development with its hope for the
future, his mind was ruled by the desire for permanence and
by the ever-present fear that some rising tide of barbarism
would close over civilization.   In the only pamphlet to
which Swift ever affixed his name, *A Proposal for Correcting, Improving, and Ascertaining the English Tongue* (1712),
his negative philosophy of history is clearly stated in linguistic terms :

. . . what I have most at heart, is, that some method should be
thought on for ascertaining and fixing our language for ever,
after such alterations are made in it as shall be thought requisite.
For I am of opinion, it is better a language should not be wholly
perfect, than that it should be perpetually changing ; and we
must give over at one time, or at length infallibly change for the
worse ; as the Romans did, when they began to quit their sim-

plicity of style, for affected refinements, such as we meet in Tacitus and other authors; which ended by degrees in many barbarities, even before the Goths had invaded Italy.

The invasions of the Goths were to Swift not only historical fact but also symbolic of the ruin which would ensue were the forces detrimental to the civilization founded in reason and nature allowed for a moment to gain headway. In his early verse it was the Progress of Dulness which evoked the most authentic emotion; if it was Pope rather than Swift who gave to this theme its final artistic statement, the latter never ceased to call upon civilized men to stand sleepless guard by their defences.

From Swift's philosophy of history radiate several lines: one leads to his aristocratic distinction of a small group of men of taste, another to his historical theory of literature as expressed in *The Battle of the Books*.

With what intensity of conviction the doctrine of taste was written up in the early verses composed at Moor Park we have already seen. Nor did Swift ever lose sight of the dualism cleaving society into two groups, one made up of the cultivated few, the other of the mass of mankind. Consistently he distinguished between these groups, assigning to the former the onerous obligation of preserving through precept and example the decencies, graces, and rationale of civilized life; to the latter the duty of obedience to superior authority. 'I am apt to think,' runs one of his *Thoughts on Various Subjects* (1706), 'that, in the day of judgment, there will be small allowance given to the wise for their want of morals, and to the ignorant for their want of faith, because both are without excuse. . .' But to the Swift of 1692 and '93, tasting life for the first time and mastered by a desire to even his score with Trinity College, the aristocratic doctrine of taste reached a good deal farther than it did in later years. For one thing, his ethical system was democratic: man without distinction of intellectual and social status lay under the curse of depravity. But it is in the equalitarianism so apparent in his political theory that the strongest check upon his aristocratic discrimination is to be seen.

The historical theory of literature which is implicit in *The*

Battle of the Books may be expressed in the following manner : The controversy in which Temple was caught concerned the question of progress in the arts and sciences. Temple, resting upon his cyclic theory of history, maintained that from early times the arts had flourished in the full bloom of perfection ; the modern arts, rather than substantiating any theory of progress, proved that culture if not sustained at the early level sinks instead of rising. When Temple was attacked by the moderns — not for his historical theory of literature but for specific philological errors and for his cool dismissal of the sciences — Swift went to his support with *The Battle of the Books*. This, too, expounds a historical theory of literature, but it is not the same as Temple's. Ancient writers are defended against modern authors, and the qualities of sweetness and light are given as the touchstones of literary perfection. It is not to say that modern letters suffer from a curse of time and place while some historical inevitability sustained ancient literature. Swift never reduced his historical theory of literature to any such theoretical lines ; what he means is that regardless of time and place feeble talents will never and true genius will always produce great art, the ingredients of which do not vary.

The general statement that Swift is a rationalist is too broad and too vague to have much definite meaning. But if rationalism be defined for the moment as that attitude which was characteristic of the Enlightenment and which embraced among others the concepts of which we have been speaking, it can be shown that Swift, on one side at least, was very much of a rationalist. He has not ordinarily been viewed in this light, for his natural intensity and his moral realism, the rigidity of his ethical doctrine, and the scorn and indignation to which he was moved by the corruptions of human nature have so fascinated his readers that they have had eyes for little else. Yet, as we have just seen, there are many elements in Swift's ideology which are characterized not by emotional and intellectual savageness but by typical neo-classical reasonableness, and this fact must not be forgotten while we are analysing Swift's ethical doctrine, which reveals another side of his mind.

4

NEO-STOICISM was a Renaissance phenomenon, which reached its height at the end of the sixteenth century and the beginning of the seventeenth.[2] The essence of the neo-Stoical doctrine is this: the passions are utterly reprehensible; reason must and can govern; the life which is proper to man is a life of unimpassioned reason. This was in part an inheritance from medieval thought. The Greek view of human nature, of the problems of conduct, and of the problems of art — these latter seen always as closely related to the problems of conduct — was one which led directly to exaltation of the rational faculties: ethically, the control of reason over the passions; æsthetically, the control of reason over fancy and imagination.[3] Because this classical view lent itself readily to Christian interpretation, it came, first through Plato and later through Aristotle, to colour deeply the moral philosophy of the Middle Ages, and in this medieval form was one of the inheritances of the modern age. Before neo-Stoicism became a commanding force among European intellectuals, Erasmus took up this older view of the conflict between reason and the passions and gave it superb satiric statement, putting into the mouth of Folly the wittiest and most ironic praise of the passions ever spoken. All is owing to me, Folly declares:

> So provident has that great Parent of Mankind, Nature, been, that there should not be any thing without it's mixture, and as it were seasoning of Folly. For since according to the definition of the Stoicks, Wisdom is nothing else than to be govern'd by reason; and on the contrary Folly, to be giv'n up to the will of our Passions; that the life of man might not be altogether disconsolate and hard to away with, of how much more Passion than Reason has Jupiter compos'd us?

Foolish wisdom, wise folly, senseless reason, sane passion — the world is turned topsy-turvy in the satiric cyclone that whirls through *The Praise of Folly.* Now, if the Erasmian flavour is not present in all of Swift's satires, it is unmistakably detectable in *A Tale of a Tub,* and this fact suggests that Swift, on one occasion at least, had viewed the dualism of reason and passion through the eyes of an early sixteenth-century satirist who was still half medieval.

But to come to neo-Stoicism proper. The Renaissance saw a quickening of the layman's interest in ethical problems, and with the Revival of Learning men began to turn back with ever-mounting enthusiasm to the original classical sources of moral philosophy, discovering in the ethical treatises of Greek and Latin writers moral doctrine of far greater appeal than that which came to them filtered through the medieval mind. For these men, the pagan Stoics supplanted the Christian clergy as instructors in the way of life ; Stoical control of the lower faculties became the high road to wisdom and virtue. The enormous popularity during the Renaissance of the classical authors treating of Stoicism and the abundance of original treatises in Latin and the vernacular setting forth Stoical doctrine all bespeak the same thing : not that this new age had come suddenly upon a point of view hitherto undiscerned, but that a point of view had already emerged during the last centuries of the Middle Ages which caused the Renaissance to find substantiation for it wherever it looked. Once, nature and grace, faith and reason had been perfectly reconciled. A growing scepticism had driven a wedge between, and by the sixteenth century there is seen a sharp severance of faith and reason. Religious faith and dogma lie on one side, inaccessible to the faulty instrument of speculative reason ; on the other side lie the problems confronting the natural man, and in these only wisdom — i.e., reason which has abandoned all claim to penetrate the supernatural — can serve as guide. This disjunction of the natural and the spiritual man, complete at the Renaissance, is reflected in the commanding position which neo-Stoicism came to occupy. Through purely natural reason it offered a way of moral conduct to men whose interests were now centred exclusively in the natural world and who without the guidance of secular wisdom were like sailors called upon to navigate unknown seas without the aid of either stars or compass.

Neo-Stoicism dwelt endlessly upon the passions, for it is these that deflect man from virtue and contentment. The passions are voluntary, born of reason but of a false reason; the will, by giving assent to these false judgments, gives life to the passions. Another source of the passions is found in the senses: these, messengers to the understanding, are often deceived; a judgment made entirely in reliance upon them without the intervention of corrective reason will, when erroneous, excite passions in the soul. The ideal which neo-Stoicism raised up is apathy, a life of unimpassioned reason. The passions, being evil, must have no play.

A Renaissance phenomenon in origin, neo-Stoicism reached its height at the end of the sixteenth and the beginning of the seventeenth century. For a long time thereafter, however, its reverberations are to be heard in the utterances of the moralists. It would be incorrect to call Swift a Stoic, yet it is against the background of neo-Stoicism that his repudiation of the passions must be viewed.

It is from the life of Swift that the most striking illustrations of his rejection of the passions are to be drawn, but we are not at this point concerned with his life but with his formal thought. Swift came closest to defining a life of unimpassioned reason in his description of the Houyhnhnms. There is also the following observation from *Thoughts on Religion* (undated), which, though it legitimizes certain passions, emphasizes at the same time the dominating function of reason.

Although reason were intended by Providence to govern our passions, yet it seems that, in two points of the greatest moment to the being and continuance of the world, God hath intended our passions to prevail over reason. The first is, the propagation of our species, since no wise man ever married from the dictates of reason. The other is, the love of life, which, from the dictates of reason, every man would despise, and wish it at an end, or that it never had a beginning.

In the neo-Stoicism of the Renaissance is found in an extreme form the insistence that reason must and can subdue the passions. But there is a broader point of view, pervading the entire period down through the seventeenth century and illustrated in Swift, which describes human nature as a dualism of reason and the lower faculties, and morality as the triumph of reason. This ethical position, however, did not occupy the field to the total exclusion of all others. Highly significant variations appeared in time. Descartes, for example, in *Les passions de l'âme,* though his tone is Stoical, reaches the conclusion that passion is good provided it serves the will. In thus coming to terms with the passions Descartes was moved by a spirit similar to that which before the end of the seventeenth century had created in 'sentimentalism' an ethical position which challenged the interpretation put upon the passions by the doctrines of which we have been speaking.[4] It is this situation which placed Swift the moralist in such striking contrast with certain contemporary moralists like Steele. Whereas these latter talked of benevolence and charity — passions essentially good — Swift remained to the end the unyielding foe of the passions. For him, the passions could only be evil, virtue only the conquest of the lower self through rational restraint. In taking up this position he was not, as we have seen, out of relation to the century into which he was born, but just as he surpassed all of his contemporaries in intensity of apprehension so did he press home his ethical theories with immeasurable harshness.

Up to this point we have been considering Swift's ethical attitude. We turn now to his æsthetic principles, our discussion of which we place at this point for the reason that they were but an extension of his moral theories. At the start it would be well to issue a general warning against drawing from what follows a too commonly held misapprehension that the literature of this period illustrates, either in theory or practice, a complete submergence of the imagination beneath a rigorously presiding reason.[5] Swift, it is true, regarded the imagination with the same hostility that he did the passions, but in this he displayed a far more austere doctrine than did his representative contemporaries. If the latter sought in reason a check upon unruly imagination, they did not believe that they were ostracizing imagination; if in their poetry they declined to 'speak out,' if they avoided giving voice to their individual moods, that was because the poet, tempering imagination with reason, addressed the general sense of mankind. Mr. T. S. Eliot has bidden us seek in their poetry for the *result* of imagination. Unlike imagination in romantic poetry, which speaks directly to us, the imaginative element in the poetry of the latter seventeenth century and of the eighteenth century is never thrust forward, but this does not mean that it has been excluded. It would be regrettable if Swift's heresy regarding the artistic imagination were given a general application to his age quite out of accord with truth.

In early seventeenth-century æsthetic theory one finds a contrast between judgment on the one side and fancy and imagination on the other, with fancy and imagination regarded with some distrust.[6] It was an inherited view, this distrust, which can be traced back through medieval writers to the Greek philosophers.[7] Francis Bacon's treatment of the imagination illustrates a late sixteenth-century point of view.[8] According to him the function of the imagination in eloquence is to stir up the affections and render them obedient to reason. Imagination, that is, has its place in literature, but it must always be regarded as a distorter of truth; if the affections were at all times obedient to reason, as they should be, there would be no need for imaginative excitation. The cautious manner in which Bacon assigns to imagination an æsthetic function only half legitimate is characteristic of the suspicion attaching to a faculty associated quite as much with insanity and morbidity as with the arts.

But it was to Hobbes that the English of the last half of the seventeenth century looked for the classic solution of the æsthetic problem. The mind, according to Hobbes, is at birth a *tabula rasa*. Upon this blank the mechanical universe, by means of the senses, inscribes impressions. All intellectual activity is in respect of these inscriptions. For instance, the æsthetic experience involved in writing a poem: 'Experience begets memory; Memory begets Judgement and

Fancy; Judgment begets the strength and structure, and
Fancy begets the ornaments of a Poem.'⁹   It mattered not
whether critics and poets accepted, repudiated, or even understood Hobbes's philosophical materialism; his statement
of the relation of literary judgment and fancy they took over
as a truism, with the result that it was he more than any other
writer who fixed the characteristic attitude of the time.
Fancy or imagination is the inventive faculty, without which
poetry cannot come to exist.   But, as Dryden wrote, 'imagination in a poet is a faculty so wild and lawless, that like an
high-ranging spaniel, it must have clogs tied to it, lest it
outrun the judgment. . .'¹⁰   There must be a happy union
of fancy and judgment, a blending of imagination with the
rational faculty.   Only the extremist like Swift would shrivel
up the imagination.

It is in *The Mechanical Operation of the Spirit* (ptd. 1704
with *A Tale of a Tub*) and *A Letter of Advice to a Young
Poet* (1720; ptd. 1721) that Swift prepared his bitterest cor-
rosives for the imagination.¹¹   'Too intense a Contemplation,' he wrote in the former piece,

is not the Business of Flesh and Blood ; it must by the necessary
Course of Things, in a little Time, let go its Hold, and fall into
Matter.   Lovers, for the sake of Celestial Converse, are but another sort of *Platonicks,* who pretend to see Stars and Heaven in
Ladies Eyes, and to look or think no lower ; but the same *Pit*
is provided for both ; and they seem a perfect Moral to the Story
of that Philosopher, who, while his Thoughts and Eyes were
fixed upon the *Constellations,* found himself seduced by his
lower Parts into a *Ditch*.

This deadly animosity towards any sort of imaginative
Contemplation does not arise, as some would have it, from a
loathsome, materialistic philosophy.   Swift neither believed
nor said that all man's faculties are purely physical in origin ;
what he was saying in the *Mechanical Operation* is that
imagination, mistaken for Celestial Converse, is founded in
matter and thus belies its pretensions.

In another passage in the same satire Swift gave of his
materialistic theory of the artistic imagination an ironically
scientific explanation which for brilliance of execution is

unsurpassed. It is the opinion of choice virtuosi, we read, that the brain is only a crowd of little animals, with teeth and claws extremely sharp, who cling together like bees:

> . . . all invention is formed by the Morsure of two or more of these Animals, upon certain capillary Nerves, which proceed from thence, whereof three Branches spread into the Tongue, and two into the right Hand. . . If the Morsure be Hexagonal, it produces Poetry; the Circular gives Eloquence; If the Bite hath been Conical, the Person, whose Nerve is so affected, shall be disposed to write upon the Politicks; and so of the rest.

It is thus, concealing himself behind a fashionable materialism of the day which he contemned, that Swift brought his ethical theories to bear upon literature. Reason should be supreme. When it is overthrown by Folly, vaporous enthusiasms arise from the lower faculties. It is so in religion, in morals, in literature.

Take, again, the *Letter to a Young Poet*. I would not despair to prove, wrote Swift,

> that it is impossible to be a good soldier, divine, or lawyer, or even so much as an eminent bellman, or ballad-singer, without some taste of poetry, and a competent skill in versification. But I say the less of this, because the renowned Sir Philip Sidney has exhausted the subject before me, in his 'Defence of Poesie,' on which I shall make no other remark but this, that he argues there as if he really believed himself.

With relentless indignation Swift pursued the shams and impostures which dupe man; pitilessly he turned them inside out, displaying their false interiors which belie their superficial fairness. It is not as you think — look! The word *cynicism*, so often applied to Swift in this connexion, will not do, for the cynic is one to whom all the contrasts which he delights to reveal between reality and pretension are merely additional evidence that the universe is an enormous cancer. It is moral realism, not cynicism, which drove Swift — the passion for seeing and for making the whole world see with eyes undimmed by folly and sentiment. The most reviled of Swift's poems, *The Lady's Dressing Room, A Beautiful Young Nymph, Strephon and Chloe, Cassinus and*

Peter (all *ca.* 1730, 1731) are not to be explained by morbidity alone. They supplement in their strange fashion
the description of the imagination found in the *Mechanical
Operation* and the ironic defence of poesie in the *Letter to
a Young Poet:* they are parodies on sentimental poetry,
styptics to the sensual imagination.

Swift's undying hatred of 'enthusiasm' and the satiric expression which he accorded this hatred stand in close relation
to his æsthetic principles.   There was in the seventeenth century a general revolt against 'enthusiasm.' [12]   In England two
treatises, the first appearing in 1655, the second in the following year, laid down the lines upon which this revolt was
to be pressed by English writers of this century.   The earlier
work is by Meric Casaubon: 'Treatise concerning *Enthusiasme,* as it is an Effect of *Nature :* but is mistaken by many
for either *Divine Inspiration,* or *Diabolical Possession.'*   It
is thus that Casaubon defined 'natural' enthusiasm: 'an extraordinary, transcendent, but natural fervency, or pregnancy
of the soul, spirits, or brain, producing strange effects, apt to
be mistaken for supernatural.'   In '*Enthusiasmus Trium-
phatus,* or a Discourse of the *Nature, Causes, Kinds,* and
Cure of Enthusiasme,' Henry More defined enthusiasm as
'nothing else but a misconceit of being *inspired'—* a misconceit due to imagination, to be corrected through rational
control.   By the time Casaubon and More wrote, the word
enthusiasm had come in England to be weighted with special
meaning.   The saints, fanatics thrown up by the innumerable religious sects of these years, were now vying with one
another in pretensions to divine inspiration.   *Enthusiasm*
did not lose its general applicability, but the extraordinary
fervency of the saints bestowed on it a particular significa-
tion which was kept alive by the undying animosity with
which the Restoration looked back upon these religious
fanatics.

The revolt again enthusiasm was pushed in several directions, not always with direct reference to religious fanaticism.   It is seen, for example, in the trend towards simplicity
in the prose style of the second half of the century [13] — a
similar trend is of course apparent in verse as well.   Sim-

plicity was demanded in pulpit eloquence. It was likewise called for by the new scientists in works on natural philosophy—in his *History of the Royal Society* (1667) Sprat gave as the ideal of style the expression of 'so many *things* almost in an equal number of *words*.' The manifold influences of the time all converged to make simplicity the canon of prose style. Here, to a greater extent than in poetry, reason must rule. Eloquence moves the passions, but it is sense that reaches the understanding; manifestly it is to the understanding that the prose writer addresses himself.

The dryness of Swift's prose style—particularly in his political and religious essays, and always to be distinguished from the genius which made of this dryness a consummate medium—derives immediately from this seventeenth-century movement. As in his unyielding ethical rigidity he is of the seventeenth rather than the eighteenth century, so in prose style his manner is not that of Addison and Steele or again of Bolingbroke but of the earlier period. The true definition of style, wrote Swift in *A Letter to a Young Gentleman, lately enter'd into Holy Orders* (1720; ptd. 1721), is 'proper words in proper places.' In his sermons the clergyman, Swift proceeds, is to avoid obscure terms and hard words: 'a divine has nothing to say to the wisest congregation of any parish in this kingdom, which he may not express in a manner to be understood by the meanest among them.' He is to shun the 'quaint, terse, florid style, rounded into periods and cadences, commonly without either propriety or meaning.' As for the 'moving manner of preaching,' calculated to work on the passions, it is one esteemed and practiced 'among all the preachers and hearers of the fanatic or enthusiastic strain.' Swift concludes the matter with this short but masterly paragraph:

I . . . entreat you to make use of this faculty (if you ever be so unfortunate as to think you have it) as seldom, and with as much caution as you can, else I may probably have occasion to say of you as a great person said of another upon this very subject. A lady asked him coming out of church, whether it were not a very moving discourse? 'Yes,' said he, 'I was extremely sorry, for the man is my friend.'

At no time, however, was the attack upon zeal — the religious form of enthusiasm illustrated in the saints — remitted.
Both psychological analysis, which soberly exposed enthusiasm as imagination gaining the control of reason and thus
denied it any supernatural source, and satire motivated by
instinctive rage were employed.[14]   It was Samuel Butler who
made of these two weapons a single one.   His miscellaneous
observations and his prose *Characters* are ample proof of his
intellectual acumen.   In nature extremes are held in balance; can the human intellect but achieve an order comparable to that which nature exhibits, reason and judgment
will operate to check man's errant impulses.   Zeal is only
one manifestation of a disease with which man and society
have at all times been consumed — the disease of presumption, bred in the lower faculties, conveyed through the febrile
imagination.   *Hudibras* is vastly more than instinctive ridicule of presbyterians and independents; it is satire intellec-
tualized by as theoretical a mind as England had produced.

Now, it has often been said that Butler is Swift's master.
This can mean several things.   One thing which it cannot
mean is that the satiric artist in Swift went to school to
Butler, for the latter failed consistently in his search for a
satiric medium which should articulate contempt and theory,
emotion and informing intellect.   What seems beyond debate is that it was Butler who more than any other taught
Swift to hate zeal and regard it as a disease of the imagination.   It might be supposed that by 1696, when Swift was
engaged on *A Tale of a Tub,* religious zeal would have lost
much of its power to rouse the satirist.   The dissenters of
these years, though they stemmed from the zealots of the
forties and fifties, had laid inspiration aside for middle-class
respectability and industry.   It will not do to lay the onus
upon the dissenters in Ulster who had surrounded Swift at
Kilroot; they, no more than their English brethren, answered
to the descriptions in *A Tale of a Tub.*   The truth is that
here again we find Swift ridden by the ideas of the seventeenth rather than the eighteenth century.   It is the voice of
Samuel Butler that speaks in *A Tale of a Tub,* a voice of the
Restoration when the idea of religious tolerance was sup-

pressed beneath contempt and vengefulness. And then again, whereas the typical neo-classical hatred of enthusiasm came to be essentially an expression of distaste for any sort of originality that opposed itself to the general sense of mankind, Swift persisted in regarding the enthusiast as one in whom the lower faculties had gained mastery over the higher and in treating him as a morally flagitious person.

In the course of the present section we have seen how Swift was conditioned by that ethical theory of the seventeenth century which distinguished between reason and the passions, and insisted that reason must subdue the lower faculties. But there is present in Swift the moralist another element, complementary to the one that we have been examining and charging it with terrific indignation — the element of anti-rationalism.[15] The pessimistic view of human nature, the insistence on man's fundamental depravity, derives from no single source. In all ages the intellectual aristocrat has regarded with a fierce contempt the stupidity, meanness, and cruelty of his unrefined fellow-creatures. The Christian comes to optimism not through a denial of man's natural perversity but through an overwhelming perception of it. The seventeenth-century atmosphere was quick to breed pessimism: reason should subdue the passions, but everywhere the passions prevail. This pessimism arising against the background of neo-Stoicism led to an analysis of human nature fitted above all else to disclose in its manifold forms, obvious and obscure, the irrationalities motivating conduct. It is for this reason that so many writers of the time — e.g., Pascal, La Rochefoucauld; in England, Butler, Wycherley, Swift — are unsurpassed in the technique of dissection but at the same time curiously limited in their explorations. Swift's pessimism settled upon two aspects of human nature and conduct: irrationality and egoism. Irrationality, according to its mode, was either contemptible or horrible. In fools it excited one's scorn, for here the vapours of zeal and enthusiasm which anæsthetized reason produced ridiculous rather than outrageous conduct; it is scorn which informs the satire in *A Tale of a Tub*. But depravity, not folly, is the disease consuming man; it is the depravity of creatures supposedly civilized that excites horror in the king of Brobdingnag and the wise Houyhnhnms.

'You are so hardy as to tell me,' Swift once wrote to Pope, 'of your intentions to write maxims in opposition to Rochefoucauld, who is my favorite, because I found my whole character in him.' Swift did not found his whole character in the writer of the famous *Maximes;* had he done so we should find the cynic in him overriding the indignant moralist. What Swift did take over from La Rochefoucauld was the latter's exposure of egoism. Swift's verses *On the Death of Dr. Swift* (1731) are headed by one of the *Maximes:* 'Dans l'adversité de nos meilleurs amis, nous trouvons toujours quelque chose, qui ne nous déplaît pas.' This unimaginative self-interest surprised and troubled Swift's heart — so great was his own sorrow when adversity, not to mention death, touched his friends. There is a note of pity — not pity for himself — in the wonderful lines on his own death :

> My female friends, whose tender hearts
> Have better learn'd to act their parts,
> Receive the news in doleful dumps :
> 'The Dean is dead : (and what is trumps ?)
> Then, Lord have mercy on his soul !
> (Ladies, I'll venture for the vole.)
> Six deans, they say, must bear the pall :
> (I wish I knew what king to call.)
> Madam, your husband will attend
> The funeral of so good a friend.
> No, madam. 'tis a shocking sight :
> And he's engaged to-morrow night ·
> My Lady Club wou'd take it ill,
> If he shou'd fail her at quadrille.
> He loved the Dean — (I lead a heart,)
> But dearest friends, they say, must part.
> His time was come : he ran his race,
> We hope he's in a better place.'

Swift's psychological analysis brought to light, however, a different kind of egoism, which kindled all the fires of his hate. The presumption of man, who in the face of corruptions of will and mind dares soar on the wings of pride, was not to be borne. *Le mythe animal* is Swift's revenge on the pride of man.[16] Men without Reason, wrote Samuel Butler, are worse than beasts : beasts have instinct, which is nothing but a kind of implicit reason 'that without understanding why, directs them, to do, or forebeare those thinges that are agreeable, or hurtful [to] their Particular Natures : while a Fool is but Half Man, and Half beast, is depriv'd of the Advantages of both, and has the Benefit of Neither.' In *The Beasts' Confession* (1732) Swift employed the comparison between man and the animals in a form quite undisguised by the artistry of A Voyage to the Houyhnhnms. The preface to these verses concludes thus :

The poem is grounded upon the universal folly in mankind of mistaking their talents ; by which the author does a great honour to his own species, almost equalling them with certain brutes ; wherein, indeed, he is too partial, as he freely confesses : and yet he has gone as low as he well could, by specifying four animals ; the wolf, the ass, the swine, and the ape ; all equally mischievous, except the last, who outdoes them in the article of cunning : so great is the pride of man !

The verses end by charging that Æsop, upon whose fables Swift has just been drawing, did as a matter of fact libel the four-foot race when he sought to illustrate human nature by stories dealing with beasts.

> Creatures of every kind but ours
> Well comprehend their natural powers,
> While we, whom reason ought to sway,
> Mistake our talents every day.
> The Ass was never known so stupid,
> To act the part of Tray or Cupid ;
> Nor leaps upon his master's lap,
> There to be stroked, and fed with pap,
> As Æsop would the world persuade ;
> He better understands his trade :
> Nor comes whene'er his lady whistles,
> But carries loads, and feeds on thistles.
> Our author's meaning, I presume, is
> A creature *bipes et implumis* ;
> Wherein the moralist design'd
> A compliment on human kind ;
> For here he owns, that now and then
> Beasts may degenerate into men.

The preceding analysis of Swift's ethical ideas has served its major purpose if it has made clear the nature of his ethical 'rationalism'—to be distinguished from the characteristic rationalism of the Enlightenment—and of his anti-rationalism, which together became in time the dominant element in his ideology. The Swift who has evoked from his critics sentiments running from admiration to inarticulate hatred is really far less the enigmatic companion of Stella and Vanessa—though one may think that one's concern is with the romantic figure—than the pessimistic moralist, dwelling incessantly upon man's depravity through a refusal to live by reason. One's ultimate judgment of Swift is bound to be affected, whether one realizes it or not, by some sort of judgment regarding his ethical theories. There are those, perhaps, who would prefer to study him only from the point of view of the history of ideas without coming to any final estimate. But an absolute suspension of judgment is impossible; indeed, it is perhaps unnatural, for the soul of Swift was more than embodiment of a certain time spirit. However we regard him, and many will find themselves unable to do so with any sympathy, so lacking was he in that Christian optimism which looks to more than restraining reason for the healing of man's corruption, it cannot be with pity. The intensity of his moral realism is too great. It is not as you think—look! To the end Swift himself looked, his eyes untouched by hope, intent only upon the ineluctable truth as it was given him to see it.

<hr />

5

BEFORE bringing to an end this analysis of Swift's controlling ideas, we should perhaps say a word about his religious position,[17] though we shall have occasion to take this up in greater detail in a succeeding chapter. In order to get at the heart of Swift's religion one must cut through a great deal that is really extraneous—the paradox, for instance, which many have found in a dean of St. Patrick's, admittedly punctilious in the performance of all the duties of his office, who was the author of *Gulliver's Travels*. Granted that

Swift was endowed with a genius better suited for literature and the world of action than for the church, the fact remains that from his youth he looked upon the established church with reverence. It is not a matter of explaining how Swift could have been a priest but of determining what as a priest he believed and taught. It is here that his anti-intellectualism is seen most clearly: the human mind was never intended by God to penetrate the mysteries of revealed religion, which are to be accepted through faith; in other respects the Christian tenets are natural and reasonable, and being so are immediately acceptable by virtue of that reason which has been conferred on all men; the established church is the venerable institution which through divine and traditional sanction symbolizes the life of reason. Beyond such simple dogma Swift rarely ventured; the classical problems of ontology and theology he dismissed with an impatient gesture. There are other aspects of Swift's religious position — his intolerance of dissenters, for example — which need not delay us at this point. It is sufficient to understand both the sincerity and the peculiar limitations of his religious views. He was never a theologian. A moralist first and foremost, he did no more than fix the church into the rigidly ordered system of ideas which he took from his age. Having done this, he worked ceaselessly to raise the church up as the chief support of the life of reason. That there was a fuller life Swift, because of his intellectual heritage, did not understand.

6

THE modern reader disposed to look upon the history of ideas as a rather remote subject will have little desire to trace Swift's controlling concepts in all their intricacy through his writings. But even to such a reader it must by this time be apparent that it is of some moment to understand the nature of Swift's ideas and the general direction in which they pressed. Yet no one conversant with Swift's mind will ever enter for it the claim of originality in the sense of ability to theorize independently. Clarity, force, and abundant power to grasp and to apply — these it had. But the terms with which it operated were of the age.   His essential genius appears not in his formal thought but in his artistic statement, infused as it is with his Dantesque intensity of apprehension which will never cease to cast its fascinating and terrible power over the reader.

CHAPTER V

THE BATTLE OF THE BOOKS AND A TALE OF A TUB

1

IN the spring of 1704 London was gratifyingly scandalized by the appearance of a book the brilliant impertinence of which became at once the subject of immense discussion. It 'has made as much noise,' one report ran, 'and is as full of wit, as any book perhaps that has come out these last hundred years.' [1] Its anonymity only served to spread its fame. From Oxford came word that it had originated there — the work of Edmund Smith and John Philips. [2] But still the rumours ran, assigning the authorship of this shocking volume with superb indifference to reputation. When 'the famous Dr. Smalridge' was touched by the voice of scandal, he declared to Sacheverell that not all they both possessed or that ever they should possess could have hired him to write it. [3] Another of those stigmatized, William King, cleared himself by issuing Some Remarks on The Tale of a Tub, in which he charged that almost every part of this gross book had 'a Tincture of such Filthiness' as rendered it 'unfit for the worst of Uses.' Some there were who having nothing to lose by being supposed the authors could afford to estimate it more judiciously: ' 'Tis very well written and will do good service,' wrote Atterbury, [4] though he recognized that its profane strokes, bound to be misinterpreted, would — as he expressed it elsewhere — do the author's 'reputation and interest in the world more harm than the wit can do him good.' [5]

In the first issue of A Tale of a Tub, as in all subsequent editions, appeared also A Full and True Account Of The Battel Fought last Friday, Between the Ancient and the Modern Books In St. James's Library and A Discourse Concerning the Mechanical Operation of the Spirit. By 1710 the authorship of the volume, which Swift never openly acknowledged, had settled definitely on him. The literary

sources of these satires were early debated and have since
been the subject of extended investigation.[6] But neither
with these nor with the minute details concerning dates of
composition — details recently studied with exacting care [7]—
are we concerned. The satiric artistry which here reaches
a high-water mark can be understood if one comes to these
three pieces with some awareness of Swift's intellectual background — this in lieu of the little which has been revealed
of their specific sources — and a knowledge of a few undisputed facts concerning dates of composition. *A Tale of a
Tub,* it is agreed, was written chiefly during Swift's third
residence at Moor Park; its composition extended over a
number of years and the final version embodied revisions
which could have been made up to the moment of publication and two additions — the dedication to Somers, and
the bookseller's notice to the reader — of 1702-1704. The
sections containing the religious allegory were written first;
then, between June 1697 and March 1698, came *The Battle
of the Books,* and thereafter the remaining sections of the
Tale. The *Mechanical Operation* appears to be contemporary with the later parts of the *Tale.* Whether Swift
worked from the start with a definite plan in mind — which
seems unlikely — or allowed a design to emerge as year by
year he added and revised is all the same — whatever the
method, its result was satire incomparable for the conjunc-
tion of matter, tone, and form.

2

The Battle of the Books was on Swift's part the forcing of
a personal issue. His patron had been attacked, so he chose
to believe, by two unmannerly pedants, William Wotton
and Richard Bentley. The insult called for revenge, and
Swift turned upon Temple's two antagonists with a concentrated fury. From end to end *The Battle of the Books* is
satire of personality, and though broader issues are brought
forward these are made to arise directly and naturally from
the affair between Temple and his critics — if Pedantry seems

to threaten Civilization, that is because Wotton and Bentley have affronted a man of taste.

Through his *Essay upon the Ancient and Modern Learning* (*Miscellany* II, 1690) Temple had set foot in a wide-spread controversy, European in extent, which had been going on since the Renaissance — the controversy regarding the relative merits of the ancients and moderns.   To the philosophic questions which were here involved Swift was supremely indifferent; it was enough that Temple had been attacked, that a man of taste had been flouted by two upstart pedants.   Yet despite Swift's lack of interest in the theoretical issues which had emerged in the course of the long controversy, these issues must be understood if Temple's essay and Swift's defence thereof are to be seen in their proper setting.   There was a time when commentators on Swift dismissed the immediate incident which called forth *The Battle of the Books* as but a repercussion of an inconsequential squabble which had taken place in France a few years earlier.   No one to-day holds such a view.

The challenge to the supremacy of the ancients and to the binding authority of tradition was thrown down when Europe, passing from medievalism into the modern age, discovered new values in secular life and a new confidence in man's unaided reason.[8]   What seemed to free men from the chains of the past was the idea of progress.   In the sixteenth century, above all in the essays of Montaigne, there is clearly foreshadowed the law of the indefinite perfectibility of the arts and sciences.   In France during the succeeding century the controversy between authoritarians and those who championed the present and future of civilization grew in intensity, reaching what may be regarded as a climax when on 27 January 1687 there was read at a meeting of the French Academy the famous poem of Charles Perrault, *Le siècle de Louis le Grand* :[9]

> La belle antiquité fut toujours vénérable ;
> Mais je ne crus jamais qu'elle fut adorable.
> Je vois les anciens, sans plier les genoux ;
> Ils sont grands, il est vrai, mais hommes comme nous ;

Et l'on peut comparer, sans craindre d'être injuste,
Le siècle de Louis au beau siècle d'Auguste.

His majesty, Louis XIV, was at the moment recovering from
a successful operation for the fistula ; it seemed an altogether
appropriate occasion to vindicate the literary glories of his
reign against the detractions of those who argued for the
superiority of ancient letters.   But Perrault did not dodge
his adversaries' philosophic arguments :

A former les esprits comme à former les corps,
La nature en tout temps fait les mêmes efforts ;
Son être est immuable ; et cette forcé aisée
Dont elle produit tout, ne s'est point épuisée :
Jamais l'astre du jour, qu'aujourd'hui nous voyons,
N'eut le front couronné de plus brillants rayons ;
Jamais dans le printemps les roses empourprées
D'un plus vif incarnat ne furent colorées. . .

De cette même main les forces infinies
Produisent en tout temps de semblables génies.

With these words he sought to drive his opponents to cover.
If the forces of nature are constant, wit and genius have
not shrunk since the days of Augustus.   It follows that
knowledge is cumulative, that the level of civilization rises,
that the arts progress with the passage of time.

Perrault's interest was in literature.   It was Fontenelle
who, coming to the aid of Perrault in the ensuing storm,
mingled the arts and the sciences — not that they had never
before been mingled in this way — and applied to them the
law of continuous, necessary, and indefinite perfectibility.[10]
In Fontenelle the modern age of science had spoken unmistakably.

In England the idea of progress was discussed throughout
the seventeenth century, but here the emphasis fell on matters relative to the sciences rather than to the arts, and it
was the scientific aspect which engaged attention when after
the Restoration the newly organized Royal Society brought
to an issue the respective merits of the old and the new
natural philosophy.[11]   This is not to say that before Temple's entrance into the controversy the literary side of the
question had been totally overlooked by the English. Dry-

den's cautious assessment of both ancient and modern writers; his weighing of the values of the literature of the past against the merits of modern writing — this is sufficient evidence that in England the question had not been confined exclusively to the sciences.

In his *Essay upon the Ancient and Modern Learning* Temple's point of departue is Fontenelle's *Poésies pastorales* — containing both a *Discours sur la nature de l'églogue* and the *Digression sur les anciens et les modernes* — and Thomas Burnet's *Sacred Theory of the Earth,* in both of which books he finds the superiority of modern learning and knowledge maintained.[12] The two arguments put forward by modern advocates Temple proceeds to rebut. In the first place, knowledge is not cumulative: it is 'the pure native force of spirit or genius, in some single men' that counts, not the cultural heritage, which extinguishes rather than feeds the flame of genius. To the second point, that since the forces of nature are constant genius cannot grow less, Temple replies with his cyclic theory of history: though man remains essentially the same, physical and social environment condition him differently —'though there are or have been sometimes dwarfs and sometimes giants in the world, yet it does not follow that there must be such in every age, nor in every country.' Having defined his position, having buttressed it with theory, Temple then goes to history for substantiation. Through the fields of human endeavour he ranges, through philosophy, grammar, rhetoric, astronomy, physic, music, architecture, geography, and more besides, supremely confident that all to which he points will show the undeniable superiority of the ancients. He comes lastly to literature — to prose, specifically. And here it is that he falls into error, thereby delivering himself into the hands of the enemy:

It may perhaps be further affirmed, in favour of the ancients, that the oldest books we have are still in their kind the best. The two most ancient that I know of in prose, among those we call profane authors, are Æsop's Fables and Phalaris's Epistles, both living near the same time, which was that of Cyrus and Pythagoras.

From this point on the story unfolds fast.[13]　Charles Boyle, afterwards earl of Orrery, undertook during the years '93 and '94 to edit anew the Epistles of Phalaris, so highly praised by Temple.　He had occasion to consult a manuscript copy of the Epistles in the Royal Library at St. James's Palace and in so doing took offence at the conduct of the library-keeper, Richard Bentley.　In 1694 William Wotton issued his *Reflections upon Ancient and Modern Learning,* in which he challenged Temple's disparagements of the moderns, though he made it clear that he was defending modern learning and knowledge, not modern literature, regarding which he yielded the superiority to antiquity.　But whatever his position, the first offence had been committed : Temple's polite scholarship had been abruptly, therefore unpardonably, called to account.　On the first day of 1695 Boyle's edition appeared, with a sarcastic reference in the preface to Bentley's remarkable courtesy.　Two and a half years thereafter (June 1697) Wotton put forth a second edition of his *Reflections,* with Bentley's first *Dissertation upon the Epistles of Phalaris* appended.　The offence had now assumed an alarming character, for, with a wealth of scholarship that put to shame all who had ranged themselves with Temple, Bentley showed that the esteemed Epistles of Phalaris and the Fables of Æsop were spurious.　The wits of Christ Church, who had abetted Boyle and of course took Temple's part, retorted upon Bentley in a clever piece which they called *Dr. Bentley's Dissertations on the Epistles of Phalaris, and the Fables of Æsop, examin'd by the Honourable Charles Boyle, Esq.*　This appeared early in March 1698.　*The Battle of the Books* was occasioned by Wotton's *Reflections* of June 1697, which included Bentley's first *Dissertation,* while the closing incident of the satire is an allegorical representation of the victory which Boyle was supposed to have gained in March 1698 through *Dr. Bentley's Dissertation Examin'd* — thus Swift's contribution is approximately dated.　And here we may end the story, though in fact the war was drawn out to amusing length by the books and pamphlets which continued to appear.　Of these only one needs mention — Bentley's second *Dissertation* (1699), where the wits of Christ Church were made to pay dearly for their cleverness, which was mercilessly turned against them by the greatest philologist of the age.

It is not altogether strange that the triumphant scholarship of Wotton and Bentley, of the historian and of the philologist, should at the moment have seemed to most but ill-mannered pedantry. Polite learning was still in the ascendant. It required a later time, cognizant of scientific methods of research, to assign the victory to the rightful party. Meanwhile Swift rode triumphantly the wave of general indignation which bore against the two scholars. To what degree does his satire suffer by the modern approval of Wotton and Bentley? Not greatly, it would seem. However dubiously we may sit down to *The Battle of the Books,* our resistance is straightway set at naught by Swift's satiric artistry. Yet it would not do to say that we are merely beguiled into taking the worse for the better cause. Though the justice of the years has long since removed the dunces' caps from the heads of Wotton and Bentley, their simulacra that indulge in such ridiculous antics throughout Swift's piece will to the end of time remain contemptible in a very real sense. Because Swift misjudged those whom he indicated as the enemy does not mean that there was — and is — no enemy. The appearance in June 1697 of Wotton's *Reflections* and Bentley's appended *Dissertation* again brought to a focus that hatred of pedantry which five years before had possessed Swift when in his verse he had described the Progress of Censure, Pedantry, and Pride ; here, in the lucubrations of Wotton and Bentley, was 'modern learning' with a vengeance, here a prime example of enthusiasm, here the dethronement of good sense, manners, and reason. Not all of Swift's terms and assumptions coincide with ours, but his description and defence of the civilized attitude will always come home.

The Battle of the Books, unlike *A Tale of a Tub,* is led into by no bewildering maze of prefatory matter ; there are only the notice of the bookseller to the reader and The Preface of the Author. The first sets forth concisely the origin of the dispute between Temple and his critics.

7

The Preface, but two paragraphs in length, may seem to
have little relevance to what follows, but in fact it an-
nounces — in paragraph 2 — the chief theme upon which the
ensuing satire is to be a series of variations:

There is a Brain *that will endure but one* Scumming: *Let
the Owner gather it with Discretion, and manage his little Stock
with Husbandry; but of all things, let him beware of bringing
it under the* Lash *of his* Betters; *because, That will make it all
bubble up into Impertinence, and he will find no new Supply:
Wit, without knowledge, being a Sort of* Cream, *which gathers
in a Night to the Top, and by a skilful Hand, may be soon
whipt into* Froth; *but once scumm'd away, what appears underneath will be fit for nothing, but to be thrown to the Hogs.*

The importunities of the early verse have vanished. We
have instead a prime example of Swift's *dolce stil nuovo* —
impertinence, deflating imagery, indirection, and implication. Wit without knowledge is a Sort of Cream. . . Thus
is the revolt against reason indicated.

In the body of the satire — the Full and True Account
of the Battel Fought last Friday, &c. — five incidents may
be distinguished. The first concerns the outbreak of the
quarrel among the books under Bentley's care. Aside from
the ingenuity displayed in investing the volumes with life
and in neatly fitting the details of the allegory to the circumstances of the real quarrel there is little that is remarkable here. The second incident is brilliantly handled.
'. . . upon the highest Corner of a large Window, there
dwelt a certain *Spider*, swollen up to the first Magnitude,
by the Destruction of infinite Numbers of *Flies*, whose
Spoils lay scattered before the Gates of his Palace, like
human Bones before the Cave of some Giant.' Into the
spider's web flies a bee, who extricates himself unharmed
and pauses at a safe distance to clean his wings. The spider,
whose web has been ruined, spies the culprit and shouts
insults at him: he is a rascal, a vagabond without house or
home, living upon a universal plunder of nature. To which
the bee replies at length: you boast that you are self-
reliant, drawing and spinning out all from yourself; '*That
is to say, if we may judge of the Liquor in the Vessel by*

*what issues out, You posess a good plentiful Store of Dirt
and Poison in your Breast. . .'* In short, the question comes
all to this:

> *Whether is the nobler Being of the two, That which by a lazy
> Contemplation of four Inches round ; by an over-weening Pride,
> which feeding and engendering on it self, turns all into Excre-
> ment and Venom; producing nothing at all, but Fly-bane and
> a Cobweb : Or That, which, by an universal Range, with long
> Search, much Study, true Judgment, and Distinction of Things,
> brings home Honey and Wax.*

Æsop overhears these recriminations and sums up the
dispute. The spider, with his love of dirt and his self-
sufficiency, is a perfect modern, whereas the bee lives as
do the ancients, bringing home honey and wax and *'thus
furnishing Mankind with the two Noblest of Things, which
are Sweetness and Light.'*
Throughout this incident the artistic economy is something to marvel at : there is not a superfluous phrase ; from
line to line the meaning is drawn out with a logical inevitability that makes of words the exact symbols of thought.
As for the satiric effect, this is gained by means which the
young versifier had understood but had not been able to
manipulate, but over which the prose satirist has gained
masterly control. The spider's every word and the entire
series of images applied to him by the bee and by Æsop
are nauseous. It is through disgust that Swift habitually
attains his most forcible effects : all that is unacceptable to
reason is given an emotional repulsiveness so strong that
it is attended by a definite visceral reaction. There is nothing quite comparable to Swift's mastery of disgust. Physical
sensations of a different sort other writers have known how
to arouse. Only Swift makes us retch at the irrational.
The third incident includes the marshalling of the two
hostile armies, the description of their respective leaders,
the engagement of the two battle lines, and a number of
hand-to-hand combats, wherein, needless to say, the ancients
are almost uniformly triumphant. Capital is the encounter
between Virgil and Dryden. The former appears in shining
armour astride a mettled horse. Towards him advances an

unknown foe 'upon a sorrel Gelding of a monstrous Size,'
old and lean, whose high trot causes a terrible clashing of
the rider's armour.   'The two Cavaliers had now approached
within the Throw of a Lance, when the Stranger desired a
Parley, and lifting up the Vizard of his Helmet, a Face
hardly appeared from within, which after a pause, was
known for that of the renowned *Dryden*.'   A former heavy-
weight boxing champion is still remembered for his short
punches ; their power was crushing but they were delivered
with such speed and at such short range that it took a slow-
motion camera to record them.   When Swift chose, he could
hit like that.   Only after we have found the pea inside the
helmet and identified it as Dryden's head do we quite understand what has happened.

The fourth incident splits the third.   In the Milky Way
the gods are convened in council to watch the momentous
battle now in progress on the library shelves.   Momus,
patron god of the moderns, takes alarm at the impending
fate of his children and rushes for assistance to the goddess
Criticism.   This deity

had Claws like a Cat : Her Head, and Ears, and Voice, resembled
those of an *Ass ;* Her Teeth fallen out before ; Her Eyes turned
inward, as if she lookt only upon herself : Her Diet was the
overflowing of her own *Gall :* Her *Spleen* was so large, as to
stand prominent like a Dug of the first Rate, nor wanted Excres-
cencies in form of Teats, at which a Crew of ugly Monsters were
greedily sucking. . .

Concerned above all for her son Wotton, Criticism flies down
to the scene of battle and in her own fashion encourages her
children.

The concluding incident impinges directly on Wotton
and Bentley.   Their last adventures on the field of battle,
recounted in mock-heroic style, are made to allegorize their
attack on Temple and their supposed defeat at the hands of
Charles Boyle.   Bravely the two moderns set out to raid
the enemy, 'resolving by Policy or Surprize, to attempt some
neglected Quarter of the *Antients* Army.'   The picture they
make as together they stalk their foes only epic simile can
give :

As when two *Mungrel-Curs,* whom *native Greediness,* and *domestick Want,* provoke, and join in Partnership, though fearful, nightly to invade the Folds of some rich Grazier ; They, with Tails depress'd, and lolling Tongues, creep soft and slow ; mean while, the conscious *Moon,* now in her *Zenith,* on their guilty Heads, darts perpendicular Rays ; Nor dare they bark, though much provok'd at her refulgent Visage, whether seen in Puddle by Reflexion, or in Sphear direct ; but one surveys the Region round, while t'other scouts the Plain. . . So march'd this lovely, loving Pair of Friends. . .

Their first adventure brings them upon the sleeping forms of Phalaris and Æsop, whose armour they steal — a goddess protects the ancients from further harm. It is then that they sight Temple and Boyle by the fountain of Helicon, where, quite unaware of danger, these two allies of the ancients are drinking deeply of the limpid water. Wotton darts his lance at Temple, but it falls harmless, whereat Boyle pursues the two marauders, lets fly 'a Launce of wondrous Length and sharpness,' and transfixes both.

As, when a skilful Cook has truss'd a Brace of *Woodcocks,* He, with Iron Skewer, pierces the tender Sides of both, their Legs and Wings close pinion'd to their Ribs ; So was this pair of Friends transfix'd, till down they fell, joyn'd in their Lives, joyn'd in their Deaths ; so closely joyn'd, that *Charon* would mistake them both for one, and waft them over *Styx* for half his Fare. Farewel, beloved, loving Pair ; Few Equals have you left behind : And happy and immortal shall you be, if all my Wit and Eloquence can make you.

So ends this epic fragment, and with it *The Battle of the Books.*

3

PRECISELY how *A Tale of a Tub* assumed its final form one can only speculate.[14] Internal evidence of dates is not entirely lacking, but the conclusions which emerge — these have already been set forth — do not allow one to dogmatize. It would seem that Swift first worked out an allegory expressing the moderate and reasonable position maintained by the church of England between the two extremes of Roman catholic presumption and error on one hand and dissenting enthusiasm on the other. It is impossible to tell at how early a date Swift's mind came to entertain this allegory, but when he returned to Moor Park in 1696 there is not much question that he set to work or continued to work on the story of the three brothers and their adventures with their coats. Then, in June 1697, came the double attack on Temple by Wotton and Bentley, and the religious allegory was set aside for a satire which should both humiliate the two moderns and raise to the level of the universal the issue between diseased learning and taste. *The Battle of the Books* was begun; finished it must have been not long after the appearance in March 1698 of *Dr. Bentley's Dissertations Examin'd*. Now, presumably, Swift returned to his earlier composition, but with a mind still bent on the pursuit of modern learning and with a pen which had just drawn blood for the first time and was eager for more; somehow the attack on the moderns must be sustained. The solution was pure genius: the religious allegory was retained, but by being cut up into sections it permitted the intercalation of a number of new sections or 'digressions' in which modern learning could be stigmatized with that satiric art born of *The Battle of the Books* and lusty from its first triumph. By any other writer such a scheme would have been rejected as soon as conceived, promising only a hopeless hotchpotch. But Swift took up the scent like a beagle: here was intellectual unity to emerge gradually, relentlessly, out of disparate themes; here was room and to spare for the leisurely and at times apparently aimless manœuvring on which the effects of indirection and implication depended; here were irrelevance, incoherence, and digression which — save for the hidden purpose — parodied the madness of modern writings.

The masterpiece of prose satire which fell on London with so much noise in the spring of 1704 no *precis* can encompass. In his Apology (1710), Swift himself gave of *A Tale of a Tub* as adequate a summary as can be hoped for: the author of the *Tale*, he wrote, '*thought the numerous and gross Corruptions in Religion and Learning might furnish Matter for a Satyr, that would be useful and diverting. . .*'

This statement leads one further than might be supposed ; it is, in fact, the guiding thread through the astonishing maze of introductions, prefaces, sections, and digressions which is *A Tale of a Tub*. A defence of the church of England as the *via media*, a defence that turns into an attack on religious corruption in the form of dissenting enthusiasm ; satire of modern corruptions of learning and parody of the modern manner — this is the double theme of the *Tale*, of which theme every portion of the work is in one way or another a variation or a developing statement.

In analysing *A Tale of a Tub*, visual aid is needed. The *Tale* is composed of sixteen parts, arranged as follows :

1. Dedication, to the Right Honourable John Lord Somers *
2. The Bookseller to the Reader
3. The Epistle Dedicatory, to His Royal Highness Prince Posterity
4. The Preface
5. § I. The Introduction [the three edifices in the air, etc.]
6. § II. [the three brothers]
7. § III. A Digression concerning Criticks
8. § IV. [brother Peter becomes insufferable]
9. § V. A Digression in the Modern Kind
10. § VI. [brothers Martin and Jack]
11. § VII. A Digression in Praise of Digressions
12. § VIII. [the æolists and Jack]
13. § IX. A Digression concerning the Original, the Use and Improvement of Madness in a Commonwealth
14. § X. [sometimes entitled 'A Further Digression']
15. § XI. [a *Character* of Jack]
16. The Conclusion

* Beginning with the fifth (1710) edition, the Gothic profusion of design was further enhanced by the addition of An Apology before the Dedication, of eight illustrations, and of a new set of notes. Marginal notes had adorned the first four editions ; to these were now added notes at the foot of the page, some of them unsigned — undoubtedly by Swift — and some of them by — of all people ! — Wotton. In 1705, in the third edition of his *Reflections*, Wotton had delivered himself of certain *Observations upon The Tale of a Tub*, from which Swift lifted a number of pat explanations, signed them each with Wotton's name, and inserted them at the foot of the page along with his own unsigned notes. *The History of Martin*, first published in 1720 and since then almost always given in editions of the *Tale*, is to be regarded as spurious.

The first five parts of the *Tale,* from the dedication to Somers through §1, the Introduction, may be regarded as a labyrinth craftily constructed to lead into the main body of the satire. They illustrate to perfection that 'new manner' of which Swift spoke in the Apology: *'He resolved to proceed in a manner, that should be altogether new, the World having been already too long nauseated with endless Repetitions upon every Subject.'* Delicious parody of literary manners 'in this polite and most accomplish'd Age,' when this writer went in heavily for dedications — see Dryden — and that for prefaces, introductions, and apologies, these five opening parts are held together chiefly by the firmness and unfaltering appositeness of line and tone, and only in a secondary way by the sustained attack on the moderns and the corruptions of modern learning — only once are religious corruptions introduced. Impertinence is foremost. Penetrate this and you find the satire, which is no longer the forthright denunciation of the early verse but an insinuating lethal gas compounded of irony, parody, and implication. This last element, implication, has been refined to its deadliest degree: like some giant in *Gulliver's Travels* bending over a body of water and aimlessly stirring it with his finger, the satirist sets in motion a veritable maelstrom, whereupon with the utmost casualness he propels his tiny victims towards the devouring whirl. Beyond this, indirection cannot go.

Taken singly, these first five parts lose much unless they are seen as segments of a whole, for they are one both through the unifying tone and the sustained attack on the moderns. The opening part, the dedication to Somers, is as clever a piece of raillery as Swift ever indulged in — raillery, as he elsewhere defined it, being 'to say something that at first appeared a reproach or reflection; but, by some turn of wit unexpected and surprising, ended always in a compliment, and to the advantage of the person it was addressed to.'

The third part — to pass over the second — is an Epistle Dedicatory, addressed to His Royal Highness Prince Posterity, and turns out to be a defence of the corporation of modern writers penned by one of them whom the indifference of Father Time to modern productions has deeply incensed. The indirection in which the *Tale* abounds is here well illustrated, for not until the sorry case of the moderns has been diagnosed in terms of the greatest generality do we have the following account of the languishing fate of certain distinguished representatives of the brotherhood:

I do . . . affirm upon the Word of a sincere Man, that there is now actually in being, a certain Poet called *John Dryden,* whose Translation of *Virgil* was lately printed in a large Folio, well bound, and if diligent search were made, for ought I know, is yet to be seen. There is another call'd *Nahum Tate,* who is ready to make Oath that he has caused many Rheams of Verse to be published, whereof both himself and his Bookseller (if lawfully required) can still produce authentick Copies, and therefore wonders why the World is pleased to make such a Secret of it. There is a Third, known by the Name of *Tom Durfey,* a Poet of vast Comprehension, an universal Genius, and most profound Learning. There are also one Mr. *Rymer,* and one Mr. *Dennis,* most profound Criticks. There is a Person styl'd Dr. *B — — tl — y,* who has written near a thousand Pages of immense Erudition, *giving a full and true Account* of a certain *Squable* of wonderful Importance between himself and a Bookseller: He is a Writer of infinite Wit and Humour; no Man raillyes with a better Grace, and in more sprightly Turns. Farther, I avow to *Your Highness,* that with these Eyes I have beheld the Person of *William W — — tt — — n,* B.D. who has written a good sizeable volume against a *Friend of Your Governor,** (from whom alas! he must therefore look for little Favour) in a most gentlemanly Style, adorned with utmost Politeness and Civility; replete with Discoveries equally valuable for their Novelty and Use: and embellish'd with *Traits* of Wit so poignant and so apposite, that he is a worthy Yokemate to his foremention'd *Friend.*

Three short discourses have been thrown together to make up the fourth part, entitled The Preface. There is, first, a dissertation on the meaning of the title *A Tale of a Tub.* Secondly, there is an essay on modern wit, certain privileges of which the author claims for himself:

There are certain common Privileges of a Writer, the Benefit whereof, I hope, there will be no Reason to doubt; Particularly,

* That is, against Temple, the friend of Time, who is governor of Prince Posterity.

that where I am not understood, it shall be concluded, that something very useful and profound is couch underneath : And again, that whatever word or Sentence is Printed in a different Character, shall be judged to contain something extraordinary either of *Wit* or *Sublime*.

Filling out the Preface is an elaborate disclaimer that the present work is satire, for which indeed the author has neither talent nor inclination :

On the other side, I am so entirely satisfied with the whole present Procedure of human Things, that I have been for some Years preparing Materials towards *A Panegyrick upon the World;* to which I intended to add a Second Part, entituled, *A Modest Defence of the Proceedings of the Rabble in all Ages.*

The fifth part — § 1. The Introduction — begins with a description of three 'oratorical machines,' the pulpit, the ladder, and the stage-itinerant. So widely does the satirist circle about his meaning that for a space the reader is thoroughly bewildered — as it is intended that he should be. But by degrees these eccentric movements close in upon a centre, and the three machines are revealed as symbols of nonsense in religion and learning, the pulpit signifying dissenting enthusiasm, the ladder and the stage-itinerant the contemptible aspect of modern letters. It is here, muffled beneath the brilliantly crazy orchestration, that the central, double theme of the *Tale* is first announced. There is nothing like a resounding proclamation; the theme is almost hidden in the inner voice. No matter which of the machines the orator chooses to mount, the manner in which he works upon his auditors is the same :

. . . in the several Assemblies of these Orators, Nature it self hath instructed the Hearers, to stand with their Mouths open, and erected parallel to the Horizon, so as they may be intersected by a perpendicular Line from the Zenith to the Center of the Earth. In which Position, if the Audience be well compact, every one carries home a Share, and little or nothing is lost.

Whether, that is, the manifestation is one of religious enthusiasm or of a false judgment fatal to learning and literature, the cause lies in a certain wind or madness which overcomes reason. The second half of the fifth part is without reference to religion, being a discourse upon the Society of Grub Street and a celebration of its prime productions.

The remaining portions of the *Tale*, amounting to ten without the Conclusion, which need not be reckoned in, divide into two groups, one — §'s II, IV, VI, VIII, XI — devoted to religion; the other — §'s III, V, VII, IX, X — to learning. But the triumph of the work is the gradual approach of these groups to one another, until in the later sections — VIII, IX, XI — the enthusiasm of Jack the dissenter and all the forms of madness in the commonwealth of empire and learning are seen as one under the aspect of universal irrationality.

The five sections given over to religion — II, IV, VI, VIII, XI, of which the first four would seem to represent the earliest part of the *Tale* in point of composition — are cast in the form of allegory. A father has three sons : Peter, Martin, Jack — i.e., the Roman catholic church, the church of England, the dissenters. To these three sons the father bequeaths on his death-bed three coats, which he promises will last for ever and, because they will grow as the sons grow, will never need alteration. After admonishing his children to look to his will for the wearing and management of the coats, and always to live in harmony together under one roof, the father dies.

In a short time the three sons come up to town, where, despite their accomplishments, they find themselves scorned by the ladies because of the great simplicity of their coats. For it happened that about this time the town was dominated by a sect who worshipped the image of a tailor as their Deity, and taught that the universe is a large suit of clothes and that 'Man himself [is] but a *Micro-coat,* or rather a compleat Suit of Cloathes with all its Trimmings.' * So gen-

* M. Pons has treated this philosophy of clothes, which he calls *l'esthéto-morphisme,* in his characteristically brilliant manner. For that reason it can here be hurried over, though it must be confessed that M. Pons finds a significance in this part of the *Tale* which the present writer has been unable to perceive. This is not to say that *l'esthétomorphisme* does not allow of universal application, nor that Swift fails to sense the implications. It is brilliant satire but it remains an impulsive sally in a direction where Swift's main objectives do not lie — it does not connect up with the attack on irrationality. To Carlyle rather than to Swift we must look for its further development.

erally accepted were these doctrines that he whose dress failed to reflect the latest fashion could look for no favour. The brothers, however, are equal to the occasion. By a forced construction of their father's will they satisfy themselves that it not only sanctions but commands the wearing of shoulder-knots, all the rage at the moment. But it is not long before they find themselves as badly off as at the beginning, so quickly does the mode change. They end by locking the will up and altering their coats at pleasure in conformity with the edicts of the town.

At this point — § IV — Peter begins to assume a superiority over his brothers. He turns 'projector,' inventing such things as a remedy for the worms and a whispering office — i.e., penance, absolution, and the confessional. Before long he is so puffed up with pride that he can endure his brothers no longer and kicks them out of doors.

Left to themselves — § VI — Martin and Jack repent their sins and follies, consult a true copy of their father's will, and guided by it begin a reformation of their lives by stripping from their coats all the false adornments. One in adversity, now that they are free of Peter they begin to show their different natures by the way they go to work reducing their coats to their original simplicity.

Martin laid the first Hand; at one twitch brought off a large Handful of *Points,* and with a second pull, stript away ten dozen Yards of *Fringe.* But when He had gone thus far, he demurred a while: He knew very well, there yet remained a great deal more to be done; however, the first Heat being over, his Violence began to cool, and he resolved to proceed more moderately in the rest of the Work. . .

But his Brother *Jack,* whose Adventures will be so extraordinary, as to furnish a great Part in the Remainder of this Discourse; entred upon the Matter with other Thoughts, and a quite different Spirit. For, the Memory of *Lord Peter's* Injuries, produced a Degree of Hatred and Spight, which had a much greater Share of inciting Him, than any Regards after his Father's Commands. . . However, for this Meddly of Humor, he made a Shift to find a very plausible Name, honoring it with the Title of *Zeal.* . .

The two last religious sections — VIII, XI — are given over to Jack. Whatever Swift's original purpose behind the story of the three brothers, it is apparent that in the final version of the *Tale* he desired more than anything else to deal ferociously with Jack. Peter scarcely comes to life ; § IV, devoted to his overbearing conduct, is purely intellectual satire, quite lacking in that emotional savageness which Swift always entertains when truly aroused. As for Martin, his appearance in the foreground is momentary, and then only for the purpose of establishing the satiric norm — the reasonable spirit of the church of England. Jack it is on whom the attack converges. § VIII procceds up to the next to last paragraph entirely by indirection. We are introduced to the curious sect of Æolists, who believe 'the Original Cause of all Things to be Wind' and who affirm 'the Gift of Belching, to be the noblest Act of a Rational Creature.' Their rites and mysteries are then described at length. It is only at the end that Jack is introduced, in this manner :

Now, whether the System here delivered, was wholly compiled by *Jack,* or, as some Writers believe, rather copied from the Original at *Delphos,* with certain Additions and Emendations suited to Times and Circumstances, I shall not absolutely determine. This I may affirm, that *Jack* gave it at least a new Turn, and formed it into the same Dress and Model, as it lies deduced by me.

§ XI is for the most part a 'character in prose,' exhibiting Jack as the perfect exemplar of æolism and zeal. In the direction of religious enthusiasm thus far and no farther can irrationality go.

Into this story of the three brothers are interpolated the digressions,— §'s III, V, VII, IX, X,— in which the corruptions of learning are discerped. Between *The Battle of the Books* and most of these sections the only transition is in the way of a heightened satiric art. Thus in § III the subject of the digression is modern critics, the most notable of whom, by direct descent from Momus and Hybris, are Bentley, Rymer, Wotton, Perrault, and Dennis. By the term *critic* was anciently understood one who drew up rules 'by observing which, a careful Reader might be able to pronounce upon the productions of the *Learned,* form his Taste to a true Relish of the *Sublime* and the *Admirable,* and

divide every Beauty of Matter or of Style from the Corruption that Apes it. . .' But the True Critic, who can trace
his family back to Momus and thus yields nothing in the
antiquity of his origin to the other sorts of critics, finds his
proper employment to be 'to travel thro' this vast World of
Writings : to pursue and hunt those Monstrous Faults bred
within them : to drag out the lurking Errors like *Cacus* from
his Den ; to multiply them like *Hydra's* Heads ; and rake
them together like *Augeas's* Dung.' He is, in short, '*a Dis-
coverer and Collector of Writers Faults.*'

A Digression in the Modern Kind — § v — continues the
vicious analysis of the modern spirit, embodied in this instance in up-to-date writers who have more sense than to
venerate the tradition of ancient letters. As the spider in
The Battle of the Books scorned the wide flight of the bee
and his universal plunder of nature and prided himself upon
spinning entirely from his own substance, so these modern
writers contemn that artistic inventiveness which comes from
wide acquaintance with the best that has been written and
are satisfied to draw their matter wholly from modern knowledge. With all taste and imagination thus disposed of,
literary composition in this enlightened age is vastly sim-
plified, the sole requirement being a florilegium of modern
knowledge, some 'universal System in a small portable Volume, of all Things that are to be Known, or Believed, or
Imagined, or Practised in Life.' It is to supply such a momentous need, adds the author, 'that I have been prevailed
on after long Sollicitation, to take Pen in Hand. . .' He
proceeds :

Particularly, I recommend to the Perusal of the Learned, certain Discoveries that are wholly untoucht by others ; whereof I
shall only mention among a great many more ; *My New help of
Smatterers,* or the *Art of being Deep-learned, and Shallow-read.
A curious Invention about Mouse-Traps. An Universal Rule of
Reason, or Every Man his own Carver ;* Together with a most
useful Engine for *catching of Owls. . .*

Along with § v should be taken §'s VII and x. Somewhat
inferior to § v they are like it exposures of the absurdities in-
herent in modern theories of knowledge and writing.

It is in § ix, a Digression concerning the Original, the Use and Improvement of Madness in a Commonwealth, that *A Tale of a Tub* reaches its climax. The satire is here raised to a degree of sheer brilliance certainly unequalled by even the greatest of Swift's later compositions, and possibly by any other work of satire. This effect is the result both of artistic execution and of informing thought, which combine to produce a dominant tone at once mordant and sombre. Inescapable is the import of the theme — the universality of madness. But more arresting than this final emergence of what through previous sections and digressions the satire has continuously been stating in ironic, fragmentary phrases, is the analysis of madness as psychological perversion, as an evil, self-imposed by man, offering irresistible pleasures of self-deception. All pre-eminent achievements in the commonwealth are owing to an acquisition of madness; is it not pure madness that causes revolutions in empire, in philosophy, in religion?

For, the Brain, in its natural Position and State of Serenity, disposeth its Owner to pass his Life in the common Forms, without any Thought of subduing Multitudes to his own *Power*, his *Reasons* or his *Visions;* and the more he shapes his Understanding by the Pattern of Human Learning, the less he is inclined to form Parties after his particular Notions; because that instructs him in his private Infirmities, as well as in the stubborn Ignorance of the People. But when a Man's Fancy gets *astride* on his Reason, when Imagination is at Cuffs with the Senses, and common Understanding, as well as common Sense, is Kickt out of Doors; the first Proselyte he makes, is Himself, and when that is once compass'd, the Difficulty is not so great in bringing over others; A strong Delusion always operating from *without,* as vigorously as from *within.* For, Cant and Vision are to the Ear and the Eye, the same that Tickling is to the Touch. Those Entertainments and Pleasures we most value in Life, are such as *Dupe* and play the Wag with the Senses. For, if we take an Examination of what is generally understood by *Happiness,* as it has Respect, either to the Understanding or the Senses, we shall find all its Properties and Adjuncts will herd under this short Definition: That, *it is a perpetual Possession of being well Deceived.*

This passage is followed by another equally remarkable, in which the satirist broods upon the deceptive fairness of

the outside covering of things, so different from the truth
that lies concealed within. Reason unreasonably insists
upon cutting through the fair exterior to the inner reality.
The senses, in contrast, are content to remain happily deceived by the false beauty of outward appearances. Therefore is the credulity of the senses infinitely more peaceful
than the curiosity of reason, infinitely preferable to 'that pretended Philosophy which enters into the Depth of Things,
and then comes gravely back with Informations and Discoveries, that in the inside they are good for nothing. . .' 'Last
Week,' the writer continues, 'I saw a Woman *flay'd,* and you
will hardly believe, how much it altered her Person for the
worse.' It is the consummate statement of that moral realism which directed Swift's entire intellectual life. It is not
as you think — look! It would be fatal to be misled by the
irony of this passage to a conclusion directly opposite to
Swift's meaning. As an anti-intellectualist he taught, it is
true, that we should restrain every impulse to indulge in
speculation outside the bounds of common sense. But the
search for moral truth beneath the concealments of false
appearances not only did not constitute intellectual aberration but was the prime function of reason.

And thus *A Tale of a Tub* draws to an end. The two
themes of zeal in religion and of enthusiasm in learning
and knowledge have been inextricably woven into one. The
impertinences of the shallow moderns, the gross manners of
the True Critics, madness in empire, philosophy, and religion, Jack's æolism — all have been reduced to single
formula: '. . . when a Man's Fancy gets *astride* on his Reason, when Imagination is at Cuffs with the Senses, and common Understanding, as well as common Sense, is Kickt out
of Doors; the first Proselyte he makes, is Himself, and when
that is once compass'd, the Difficulty is not so great in bringing over others. . .' London was bewildered, finding in
this great satiric work an unforgiveable audacity and a tone
of rankest impiety. But the shade of Erasmus smiled.

4

A Discourse Concerning the Mechanical Operation of the Spirit is really a fragment of *A Tale of a Tub* which instead of being fitted into that work was left standing by itself. It is a further analysis of zeal. It begins with the statement that many English desire to go to Heaven not in the conventional fiery chariot but on an ass. The ass, it is explained, here signifies a gifted or enlightened teacher, the rider a fanatic auditory. The question to be disposed of is how such a teacher arrives at his gifts, or spirit, or light. Now, there are three aspects of religious enthusiasm which have commonly been distinguished : first, prophecy, or an immediate act of God ; secondly, possession, or the act of the devil ; thirdly, enthusiasm springing from causes purely natural. Since, however, these aspects have been discoursed on at length by others, the present writer intends to treat of zeal as 'purely an Effect of Artifice and *Mechanick Operation,*' hitherto sparingly handled. By zeal or Spirit — the author uses the latter word — is not meant that supernatural Assistance approaching from without but a movement which proceeds entirely from within, and this being understood it is to be accepted as fundamental that the generation of Spirit lies in the corruption of the senses. The remainder of this curious discourse is largely an explanation of the artifices resorted to by the enlightened teacher to hasten this corruption and a description of the strange physical behaviour of both teacher and auditory when together they labour to kindle the fires of enthusiasm. Notable is the ironically materialistic explanation of how poetry, eloquence, and political discourse come to be written through the morsure on certain capillary nerves, of the little animals who cluster together to form the human brain.

The terminal position occupied by the *Mechanical Operation* would indicate that the canny artist perceived how effectively it would cope the two great satires preceding it. Never has imagination — a corruption of the senses which drives out reason — been so utterly discredited as in this closing piece.

8

BOOK II

1699–1710

BIOGRAPHICAL SYNOPSIS

1699 - 1710

27 Jan. 1699 :	Death of Sir William Temple.
July 1699 :	Appointed chaplain to Lord Berkeley, recently made a lord justice of Ireland, and with him to Dublin.
Feb. 1700 :	Appointed to vicarages of Laracor and Rathbeggan and rectory of Agher, and in the autumn of this year to the prebend of Dunlavin in the Chapter of St. Patrick's Cathedral.
Feb. 1701 :	Received the degree of D.D. from Dublin University.
April 1701 :	To England in Lord Berkeley's train, publishing thereafter *A Discourse of the Contests and Dissensions in Athens and Rome.* Returned to Ireland in September.
April-Oct. 1702 :	In England.
Nov. 1703-June 1704 :	In England. *A Tale of a Tub* published.
Nov. 1707-June 1709 :	In England, officially negotiating with the government for the remission of the first-fruits and twentieth parts to the Irish clergy, writing much on matters of church and state, and soon known to Addison and his circle as a wit and man of letters of the first water, a maker of graceful verses, and the tormentor of Partridge the astrologer.
June 1709- August 1710 :	In Ireland.

CHAPTER I

YEARS OF ACTIVITY AND SUSPENSE

1

THE death of Sir William Temple altered abruptly the course of Swift's life. Surely no unforeseen eventuality, the breaking up of the Moor Park *entourage* came nevertheless as a shock to the secretary who for the greater part of ten years had been enjoying a position which brought him in touch with the world without the necessity of wringing from it an acknowledgement of his genius. Security was suddenly removed and at the age of thirty-one Swift was cast upon the world, there to force his way. Fate had betrayed him, and while this treachery was still fresh he smarted from resentment. The words which his sister wrote to her cousin Deane Swift four months after Temple's death are doubtless an accurate indication of Jonathan's mood during the early half of 1699: 'My poor brother has lost his best friend Sir William Temple, who was so fond of him whilst he lived, that he made him give up his living in [Ireland], to stay with him at Moor Park, and promised to get him one in England. But death came in between, and has left him unprovided both of friend and living.' It was like Swift to lay his plight to the indifference of Temple. But he knew perfectly well that he had chosen with open eyes to remain a nonentity at Moor Park rather than struggle for distinction in London. When his choice came home his first feeling was one of bitterness. This, however, soon passed off.

The twelve ensuing years of Swift's life, from Temple's death early in 1699 down to September 1710, when he crossed the Irish Sea to become before the year's end one of the greatest political journalists in England, are the record of a genius arrived at the full measure of his powers who was as yet unacknowledged and thus compelled to lay systematic siege to the world of letters and action. Unquestionably his behaviour during this period lends itself to the most uncharitable interpretation: his dread of poverty, his contempt for the humble ways of life, his total lack of sympathy for those of his brethren who could rest content with a poor parish and a growing family — these were the emotions that drove him in his restless search for worldly distinction. It is much easier, however, to write all this down to his discredit than to take account of the tremendous energy seeking through conquest of an indifferent world to force channels for itself. His genius was not of the contemplative order, but demanded forms of expression through which it could act directly upon passing affairs. Swift regarded as his right a position in society from which he could raise his voice with authority.

The perfect candour with which in his letters and in *The Journal to Stella* he discussed social advancement and preferment in the church has told heavily against him. Because we are not accustomed to frankness in such matters, instinctively we judge open avowal more reprehensible than concealed desire. As a matter of fact, Swift wrote of his hopes and ambitions with a dignity and again a naïveté that disallow the impurity of motive that has so often been attributed to him. If in the days following Temple's death he felt that he had been cheated, he was quick to accept his fate and put all bitterness behind. In the twelve ensuing years, when his efforts to gain recognition were meeting with but indifferent success, he raised no plaintive cry. He was too certain of his powers to feel other than impatience with a world that was reluctant to give them full scope.

This impatience bred a nervous activity of which the signs are everywhere during the period from 1699 to 1710. Within six months after Temple's death he secured the post of chaplain to a newly appointed lord justice of Ireland and in the latter's train proceeded to the Castle in Dublin. A modest preferment in the Irish church was shortly forthcoming, yielding an annual income of about £260, which gave him an independence that he had not previously enjoyed. Another might have accepted such a living as a life settlement, but Swift could regard a country vicarage as no better than exile from the scene where he rightfully belonged. To that scene he hastened whenever opportunity allowed. He was in England, for the most part in London, from April to September 1701 ; from April to October 1702 ; from November 1703 to June 1704 ; and from November 1707 to June 1709.

Nor was his nervous activity confined to journeying to and from London. His pen was never still for long. During this period he wrote almost fifty pieces, which in their diversity enforce the impression of one searching impatiently for an opening.

Behind the restlessness of mind and body, however, the mounting commitments of a life no longer insulated as at Temple's against the necessity of decisions were giving to his character a solidity comparable to that which Moor Park had given to his intellect. This increasing substantiality of the man himself is in part, to be sure, no more than an impression owing to the fuller documentation of his life. Up to 1699 Swift is a very dim figure, authentic only as we sense him behind *A Tale of a Tub* and *The Battle of the Books;* no sooner does he return to Ireland a lord justice's chaplain than the shadows disappear and we see him as a man very much alive — a gentleman with a baudy and sarcastic tongue, a wit of the first order, an Irish vicar bent on the conquest of London. But our fuller information does not solely account for this clearer picture. The Swift of Moor Park was mostly intellect, for little had happened to evoke his moral character. When in 1699 the insulation was torn away he began to live.

Not only had he recommitted himself to a life within the church and thereby entered upon a long struggle for such power as a clergyman could command in the world, but he had also determined the circumstances of his private life. Varina, who in 1696 had resisted his importunities, turned up with different ideas about marriage. One letter disposed of her. In the following year Hester, accompanied by the inseparable Rebecca Dingley, came to Ireland and her presence, whether as a lover who was to wait fifteen years for a secret and empty marriage or more reasonably as a friend, had all the nature of a major decision on Swift's part.

If impatience with the obscurity of his position is the

dominant note through the years from 1699 to 1710, the
man whom Hester joined in Ireland must not be thought
of as a morose and perplexed figure.   Perhaps it was revenge upon the mirthless Temple, perhaps it was relief on
facing at last the reality of unsheltered life, but in any event
the Swift of these days was a gay person for all his restless
stirrings.   It was an irrepressible humorist who in 1701 described life in the servants' quarters at the Castle in those
matchless verses which go by the name of *Mrs. Frances Harris's Petition,* and in 1708 and 1709, when London was
laughing hysterically at the predicament of Partridge the
astrologer, the humorist was still in the ascendant.   In a
sense this period of twelve years is seen as an energetic scherzo
preceded by the intellectual rigours of *A Tale of a Tub* and
followed by increasingly grim controversy and satire.   Swift
was happy as he had never been before and was never to be
thereafter.   The satirical mood he could not put entirely
from him, but the spirit in which he accepted life gave
laughter rather than indignation to his moral realism.

It was not until the end of 1710 that Swift at length gained
entrance to the world of affairs and a rôle of some consequence in the political drama then in progress.   As everyone knows, this change in his fortunes came as the direct
result of his conversion to the tory party.   Now, it is true
that he did not formally renounce his allegiance to the whigs
until the autumn of 1710; but it is not true, as many have
believed, that he changed his political colours on a sudden
impulse and out of a spirit of pure opportunism.   One has
but to follow the workings of his mind during the twelve-
year period that we are speaking of to see how he was forced
step by step to the conviction that adherence to the whigs
was incompatible with loyalty to the church.

It was in a purely intellectual manner that he arrived at
this conviction.   In the reign of Queen Anne the relations
of church and state were still a vexing problem.   The issues
involved had in the seventeenth century drawn blood, and
although the subjects of Queen Anne were agreed that the
violence which had set cavalier against roundhead should be
evermore outlawed they had by no means succeeded in work-

ing out a settlement acceptable to all shades of opinion.   It
was inevitable that a churchman like Swift, attracted by his
whole nature to the practical aspect of affairs, should have
seen in the questions pertaining to the relations of church
and state the central problem confronting his times.   Thus
it was that he entered the controversy, reducing his ideas to
clear and incisive form in a series of six pamphlets written
in 1708 and 1709, of which five saw publication at the time.
In these he was bent solely on intellectual statement, and
accordingly the position which he defined did not call for
immediate translation into action; formally he was still a
whig.   Every experience, however, which now befell him
made it clear that only as a tory was his position unequivocal.
His open confession of the tory faith at the end of 1710
was a response to clear conviction.   This is not to say that
his action was not also motivated by frank self-seeking, for
undoubtedly it was.   The great ones of the whig party
played their cards so far as Jonathan was concerned with
unbelievable ineptitude.   They kept him waiting out of all
measure in the ante-room, only to treat him, when finally
admitted, with an indifference which would have goaded a
fool.   When he laid before them his desires for the church
they hedged and showed him the door.   It was with a sense
of delicious revenge that a few years later he took over tory
propaganda and proved to his erstwhile friends the measure
of the man whom they had spurned.   In the earlier passages of *The Journal to Stella* Swift makes no concealment of
his huge satisfaction in evening the personal score.   What
is often forgotten, however, is that in the entire absence of
such a score, Swift must sooner or later have renounced
his early political loyalties.   His concern for the church,
so clearly indicated in the pamphlets of 1708-1709, would
have brought him to toryism whether or no it was to his
own advantage.

Such are the general characteristics of this twelve-year
period in the life of Swift.   Critically, our interest is divided
between the pamphlets treating of church and state and the
productions in prose and verse of the wit and man of letters,
and to each of these subjects a chapter will be given.   Un-

fortunately, however, we cannot dismiss Swift's life during these years with but a brief characterization. As he became engaged in national events the history of the times comes to stand more and more as essential commentary on his life. For this reason we must follow his activities during these twelve years in some detail, with a history of Queen Anne's reign at hand for ready reference.[1]

2

SHORTLY after Temple's death Swift went up to London to press his claims to preferment in the church. Precisely what these were one does not venture to assert. In the autobiographical fragment (*ca.* 1727) we read that King William had promised Temple to give Swift a prebend of Canterbury or Westminster. Now, Swift's memory for such matters was not of the clearest, and it is altogether likely that twenty-eight years after the event he had come to exaggerate the nature of the king's commitments, though passages in his letters written from Moor Park incline one to the belief that something in the way of assurances had in fact been given. Whatever they were, Swift made no headway at court. 'After long attendance in vain,' the autobiographical passage proceeds, '[he] thought it better to comply with an invitation, given him by the Earl of Berkeley, to attend him to Ireland, as his chaplain and private secretary. . .' There follows the story, to be taken *cum grano,* of another of the earl's attendants who by persuading Berkeley that it was improper for a chaplain to act also as secretary gained the latter post for himself and succeeded a few months later in diverting the vacant deanery of Derry from Swift to another applicant who had bolstered his claim with a bribe. What is beyond doubt is that on 16 February 1700 Swift was preferred to the vicarages of Laracor and Rathbeggan and the rectory of Agher in the Diocese of Meath, and in October to the prebend of Dunlavin in the Cathedral of St. Patrick's. But in his capacity of chaplain to the lord justice, Swift continued to reside at Dublin Castle. If the earl had failed him in the matter of the secretarial post and the deanery

of Derry, that did not interfere with Swift's establishing the
heartiest relations with all the Berkeleys and taking his ease
among them.   True, he had no hesitation in holding up his
new patron to ridicule in two filthy squibs in verse, *The
Discovery* and *The Problem ;* but the barrack-room tone of
these pieces probably reflects something of the earl's own
humour and is at any rate a sign that Swift now stood on a
footing different from that of the Moor Park days.   For
Dublin Castle appreciated the wit who had been smuggled
in under a cassock and the wit responded.   Upstairs and
below there was nothing that escaped his sharp eyes, nothing
which was safe from his puns and his verses.   His astonishing comprehension of manners in the servants' hall was translated into the rhythm and idiom of *Mrs. Frances Harris's
Petition.*   With such a performance as warning, only people
with a higher respect for wit than for their own dignity
could have tolerated such a chaplain in their midst.

On 16 February 1701 Swift took his degree of Doctor of
Divinity in the University of Dublin, and in the following
April, when Berkeley's office came to a close, he accompanied
him back to England.

Of his correspondence of this time there is one letter
which must be mentioned — that written from Dublin on 4
May 1700 to Jane Waring, otherwise Varina.   In this Swift
was refusing her offer of marriage.   The manner in which he
did so has seemed to many unforgivably brutal.   Brutal it
may have been, but we are here moving in uncharted waters
for the reason that Anglo-Saxon society, until recently perhaps,
has refused to consider the terms in which a man is to reject
a suitor.   The passage of greatest interest is this : '. . . you
would know . . . whether this change of style be owing
to the thoughts of a new mistress.   I declare, upon the word
of a Christian and a gentleman, it is not ; neither had I ever
thoughts of being married to any other person but yourself.'
It has been argued that these words were thoroughly dis-
ingenuous — that Stella had everything to do with his change
of heart.   One cannot, to be sure, prove that Swift spoke
the simple truth ; one can only insist that it is possible for
a man to discover that he does not want to marry anyone.

But whether Swift was equivocating or not when he declared that he had no thoughts of a new mistress, his feeling for the old one is clear enough. Chivalry aside, it was better, surely, to repulse Varina than to submit and thereby doom himself and her to years of misery.

3

SWIFT had chosen an exciting moment for his return to England. The terms *whig* and *tory* had had their origin in the time of Charles II. The whig party brought together under its sheltering wings several groups of opinion : the dissenters — men who chose to suffer the disabilities imposed by Restoration laws rather than betray their loyalty to the defeated puritan cause; those church of England men, clerical and lay, whose 'rational' attitude towards political and religious matters turned them from dogmatism to empirical acceptance of events and to reasonable compromise; quakers, unitarians, and philosophical deists; middle-class tradesmen, and in increasing numbers the monied men of the City. Far more homogeneous was the tory party, which in a new age clung to the established social and religious traditions of the past, drawing its strength from the land-owners and gentry and from the majority of the clergy. Though both parties had backed the Revolution of '88, the ensuing years of William III's reign did not break down party spirit. As was natural, the king inclined to the whigs, but there was much confusion because as yet no one had perceived that only with a ministry that could command a majority in the commons could government run smoothly. While the swing of public sentiment was reflected — less quickly and less sharply than later, to be sure — in the election of members to the house of commons, the ministry was still appointed by the sovereign. Thus, when the popularity of the foreign-born king was suffering a decline in the last years of the century, the whig ministry continued intact, and it was only when the commons voted against William that at last he saw the necessity of replacing certain of his whig ministers with representatives of the opposition. Parliament was dissolved and in the new one which met early in 1701 it was the tories who held the reins. Such was the tory desire for vengeance that action was taken to impeach the whig grandees — Somers, the earl of Portland, the earl of Orford, and Halifax — for their past actions. These proceedings were still going forward when Swift arrived in London.

To him this critical moment was an opportunity ripe for plucking. It was his first venture in political controversy, but he was fully armed — he had not sifted the problems of government with Temple and read history for days on end and in the library at Moor Park for nothing. *A Discourse of the Contests and Dissensions Between the Nobles and the Commons in Athens and Rome, With the Consequences they had upon both those States* (1701) will strike the modern reader as a dull discourse, a show of pedantry rather than a timely comment. To the reader of 1701 there was nothing dead about it : the analogy between classical and modern times seemed apt, and there were references and implications, meaningless to us, which events of the moment charged with significance.

The political ideas which Swift set forth in this pamphlet we shall take account of in the next chapter. Here it is enough to understand that he was calling upon both factions to forego their hostilities and scent the common danger — the utter loss of political freedom which these discords threatened by breeding popular discontent and thus reducing the commonwealth to a state of anarchy, out of which, as history showed, the tyrant was sure to arise. He spoke as a whig, and in defence chiefly of Somers, to whom he was to dedicate *A Tale of a Tub*. But he gave way to no intemperate partisanship.

Had Swift at this stage been other than a whig he would have been anomalous. Born in Ireland, reared in Trinity College, toryism still meant to him as to all of his class the pretender, catholic dominance, an uprooting of the English interests in Ireland. His intercourse with Temple had confirmed his whig prejudices. One fundamental doctrine of the whig philosophy he never, in fact, renounced : the Revolutionary settlement, by which an hereditary king of Eng-

land had been cast out to make way for a foreigner, he
defended even in his tory pamphlets. And in regard to the
church of England, his position was to remain in certain
respects that of a moderate whig. It can be said that his
early political convictions were never entirely broken down,
and, as we shall see, they were in later years to hold his tory
enthusiasm in check. When as the agent of Oxford and
Bolingbroke he was raising political controversy to ear-split-
ting pitch, he decried partisanship, insisting that the tories
represented a national party and were opposed only by a
paltry, head-strong faction. Like other politicians before
and since, he actually believed his wish — the signal instance
in his life of complete self-delusion. But to the extent that
he spoke for a party which existed only in his own mind, to
the extent that his political principles surpassed in clarity
and nobility those embodied by the politicians whom he
served, he was right. His own toryism was not denial of all
that the whigs stood for, not fear of all save the past; it was
faith in history, in experience, and in the moderation of
average Englishmen when intelligently informed.

The *Contests and Dissensions* impressed the whigs. Swift
gained the acquaintance of Somers, Burnet, and Halifax,
and seems in some way to have been brought to the king,
with whom he discussed politics. But the only reward which
he desired — a settlement in England — did not in 1701 lie
in the gift of the whigs, and in September he returned to
Ireland, still vicar of Laracor. At Laracor he took up residence and busied himself with building a parsonage to re-
place the ruined one he found, repairing his dilapidated
church, conducting services for his congregation of no more
than half a score,—'most gentle and all simple,'— laying out
a garden, planting willows, and constructing a Dutch canal
after the fashion of Moor Park. Near at hand were Hester
Johnson and Mrs. Dingley, who had recently come over
from England.

4

IN the following year — 1702 — Swift was again in England
from April to October, but of his activities almost nothing

is known. We can only be certain that he was observing the political scene with eyes which missed little. There was a great deal to observe. In November 1701 the king had dissolved parliament. In the new one meeting early in 1702 the two parties were evenly balanced — England had now entered the war against France, and partisanship had for a space given way to common purpose. But the year was not old when William was thrown from his horse, suffering fatal injury. Anne succeeded, extreme tories toasted 'the little gentleman in black' who had ended the life of a spurious sovereign, and in the new parliament the whigs found themselves outnumbered. The tories, ever the foes of the dissenters, now took the opportunity to introduce a bill forbidding the further practice of occasional conformity. To understand the significance of this bill one must go back to the Restoration. The Clarendon Code, enacted between 1661 and 1665, had quite contravened the promise of religious toleration implied in the events of 1660. Parliament, actuated by a sentiment heartily shared by the average Englishman, who had been repressed too long by the saints to know mercy, passed a series of laws rigorously penalizing all forms of dissent from the established church. Though the Toleration Act of 1689 repealed most of these laws, it left standing the Test Act of 1673 and the Corporation Act, and the effect of these measures was still to exclude from civil and military office anyone who would not take sacrament in the church of England. But among dissenters ambitious to hold office and not too strict in conscience there arose the practice of meeting the letter of the law by receiving sacrament by the rite of the established church and, having thus qualified for office, of rejoining the dissenting congregation. The bill against occasional conformity was designed to end this evasion. In presenting the dissenters with the choice of strict conformity or the disabilities of the Tests, the tories spoke for a large element within the church. The whigs, who regarded occasional conformity as a means towards that religious toleration for which they had always stood, opposed the bill.

If at this stage Swift had opinions regarding occasional

conformity he kept them to himself. The final defeat of
the bill came in February 1703, some months after he had
departed for home.

Throughout the summer of 1703 he remained in Ireland
wrapped in obscurity, from which he emerged in November, when he again journeyed to London. That thoughts
of preferment were still uppermost we know from his letters
of this date to the Reverend William Tisdall in Ireland.
'I have here the best friends in nature,' he wrote, 'only want
that little circumstance of favour and power; but nothing
is so civil as a cast courtier' (16 December 1703). And
again: 'I find nothing but the good words and wishes of a
decayed Ministry, whose lives and mine will probably wear
out before they can serve either my little hopes, or their
own ambition' (20 April 1704). In other words, the whigs
were not above taking some notice of him but being out of
office they had no English living with which to reward the
author of the *Contents and Dissensions*.

It was disturbing that his friends should be completely
without power, but he could enjoy the political fracas that
was now diverting London. This he described to Tisdall
with gusto: '. . . I observed the dogs in the streets much
more contumelious and quarrelsome than usual; and the
very night before the bill [against occasional conformity]
went up, a committee of Whig and Tory cats, had a very
warm and loud debate upon the roof of our house' (16 December 1703). The parliamentary session of the winter of
1703-1704 was marked by the introduction of a second
bill against occasional conformity. It suffered the fate of
the previous bill, being rejected 14 December, but the debate split the still firmly entrenched tory party, and the high
tories found themselves faced not only by the whigs but by
the moderate element within their own ranks, who were to
take the lead during the next two years, yielding in 1707-
1708 to the rising whigs.

It appears that the whigs called for the assistance of
Swift's pen in the fight against the bill of 1703. For the
first time Swift's confidence in the party of his inheritance
faltered — the wedge which ultimately was to sunder him

from the whig cause had found entrance. So long as being a whig meant rejection of the pretender, he was a whig without qualification; but if the whigs should reveal themselves as the foes, and the tories the friends of the established church he could no longer be sure where he stood. He turned to his whig friends for assurance.

I put it close to my Lord Peterborough just as the bill was going up, who assured me in the most solemn manner, that if he had the least suspicion the rejecting this bill would hurt the Church, or do kindness to the Dissenters, he would lose his right hand rather than speak against it. The like profession I had from the Bishop of Salisbury, my Lord Somers, and some others; so that I know not what to think . . . (To Tisdall, 16 December 1703.)

His desire was to believe that in standing out against the tories' efforts to end occasional conformity the whigs had no thought of extending comfort to the dissenters. But he was not convinced. Meanwhile, should he or should he not write against the tories' bill? Finally he yielded to pressure and wrote a pamphlet against it, but the day before it was finished the bill was defeated and he refused to print. It was most unlike Swift to be caught dallying. Had he, perhaps, resorted to subterfuge to save his face?

For some months he lingered on in London. By 1 June 1704 he was back in Ireland. But before his departure from England he had shot an arrow into the future. Its eventual mark was not to be the one he had sighted at, but this he had no way of knowing in 1704. The unsuspected author of *A Tale of a Tub,* observing from beyond the Irish Sea London's response to his genius, had cause as yet only for secret exultation.

5

AFTER the visit to England of 1703-1704 Swift did not stir out of Ireland for three and a half years. Perhaps he was deterred from making the journey from Dublin to London — then a long and wearying one — by the continued exclusion of the whigs from power, perhaps he was reluctant

9

to lay out the money, perhaps he was content for the moment, now that the anonymous *Tale of a Tub* had vindicated his genius, to relish the pleasures of an obscure life.   Even his pen was comparatively inactive.   It is of course possible that he committed many of his writings of this period to the fire or that they have not come down to us, but those which we have are inconsiderable in number : a few pieces in verse — one the earlier version of the famous *Baucis and Philemon* — and the first portion of *Thoughts on Various Subjects*.   Quite as slender is the correspondence of these three and a half years.   One letter there is, addressed on the last day of 1704 to Archbishop King of Dublin, which introduces us to a matter of much importance in Swift's life a few years later.   The archbishop was then in London and Swift urged him to take this opportunity of pressing a certain measure of benefit to the church in Ireland : 'I would . . . beg of your Grace to use some of your credit toward bringing to a good issue the promise the Queen made . . . to remit the first-fruits and tenths of the clergy. . .' In both England and Ireland the church had since the Reformation paid an annual tax to the Crown in the form of first-fruits and tenths,— first-fruits and twentieths in Ireland,— the first-fruits being paid by incumbents upon their promotion, the tenths being paid yearly out of all benefices. In February 1704 was announced Queen Anne's Bounty, which remitted these taxes, estimated at about £16,000 a year, to the English clergy.   The church in Ireland was naturally eager for a similar remission of its first-fruits and twentieths.   The entire sum did not amount to much more than £950 yearly, but if its remission meant inconsiderable relief to the clergy it seemed a small favour to ask and the Irish clergy were eager for the grant, regarding it as a sign of that good will which they so earnestly desired from the powers in England.

Having broached the subject in his letter to the archbishop, Swift pursued it no further at this time, but three years later, when he was again in London, he was commissioned by the Irish clergy to negotiate with the government for remission of the first-fruits and these negotiations were to have not a little to do with his subsequent political apostasy.

Dublin Castle during the early years of the century saw a succession of lords-lieutenants. Rochester had been followed early in 1703 by the duke of Ormond, who four years later gave place to the earl of Pembroke. Since the days of Berkeley's incumbency as a lord justice, Swift seems to have had easy access to the Castle, but during Pembroke's term of office he became one of a group who gathered there regularly to amuse themselves and the lord-lieutenant with a display of Irish wit. Besides Swift the circle included the two Ashe brothers, one of whom had been Swift's college tutor; Dr. Stearne, dean of St. Patrick's; Dr. Raymond of Trim, and Archdeacon Walls. Their chief amusement was practising the 'Castilian language,' in which it was possible to suggest that parliament could be dissolved in vinegar and that a puss tied to a post in a library might serve as a catalogue. From his bagatelles and puns Swift withheld nothing of his characteristic intensity.

Late in November 1707 Lord Pembroke sailed for England, and Swift, resolved to adventure once more in London, sailed with him. At Leicester he paused for a brief visit with his mother, and as he breathed deep of English air he realized as never before the hatefulness of the scene to which his misfortune of being born in Ireland seemed to doom him. 'I came round by Derby to this town,' he wrote on 6 December to Archbishop King, 'where I am now upon a short visit to my mother, and I confess to your Grace that after an absence of less than four years, all things appear new to me. The buildings, the improvements, the dress and countenance of the people put a new spirit into one, *et tacite circum praecordia ludit.*' He was forty now. The balance of power was swinging steadily towards the whigs. His own star, for whose rise he had been watching impatiently since the death of Temple nine long years ago, was perhaps ascendant at last. The new year found him in London, poised expectantly for the turn of events.

For Swift the wit and man of letters the ensuing year and a half was a period of triumph. When he returned to

Ireland in June 1709 the names of Addison, Steele, and Swift were joined wherever contemporary letters were known. There is no evidence that the recognition of his literary talents antedates the forty-first year of his life (1708) or that he had in any way become known during previous visits to London to the brilliant group of whig writers who now with acclaim admitted him to their circle. It is supposed that the discovery of his authorship of *A Tale of a Tub* had much to do with this reception, and this may have been the case. Having once won consideration, however, it was not necessary for Swift to make his way by virtue of past achievement. At any time during the last nine years the slightest encouragement would have set his energies athrob. His genius now spoke and the world applauded. It spoke in verse, with some prompting by Addison : the revised versions of *Baucis and Philemon* and *Vanbrugh's House* appeared, and the piece *On Mrs. Biddy Floyd,* of exquisite polish, and the lines *Apollo Outwitted,* addressed to Anne, countess of Winchelsea, were composed. It spoke in a different accent in *Predictions for the Year 1708* and the subsequent Partridge pamphlets. When on 12 April 1709 Steele began to issue his *Tatler,* he could think of no better means to ensure its popularity than by assuming the character of Isaac Bickerstaff, author of the *Predictions* and their famous sequels. And it was to this new periodical that Swift contributed (30 April 1709) his last literary triumph before he made his way back to Dublin and Laracor — the nine-couplet *Description of the Morning,* a parody so consummate that it creates an attitude which stands in its own right.

Yet wit and letters were the lesser half of his life during these months of association with Steele and Addison. Since his previous residence in London in 1703-1704 the national scene had changed greatly. The elections during the summer of 1705 had placed the moderate tories and the whigs in control. The latter were now on the rise, and by 1707 the traditional whig sentiment in favour of religious toleration began to make itself felt. But no one dared to extend aid to dissenters in England until public feeling could be tested elsewhere. Ireland was regarded as a fit place to release a trial balloon, and to this end Lord Pembroke was sent over in 1707 to suggest the abolition of presbyterian disabilities in Ireland. He made no headway, for the governing classes in Ireland, whig and tory alike, distrusted the dissenters even more than the catholics. In England, meanwhile, the elections of 1708 had resulted in such a strengthening of the whigs that the tories were completely dislodged from power. The whig supremacy for which Swift had been waiting had now come to pass.

In the earlier years of Anne's reign the war had been more or less taken for granted, but by 1708 it was becoming a political issue. Late in 1701 England had joined the Allies, who were seeking to check the ever-expanding dominance of France in European affairs. England contributed money, men, and one of the greatest military geniuses of all time. Under Marlborough's superb command the Allies in 1704 had crushed Louis's army at Blenheim, in 1706 they had dislodged the French from their positions in the Spanish Netherlands and swept them south towards the French border, and at Oudenarde, in 1708, they had brought Louis almost to the end of his resources. Yet the war went on and the whigs backed it to the limit, raising the cry of 'No peace without Spain'—from the beginning the declared purpose of the Allies had been to prevent Spain's going to Louis's grandson Philip, thus putting European power out of all balance. By 1709 Louis was ready to yield to the Allies on almost any terms save the surrender of Spain. But the whigs, blind to the fact that the Allies could now emerge from a treaty of peace with riches of other sorts undreamt of at the beginning of hostilities, still regarded Spain as a *sine qua non,* and to ensure the continuance of the war were driven to the necessity of propitiating their allies in the Netherlands by signing in October 1709 the Barrier Treaty, whereby Holland was guaranteed eventual peace terms exceeding what otherwise she could have expected. By this time the enthusiasm of the average Englishman for the war, an enthusiasm sustained up to now by triumph after triumph of Marlborough's arms, was beginning to diminish. How

much longer, it was asked, must the Allies go on beating
Louis's armies? Indirect taxation began to weigh heavily.
Bad harvests increased the price of corn. By 1709 there
were audible rumblings and talk of the 'butcher's bill,' all
of which the whigs would have done well to heed.

In touching upon the war as an emergent political issue
in England we have passed beyond the limits within which
Swift's interests were as yet confined. The war meant nothing to him until he embraced toryism and was primed by
the tory leaders with all the arguments for peace. During
1708-1709 his thoughts, outside literature, were given over
to the matter of the first-fruits, to the whigs' attempt to cut
down religious disabilities, and to his own preferment.

Concerning the first-fruits, he had written to Archbishop
King on 6 December 1707, signifying his willingness to
undertake negotiations with the whigs; his credit with Lord
Somers and Lord Sunderland seemed to promise success.
Archbishop King gave him his blessing, which was later
confirmed by an authorization from the Irish clergy to proceed with the business. But scarcely had Swift arrived in
London when disquieting rumours reached him. Though
the whigs had only recently witnessed Lord Pembroke's
failure to effect the abolition of presbyterian disabilities in
Ireland, it seemed that they had by no means abandoned
their plan of using that country as a proving-ground for
their schemes of broader toleration. The wise ones hinted
to Swift that the ministry would, perhaps, grant remission
of the first-fruits only on condition that the Irish clergy
withdraw their opposition to the removal of the Test. This
disturbing aspect of affairs Swift reported immediately to
Archbishop King:

I have heard it whispered by some who are fonder of political
refinements than I, that a new difficulty may arise in this matter,
that it must perhaps be purchased by a compliance with what
was undertaken and endeavoured in Ireland last sessions, which I
confess I cannot bring myself yet to believe, nor do I care to
think or reason upon it. (1 January 1708.)

For two and a half months Swift was held up in his negotiations, but on 15 April he reported progress to Archbishop

King: through the good offices of Lord Somers and Lord Sunderland he was to attend Godolphin, lord treasurer and head of the ministry, and lay before him the desires of the Irish church. There was a further delay, but early in June Swift was finally admitted to Godolphin. What took place during this conference confirmed Swift's worst fears. Godolphin opened by belittling the entire matter: in England, not one clergyman was a shilling the better for the queen's grant. He came finally to the point: he would give his consent if assured that the grant would be received by the subjects in Ireland with due acknowledgments. By that, Swift asked, had he in mind any particular acknowledgments?

He replied, 'By acknowledgments, I do not mean any thing under their hands; but I will so far explain myself to tell you, I mean better acknowledgments than those of the clergy of England.'

I then begged his Lordship, to give me his advise, what sort of acknowledgments he thought fittest for the clergy to make, which I was sure would be of mighty weight with them. He answered, 'I can only say again, such acknowledgments as they ought.' We had some other discourse of less moment; and after license to attend him on occasion, I took my leave. (To Archbishop King, 10 June 1708.)

Godolphin, for all his evasions, had spoken only too clearly. The church in Ireland was to be bribed into consenting to the removal of the Test.

And so the affair stood. So long as the ministry chose to tie the business up until the clergy came to time, Swift could do nothing more. But it was exacerbating to hear from Archbishop King that my Lord-Lieutenant Pembroke was pressing the business with success and that the queen might be expected to act as soon as there was peace in Europe. He, Swift, was in charge, and a far more effective agent he was than any fool of a lord-lieutenant; the talk about waiting for peace was pure moonshine — the grant would be forthcoming the instant the Test was removed. The mean tergiversations of the world were getting under his skin:

. . . in the small conversation I have had among great men, there is one maxim I have found them constantly to observe, which is, that in any business before them, if you enquire how it proceeds, they only confide what is proper to answer, without one single thought whether it be agreeable to fact or no. For instance, here is Lord Treasurer assures me that what you ask is a trifle, that the Queen would easily consent to it, and he would do so too ; then adds some general condition, etc., as I told you before ; then comes Lord Lieutenant assures me that the other has nothing at all to do with it, and that it is not to come before him, and that he has made some progress in it ; and hints to you, it seems, that it will be hardly done before a peace. The progress he means, must be something entirely between the Queen and himself, for the two chief Ministers assure me they never heard of the matter from him ; and in God's name, what sort of progress can he mean? (To Archbishop King, 28 August 1708.)

His solicitation of the first-fruits, so he had assumed when he came up to London, would be a short and successful battle ; it would redound to his credit at home, and at London would establish him within the sphere of influence. But the human race was stupid and corrupt. Godolphin had imposed impossible conditions ; the jealous clergy in Ireland whispered that Swift was not the man for the job ; Pembroke suavely insinuated that a lord-lieutenant's word would suffice. Late in November Swift learned that Pembroke had indeed prevailed and that the queen would shortly announce the Bounty. Here was the victory — that was to have been his. '. . . his Excellency [i.e., Lord Pembroke] had it at heart, and the thing is done, of which, I suppose, you have an account'—thus did he announce the news to Archbishop King.

It turned out, however, that no grant had been bestowed, and in the absence of victory Swift had at least the enjoyment of complete vindication. The reverend gentlemen of Ireland who had distrusted his powers and pinned all on Lord Pembroke might now perceive with what competence the latter had proceeded. '. . . Lord Pembroke,' he wrote to Archbishop King,

sent me word . . . , that the Queen had granted the thing, and afterward took the compliment I made him upon it. He like-

wise, I suppose, writ to the same purpose himself to [you]. . .
I . . . desired Mr. Addison to inquire at the Treasury, whether
such a grant had then passed; and finding an unwillingness, I
enquired myself, where Mr. Taylour assured me there were
never any orders for such a grant. (26 March 1709.)

When on 5 May Swift left for Leicester the first-fruits were
as far to seek as they had been on the day of his arrival in
London. The morning of 1 August he landed at Dublin
and 'went straight to Laracor without seeing anybody.'
Though he returned an eminent man of letters he was not
thinking of his literary triumphs but of his failure to secure
the first-fruits, of the loathsome inside of the great world
which so belied its pompous show, and of his own star
which had not risen after all.

His futile solicitation of the first-fruits is, however, but
part of the story. The comfort which the whigs were determined to accord the dissenters touched Swift's most
deeply implanted prejudice. Four years previously when
his party had opposed the bill against occasional conformity
he had been perplexed. All perplexity now vanished before
the open assault upon the Test in Ireland. When Brodrick,
speaker of the Irish house, was in London in April 1708,
urging relief for the Irish dissenters, Swift wrote, 'I hope
he will be impeached when your Parliament meets again'
(To Stearne, 15 April 1708). He warned Archbishop King
that 'counter-addresses should be sent both from the clergy
and conforming gentry of Ireland, to set the Queen right
in this matter' (15 April 1708). In November of this year
things took a more serious turn. It was fixed that Lord
Pembroke should be succeeded as lord-lieutenant in Ireland
by Lord Wharton, and this, as everyone knew, meant that
the whigs were redoubling their efforts to secure a removal
of the Irish Test preparatory to extending greater freedom
to English dissenters. Swift was not yet prepared to break
with his party; he still stood ready to serve it with his pen
in matters to which he could assent; but never would he
abet it in its present religious policy. On this he made
himself clear to Archbishop King:

. . . not knowing how far my friends may endeavour to engage me in the service of a new Government, I would beg your Grace to have favourable thoughts of me on such an occasion ; and to assure you, that no prospect of making my fortune, shall ever prevail on me to go against what becometh a man of conscience and truth, and an entire friend to the Established Church. (9 November 1708.)

One of the surest ways to preferment in the Irish church was to secure the post of chaplain to the lord-lieutenant. Archbishop King, who professed to have Swift's fortunes at heart, urged him to return chaplain to Lord Wharton. On 16 November 1708 Wharton took office but Swift would have given his right hand rather than solicit from this man whom he already hated like poison. To Dean Stearne Swift wrote : 'I made no manner of application for that post, upon certain reasons, that I shall let you know, if ever I have the happiness to see you again' (30 November 1708). Wharton's choice of chaplain fell on the Reverend Ralph Lambert, and when the deanery of Down became vacant a few months later, it was Lambert who was preferred, not Swift. Lambert had complied with the ministry by changing his ideas concerning toleration.

The crucial nature of Swift's reactions to the events of 1708-1709 should now be apparent. His behaviour at this time has not always been judged approvingly. Particularly has suspicion attached to the religious pamphlets which he now wrote. But such suspicion can arise only from an insufficient grasp of Swift's character. Undoubtedly he meant the world to take note that he was not only a wit but a clergyman entirely competent in the field of religious controversy. To see only the self-seeking intention is, how-ever, quite to overlook the disinterested, intellectual aspect of these writings. Circumstances had brought him head on against the old but by no means dead problem of state *versus* church. His mind closed upon the problem, it had the solution without searching for it, but clarification and statement were needed.

The five pamphlets which were apparently written dur-ing the latter months of 1708 are what we might expect:

a splendidly economical, clear, and vigorous statement of his position as a churchman, addressed to the general sense and hence original only in the magnificent ordering of commonplace ideas. In but one of the pamphlets did he lay aside straightforward exposition ; when he did, it was to achieve in *An Argument against Abolishing Christianity* a masterpiece of ironic disputation. *The Sentiments of a Church of England Man* and the incomplete and unpublished *Remarks upon 'The Rights of the Christian Church'* are remarkable for their candour, the former elucidating once and for all his conception of the church. *A Letter concerning the Sacramental Test,* dated as from Dublin 4 December 1708, was his answer to the whig ministry — an attack on the Irish dissenters and a fierce defence of the Irish Test. The last of these five pamphlets, which was not issued before March 1709, is of a somewhat different nature. As mentioned in a previous chapter, Swift has been suspected quite erroneously of writing *A Project for the Advancement of Religion and the Reformation of Manners* with his tongue in his cheek. He was, as a matter of fact, entirely in earnest, and his old friend the earl of Berkeley urged that the bookseller enable the archbishop of York to give the queen a copy — not only that Anne might be instructed how to promote piety but also, one suspects, that she might learn of the existence of one Jonathan Swift. It would have been well for Swift had he complied with Berkeley's suggestion, but apparently he did not, for it seems certain that Anne's first knowledge of him was conveyed some years later by those who took care to represent him in the worst possible light.

But whether conversing with Addison and Steele, or soliciting for the first-fruits, or engaged in writing pamphlets, Swift was ever in an agony of suspense over his own fortunes.[2] He had, he believed, made good his claim to preferment in the church. He had served the establishment in Ireland ; he had entered the lists for the whigs. What more was demanded ? It can only be said that Swift's question was reasonable. He was lacking, so it seems to us, in spiritual humility and fineness, but so were large numbers who in his day received recognition from the church. He had not engaged in recondite speculations in theology, but neither had many on whom preferment was bestowed. In blunt sincerity, in intellectual good will, in practical ability, and in talent he was behind no man; by the standards of the time he was fully qualified.

Why, then, was he held in suspense throughout these months in London and tantalized by promises of preferment which never materialized? It was not his authorship of *A Tale of a Tub*. At a later period the cry was raised by his enemies that the man who had written this book was little better than an infidel, but in 1708-1709 such malice had not begun to work against him. His ill success seems due in part to the fact that he had been born in Ireland and now held a modest Irish living — the ministry habitually reserved rich preferment in the church in Ireland as reward for services rendered by clergymen of the church in England. Again, the jealousy of those in Dublin probably worked in petty ways against him. But the reason which outweighed all others was his refusal to support the whigs in their endeavour to remove the Irish Tests. Had Swift proved as supple as Lambert, Wharton's chaplain,— but instead he wrote *A Letter concerning the Sacramental Test*.

His first great disappointment came, however, before he had offended the ministry. Early in January 1708 the see of Waterford was vacant, and Swift was encouraged to hope. But before the end of the month he learned that one Thomas Milles, who had gone over to Ireland in the train of Lord Pembroke, was to be appointed. 'Your Grace,' he wrote to Archbishop King, 'knows long before this, that Dr. Milles is Bishop of Waterford. The Court and Archbishop of Canterbury were strongly engaged for another person [Swift himself, without much question], not much suspected in Ireland, any more than the choice already made was, I believe, either here or there' (5 February 1708). It was a clear case of the advantage enjoyed in these days by a clergyman attached to a lord-lieutenant ; as yet the court and Archbishop Tenison had apparently taken no alarm at *A Tale of a Tub*.

In November 1708 a plan was afoot to send Lord Berkeley
to Vienna on a diplomatic mission.   The ministry promised
Swift the post of queen's secretary in Berkeley's train.
Heartily sick by this time of waiting for preferment which
never came, and out of patience with Godolphin and the
rest who, as it seemed to him, were threatening the security
of the church, Swift resolved to accompany Berkeley. '. . .
I shall be out of the way of parties, until it shall please God
I have some place to retire to, a little above contempt,' he
wrote to the archbishop (9 November 1708) ; and to Archdeacon Walls, '. . . if they carry things too far, I shall go to
Vienna, or even to Laracor, rather than fall in with them'
(9 November).   But the plan collapsed ; Berkeley never
went to Vienna, Swift was never made queen's secretary.

It was also in November 1708 that Wharton took office
as lord-lieutenant.   When Swift refused to solicit the post
of chaplain, he thereby ruined his chance of appointment to
the deanery of Down, which fell vacant early in 1709 and
was bestowed on Wharton's chaplain, Lambert.   Swift had
no more illusions.   'I shall go for Ireland some time in
summer,' he wrote, 'being not able to make my friends in
the Ministry consider my merits, or their promises, enough
to keep me here' (To Robert Hunter, 22 March 1709).

Nothing occurred to alter his resolution, and on 5 June
he left London, pausing in his journey back to Laracor for
a week's visit with his mother in Leicester.   From here he
addressed to Lord Halifax a letter which somewhat impairs
the dignity which had marked his previous conduct.   Pray
keep Lord Somers in mind of me, he asks, and do you duly
once a year 'wish me removed to England.'   If Dr. South
should die — he was then eighty but survived till 1716 —
he has a prebend of Westminster 'which will make me your
neighbour' and 'which my friends have often told me would
fit me extremely' (13 June 1709).   Was it that the wholly
unpleasing prospect of returning to Ireland had reduced
Swift to such a tone of solicitation ?   Perhaps, for henceforth it was preferment in England that his heart was doubly
set upon.   But there is no use in dodging the truth that Swift
was never averse to using a slightly undignified tone when

pushing his claims.   His defence lies in the grand independence of his mind, shown through all the cruelly trying events
of 1708-1709.

6

FROM the first day of July 1709 to the last day of August
1710 Swift remained in Ireland.   Sometime subsequent to
December 1709 he followed up *A Letter concerning the
Sacramental Test* with a pamphlet entitled *A Letter to a
Member of Parliament, in Ireland, upon the choosing a New
Speaker there,* in which he again attacked the efforts of the
whigs to do away with the Test.   Little else came from his
pen.

He had recently issued the third part of Temple's
Memoirs.   Lady Giffard took exception to his act, and the
means she employed of publicly expressing her resentment
stung Swift to the quick, as his letter to her of 10 November
1709 shows.   The following summer he received the news
of his mother's death.   He wrote in his account-book, 'I
have now lost my barrier between me and death ; God grant
I may live to be as well prepared for it, as I confidently
believe her to have been !   If the way to Heaven be through
piety, truth, justice, and charity, she is there.'

While Swift, at Laracor, was dreeing his weird, excitement
was running high in London.   From November 1709 to
April 1710 the last whig parliament was in session.   Godolphin's ministry was still in the saddle, but they rode an
increasingly unruly beast.   Instead of propitiating public
sentiment, they held to a policy which rapidly turned the
nation against them.   The unpopular Barrier Treaty, rising taxes, and a bad harvest had sapped enthusiasm for the
war.   But their unforgivable blunder was their action
against Sacheverell.   A genuine fear was already abroad that
the church was in danger from the whigs, and when they
ventured to bring the Reverend Henry Sacheverell to trial
for a high-flying tory sermon preached before the lord mayor
of London they sealed their fate.   The London mob rose
to the defence of a new martyr, and in every shire the cry
went up that the whigs were enemies of the church.   By

the end of 1710 the commons and the ministry had been delivered into the hands of the tories.

How did the news which came to Ireland during the winter of 1709 and the summer of 1710 affect Swift? Did it raise in his mind thoughts of desertion from a sinking party? His correspondence indicates that it did not. His whig friends, it seemed, had awakened to their neglect of him. Lord Halifax wrote, 'I am quite ashamed for myself and my friends, to see you left in a place so incapable of tasting you . . .' (6 October 1709.) Steele had words of comfort: 'No opportunity is omitted among powerful men, to upbraid them for your stay in Ireland' (8 October 1709). Such assurances Swift accepted as more than idle flattery, for in November 1709 he asked Halifax to think of him for the vacant bishopric of Cork. Of this request nothing came; another was appointed. Casting up his score against the whigs, he caught a momentary glimpse of the revenge which might be his if a new party were to come into power. '. . . I hope to see you ere it be long,' he wrote to Tooke, his publisher; 'since it is likely to be a new world, and since I have the merit of suffering by not complying with the old' (29 June 1710). But it was a passing thought, for only nine days before his unexpected departure for England he wrote Addison, asking whether it would be worth while to proceed to London—he was still, that is, looking to the whigs.

CHAPTER II

CHURCH AND STATE

1

THE clash between the church and the state as rival claimants to supreme authority is written large over the pages of medieval history. The Reformation, instead of resolving these issues, gave them new life, and in a variety of forms they continued throughout the sixteenth and seventeenth centuries to excite passion and irreconcilable sentiments. Meanwhile two other problems came to stand in close connexion with this which centred in the relations of church and state: the problem of the nature and source of authority in the state, and the problem of religious toleration.

Of these three problems the Elizabethans were by no means unaware, but it remained for Englishmen of the seventeenth century to experience the full measure of violence which these questions were capable of arousing. The Restoration was hailed as bringing to an end not only the hostilities of armed men but a bitter struggle of ideas: the restored monarchy and the restored church were intended as a final solution of political and theological difficulties. It became clear, however, as Charles II's reign wore on, that the underlying difficulties had not been obviated, and under James II each day brought closer a renewal of open violence. But the timely abandonment on the part of tories of their cherished principle of non-resistance, and opportune desertions from the ranks of James's supporters made the Revolution of 1688 a bloodless one. In the end, the Revolution proved to be the triumph of good sense over the heroic loyalties which a generation earlier had set cavalier against roundhead, and this time a relation between church and state was effected which held. Nevertheless, the issues which had been before men's minds for two centuries were not immediately laid to rest; down to 1714, in fact, they proved to be very much alive.

How the events of 1696-1710 forced upon Swift's attention the conflicting interests of church and state we have already seen. It remains to show how his mind grappled not only with the problem thus presented, but also with the two cognate problems of the nature and source of authority in the state and of religious toleration. The incisiveness of his analysis and the clarity of his exposition are not the only things which sustain one's interest, for his entire concept of religion is involved and behind this lies the complex of his controlling ideas. Yet it is fair to ask whether the writings now before us are, all things considered, of any lasting importance. It should be understood from the beginning that they cannot stand as original contributions to the thought of the time. All that they afford is a wonderfully clear statement of what had often been said. But in doing this they exhibit, even when allowance is made for Swift's individual prejudices and those of his class, so much of the characteristic temper of his age that they assume something of historical value. However, their chief importance is in respect of Swift himself: they tell us so emphatically that the intellectual energy transformed into great art in *A Tale of a Tub* and *Gulliver's Travels* was also directed towards the living world in which he moved. Only through taking account of his writings like these on church and state does one come to an adequate appreciation of the diversity of Swift's interests, a diversity which is no sooner understood than the romantic view of a misanthrope who lived in a hot-house atmosphere of dark and dubious passion is shattered once and for all.

It was in 1701, in the *Contests and Dissensions in Athens and Rome,* that Swift first turned to the problems of which we have been speaking. In this pamphlet he was concerned with the nature and source of authority in the state. Some seven years later, in *The Sentiments of a Church of England Man* and *Remarks upon 'The Rights of the Christian Church,'* he took up the central problem of the relations of church and state, and at about the same time he found occasion to express his views concerning religious toleration in *A Letter concerning the Sacramental Test* and *A Let-*

*ter to a Member of Parliament, in Ireland. An Argument
against Abolishing Christianity* and *A Project for the Advancement of Religion and the Reformation of Manners*
lead us towards his conception of religion as a practical and
ethical force. Since the attitudes disclosed in this whole
series of pamphlets are in direct relation to his fundamental
religious beliefs, the closing section of the present chapter
will be devoted to an analysis of these beliefs. It will be
found that *Mr. Collins's Discourse of Freethinking* (1713),
*A Letter to a Young Gentleman, lately enter'd into Holy
Orders* (1720; ptd. 1721), together with the undated *Sermons*
and *Thoughts on Religion* will, when taken along with the
pamphlets of 1701-1709, supply what is necessary for an understanding of Swift's religious position.

2

READ in the light of Swift's later writings the *Contests and
Dissensions* is a curious performance. In 1701 Swift's whig
philosophy had not passed through fire; there were elements
in it which were later to be refined away. When he undertook a defence of the whig lords threatened with impeachment he did so by way of an attack on the 'unruly' tory
commons. His surprising identification of a tory house
with the turbulent popular assemblies of Athens and Rome
seems downright naïve. Yet despite much that is callow,
the *Contests and Dissensions* does express, as we shall see,
Swift's mature ideas on the nature and source of authority
in the state, ideas unshaken by later experiences.

The political spirit which pervades the pamphlet is that of
the post-Revolution period, when the commonly accepted
political doctrine, which seemed to explain the actual events
of recent history, was the contract theory, according to which
men had at some remote time surrendered their unsocial
liberties in order to enjoy mutual peace and security in an
ordered state, but retained the right, in the face of tyranny,
to overthrow their ruler. Powers within the state, it was
believed, should exhibit a balance corresponding to that
which Europe was striving to maintain between nations.

Such assumptions and the enclosing atmosphere of post-Revolution thought Swift, attaining maturity in the years following 1688, had absorbed naturally, nor did he ever lose this whig temper received during his formative years. The tone of reasonableness runs through the *Contests and Dissensions*: though there is fear of popular disturbance, there is faith in the good will of average men; the theory of a balance of power is accepted. Only in his eschewal of the Lockian theory of contract does Swift offer any resistance to the Revolution's assumptions — like Temple, he preferred to work backward over the course of history for an explanation of social institutions.

At the beginning of the pamphlet Swift lays down two basic principles: (1) ' 'Tis agreed, that in all government there is an absolute unlimited power, which naturally and originally seems to be placed in the whole body, wherever the executive part of it lies;' (2) not to be confused with this absolute power is the administrative or executive power. (Swift would have achieved a clearer statement had he made a further distinction, which he later adopted, between the administrative or executive power of the Crown and the legislative power as held by king, lords, and commons. When speaking in the *Contests and Dissensions* of the administrative or executive power he seems to have had in mind what he later would have called the legislative power, but on this point his thought is frequently cloudy.) In a 'mixed government' like that of England this executive power is shared by king, nobles, and commons, and between these three it should ever be held in balance.

The interesting and fundamental thing in these opening statements is the insistence that the whole people constitutes the source of all power in the state. Had Swift taken any other view he would have done violence to his belief in the universality of reason — the authority of the state being but the political aspect of the general sense of mankind. And it is important to see how this creed conditioned Swift's historical outlook, exposed as clearly in the pages of this pamphlet as in any of his later writings. On the side of English history, his interest in events before the Tudors was per-

functory, but beginning with Elizabeth he was on familiar
ground. The middle of her reign, he held, marked the
most delicate balance of administrative power which England had ever effected; it was then that nobles and commons weighed equally. In the first half of the seventeenth
century this balance was upset by the puritans, who arro-
gated all power to themselves and prepared the way for the
single tyrant in the person of Cromwell — never, it should be
remembered, did Swift look upon the puritans as other than
a savagely persecuting minority. In 1660 the old government was restored, but for the next thirty years two weak
princes continually threatened to disturb the balance, but
this danger was at last removed by the Revolution. Historically, Swift's mind moved between 1558 and his own age.
But it was also guided — on the side of theory — by a very
definite philosophy of history, which again is given clear
expression in the *Contests and Dissensions*. It is, as we have
previously seen, a negative philosophy. In certain respects
it shows a thorough comprehension of Machiavelli. Every
form of government is limited in time, and will eventually
come to an end through the decree of Heaven and nature.
No human endeavour can prolong a state beyond this fixed
mark, but if men will break down the art of government
into its first principles they will be enabled to prevent accidents and render the state longer lived though not immortal — Machiavelli's point, precisely. In such an attitude
there is a splendid realism which we of the present century
can understand better than did our parents of the nineteenth : instead of reliance upon a law of melioration there
is the grand hope that man's powers will prove equal to
events.

Having announced his first principles, Swift proceeds to
apply them, and in doing so he preaches a sermon, amply
footnoted from history, at the tory commons, who by their
actions are bringing the commonwealth into danger. The
administrative or executive power has in different states at
different times been held preponderantly by the one, by the
few, and again by the many, 'but . . . in the last resort
was always meant by legislators to be held in balance among

all three.' For this maintenance of balance three things are necessary: the hand which holds the scale — the king — and the two counterpoised weights — the lords and the commons. When there is equilibrium in the state, the holding hand is not necessarily the strongest; when the equilibrium is destroyed and tyranny replaces liberty it is not always the 'one' who usurps. Any one of the three elements in the state can by headstrong action break the balance, and history points to quite as dreadful tyrannies established by the populace as by single men or oligarchies. The implication is evident: as in the 1640's and '50's the puritans broke the balance and set up a persecuting Commonwealth, so now a tory commons threatens to arrogate an undue share of power with the inevitable result.

In the closing paragraphs of the first chapter Swift gives a short psychological analysis of the motives which render men ever ready to disrupt the political equilibrium, and the voice of Machiavelli is heard again:

So endless and exorbitant are the desires of men, whether considered in their persons or their states, that they will grasp at all, and can form no scheme of perfect happiness with less. Ever since men have been united into governments, the hopes and endeavours after universal monarchy have been bandied among them. . .

But experience teaches that whenever the struggle for domination lies between nobles and commons, both are cheated in the end, for oppression by either the few or the many leads in short space to the tyranny of a single person.

The second and third chapters are packed with historical parallels between ancient and present times. The usurpation of power by the Athenian populace is described, together with their jealousy and persecution of their great generals. At this point the *Contests and Dissensions* is full of suppressed analogies: Lord Orford is indicated in Miltiades, Halifax in Pericles, and Somers in Aristides. From all this the familiar moral is drawn: the unruly populace by destroying the commonwealth paved the way for the single tyrant. To the same effect chapter three deals with Roman history: 'Here ended all show or shadow of liberty in Rome.　Here was the repository of all the wise contentions and struggles for power between the Nobles and Commons, lapped up safely in the bosom of a Nero and a Caligula, a Tiberius and a Domitian.'

The fifth and final chapter of the pamphlet is perhaps the most interesting.　If any doubt were to be entertained whether the hand that wrote *A Tale of a Tub* also penned the *Contests and Dissensions,* this closing chapter would dispel it.　In fact, the similarity of tone between the Digressions in the former work and the last pages of the political pamphlet lends much weight to M. Pons's contention that a considerable part of the satiric piece dates from the years immediately preceding its publication in 1704.　The evils in popular assemblies, we are informed, are not owing to innate perversion in the run of men, but rather to the baleful influence exercised by some private person — in political jargon a 'leading man'— and by party.　Without these, popular assemblies would not run amuck:

Because, this must be said in behalf of human kind, that common sense and plain reason, while men are disengaged from acquired opinions, will ever have some general influence upon their minds; whereas the species of folly and vice are infinite, and so different in every individual, that they could never procure a majority, if other corruptions did not enter to pervert men's understandings, and misguide their wills.

There follows a description of the working of party spirit which immediately carries us back to Jack, the æolists, and the madmen in a commonwealth:

To describe how parties are bred in an assembly, would be a work too difficult at present, and perhaps not altogether safe. *Periculosæ plenum opus aleæ.* Whether those, who are leaders, usually arrive at that station more by a sort of instinct or secret composition of their nature, or influence of the stars, than by the possession of any great abilities, may be a point of much dispute; but when the leader is once fixed, there will never fail to be followers.　And man is so apt to imitate, so much of the nature of sheep, (*imitatores, servum pecus,*) that whoever is so bold to give the first great leap over the heads of those about him, (though he be the worst of the flock,) shall be quickly followed by the rest.　Besides, when parties are once formed, the

stragglers look so ridiculous and become so insignificant, that
they have no other way but to run into the herd, which at least
will hide and protect them ; and where to be much considered,
requires only to be very violent.

In *A Tale of a Tub* it is shown how infinitely the outside
of nature differs from the inside ; we now see to what degree
a man in his everyday capacity differs from the same man
when inflamed with party zeal :

> . . . I think, there is hardly to be found through all nature a
> greater difference between two things, than there is between a
> representing commoner in the function of his public calling, and
> the same person when he acts in the common offices of life.
> Here he allows himself to be upon a level with the rest of
> mortals ; here he follows his own reason, and his own way ; and
> rather affects a singularity in his actions and thoughts, than ser-
> vilely to copy either from the wisest of his neighbours.   In short,
> here his folly and his wisdom, his reason and his passions, are
> all of his own growth, not the echo or infusion of other men.
> But when he is got near the walls of his assembly, he assumes
> and affects an entire set of very different airs ; he conceives him-
> self a being of a superior nature to those without, and acting in
> a sphere when the vulgar methods for the conduct of human life
> can be of no use.   He is listed in a party where he neither knows
> the temper, nor designs, nor perhaps the person, of his leader ;
> but whose opinions he follows and maintains with a zeal and
> faith as violent as a young scholar does those of a philosopher
> whose sect he is taught to profess.   He has neither opinions, nor
> thoughts, nor actions, nor talk, that he can call his own, but all
> conveyed to him by his leader, as wind is through an organ.
> The nourishment he receives has been not only chewed, but
> digested, before it comes into his mouth.   Thus instructed, he
> follows the party, right or wrong, through all his sentiments, and
> acquires a courage and stiffness of opinion not at all congenial
> with him.

Swift brings his sermon to an end by expressing the hope
that when the members of the present house of commons
return to their homes they will seriously consider their recent conduct.   In retirement they will, perhaps, discern how
strongly the nation, moved by gratitude to King William
and fear of the French monarch, resents their behaviour.

The *Contests and Dissensions* is significant at many points.
It testifies not alone to the firm hold which the Revolution's

principles had upon Swift, but to his realistic analysis of political conduct, to his reduction of party spirit to the level of enthusiasm, above all to his concept of liberty, the possession of rational human beings to be defended at whatever cost against the tyrant's destroying passion.

3

THE ideas expressed in the series of pamphlets begun in 1701 and completed in 1709 are seen gradually to form themselves into a carefully designed structure. In this structure *The Sentiments of a Church of England Man* (1708) may be regarded as the keystone. Here Swift proceeded with unfaltering directness to the central problem about which all the others lay grouped : the relations of church and state.

Some have regarded the *Sentiments* as a piece of self-advertising. Temple Scott, the editor of the *Collected Prose Works*, believed that it was rather a warning to both whigs and tories. A more reasonable view is that Swift desired to clarify his mind by marking out his own position with the greatest exactness. It will be remembered that in the latter months of 1708, when presumably he wrote the *Sentiments*, he was bewildered by conflicting loyalties : committed to the Revolution's principles, he had assumed hitherto that his natural place was in the whig party, but the ministers' increasing hostility towards the church had begun to unsettle him. In such a mood he shifted his gaze from parties to himself, seeking as it were to confirm once and for all that body of assured principles to which he was committed and which partisanship, he felt sure, would be powerless to shake.

His desire to transcend mere party issues is apparent throughout the *Sentiments,* and gives to it a tone of moderation and reasonableness which we have come to assume, quite erroneously, was at all times and in all matters foreign to Swift. He opens with the declaration that he will not believe that either of the parties desires to push matters to extremes in religion and government as charged by its enemies ; he will not believe that the whigs are working for a presbyterian church and a republican government; he will not believe that the tories aim at Roman catholicism and arbitrary power.   If each party suffers from enthusiasts who would drive it to some wild extremity, its strength and its numbers lie in moderate members.   As a moderate clergyman standing for the time being aloof from both parties, he will, he seems to say, lay down his own principles, with regard first to religion and then to government, offering them as those to which all men must give immediate assent so long as reason prevails in the nation.

The adroitness with which Swift handles all the delicate problems arising out of the relations of church and state, his reasonableness, and the extent to which the principles of the Revolution controlled his thinking cannot be understood without some knowledge of the positions relative to one another which the church and the state had occupied in England during successive periods since the Reformation.

The Elizabethan Settlement had resulted in an Erastian state-church. The relations thus established between the state and the church can be indicated by saying that they were in contradiction to those posited by the ideological church-state with which medieval catholicism had answered the emperors' claims to supreme power: above the laws of the state there is, the church held, a law of God, to which princes like all others are subject and which allows the deposition of tyrannical kings.   When the English Calvinists of the earlier seventeenth century found themselves in bondage to the Elizabethan state-church, they fell back upon the opposing theory of the Middle Ages and gave it a new expression: by God's law speaking through the people Charles I merited punishment.   In the face of this, conservatism was compelled to redefine its position regarding church and state, and the result was anything but a liberalizing of its previous views.   In the church, Laudianism came to rule; in both ritual and doctrine there was a recessive movement which in certain respects seemed to challenge the Reformation.   Politically, the king became the mainstay and was endowed with a divine right.   This philosophy, in which high church and royalism were united, shone the more brightly for the material triumphs of the puritans, and in 1660 it was in a measure translated into fact in a restored church and king. But the events of 1688 proved its undoing, the *de facto* government then set up splitting the tories. The non-jurors refused to recognize William; those who accepted him and the historical actualities of the day were forced to temporize regarding theory. The whigs, on the other hand, were compromised in no such way by the Revolution, for their doctrine now defined a state-church, deriving its authority from the general voice. It was in the latter years of Queen Anne's reign that the old spirit of toryism flared up for the last time. In this revolt against the principles and spirit of the Revolution, high church took the lead. There was revival of Laudianism, a reassertion of the sacred character of the priesthood and the divine right of bishops, and a branding of other protestants as schismatics; politically, Jacobitism rekindled royalist fervour. The whigs' reaction to this movement was determined by their entire previous history: threatened with a return of a church-state they became increasingly Erastian, extremists like Hoadly describing a state-church in which other powers almost vanished before political authority.

Swift's settled course in respect of religion and government lay between high-flying conservatism and whig radicalism. For him the *de facto* character of William's reign constituted no problem; from the first he had accepted the principle that sovereignty resides in the body of the people. The episcopal church claimed his loyalty because of its venerability and its historical sanctification, but to the catholic theory of the right divine of bishops he did not accede; while the church stood in its own right and not merely by authority of the state it was not so narrowly calculated 'that it [could] not fall in with any regular species of government.' Swift sought neither a whig state-church nor a tory church-state: politically, the state was supreme; but the church, because its principles were of quite another order, was, in all that concerned religion proper, inaccessible to civil decrees. It was such a middle course, dictated by his entire system of controlling ideas, which *The Sentiments of a*

Church of England Man was intended to define.   To doubt the sincerity of this pamphlet is to reduce all the operations of his mind to a ghastly form of intellectual dishonesty.

The *Sentiments* consists — aside from introductory paragraphs — of two sections, in the first of which is set forth a typical, non-partisan attitude towards religion, in the second a similar attitude towards government.   In the first section we read :

A Church of England man hath a true veneration for the scheme established among us of ecclesiastic government ; and though he will not determine whether Episcopacy be of divine right, he is sure it is most agreeable to primitive institution, fittest of all others for preserving order and purity, and under its present regulations best calculated for our civil state : He should therefore think the abolishment of that order among us would prove a mighty scandal and corruption to our faith, and manifestly dangerous to our monarchy ; nay, he would defend it by arms against all the powers on earth, except our own legislature ; in which case he would submit as to a general calamity, a dearth, or a pestilence.

The nature of the church and the position which he conceived it to hold in relation to the state could hardly be put more neatly.

Before bringing the first section to an end, Swift broaches the problem of religious toleration.   So large does his later harrying of the dissenters bulk in the minds of modern readers that an exact appreciation of his conduct in this respect will not be attained until it is seen how widely he diverted from the high-church definition of schism.   As a church of England man 'doth not reckon every schism of that damnable nature which some would represent; so he is very far from closing with the new opinion of those who would make it no crime at all, and argue at a wild rate, that God Almighty is delighted with the variety of faith and worship, as He is with the varieties of nature.'   Once schisms develop, the question quickly arises, who are the real schismatics?   Swift rests his answer not on dogma but on civil decree.   '. . . 'tis certain, that, in the sense of the law, the schism lies on that side which opposes itself to the religion of the state.'   The schismatics are to be accorded freedom to

worship as they choose, but since their dissent is a non-com-
pliance with the will of the state they should be rigorously
excluded from positions of civil power. These opinions
Swift never altered, nor in his attacks against the dissenters
did he ever go beyond them; he sought not to persecute
them into conformity, merely to exclude them from political
power through maintenance of the Tests. It will perhaps
be suggested that in defining dissent as opposition to the
religion of the state he was, by appealing to civil law, doing
violence to his theory of church. The contradiction is more
one of words than of thought. What lay at the back of his
mind was this : reason expresses itself politically through the
sovereign voice of the people, religiously through that church
which, *because* it embodies the beliefs accepted by every reasonable man, wins recognition from the state. When he
said that dissent was opposition to civil decrees Swift meant
two things : one, that no law of God gives any church the
right to persecute ; two, that the law of reason establishes
in the commonwealth a church that can be unacceptable
only to enthusiasts.

The second section of the *Sentiments* is devoted to government. The fundamentals to which all agree are loyalty to
the queen, abjuration of the pretender, the settlement of the
Crown in the protestant line, affection to the established
church, toleration of dissenters. But beyond these there is
much which is still disputed. Now, a church of England
man 'doth not think the Church of England so narrowly
calculated, that it cannot fall in with any regular species of
government ; nor does he think any one regular species of
government more acceptable to God than another.'

In the pages which follow he restates what he had said
before in the *Contests and Dissensions*.

Where security of person and property are preserved by laws
which none but the Whole can repeal, there the great ends of
government are provided for whether the administration be in
the hands of One, or of Many. Where any one person or body
of men, who do not represent the Whole, seize into their hands
the power in the last resort, there is properly no longer a government, but what Aristotle and his followers call the abuse and
corruption of one. This distinction excludes arbitrary power

in whatever numbers; which notwithstanding all that Hobbes, Filmer and others have said to its advantage, I look upon as a greater evil than anarchy itself; as much as a savage is in a happier state of life than a slave at the oar.

This sovereign power speaks through the legislature, which must never be confused with the administration. Whereas the legislature is rightly a universal voice, it is the part of wisdom to confine the administrative powers—'I believe it may pass for a maxim in state, that the administration cannot be placed in too few hands, nor the legislature in too many.' In this material point the English government exceeds all others.

Swift's unpublished *Remarks upon 'The Rights of the Christian Church,'* of the same date as the *Sentiments,* continues the line of argument taken up in the latter pamphlet. It is an answer to a book by Tindal, the deist, who represented religion as the imposture of cunning priests and who would free men from this incubus by showing that the church and Christianity are in fact but a contrivance of civil power. There is genuine indignation in Swift's rebuttal, but the abusive epithets which he allowed himself are less effective than the force of his logic, which produces a masterly and at the same time humorous statement of the civil-religious relationship. Here again Swift succeeded in giving a pellucid statement of the authority which he believed the church retained above and beyond the supreme civil power.

4

A Letter concerning the Sacramental Test (dated as from Dublin 4 December 1708) and *A Letter to a Member of Parliament, in Ireland, upon the choosing a New Speaker there* (subsequent to December 1709) mark Swift's first open rupture with his party. The severance was not yet a complete one, but he was washing his hands of those whig extremists whose Erastianism dictated as an opening move the repeal of the Test in Ireland.

As we have seen in the preceding section, the principle of religious toleration was one to which Swift genuinely believed that he assented, and it must be said that he never allowed what we should call his intolerance to trample down the precise definitions and distinctions with which he began. The dissenters should be free to worship as they choose, but because their dissent is a sign that they deny the general sense of the nation they must be excluded from all power in the state.   This was the intellectual ground of his implacability.   His emotional fury arose from his belief that the dissenters aimed at power in order to destroy the church of England and that as in the days of the Commonwealth they would, given the opportunity, establish themselves as a persecuting minority.   The large measure of reasonableness which Swift drew from the era of the Revolution was insufficient to dissolve his hatred of enthusiastic sectarianism, a hatred conveyed into his blood by the writers of the earlier seventeenth century.

A Letter concerning the Sacramental Test says in substance everything which Swift ever uttered of the dissenters, and says it with some temperance.   One passage, often quoted, owes its interest not to references to the Test but to an ironic statement of the consideration which the English may count on from Ireland.   Do the advantages which will follow from a repeal of the Test lie entirely on the English side of the Irish Sea?   If they do, the powers in England need only say so.   Has Ireland ever advanced her own interests before England's?

> 'Forbid it Heaven my life should be
> Weigh'd with her least conveniency:'

In short, whatever advantage you propose to yourselves by repealing the Sacramental Test, speak it out plainly, 'tis the best argument you can use, for we value your interest much more than our own: If your little finger be sore, and you think a poultice made of our vitals will give it any ease, speak the word and it shall be done; the interest of our whole kingdom is at any time ready to strike to that of your poorest fishing towns; it is hard you will not accept our services, unless we believe at the same time that you are only consulting our profit, and giving us marks of your love.   If there be a fire at some distance, and I immediately blow up my house before there be occasion, because you are a man of quality, and apprehend some danger to a corner of your stable; yet why should you require me to attend next morning at your levee with my humble thanks for the favour you have done me?

Thus spoke the Drapier some sixteen years before his time.

But irony is quickly dropped and the argument becomes straightforward. Have not the dissenters toleration? Have they not liberty, property, and religion? What they have not and what they now demand is power and employment, and no sooner will they come into possession of these things than they will straightway carry out their designs against the established church. Those who cry up repeal talk of the expediency of uniting all protestants in Ireland against the catholic danger. But where is this danger? '. . . we look upon [the Papists] to be altogether as inconsiderable as the women and children. Their lands are almost entirely taken from them, and they are rendered incapable of purchasing any more; and for the little that remains, provision is made by the late act against Popery, that it will daily crumble away. . .' As for uniting all protestants, ' 'Tis an odd way of uniting parties, to deprive a majority of part of their ancient right, by conferring it on a faction who had never any right at all, and therefore cannot be said to suffer any loss or injury if it be refused them.' In any case, before you grant these protestants what they are now clamouring for, put the question 'whether, these same Protestants, when they have by their dexterity made themselves the national religion, and disposed the Church revenues among their pastors or themselves, will be so kind to allow us dissenters, I do not say a share in employments, but a bare toleration by law?'

In December 1709 the speakership of the Irish house of commons became vacant. Thereupon Swift issued *A Letter to a Member of Parliament, in Ireland,* in which he adjured the commons not to vote for any candidate siding with those extreme whigs in England who were attempting a repeal of the Test.

Swift believed that these two pamphlets in support of the Test had ruined his chance of promotion at the hands of the whig ministers, and perhaps he was right. Certainly no man who valued advancement above principles would have ventured at this juncture to speak his mind so boldly.

5

THE two other pamphlets of this series are *A Project for the Advancement of Religion and the Reformation of Morals* (not issued before March 1709) and *An Argument against Abolishing Christianity* (1708). It has so often been said that Swift discerned in religion little more than a morally restraining force that the statement is generally believed. It is a particularly insidious statement because it comes near enough to the truth to deceive honest but hostile critics of Swift, for unless his religious beliefs are seen as native to his entire ideology, they are open to misinterpretation at the hands of even his most sympathetic commentators. Now, Swift would have been the first to agree that he was above all a moralist. And as the *Project* and the *Argument* show, he was ready enough to meet the world on its own secular terms and to appeal on grounds that are largely moral for decency in conduct and for respect for the church as a social institution. But from this, as we shall see in the closing section of this chapter, it is inaccurate to conclude that his religion terminated in ethics.

The *Project* is a surprising work. Here Swift's ethical rigidity takes absolute control. Immorality in the kingdom is to be uprooted by a moral crusade, led by the queen. Conformity at least to the outward decencies is to be enforced by the officers of the Crown, who are to function like the Roman censors :

There are several pernicious vices frequent and notorious among us, that escape or elude the punishment of any law we have yet invented, or have had no law at all against them ; such as atheism, drunkenness, fraud, avarice, and several others ; which, by this institution, wisely regulated, might be much reformed. Suppose, for instance, that itinerary commissioners were appointed to inspect everywhere throughout the kingdom, into the conduct (at least) of men in office, with respect to their morals and religion, as well as their abilities ; to receive the complaints and informations that should be offered against them, and make their report here upon oath, to the court, or the ministry, who should reward or punish accordingly. I avoid entering into the particulars of this, or any other scheme, which, coming from a private hand, might be liable to many defects, but would soon be digested by the wisdom of the nation; and surely, six thousand pounds a year would not be ill laid out among as many commissioners duly qualified, who, in three divisions, should be personally obliged to take their yearly circuits for that purpose.

At the end of the tract these extreme measures are justified by certain first principles derived from Machiavelli:

Whether the proposals I have offered toward a reformation, be such as are most prudent and convenient, may probably be a question; but it is none at all, whether some reformation be absolutely necessary; because the nature of things is such, that if abuses be not remedied, they will certainly increase, nor ever stop, till they end in the subversion of a commonwealth. As there must always of necessity be some corruptions, so, in a well-instituted state, the executive power will be always contending against them, by *reducing things* (as Michiaevel speaks) *to their first principles;* never letting abuses grow inveterate, or multiply so far, that it will be hard to find remedies, and perhaps impossible to apply them.

Of an altogether different tone is the incomparable *Argument against Abolishing Christianity,* by all odds the greatest of these pamphlets in point of artistry. The master of ironic logic is here in full command. The intellectual sleight-of-hand whereby the arguments of the deists against religion and the church are turned inside out and drolly tossed back at the enemy is not to be analysed — the effect owes as much to the prestidigitator's mien as to his nimbleness. He would not think, he freely admits, of undertaking to justify real Christianity; his concern is entirely with nominal Christianity. Nor will he attempt to defend the latter save on the grounds of pure expediency: were we to cast off the name and title of Christians, 'I will beg leave to shew what inconveniencies may possibly happen . . . in the present posture of our affairs.'

The natural religion which the deists maintained against

revealed religion excited only contempt in Swift. It was a
species of enthusiasm, a bugaboo born of crack-brained speculations. All his hatred of empty theorizing rose up in
revolt against these philosophers, with whom he disdained to
enter into serious controversy. It was sufficient to expose
their morals :

. . . of what use is freedom of thought, if it will not produce
freedom of action, which is the sole end, how remote soever in
appearance, of all objections against Christianity? And therefore, the freethinkers consider it as a sort of edifice, wherein all
the parts have such a mutual dependence on each other, that if
you happen to pull out one single nail, the whole fabric must
fall to the ground. This was happily expressed by him who had
heard of a text brought for proof of the Trinity, which in an
ancient manuscript was differently read ; he thereupon immediately took the hint, and by a sudden deduction of a long
sorites, most logically concluded; 'Why, if it be as you say, I
may safely whore and drink on, and defy the parson.' From
which, and many the like instances easy to be produced, I think
nothing can be more manifest, than that the quarrel is not
against any particular points of hard digestion in the Christian
system, but against religion in general ; which, by laying re-
straints on human nature, is supposed the great enemy to the
freedom of thought and action.

This was the line which Swift took at all times with the
deists. Undeniably it may be made to bear out the view
that his religion was mere morality. The fallacy of such
an interpretation lies in the assumption that Swift overlooked doctrine. He did not. He merely refused to dig-
nify the deists by engaging them on the intellectual plane ;
against paltry immoralists what more was needed than the
moral argument?

6

IT is centrality which is the foremost characteristic of Swift's
thought. Thus, when he wrote of the relations to be observed between church and state, when he wrote of matters
connected with religious toleration, when he wrote against
the deists and in behalf of religion as a moral check, he was
expressing not occasional ideas but convictions stemming

from a perfectly ordered system of thought. It is within this system that his primary religious beliefs must be sought.

In order to round out our present discussion, we shall first consider two compositions not to be omitted from any conspectus of Swift's religion. After these, we shall refer to the *Sermons* and the *Thoughts on Religion*.

Mr. Collins's Discourse of Freethinking; put into plain English, by way of Abstract, for the Use of the Poor was written in 1713, when for over two years Swift had headed the tory journalists. *A Letter to a Young Gentleman, lately enter'd into Holy Orders* is dated 1720. The earlier of these is to be bracketed with *An Argument against Abolishing Christianity*: it is a blast against the deists, its force lies in ironic logic, and the argument rests upon the disciplinary value of the church. The chief difference between the two pieces lies in tone, the drollery of the *Argument* becoming in the *Discourse* undisguised asperity. One by one Collins's arguments are taken up, translated into the language of irony, and then through what profess to be legitimate extensions pushed into the realm of nonsense. Political animus there also is, for one of Swift's purposes throughout these pages is to fasten upon the whigs the stigma of deism and irreligion, and with journalistic unscrupulousness he lets slip no opportunity of identifying his political with his religious enemies.

The chief points at which Swift breaks through the lines of the deists are these: their talk of cunning priests, their arguments based on doctrinal disagreements, and their contempt for any sort of conformity. The Bible, because it is the most difficult book in the world to understand, is the source of those impostures by which cunning priests beguile mankind. Deliverance lies through free-thinking. The more difficult the matter, the greater the necessity of free-thinking.

How can a man think at all, if he does not think freely? A man who does not eat and drink freely, does not eat and drink at all. Why may not I be denied the liberty of freeseeing, as well as freethinking? Yet nobody pretends that the first is unlawful, for a cat may look on a king; though you be near-sighted, or have weak or sore eyes, or are blind, you may be a free-seer; you ought to see for yourself, and not trust to a guide to choose the colour of your stockings, or save you from falling into a ditch.

Again, because there is much disagreement among the clergy on points of doctrine, it follows that every man should arrive at the truth through his own free-thinking and maintain his conclusions against the world, no matter who challenges him. The bishops will say that when the church's judgment is against you, you should maintain the peace of the church by silence.

Now my opinion is directly contrary; and I affirm, that if ten thousand freethinkers thought differently from the received doctrine, and from each other, they would be all in duty bound to publish their thoughts (provided they were all sure of being in the right) though it broke the peace of the Church and state ten thousand times.

Lastly, as for conformity of any sort, it is a sign of limitation.

It is the indispensable duty of a freethinker, to endeavour forcing all the world to think as he does, and by that means make them freethinkers too. You are also to understand, that I allow no man to be a freethinker, any further than as he differs from the received doctrines of religion. Where a man falls in, though by perfect chance, with what is generally believed, he is in that point a confined and limited thinker. . .

In these ways did Swift illuminate the principle of discipline in thought and action. Most, he was saying, are ready enough to be guided by the general sense; those who do not know the meaning of submission must be checked by common morality and by institutional religion.

A Letter to a Young Gentleman, lately enter'd into Holy Orders carries us somewhat farther towards the centre of Swift's religious position. The advice which he has to give in this admirable composition is much of it concerned with pulpit eloquence. The preacher should avoid the use of obscure terms, above all those peculiar to divinity. '. . . I defy the greatest divine to produce any law either of God or

man, which obliges me to comprehend the meaning of
*omniscience, omnipresence, ubiquity, attribute, beatific
vision,* with a thousand others so frequent in pulpits. . .'
On the other hand, the desire to avoid pedantry is in some
clergymen so great that they affect the polite style of the tea-
table and coffee-house :

These accomplishments, when applied to the pulpit, appear by
a quaint, terse, florid style, rounded into periods and cadences,
commonly without either propriety or meaning. I have listen'd
with my utmost attention for half an hour to an orator of this
species, without being able to understand, much less to carry
away one single sentence out of a whole sermon.

But of all evils, the greatest is attempting to move the
passions of one's auditors.

A plain convincing reason may possibly operate upon the
mind both of a learned and ignorant hearer as long as they live,
and will edify a thousand times more than the art of wetting the
handkerchiefs of a whole congregation. . . I take it, the two
principal branches of preaching are first to tell the people what
is their duty, and then to convince them that it is so.

Further, the young clergyman should not fall into the
common cant of disparaging the heathen philosophers.
True, their system of morality falls very short of that contained in the Gospel and wants divine sanction. 'But I am
deceived, if a better comment could be anywhere collected,
upon the moral part of the Gospel; than from the writings
of those excellent men. . .' As for attempting in one's sermons to explain the mysteries of the Christian religion, not
only is this not directed in the canons or articles, but 'since
Providence intended there should be mysteries, I do not see
how it can be agreeable to piety, orthodoxy or good sense,
to go about such a work.'
The *Letter* is a very meaty discourse, opening up several
inviting avenues to explore. A great deal might be written
concerning Swift's observations on style, and again concerning his denunciation of moving oratory. We must confine
ourselves, however, to the anti-intellectualism which he here
applies to matters of religion. No law of God or man

obliges us to understand terms like *omnipresence, ubiquity,* and *beatific vision;* God intended that the mysteries of the Christian religion should remain incomprehensible to man. Here we have direct insight into Swift's religious thought. The intellectual subtlety and the emotional ardour which are combined in different patterns in the divine and the religious mystic lay quite beyond Swift's experiences. Both in intellect and emotion his range was confined within the limits imposed by his own nature and by his age. What did it avail, he asked, to search beyond the truths made clear to all men by the light of reason?

And this brings us to our closing observations. In so far as Swift's religion was intellectual definition, its two all-important statements had to do (1) with the relations between man and God effected through the mysteries of re-vealed religion, and (2) man's apprehension of God through beliefs arrived at purely through reason. Concerning these beliefs: man's reason is God-given, and would therefore be quite trustworthy were it not that 'the reason of every par-ticular man is weak and wavering, perpetually swayed and turned by his interests, his passions, and his vices' *(Sermon on the Trinity).* That is, the anti-rationalistic element in the individual stands in the way of a perfect apprehension, through reason, of truth and God, and it follows that the discipline of society, of the state, and above all of the church must intervene. 'I am not answerable to God,' runs one of the *Thoughts on Religion,* 'for the doubts that arise in my own breast, since they are the consequence of that reason which He hath planted in me ; if I take care to conceal those doubts from others, if I use my best endeavours to subdue them, and if they have no influence on the conduct of my life.' Time and again this passage, interpreted as a confes-sion, has been quoted against Swift. It is, of course, not in any way an admission of personal weakness but a general observation : *all* men know such doubts, for the individual's reason is rendered fallible by the disturbances of self-interest and of the passions ; *all* men must bow to the discipline im-posed by the institutions which nature, history, and God have sanctified.

As for the mysteries of revealed Christianity: man's reason, even when free from the disturbances of the passions, is limited by the will of God to the truths of nature. Beyond nature lies the supernatural, incomprehensible to the human intellect, but signified through the Christian mysteries. What reason is powerless to explain, we must accept through faith.*

It will be seen that the chief elements in Swift's religious ideology are (1) the doctrine of reason and nature, (2) anti-rationalism, and (3) anti-intellectualism.

It should not be imagined that this treatment of Swift's religion is in any way exhaustive. Thick are the shadows which we have left unexplored — for instance, his meditations on evil. But enough has been uncovered to indicate the quality of his thought, the general nature of his religious concepts, and the manner in which these concepts were mortised into his controlling ideas. And while interpretation has been the single aim of this chapter, in the course of it Swift has, it is believed, been vindicated of certain charges commonly brought against him. He was not a spiritual man. But his writings on church, state, and religion disclose an intellectual sincerity and consistency which challenge a great many of the criticisms to which on the side of religion he has been subjected. Take him on his own plane, bear in mind the character of his period, and he is seen as an honest and devout man. There is, of course, a quite different point of view from which it may be proper to judge him, but our task has been that of exploration at the level of his own age.

---

* This bifurcation of reason and faith seems to the present writer, who speaks merely as a historian and from a purely historical point of view, to be the central weakness in Swift's religious system. The chapter on controlling ideas in Book I suggests something of the Renaissance background of the disjunction of reason and faith, nature and grace.

CHAPTER III

WIT AND MAN OF LETTERS

1

HOWEVER earnest life was for Swift during the trying and critical twelve years preceding the political upset of 1710, however severe the disappointments which he suffered, he achieved a greater freedom in the face of circumstance than at any other time in his life. His good spirits refused to be put down by annoyances, misfortunes, and the perversities of the human race. During lighter moments, of which there were many, humour held sway freely. Exclusive of *A Tale of a Tub*, with its conjoined matter, and the pamphlets on church and state, Swift's compositions between 1699 and September 1710 number more than thirty-five, and with few exceptions these bear witness to his exuberance.

Of these pieces wherein the wit and man of letters is represented those in verse take foremost place. Swift had come upon the familiar style while yet at Moor Park, and his lines on the burning of Whitehall (1698) and *Written in a Lady's Ivory Table-Book* (1698; probably revised 1706) were both assured and convincing. From this point on his progress in the familiar style was triumphant. To mention only productions of outstanding importance: first came *Mrs. Frances Harris's Petition* (1701), a few years later *Vanbrugh's House* (1703-04) and *Baucis and Philemon* (1706); his association beginning early in 1708 with the Addisonian circle resulted in the polishing and refinement of the familiar style which are to be seen in the revised versions of the two poems last mentioned and in *On Mrs. Biddy Floyd* (1708); and as a fitting climax came the masterly *Description of the Morning* (1709).[1]

The prose is of course headed by the Bickerstaff pamphlets (1708, 1709), of immortal humour. After these the most interesting of the many prose productions are *A Meditation upon a Broomstick (ca.* 1704), and in the serious vein the *Hints towards an Essay on Conversation* (*ca.* 1709 or 1710), the *Thoughts on Various Subjects* (the first *Thoughts* are dated October 1706; others of later date follow), and the Apology for *A Tale of a Tub* (1709).

A critical survey of all which came from Swift's pen during intervals of relaxation between the serious business appertaining to church and state is here out of the question. We must limit ourselves to the items of major importance, of which all but a few have just been cited.

2

SWIFT's residence at Dublin Castle during Lord Berkeley's term of office was marked by several compositions in verse, three of which deserve notice. The first two are *The Discovery* and *The Problem,* written shortly after arrival in Ireland and portraying the lord justice in a humorous and coarse manner. Swift's mastery of the familiar style is here shown in the perfect command of rhythm and rhyme, in the control of detail, in the matching of tone with the occasions described. But it is the scatological element which is arresting. In *The Problem,* a forewarning of whose contents is given in the subtitle, 'That My Lord Berkeley stinks when he is in love,' we have the first clear case — unless it be in *A Tale of a Tub* or *The Battle of the Books* — of that obsession by excremental details which grew upon Swift until in many of the verses of the 1730's he gave way to it completely. What is to be made of this strange fascination which the emissions of the human body held for Swift? Countless are the recorded attitudes towards this problem, Taine's overpowering disgust lying at the emotional extreme and the impassive observations of the psychiatrists at the scientific. If one reviews everything that has been said on the subject, one will come upon any number of propositions, representing as many shades of opinion, to which one partially assents, but to fit these together into a critically satisfying statement is a different matter; one's perceptions may not have reached home, but they have penetrated far enough to bear witness against any of the conclusions thus far advanced. It is true that Swift's age was not squeamish, true that Swift himself never sought to conceal his most repulsive writings, but there is more than frank coarseness to reckon with. Again, it is true that his imagery is calculated to the last degree to disgust rather than to excite; we have already seen that he used disgust to rebuke man's passions, and that in his foulest pieces he was sometimes parodying the high romantic strain, exposing mercilessly the physical ugliness above which imagination would soar; but the moral purpose does not account for the peculiar intensity. His scatology may be as flagitious as Taine would have it, but the critic who can only retreat upon the decencies may be suspected of lacking any desire or ability to analyse sanely that which lies outside the normal yet bears the stamp of genius. And as for the diagnoses of the psychiatrists, they leave one to seek in the point above all others of moment to the critic—the artistry which is greater than any psychosis. One can only admit defeat.

The scatological aspect becomes more pronounced as Swift ages. It is present clearly enough in *The Problem,* but here as in all the earlier pieces of the sort there is an admixture of humour, however coarse, which shows that Swift laughed as he wrote. In later years there was no laughter.

The third piece composed at Dublin Castle is the delicious *Mrs. Frances Harris's Petition.*

> To their Excellencies the Lords Justices of Ireland,
>   The humble petition of Frances Harris,
> Who must starve and die a maid if it miscarries;
> Humbly sheweth, that I went to warm myself in Lady
>   Betty's chamber, because I was cold;
> And I had in a purse seven pounds, four shillings, and
>   sixpence, (besides farthings) in money and gold. . .

So begins the story told by Lady Berkeley's gentlewoman, a story recounted with breathless prolixity and setting forth the loss of her purse, her distress thereat, and her efforts to detect the thief among the lower servants. Never has a comedy of manners been written with greater insight: Mrs.

Harris comes to life not only because the words and intonations are hers, but because we recognize instantly that only she ever thought precisely so. It is equally as good if judged simply as a *tour de force* of words and rhythms, for the waves of sound quite apart from any recognizable meaning make a kind of sense which the ear delights in.

3

FROM April 1701 down to November 1703, during which time Swift was twice in England — in 1701 from April to September, in 1702 from April to October — his occasional productions were few and of minor importance. During his next visit to England, which lasted from November 1703 to June 1704, he seems to have written the early version of *Vanbrugh's House* and the *jeu d'esprit* entitled *A Meditation upon a Broomstick*.

Vanbrugh, remembered today as the author of *The Provoked Wife*, was not only a playwright but an architect. In this latter capacity he had aroused the mirth of the town by erecting on the site of the palace at Whitehall, destroyed by fire early in 1698, a house so small that to look at it was to laugh. It is on this incident that Swift's verses entitled *Vanbrugh's House* rest. In days of old, we learn, poetry was endowed with a peculiar power; at the sound of verse the builder's materials would assemble themselves into the desired structure:

> Heroic strains could build a tower;
> Sonnets and elegies to Chloris,
> Might raise a house about two stories;
> A lyric ode would slate; a catch
> Would tile; an epigram would thatch.

But Jove, considering the case, thought a change advisable in the interests of the building trade, and he took steps to confine the operations of poetry to the erection of castles in the air. Vanbrugh, however, in view of his achievements as dramatist, obtained a special dispensation from Apollo to build for once in the old way.

After hard throes of many a day
Van was delivered of a play,
Which in due time brought forth a house,
Just as the mountain did the mouse.
One story high, one postern door,
And one small chamber on a floor,
Born like a phœnix from the flame :
But neither bulk nor shape the same ;
As animals of largest size
Corrupt to maggots, worms, and flies ;
A type of modern wit and style,
The rubbish of an ancient pile ;
So chemists boast they have a power,
From the dead ashes of a flower
Some faint resemblance to produce,
But not the virtue, taste, nor juice.
So modern rhymers strive to blast
The poetry of ages past ;
Which, having wisely overthrown,
They from its ruins build their own.

A Meditation upon a Broomstick, as everyone knows,
was a 'bite' at the expense of Lady Berkeley, whose enthusiasm for Robert Boyle's *Occasional Reflections* led her
frequently to request Swift to read aloud from these discourses for her edification.   Wearying of Boyle's flatulence,
Swift inserted his own *Meditation* into the book and took
the next occasion to read it to the countess, who received
it in perfect faith, exclaiming that 'there is no knowing
what useful lessons of instruction this wonderful man may
draw from things apparently the most trivial.' Swift's
humour is, in all conscience, innocent enough.   Nevertheless, in a life of Boyle which appeared the year before
Swift's death, the author felt constrained to defend the
Occasional Reflections 'against the insult upon it in Dr.
Swift's pious Meditation on a Broom Staff,* who has certainly not shewn in that piece a just regard to the interests
of religion.' [2]

4

DURING his long residence in Ireland from June 1704 to
November 1707 Swift does not appear to have taxed himself.

Less than ten pieces are now assigned to this period. Of these the more important are three metrical compositions and the *Thoughts on Various Subjects*.

In 1705 Lord Cutts, dubbed the Salamander because of his coolness under fire, was sent over to Ireland as commander of the forces, and during the absence of the lord-lieutenant he also served as a lord justice. Swift was enraged that one of Lord Cutts's character and conduct should be raised to a position of such eminence, and expressed his indignation in the withering satiric lines of *The Description of a Salamander*. Are there detractors who object to Lord Cutts's sobriquet? Let Pliny's description of the salamander prove how well the name suits: this reptile has a gaudy coat and a shining train, but his body is marked with loathsome spots; during rain and tempest he flies out from an obscure hole, but when the air clears he crawls back into his den:

> So, when the war has raised a storm,
> I've seen a snake in human form,
> All stain'd with infamy and vice,
> Leap from the dunhill in a trice,
> Burnish and make a gaudy show,
> Become a general, peer, and beau,
> Till peace has made the sky serene,
> Then shrink into its hole again,
> 'All this we grant — why then, look yonder,
> Sure that must be a Salamander !'

Pliny affirms further that this serpent is so cold that placed in the midst of fire it will extinguish the flames, and that its purulent spume spreads leprosy and baldness:

> So have I seen a batter'd beau,
> By age and claps grown cold as snow,
> Whose breath or touch, where'er he came,
> Blew out love's torch, or chill'd the flame:
> And should some nymph, who ne'er was cruel,
> Like Carleton cheap, or famed Du-Ruel,
> Receive the filth which he ejects,
> She soon would find the same effects
> Her tainted carcass to pursue,
> As from the Salamander's spue;

A dismal shedding of her locks,
And, if no leprosy, a pox.
'Then I'll appeal to each bystander,
If this be not a Salamander?'

This *Description* is the earliest example of the unmitigated
satiric fury with which Swift could blast a single adversary.
The repulsiveness, it will be seen, has increased in direct
proportion to the animosity. In this case *le mythe animal*
was already at hand, but the loathsome details with which
this is elaborated come solely from an imagination possessed
of a terrible power to transfer our disgust from physical
things to some object of moral reprobation.

It was probably also in 1705 that Swift animadverted for
a second time in verse upon Vanbrugh's architectural accomplishment. The occasion of this piece — *The History
of Vanbrugh's House* — was Vanbrugh's employment by
Marlborough as an architect at Blenheim, then being erected
as a token of the nation's gratitude to her great general. If
the construction at Whitehall of a pile so monstrous that
two chairmen are unable to lift it qualifies Vanbrugh to
build Blenheim, what may we not expect?

But raillery at once apart,
If this rule holds in every art ;
Or if his grace were no more skill'd in
The art of battering walls than building,
We might expect to see next year
A mouse-trap man chief engineer.

In the following year Swift achieved a signal triumph
in the familiar style. *Baucis and Philemon* tells the story,
imitated from Ovid, of a farmer's cottage which miracu-
lously becomes a church, and of the farmer and his wife
who are turned into parson and dame and finally into two
yews. Swift's art is seen in the wealth of detail brought
to the story, in the almost Chaucerian humour pervading the
narrative, and in the subtlety with which the atmosphere
of an English village is created. To understand why *Baucis
and Philemon* is generally regarded as one of the finest of
Swift's metrical compositions one must read it in its entirety.

About a fourth of the *Thoughts on Various Subjects, Moral and Diverting* was written down, it is supposed, in October 1706 ; the remainder is of a later date. But since nothing would be served by distinguishing the earlier from the later observations, we may treat of them all at this point. Swift's *Thoughts* are worlds removed from Pascal's *Pensées ;* their similarity to La Rochefoucauld's *Maximes* and to *Les caractères* of La Bruyère is of the slightest. It is perhaps unfair to call attention to these facts, inasmuch as Swift, unlike the three French writers, harboured absolutely no artistic intentions ; he was but jotting down a few random thoughts. On the other hand, the comparison rightly reminds us that the strength of Swift's mind lay not in subtlety or originality but in its firm grasp upon generalities. Had he chosen to work in the French manner, only La Bruyère could he have approached.

If there is almost nothing in the *Thoughts* which casts new light upon Swift's mind, there is little which does not underscore one or another of his controlling ideas. Thus is æolism dealt with : 'The chameleon, who is said to feed upon nothing but air, has of all animals the nimblest tongue.' Again :

The common fluency of speech in many men, and most women, is owing to a scarcity of matter, and a scarcity of words ; for whoever is a master of language, and has a mind full of ideas, will be apt, in speaking, to hesitate upon the choice of both ; whereas common speakers have only one set of ideas, and one set of words to clothe them in ; and these are always ready at the mouth ; so people come faster out of a church when it is almost empty, than when a crowd is at the door.

The literary judgment and taste defended in *The Battle of the Books* are obliquely described in these words : 'Would a writer know how to behave himself with relation to posterity, let him consider in old books what he finds that he is glad to know, and what omissions he most laments.' His fear lest the canons of taste and learning perish in a world eager for multiplicity, and his consequent desire for codification is likewise expressed : 'If books and laws continue to increase as they have done for fifty years past, I am in concern for future ages, how any man will be learned, or any man a lawyer.'

In the *Thoughts*, as always, it is the moralist who stands forth. Momentarily he is the cynic: 'If a man will observe as he walks the streets, I believe he will find the merriest countenances in mourning coaches.' But we find little of La Rochefoucauld in him; ordinarily he is a moralist content to deliver straightforward observations. Now he dwells upon the respective moral obligations of the wise and the simple:

I am apt to think, that, in the day of judgment, there will be small allowance given to the wise for their want of morals, and to the ignorant for their want of faith, because both are without excuse. This renders the advantages equal of ignorance and knowledge. But some scruples in the wise, and some vices in the ignorant, will perhaps be forgiven, upon the strength of temptation to each.

But of wisdom he writes in no spirit of pride or vanity; rather is he overcome by the humility which wisdom enforces: 'The latter part of a wise man's life is taken up in curing the follies, prejudices, and false opinions he had contracted in the former.' And just as wisdom brings to light past follies, so it is always reminding us of the fallibility of our minds: 'If a man would register all his opinions upon love, politics, religion, learning, &c., beginning from his youth, and so go on to old age, what a bundle of inconsistencies and contradictions would appear at last!'

The only passages which seem in any way personal are those on marriage. Two of these will do. 'Matrimony has many children; Repentance, Discord, Poverty, Jealousy, Sickness, Spleen, Loathing, &c.' 'What they do in heaven we are ignorant of; what they do *not* we are told expressly, that they neither marry, nor are given in marriage.'

There are, however, two *Thoughts* which are something more than mere restatements of familiar ideas. One calls to our attention the distance which separates La Rochefoucauld and Swift as psychologists. The former, seeing self-interest dominant in all man's actions, could regard human behaviour only with cynicism. Swift, on the contrary, though ever aware of *amour-propre,* never truly embraced the cynic's conclusions, from which he was diverted by the force of several ideas. It is the moralist's solicitude for the *results* of our actions which is seen in the following passage :

The motives of the best actions will not bear too strict an inquiry. It is allowed, that the cause of most actions, good or bad, may be resolved into the love of ourselves ; but the self-love of some men, inclines them to please others ; and the self-love of others is wholly employed in pleasing themselves. This makes the great distinction between virtue and vice. Religion is the best motive of all actions, yet religion is allowed to be the highest instance of self-love.

The last of the *Thoughts* which we shall here quote goes as follows :

One argument used to the disadvantage of Providence, I take to be a very strong one in its defence. It is objected, that storms and tempests, unfruitful seasons, serpents, spiders, flies, and other noxious or troublesome animals, with many other instances of the same kind, discover an imperfection in nature, because human life would be much easier without them ; but the design of Providence may clearly be perceived in this proceeding. The motions of the sun and moon, in short, the whole system of the universe, as far as philosophers have been able to discover and observe, are in the utmost degree of regularity and perfection ; but wherever God hath left to man the power of interposing a remedy by thought or labour, there he hath placed things in a state of imperfection, on purpose to stir up human industry, without which life would stagnate, or indeed rather could not subsist at all : *Curis acuuntur mortalia corda.*

Here Swift was driving close to the problem of evil. At the time when this observation was written, many minds were discovering in the evils exhibited by nature a more fascinating problem than the one presented by the evils identified with man's immorality.[3] Not so Swift. Accepting the concept, created by seventeenth-century science and philosophy, of the mechanical perfection of the universe, he was content to explain the presence of natural phenomena at odds with this perfect design by appeal to the wisdom of God ; in effect, he brushed aside the cruelties, injustices, and holocausts visible in the natural order, sens-

ing here no basic hostility to the forces of life and to
human hopes.   Evil he saw only as the corruption of man's
reason, and for this moral aberration man alone, he believed, was answerable.   It was at once a terrible and a magnificent creed; it was oblivious of any principle of love, but
from the indissoluble conditions on which life is given to
man it refused to turn in whimpering self-pity.

5

SWIFT's residence in England from November 1707 to June
1709 was a richly productive period.   It was then that five
of the six pamphlets relating to church and state were
written, then that his Muse, prompted by Addison, went
on to win the ear of the town, then that his wit conceived
and gave birth to the inimitable Bickerstaff papers.

It was Swift the writer of verse whom Addison took in
hand.   Addison seems to have been the first distinguished
man of letters fully to recognize the genius of this Irish
parson who for some years now had been coming and going
without anyone's paying him much attention despite the
fact that he had written prose which no living man could
equal and verse which the best might be proud to own.
Addison, perhaps, had knowledge before others of the authorship of *A Tale of a Tub*.   Even so, the credit for raising
a great wit from obscurity is his.   Soon Swift was submitting his verses to him.   Thus did *Baucis and Philemon* and
Vanbrugh's House pass beneath Addison's searching eyes,
to be approved for publication only after extensive revisions.
But as it happens, the original versions of these two pieces
are much more to the modern taste than the later versions
exhibiting the Addisonian correctness and polish.   One cannot say that Swift did not profit from his new association;
he did, as his exquisite lines addressed to Mrs. Biddy Floyd
bear witness.   Yet although his familiar style in verse was
given a classical purity which it had lacked before, it lost
much — as the 1708 version of *Baucis and Philemon* shows
— in the way of coarse-textured humour and raciness.   For
example, in *Baucis and Philemon* Swift had originally swung

into the narrative — after four introductory lines — in this manner:

> It happen'd on a winter's night,
> As authors of the legend write,
> Two brother hermits, saints by trade,
> Taking their tour in masquerade,
> Came to a village hard by Rixham,
> Ragged and not a groat betwixt 'em.
> It rain'd as hard as it could pour,
> Yet they were forced to walk an hour
> From house to house, wet to the skin,
> Before one soul would let 'em in.

At Addison's advice, these couplets were revised to read as follows:

> It happen'd on a winter night,
> As authors of the legend write,
> Two brother hermits, saints by trade,
> Taking their tour in masquerade,
> Disguis'd in tatter'd habits, went
> To a small village down in Kent;
> Where, in the strollers' canting strain,
> They begg'd from door to door in vain,
> Try'd ev'ry tone might pity win;
> But not a soul would let them in.

The 1706 version goes on to describe the saints' misadventures as they knock from door to door in search of shelter, and through sixteen couplets one almost fancies that he is listening to Chaucer. But this entire passage, beginning

> They call'd at every door: 'Good people,
> My comrade's blind, and I'm a creeple!',

offended beyond possibility of correction, and was lopped away!

When, however, it was a case not of revision but of fresh composition, Swift's compliance with the Addisonian canons yielded verse for which there can be only praise. The lines addressed to Anne, countess of Winchelsea, and entitled *Apollo Outwitted* show the new influence to advantage. But the finest of Swift's metrical compositions dating from this period is *On Mrs. Biddy Floyd*, in which Lady Betty

Germain's companion — Lady Betty was Lord Berkeley's daughter — is complimented in the grand manner. The piece is only twelve lines long:

> When Cupid did his grandsire Jove entreat
> To form some Beauty by a new receipt,
> Jove sent, and found, far in a country scene,
> Truth, innocence, good nature, look serene:
> From which ingredients first the dext'rous boy
> Pick'd the demure, the awkward, and the coy.
> The Graces from the court did next provide
> Breeding, and wit, and air, and decent pride:
> These Venus cleans'd from ev'ry spurious grain
> Of nice coquet, affected, pert, and vain.
> Jove mix'd up all, and the best clay employ'd;
> Then call'd the happy composition FLOYD.

Never did Swift's peculiar drollery work to happier effect than in the Bickerstaff pamphlets. Here was wit for the gods, and from Olympus to London there was hilarious laughter. How Swift baited poor Partridge in *Predictions for the Year 1708* and in *The Accomplishment of the First of Mr. Bickerstaff's Predictions,* and finished him off in *A Vindication of Isaac Bickerstaff, Esq.* everyone knows. But only recently has anything like an accurate account of the whole affair been available to the modern reader.[4] Not only does this account heighten the flavour of Swift's wit, but it disposes of the charge that Swift was playing a rather contemptible joke on an ignorant but harmless charlatan.

Partridge was an assumed name, for Swift's antagonist was born John Hewson. About 1679 the fellow went up to London, changed his name, and setting up as an astrologer and almanac maker was soon riding to success. His handbooks of astrology and his annual almanac, *Merlinus Liberatus,* carried his fame far and wide and lined his pockets. His violent protestantism took the form of a continuous hue and cry against papists, and when the Rye House Plot fell through he turned opportunity to account by bearing false witness and securing the title of physician royal. With James's accession royal favour was abruptly transformed to displeasure; Partridge fled to Holland, where he lived with John Dunton. At the Revolution he returned to London, where he continued to enjoy his former success. Had it not been for the wits all would have been well. As early as 1685, however, they fell foul of him, and from that time on, until Swift finished the business, they plagued him without intermission. Tom Brown seems to have led the way, following up his first thrusts with a parody of the *Merlinus Liberatus* called *Prophecies out of Merlin's Carmen* (1690). Other wits now took a hand, and Partridge saw himself ridiculed in the *English Lucian* (1698), a periodical; in Ned Ward's *The London Spy* (1698); and in three new parodies (1704-1706) of the *Merlinus Liberatus*. Tom Brown, however, was not to be outdone; in 1700 he printed at least eighteen weekly installments of *The Infallible Astrologer, or Mr. Silvester Partridge's Prophesie and Prediction of what shall infallibly happen* (rptd. 1705 and 1707 in Brown's *Works*),[5] quite the most formidable attack on Partridge before Swift's pamphlets of 1708-1709.

Thus, when Swift turned his wit loose upon Partridge, it was no obscure man whom he was seeking to overpower but an eminent quack who had hitherto outfaced a multitude intent upon exposing him. And unquestionably Swift's humour was edged with moral purpose — it was not right that such a charlatan should pander year after year to ignorant superstition.

As the year 1707 drew to a close, Partridge, true to custom, issued a new edition of his almanac, calculated for the approaching year. But this time he found himself challenged by a new rival, and this latest addition to the company of astrologers gave one pause. When had there appeared such daring prognostications as these in *Predictions for the Year 1708?*[6] On the fourth of April will die the Cardinal de Noailles, archbishop of Paris; on the seventh there will be an insurrection in Dauphine; July will bring the death of no less a personage than King Louis XIV. And heading these momentous prophecies this 'trifle': on the twenty-ninth of March, about eleven at night, John Partridge the almanac-maker will infallibly die of a raging fever. Promptly on the morning of 30 March 1708 there

appeared on the streets of London an *Elegy* announcing
the death of Partridge in full accordance with Bickerstaff's
prediction.   A few days later came *The Accomplishment of
the First of Mr. Bickerstaff's Predictions,* which informed
the reader that Partridge had indeed died on the night
foretold by Bickerstaff, but not at eleven as predicted but
about five minutes after seven, 'by which it is clear that
Mr. Bickerstaff was mistaken almost four hours in his cal-
culation.'   The town now rose to the sport.   Of the deluge
of pamphlets in which Bickerstaff was now attacked and
again defended, the gem is *Squire Bickerstaff Detected*
(1709 ? 1710 ?), which authoritative opinion now holds was
written by Swift and Congreve, was conveyed by their friend
Thomas Yalden to Partridge, and was printed by the latter,
who in perfect innocence took the thing for a strong testi-
monial in his own favour.   It tells of the sufferings put
upon Partridge by this villain Bickerstaff; how bellman,
undertaker, joiner, and sexton have turned deaf ears to
all the astrologer's protests that he is, printed notices to
the contrary, alive; and how, as a last indignity, he has
been dunned for his own funeral expenses.   But Partridge,
to his misfortune, did not rest his case here; in his almanac
for 1709 he came forward with the solemn declaration that
he was now alive and had been alive on the preceding
twenty-ninth of March.   To which Swift replied in *A Vindication of Isaac Bickerstaff, Esq.* that this is perfect cavil-
ling: Partridge 'declares his opinion, that a man may be
alive now who was not alive a twelvemonth ago,' and here
lies the sophistry of his argument, for he dares not assert
that he has been alive ever since the twenty-ninth of March;
dead he was on that day — let the world judge whether he
be since revived.

   A Famous Prediction of Merlin (early 1709) brought
Swift's game to an end.   It had had its effect.   Whether or
no the Inquisition in Portugal burned the *Predictions for
the Year 1708,* it is a matter of record that a certain French-
man was so offended by the freedom with which his country
had been handled by Bickerstaff that he denounced him in
a work entitled *Renversement des Predictions . . . d'Isaac*

Bickerstaf. As for poor Partridge, he had as good as been killed. For when the Company of Stationers struck his name from their rolls and laid claim to all rights of publication over *Partridge's Almanac,* the astrologer's protest was turned down by no less than the lord chancellor !

On Saturday 30 April 1709, five days before Swift left London, his *Description of the Morning* was printed in the ninth *Tatler*[7] with an introductory note stating that the author of these verses, to avoid the strain of those scribblers who are so justly laughed at for their sonnets on Phillis and Chloris and fantastical descriptions of them, has 'run into a way perfectly new, and described things exactly as they happen.' There was small chance, with these words before him, that even the dullest reader could take Swift's lines *au grand serieux* — as many a modern reader seems only too likely to do.

> Now hardly here and there an hackney-coach
> Appearing, show'd the ruddy morn's approach.
> Now Betty from her master's bed had flown,
> And softly stole to discompose her own ;
> The slip-shod 'prentice from his master's door
> Had pared the dirt, and sprinkled round the floor.
> Now Moll had whirl'd her mop with dext'rous
> airs,
> Prepared to scrub the entry and the stairs.
> The youth with broomy stumps began to trace
> The kennel's edge, where wheels had worn
> the place.
> The small-coal man was heard with cadence deep,
> Till drown'd in shriller notes of chimney-sweep :
> Duns at his lordship's gate began to meet ;
> And brickdust Moll had scream'd through half
> the street.
> The turnkey now his flock returning sees,
> Duly let out a-nights to steal for fees :
> The watchful bailiffs take their silent stands,
> And schoolboys lag with satchels in their
> hands.

On 7 May Swift arrived in Leicester, leaving on 14 June to continue his journey back to Dublin and Laracor. The Apology for *A Tale of a Tub,* which was printed for the first

time in the fifth (1710) edition of the *Tale,* is dated 3 June
1709.   Like the satire itself, it was never openly acknowledged by Swift, but his authorship is beyond dispute and
up to a certain point his motives are clear.   For one thing,
he had an altogether natural desire to retort upon the cen-
sorious critics who had written against the *Tale.*   He confined himself to two of these, William King, the author of
Some Remarks on The Tale of a Tub (1704), and Wotton,
who into the third (1705) edition of his *Reflections* had
inserted 'Some Observations upon the *Tale of a Tub.*'   With
King Swift dealt lightly; it was Wotton who had nettled
him.   Wotton had censured the design of the satire; Swift's
reply is that *'there is not a Person in England who can
understand that Book, that ever imagined it to have been
anything else, but to expose the Abuses and Corruptions in
Learning and Religion.'*   Wotton had asserted furthermore
that in the *Tale* the wit is not entirely the author's own,
and had cited three instances of plagiarism.   Swift glanced
at all three to refute them, and entered a general denial by
insisting *'that through the whole Book he has not borrowed
one single Hint from any Writer in the World; and he
thought, of all Criticisms, that would never have been one.'*
Lastly — and here was the imputation that rankled most —
Wotton had hinted that the author was dead while at the
same time he had laid the suspicion, as Swift wrote, *'upon
somebody, I know not who, in the Country; to which can
be only returned, that he is absolutely mistaken in all his
Conjectures. . . '*   Now, in dealing with the question of
authorship, Wotton had implied that the satire was Temple's work, erroneously attributed by rumour to Dr. Swift's
'brother,' a clergyman preferred through Sir William's influence to 'a very good Benefice in one of the Delicious
Parts of one of the Pleasantest Counties of *England.*'
Swift's cousin, Thomas Swift, late chaplain to Sir William
and now rector of Puttenham, was indicated.   It was ridiculous that anyone should conceive Cousin Tom equal to
A Tale of a Tub; but when Cousin Tom was in no way
reluctant to be taken for the author, it was time to give
his pretensions a jolt.   This, at least, is how one now reads

Swift's statement that Wotton '*is absolutely mistaken in all his Conjectures*,' and one's interpretation is borne out by the Postscript to the Apology, which was added in 1710 under the spur of Edmund Curll's *Complete Key to the Tale of a Tub ; With some Account of the Authors* (1710), where the composition of the *Tale* was apportioned between Jonathan and Thomas. In the *Key* Swift obviously believed that his cousin had had a hand, for in the Postscript he protested that '*the Writer of* [the *Key*] *is utterly wrong in all his Conjectures*,' and he closed with these words : '. . . *if any Person will prove his Claim to three Lines in the whole Book, let him step forth and tell his Name and Titles, upon which the Bookseller shall have Orders to prefix them to the next Edition, and the Claimant shall from henceforward be acknowledged the undisputed Author.*' It was clearly a challenge to Thomas.

The rest of the Apology is devoted to a careful explication of the author's satiric purpose. The *Tale* seems calculated to live '*at least as long as our Language, and our Tast admit no great Alterations*,' and, despite the treatises written expressly against it, is approved by the great majority of men of taste. True, it was written while the author was still young, and it is to be granted that he '*gave a Liberty to his Pen, which might not suit with maturer Years.*' But there is nothing in it contrary to religion and morality ; the satire is directed solely at '*the numerous and gross Corruptions in Religion and Learning* . . .' Why, then, should any clergyman of the established church resent this work ? Is he angry to see the follies of fanaticism and superstition exposed, or the church of England celebrated as the most perfect of all others in discipline and doctrine ? It is in this portion of the Apology that Swift's motives remain partially obscure. Doubtless he was actuated by resentment at the stupid misinterpretations forced upon his great satire. But was his defence perfectly candid ? Was he altogether innocent of seeking, through explanations sometimes forced, to represent his work as less provocative than he knew it to be ? And if he was guilty of sophistry, are we to conclude that as early as 1709 he had learnt what an obstacle to preferment the *Tale* could be? Such questions will perhaps never be answered with assurance.

6

BY early July 1709 Swift was back at Laracor. The contrast between the provincial scene, which had long since lost whatever charm it once held for him, and the fascination and excitement of the great city which he had just left must have brought him close to despair. After months of intense activity, he was again a country vicar. There was only too much time for brooding over the triumphs and defeats of the recent London sojourn. What with his meditations on past events and his half-hearted interest in the progress of English politics he was disposed to leave letters alone. He did, it is true, compose *A Letter to a Member of Parliament, in Ireland.* And he may have written at this time the *Hints towards an Essay on Conversation.* Aside from these, his only other production seems to have been a piece in verse entitled *On the Little House by the Churchyard of Castleknock.*

This metrical composition is a charming trifle, in which, as has frequently been pointed out, the Lilliputian theme makes its first appearance. 'The little house' here described was the microscopic vestry of the parish church of the Phoenix Park, of which church Swift's friend, Archdeacon Walls, was incumbent. A western blast, we are informed, once toppled the spire off the church steeple and deposited it upright on the ground, and it is this 'little strutting pile,' at least twelve inches tall, which now serves the vicar as a vestry.

> A traveller, who by did pass,
> Observed the roof behind the grass;
> On tiptoe stood, and rear'd his snout,
> And saw the parson creeping out:
> Was much surprised to see a crow
> Venture to build his nest so low.
>
> .   .   .   .
>
> The doctor's family came by,
> And little miss began to cry,

Give me that house in my own hand !
Then madam bade the chariot stand,
Call'd to the clerk, in manner mild,
Pray, reach that thing here to the child :
That thing, I mean, among the kale ;
And here's to buy a pot of ale.

The *Hints towards an Essay on Conversation* has been completely overshadowed by its astonishing sequel, *Polite Conversation (ca.* 1731; ptd. 1738). The earlier work is not, however, without merit. Properly it should be read along with *A Treatise on Good Manners and Good Breeding* (date of composition unknown; ptd. 1754) and *Hints on Good Manners* (date of composition unknown; ptd. 1765), all of which are notable for keen observation of manners, rugged common sense, and a highly civilized conception of social intercourse. The *Hints on Good Manners* opens with this observation : 'Good Manners is the art of making every reasonable person in the company easy, and to be easy ourselves.' This is also the tone of the *Hints towards an Essay on Conversation*. The faculty of speech is the great distinction between men and brutes; when conversation is abused, not only do we fail to take advantage of that which might be the greatest, as well as the most useful pleasure of life, but human nature is debased. Good conversation lies within the power of every man, if he will but avoid a few faults, of which the commonest are talking too much, talking only of oneself, attempting always to say witty things, and pedantry or 'the too frequent or unseasonable obtruding our own knowledge in common discourse, and placing too great a value upon it.' Among other causes, the degeneracy of conversation and its pernicious consequences are owing to the exclusion of women from all save social frivolities. In England politeness reached its highest point in the peaceful part of Charles I's reign, when *salons* were maintained by several ladies. We are apt, adds Swift, to ridicule the platonic notions of these women, but 'their refinements were grounded upon reason.' No, Swift was not a hater of women. The same piercing eyes which saw delusion in romance, *ennui* in marriage, and indignity in the necessities of the body, saw also the chief, if hidden, attribute of cultivated woman — her realism. What man talked — or thought — better sense than Stella?

Here, for a space, we leave the wit and man of letters. If the verse and prose which we have just examined do not exhibit the great and original artistry which distinguishes the later writings at Moor Park, that is because Swift came to terms with the world and for some years consented to play such airs as pleased it. But his nature was not a compliant one. Tragedy already had her eye upon him, and when, after pursuing him through four years she brought him down at last about the time of the queen's death, she killed a fine gentleman but restored to life the defiant, incalculable artist.

BOOK III

1710 — 1714

BIOGRAPHICAL SYNOPSIS

1710-1714

1 Sept. 1710 :	To England again, having once more been commissioned by the Irish bishops to solicit for the first-fruits.
7 Sept. 1710 :	Arrived in London, and received with open arms by all the whigs save Godolphin.
4 Oct. 1710 :	First conference with Harley, now head of the tory ministry ; sent to the printer a lampoon on Godolphin.
2 Nov. 1710 :	Took up the editorship of the *Examiner*, the tory journal, having definitely renounced the whigs.
7 June 1711 :	Gave over the editorship of the *Examiner*, in order to work on *The Conduct of the Allies,* a tory pamphlet in support of the peace proposals.
27 Nov. 1711 :	*The Conduct of the Allies* published.
23 Dec. 1711 :	Attacked the duchess of Somerset in *The Windsor Prophecy.*
29 Dec. 1711 :	The tories saved from apparent disaster by a political coup.
Summer 1712-early 1713 :	At work on *The History of the Four Last Years of the Queen,* an account of events leading up to the peace.
23 April 1713 :	Made dean of St. Patrick's ; left for Ireland 1 June ; installed 13 June.
9 Sept. 1713 :	In London again, summoned back to reconcile the warring ministers.
Early 1714 :	The Scriblerus Club in session.
1 June 1714 :	Left London, having abandoned all hope for the ministry ; took refuge in a Berkshire parsonage.
1 Aug. 1714 :	Death of Queen Anne and fall of the tories.
Mid-Aug. 1714 :	Left his Berkshire retreat and went into exile in Ireland.

CHAPTER I

THE FOUR LAST YEARS OF QUEEN ANNE

1

ON the last day of August 1710 a sudden decision by the Irish bishops snatched Swift from the obscurity in which he had been passing his days since his last return to Ireland, and established him once more close to the heart of English political life. Could the bishops have foreseen the consequences of their act they would have moved heaven and earth to keep him chained in Ireland. That the whigs were doomed they knew when they dispatched him. What they failed to take account of was Swift's ripeness for apostasy and the consummate talents he was ready to offer a ministry willing to give assurances in place of the open threats of Godolphin and Wharton. Swift reached London on 7 September. Before two months had passed he had not only been snared by the tories, but had been set up by them as their factotum in charge of propaganda. From this date until the tory *dénouement* in July 1714, Swift's life, a few incidents of an entirely personal character excepted, is recorded in terms of the political party of his adoption.

The intensity of Swift's life during these four years, his incredible energy as a controversialist, his melodramatic rôle in the thrilling events following the tory victory of 1710, his intimate association with those who in politics and letters gave to the London of Queen Anne the characteristics on which our imagination still dwells — these lend to his brief period of complete worldly triumph a kind of fascination attaching to no other part of his life. If our interest is disproportionate, Swift himself must bear not a little of the blame, for his letters of this date and particularly *The Journal to Stella* are so instinct with excitement that reading them we are beguiled of historical perspective and follow the unfolding of events upon which the fate of Christendom seems to hang.[1]

2

THROUGHOUT the summer of 1710 Queen Anne, in response
to the clearly indicated sentiment of the country, was re-
moving whigs from the ministry to make way for men of
moderate opinion or of definitely tory stamp.   In this manner was the great political reversal begun.   The general
election in October completed the change by returning the
tories in overwhelming majority to the commons.   The
queen and not a few prominent leaders anxious to allay
extreme partisanship had hoped for a moderate house to
match a moderate ministry.   The defeat of the whigs spelt
the end of moderation, while at the same time it lay the
triumphant party open to the most insidious of all political
dangers — internal dissensions, inevitable from the moment
that opposition crumbles.

    Thus was the new tory ministry which set sail in the
autumn of 1710 with every apparent good omen doomed
within a short time to the destruction which finally overtook
it four years later.   It was a coalition ministry, its centre of
gravity lying in a kind of middle party between whig and
tory.   Because it never quite lost this early character it was
unable to bear up under the strains imposed in the first
instance by the sweeping electoral victory of October 1710,
and thereafter by the steadily rising zeal of the high tories.
In its two leaders the ministerial dissonance was symbolized :
Oxford, desirous of a middle course, resisting the pressure
towards the right ; Bolingbroke, the tory hot-head, impatient
of all moderation.   Nor did the queen — a stronger force
in these affairs than all but a few then realized — exercise
her power in a way calculated to heal these differences ; with
glum stubbornness she was bent upon preserving moderation, but when it came to an open declaration regarding her
successor she maintained silence where a forthright statement would have done much to stabilize the ministry.

    The hub about which all revolved during these four years
was the question of peace.   The tories were successful in
bringing the war to a conclusion and by the Treaty of
Utrecht (1713) they secured peace for England on highly

advantageous terms.   But this triumph in diplomacy they
purchased at the cost of a yet wider dissension in party
and ministry.   The whig resurgence of August 1714 was
less a triumph of the opposition than the end of a slow
process of self-destruction to which the tories had from the
beginning committed themselves.

FROM November 1709 to April 1710 the last whig parliament was in session.   It was during these months that the
Godolphin ministry was going through with the trial of
Sacheverell.   By summer the increasing unpopularity of the
war and the fear for the safety of the church aroused by
the ill-considered measures against Sacheverell had lost the
whigs the last vestige of popular support.   The outcome of
the elections of October was scarcely surprising.

Well before October, however, the whigs had seen the
reins slipping from their hands.   A middle party, led by
the duke of Shrewsbury, the duke of Somerset, and the duke
of Argyll had taken form, its avowed aims being to displace
the whig ministers, to bring about peace, and to protect
the Hanoverian succession.   Then Queen Anne acted.
The first blow fell in April, when the marquis of Kent was
replaced by the duke of Shrewsbury as lord chamberlain.
Other changes followed, climaxed by the dismissal of Godolphin on 8 August when Harley, as chancellor of the exchequer, succeeded the lord treasurer.   In September St.
John went in as secretary of state.

As yet Harley counted for much more than his later rival.
Harley it was who had worked for months to undermine the
whig junto through backstairs intrigue.   With no intention
of falling under the sway of tory zealots, it was he who had
supported Shrewsbury and the middle party.   And finally,
it was his presence in the ministry that was intended to
stamp it as a 'queen's ministry above party.'   But the October elections threw all askew.   Moderates of the middle
party, like Shrewsbury and Somerset, were left high and
dry; Harley had perforce to compromise with the tory zealots ; and St. John, nothing if not an extremist, came gradually into the lead.

13

The first parliamentary session extended from November
1710 to June 1711. But it was outside parliament that
events of first importance were taking place. In January
the duchess of Marlborough was put out of her places at
court — a stunning blow, which removed from the circle of
influence the invaluable ally of the old junto, struck at the
duke, and announced clearly that all support of the war
was about to be withdrawn. The relinquished offices were
divided between Mrs. Masham, representing the tories, and
the duchess of Somerset, identified with the moderate whigs
— the queen would distribute the ballast evenly. Harley was
glad enough, but his party raged, seeing in the duchess's
presence at court a betrayal of their interests by the queen
herself, and from this time on 'Carrots' — the duchess of
Somerset had red hair — was the object of their most offensive obloquies.

Then, on 8 March 1711 Harley was struck down by the
Marquis de Guiscard. This man, once in the employ of the
English government, had that day been arrested for high
treason, and during his examination before a committee of
the privy council had seized a pen-knife and stabbed Harley
in the breast. The wound was not serious, but for two
months Harley was confined. The attack upon him, and
the inference that he had been singled out because of hostility to France, increased his popularity tremendously. He
emerged from convalescence as the earl of Oxford. But
the true import of this incident came only gradually to light.
Lying ill, Harley lost his grip on the situation; thereafter
he lacked purpose and strength, seemingly content to drift
from moment to moment. The power that he let slip was
snatched up by St. John, jealous of his associate's elevation
to the peerage and burning to harness the ministry to extreme toryism.

Otherwise, the year 1711 was one of excitement attendant
upon the opening negotiations for peace. The first steps
towards a peace had, in truth, been taken secretly as early
as August 1710, but it was not until April 1711 that the
English public knew that France was submitting official proposals. In September, preliminary articles were signed. In

the course of these proceedings the tories renounced the policies which the whigs had carefully built up during the first nine years of the war, and sought by deserting their Allies and joining France in diplomacy to force a peace, thus assuring England of more favourable terms than could be gained through negotiations in concert with the Allies — besides, intrigue with France held fascination for those tories whose imaginations were still touched by the romance of Jacobitism. The tory strategy bore particularly hard upon the Dutch, whose previous reluctance to support the war had in 1709 been overcome by the whigs only through the assurances given in the Barrier Treaty. Having settled upon peace through betrayal of their Allies, the tories faced the necessity of winning popular support of their policy not only by silencing the rumblings of the whigs but by turning sentiment strongly against the Allies, particularly the Dutch. It was Swift to whom they turned at this all-important juncture, and his wonder-working pen produced in November, just before the parliamentary debate was due to begin, that masterpiece of propaganda, *The Conduct of the Allies*.

The month of December 1711 was all melodrama. If parliament rejected the peace proposals, the tories fell; if the vote was for peace, their future was secure. Parliament met, and the whigs rallied for a final attack upon the ministerial policy. At this moment the tory ranks broke as the earl of Nottingham — in return for the whigs' support of a new bill against occasional conformity — deserted to the enemy and headed the attack in the lords upon the peace proposals. On 7 December an anti-ministerial vote was carried in the lords. The crisis was fast approaching. With consternation the tories watched the progress of the debate. They shot at the earl of Nottingham with lampoons — one of them of Swift's fashioning. They cried 'Betrayal!' and pointed at the duke and duchess of Somerset whispering in the royal ear, while Swift, in *The Windsor Prophecy*, breathed poison upon 'Carrots.' Then, suddenly, deliverance and victory — at the very end of the year the announcement of the creation of twelve new peers, a number sufficient to carry the vote for peace in the lords. At the same time the duke of Marlborough was dismissed from his offices. The ministry had been saved by a hair's-breadth.

Through the ensuing year negotiations for peace went forward. But in these it was St. John — created Viscount Bolingbroke in July 1712 — who took the lead, not Oxford. The latter's degeneration was now apparent, and by his refusal to renounce moderation by turning the last whig out of office he exposed his weakness only too clearly to an impatient party. This was playing straight into the hands of Bolingbroke, who now became the recognized leader of the high tories, and whose influence mounted as he assumed leadership in the negotiations for peace.

There was not in this year the desperate need of propaganda that had existed some months before. Two tory writers, nevertheless, were at work. Between 6 March and 31 July Arbuthnot issued the five pamphlets later known as *The History of John Bull*. Swift, meanwhile, was slaving away at *The History of the Four Last Years of the Queen*,— a misleading title, for the piece is entirely concerned with events leading up to the Treaty of Utrecht,— which was designed to aid the ministry but was suppressed as injudicious (ptd. 1758).

Early in 1713 the Treaty of Utrecht brought to an end the War of the Spanish Succession. The ministry had now accomplished the chief task to which they had committed themselves upon taking office. But while concluding the war they had, in varying degrees, implicated themselves in the Jacobite conspiracy. Bolingbroke's complicity was clear-cut; Oxford was willing enough to support a triumphant Hanoverian cause, but so long as the Stuarts held any claim upon the future he did not intend to burn his bridges. The danger of the pretender's return at the queen's death, a danger cried up by the whigs in season and out of season, and as often scoffed at by Swift, was not a very great one, but present it was.

1713 marked also the final break in the ministry. That summer the whigs won their first popular success in parliament by forcing the rejection of the commercial treaty with France. Bolingbroke could contain himself no longer. He had been at odds with Oxford off and on since the Guiscard incident; his impatience had mounted steadily since the latter's refusal to sweep all moderates from office; he could now point to the whigs' success as a fore-token of the disastrous consequences to follow from Oxford's weakness. Early in September he was setting Lady Masham to undermine the lord treasurer's credit with the queen. The election that autumn saved the tory majority, but it was no longer a secret that the party was rotting asunder. Already the political ranks were astir, and a new name had appeared — the 'whimsicals,' by which were designated Hanoverian tories like Nottingham, who were now drawing together with the middle party of Shrewsbury and Somerset.

From this time on the ministry, torn by dissension, drifted slowly to destruction. Swift had worked ceaselessly to reconcile Oxford and Bolingbroke, but at the beginning of June 1714 he gave up hope and retreated to Letcombe in Berkshire. Here, at intervals during the next two months, letters from London — like messengers in a Greek tragedy — brought him bit by bit the news of the inexorably unfolding catastrophe. The Dragon — an ironic name for Oxford, who was notoriously mild — has now lost all favour with the queen. The Dragon will be out at any moment. The Dragon has to-day been dismissed as lord treasurer; Bolingbroke commands (27 July). The queen is ill (29 July). The queen's condition is alarming; the privy council has met; the lord treasurer's staff has been given into Shrewsbury's hands — not Bolingbroke's (30 July). The queen is dead (1 August). And then, two days later, Bolingbroke's note: 'The Earl of Oxford was removed on Tuesday; the Queen died on Sunday. What a world is this, and how does Fortune banter us.' From the tories Fortune had, indeed, turned her face. They were soon no party at all — only scattered adherents of a cause hopelessly lost.

3

WITHOUT much question Swift would sooner or later have forced his way into the drama just described. That he was present from the start was owing to the bishops in Ireland. Mindful of impending changes, they determined to press once more for the remission of the first-fruits. Whom should they send to London? Swift, as their last emissary, was naturally considered. Some of the bishops opposed him — he was too much of a whig, they said, to negotiate successfully with the rising tories. But Archbishop King was for Swift, and the archbishop finally prevailed.

Swift was given short notice, but immediately on the receipt of his credentials he hastened aboard the lord-lieutenant's yacht, which was on the point of sailing, and thus reached Parkgate on Friday 1 September. Six days later he was in London.

At once began the stream of letters — mostly to Archbishop King — and *The Journal to Stella* — a magnificent correspondence, taken all together. Now the great events in council, court, and parliament are narrated with terse vigour. Now Swift is seen arising in his cold lodgings, proceeding to Whitehall or to some printer in the City, dining with the great, and then returning home to work at a pamphlet or a lampoon. Of surpassing interest are those numerous passages in the *Journal* in which Swift writes of his motives and ambitions. If in these he reveals a side of his character which has repelled many who have sat in judgment upon him, it should be remembered that Stella's correspondent was a great realist who could no more misread or disguise the promptings of his own heart than he could mistake the outside of nature for its inner reality. His candour — amounting almost to naïveté — does not explain away his ambition, it does not exculpate him of intemperance towards men and affairs. But how many worldly men have achieved such clarity of desire, have learned to look within themselves with such unfaltering realism, or have exposed themselves so minutely?

Arrived in London, Swift felt no such thrill of expectation as he had experienced four years earlier when, as emissary for the first time of the church in Ireland, he had searched the future with such eager eyes. The previous months in Ireland had bred a stoical passivity; it mattered little what happened. 'I neer went to Engd with so little desire in my Life,' he confessed to Stella. Yet he found himself caressed as never before by men of both parties. The whigs received him as a lost brother restored to them at a moment of direst need, the tories 'as one discontented with the late men in power, for not being thorough in their designs, and therefore ready to approve present things' (To Archbishop King, 9 September). The tory blandishments at first merely amused him, and as a matter of course he fell into the old way with his whig friends — Addison, Steele, Congreve, Lord Somers, Lord Halifax. He was still the whig man of letters, contributing to the *Tatler* (No. 230, 28 September) a paper on style and a few weeks afterwards (No. 238, 17 October) a new poem, *A Description of a City Shower*.

But there was one whig who refused to add his voice to the chorus of welcome — his old enemy Godolphin. 'I was to visit my Lord Godolphin,' Swift wrote to the archbishop on 9 September, 'who gave me a reception very unexpected, and altogether different from what I ever received from any great man in my life ; altogether short, dry, and morose. . .' The same day Swift confessed to Stella, 'I am almost vowing revenge.' Had Godolphin, reading the future accurately, seen in his visitor the tory propagandist still two months from birth and treated him accordingly? Probably not ; the chances are that the deposed lord treasurer was merely thinking of *A Letter concerning the Sacramental Test*. But in any case, it was this ill-timed surliness that led directly to Swift's first overt act against the deposed party, for it was only a matter of hours before his poisonous verses on Godolphin were shaping themselves in his mind.

And now Erasmus Lewis, Harley's crafty henchman, was seeking the Irish vicar out. Swift had come to London on the first-fruits business? He must, at the first moment, talk with Mr. Harley, who unlike his predecessor was all eagerness to serve the church. On Wednesday 4 October Swift had his first interview with Harley, and was with him again on the seventh and on the tenth. The world had indeed altered — here was a minister who, instead of drawing back in cold disdain at the first mention of the church, listened attentively, asked for full details, and within six days gave assurance that the first-fruits would be granted. At this unexpected triumph, the disappointments of the past years were wiped out; Swift was again on his mettle, eager for what was to come. As the past lay revealed for a moment under the flash of victory, he drew that sharp breath which attends the sudden conviction that all has been for the best: 'They may talk of the *you know what* [i.e., *A Tale of a Tub*]; but, gad, if it had not been for that, I should never have been able to get the access I have had; and if that helps me to succeed, then that *same thing* will be serviceable to the church' (*The Journal to Stella*, 7 October).

The day he first met Harley — 4 October — Swift took an irrevocable step — he sent to the printer *The Virtues of Sid Hamet the Magician's Rod*, his lampoon on Godolphin. This he followed up, some two months later (8 December), with *A Short Character of His Ex. T[he] E[arl] of W[harton]*, a ferocious attack upon the second of his enemies in the previous ministry.

The successful outcome of the negotiations for the first-fruits Swift was not permitted to announce to Archbishop King at once; not until 4 November did he send the good news. Had Swift's fortunes depended upon the gratitude of the bishops, he would, as things turned out, have been as far to seek as some obscure cleric never outside of Ireland. Following Swift's announcement the grant was held up for some months. In the meantime the duke of Ormond had taken office as lord-lieutenant, and the Irish bishops directed Swift to hand over all his powers to those who could treat directly with Ormond. Swift was inarticulate with rage. But worse was in store, for when in the summer of 1711 the grant was at last announced the bishops outdid themselves in protestations of gratitude to the lord-lieutenant. So far as they were concerned, Swift's part in the negotiations had amounted to exactly nothing. Long before this, however, Swift had whistled the Irish bishops down the wind. When on 4 November he wrote to the archbishop that the first-fruits were granted, he had two days previously taken over the editorship of the *Examiner,* the tory journal.

It had taken Erasmus Lewis and Harley not quite two months to win him over. Like most converts, Swift embraced the faith with excessive ardour. The pages of the *Examiner* were an insufficient outlet for his zeal, and accordingly during the closing weeks of 1710 he plied Grub Street with political verse much of which he had written himself and the rest inspired.

Through 1711 Swift worked at top speed. Until early June, when the *Examiner* was entrusted to other hands in order to free Swift's for a more important task, each weekly issue of the periodical was of his composing. Swift met the enormous demand upon his journalistic resourcefulness without a quiver, turning out with clock-like regularity article upon article in which the fierce clarity and energy of his opening numbers were perfectly sustained. He was not, in this instance, forcing an opportunity by an unexpected display of talent. Harley and the rest had counted on his genius, for they had need of just such a writer as Swift to make of the *Examiner* the very spear-head of the tory attack. 'Peace!' was the cry, and week after week Swift took it up, at one moment indicting the whigs on the charge of prolonging the war for their own interests, falling at the next upon the greed of the Marlboroughs, and with every breath calling upon the nation to support the queen's ministry to the limit.

It was imperative, if Swift's propaganda was to reach its mark, that he should be always within call of Harley and St. John. But the vicar of Laracor was a formidable person, who made it very clear that he would serve no man, whatever his position or title, as lackey. And he backed his demands with wit and charm enough for any company. It was on 17 February that he was first admitted to the Saturday dinners at Harley's, where the chancellor of the exchequer sat down with St. John and the lord keeper, Sir Simon Harcourt, to plan the campaign for the week to come. It was precisely ten days after this triumph that John Morphew brought out the *Miscellanies in Prose and Verse,* in which were gathered up Swift's principal compositions — thirteen metrical and twelve prose pieces.   Despite Swift's protestation in *The Journal to Stella* that ' 'twas without my knowledge or consent' he had projected such a *Miscellany* as early as 1708, and Steele had at that time agreed to usher it into the world with a preface.   Although every item in it, with the exception of *A Description of a City Shower* and *Sid Hamet the Magician's Rod,* antedated the author's conversion to the tory party, there was nothing here which compromised his new position.   Indeed, the reappearance of the *Sentiments,* the *Argument,* the *Project,* and *A Letter concerning the Sacramental Test* had about it a certain timeliness — not uncalculated, perhaps ; if the writer had changed political colour, he was now as then the church's champion.

The stabbing of Harley on 8 March threw Swift into indescribable consternation.   For several days he could write of nothing save poor Harley and that villain Guiscard, and when it was apparent that Harley was out of danger, he continued to dwell mercilessly upon the assassin, even describing how Guiscard's body was pickled in a trough and shown for twopence.

A few weeks before this and Swift had been writing to Peterborough that whatever else threatened the ministry it was not internal disharmony, for Harley, St. John, and Harcourt 'seem heartily to love one another.'   It was when Harley, now earl of Oxford, returned to the scene after recovering from his wound that the first signs of enmity between him and St. John began to show.   Instantly Swift intervened, and from this moment until his retirement to Letcombe in June 1714 he worked ceaselessly to reconcile the two men upon whose mutual amity he believed that England's welfare depended.

On 7 June Swift gave over the editorship of the *Examiner.* During all the months in which he had been thundering in its pages, he had found time for yet other writing : having set his friend Harrison up in a new *Tatler,* one of the many imitations of Steele's now defunct periodical, he had come to the young man's aid with several essays and had

had a hand in the verses printed by Harrison and entitled *A Town Eclogue;* and he had probably inspired, if not written, several metrical pieces of a political nature issued from Grub Street. Now the ministers were saddling him with a new commission, of an importance outdistancing anything hitherto entrusted to him. The *Examiner* had been preparatory propaganda; through its columns the nation had been turned towards peace. The time was now approaching for the submission of actual proposals to parliament, and there was need of a handbook which would sum up the tory policy and, being sown far and wide, give the debate the right bias on the eve of the meeting of parliament. Through the summer Oxford and St. John kept Swift close by them, informing him of every necessary detail, priming him with arguments, making certain that no breach should remain unprotected. The queen, as was her custom in the summer months, was at Windsor, and the ministers usually travelled down in their coaches from London for the weekend. Swift accompanied them repeatedly, sometimes returning the following Monday or Tuesday, again remaining for as long as a fortnight. (With characteristic energy, Swift found time in the midst of his new labours for several occasional pamphlets, of which the best known is *A New Journey to Paris* (September), the purpose of which was to divert public suspicion from Prior's recent sojourn in France, where he had gone on a secret mission connected with the peace negotiations, only to have the fact discovered at his return by the blundering of an English custom official.) Day by day the pamphlet grew. Finished at last, it was released at the critical moment (27 November). Its appearance, preceding by a few days the meeting of parliament, was so timed that the reverberations from readers throughout the nation would be reaching highest pitch precisely as the ministry opened the debate. Oxford and St. John had not mistaken their man; Swift had surpassed himself in *The Conduct of the Allies.* Edition followed edition, until before the end of December an estimated eleven thousand copies had been bought — a tremendous sale for those days.

But during the closing weeks of the year Swift had scant

opportunity to contemplate the triumph of his pen. No sooner did parliament meet than the tories were seized with panic terror at the strength and, as they believed, the treachery of their opponents. When Nottingham went over to the enemy, they called on Swift to exact vengeance for this desertion, which he promptly did in *An Excellent New Song, Being the Intended Speech of a famous Orator against Peace.* The queen, they said, was unfaithful, swayed as she was by the duke and duchess of Somerset, and no one believed this more implicitly than Swift. He took up Arbuthnot's quotation, the 'hearts of kings are unsearchable,' and with each new day fulminated more terribly against the Somersets, until he could no longer bear the thought of the duchess's insidious presence by the royal side. On the twenty-third he wrote to Stella, 'I have written a *Prophecy,* which I design to print. . .' This was the famous *Windsor Prophecy,* that distillation of all hateful rumours attaching to the duchess of Somerset's dubious past. Mrs. Masham took alarm and prevailed upon him to suppress the verses, but many printed copies got about and the harm was done.

Christmas came and went, and Swift could see no hope of a tory victory. It is clear that he had not the slightest intimation of the coup about to be sprung. Oxford's cheerfulness he found unaccountable. Then, on the twenty-ninth, news of the creation of the twelve peers sped through London. Swift received it in a coffee-house and in his great elation tore open the letter to Stella lying in his pocket and scribbled a postscript, 'to let you know, that we are all safe' and that the duchess of Somerset is to be turned out, for the queen 'is awaked at last, and so is lord treasurer. . .' For Swift it was a supreme moment — the *Examiner, The Conduct of the Allies,* countless political pamphlets and squibs, even *The Windsor Prophecy,* had issued at last in dazzling success. It was well that he sensed the triumph to the full; for from this, their highest point, his own fortunes and those of his party were to be swung rapidly downwards.

1712 was full of signs telling unmistakably that the best of the adventure was now over. The bickering between Oxford and Bolingbroke ceased to be an annoyance and became a veritable death's-head gaping down upon every ministerial council.   As for Swift himself, his old enemy — 'giddiness' — now began to overtake him, and a painful illness of another nature laid him up for the better part of two months.   And then there was the matter of his preferment.

Swift, unmindful as yet of the difficulties that lay ahead, strode into the new year with the splendid energy awakened by the journalistic discipline of the previous months still tingling in his nerves.   The political triumph of the closing days of 1711 had rekindled the zeal of the extreme tories, a group of whom were now foregathering in what they called the October Club to press for the thorough-going measures which their party's undisputed power seemed to call for.   If such a line coincided with Bolingbroke's plans, it threatened in every way the policy of moderation to which Oxford was committed and had managed thus far to impose on the ministry.   Swift, engaged on the side of Oxford, now published *A Letter of Advice to the Members of the October Club* (January 1712), a general warning to all those clamouring for a full display of tory strength that the leaders of the party were still impeded by clogs — of which the outsider knew nothing — and could only be embarrassed by impolitic agitations for measures as yet impossible to carry through. At about the same time he issued another pamphlet, entitled *Some Remarks on the Barrier Treaty*, designed to supplement *The Conduct of the Allies*.   Meanwhile, for good measure, he was plying Grub Street hard with political verses, the most pointed of which celebrated the fall of Marlborough in a spirit thoroughly ignoble (*The Fable of Midas*).   Of an entirely non-political character was *A Proposal for Correcting, Improving, and Ascertaining the English Tongue*, dated 22 February — the only pamphlet which Swift ever printed under his own name.

There are frequent references in the earlier parts of the *Journal* to seizures of giddiness, the periodic recurrence of which Swift had long since come to expect.   But at the end of March he was complaining to Stella of a pain in his shoulder — the first symptom of shingles, which kept him in agony for the next two months and caused him on several occasions to interrupt his entries in the *Journal*.

The last of May, on his feet once more, Swift went to Kensington for a fortnight to be near the tory leaders, and during the summer he was frequently at Windsor for the same purpose. For one reason or another his friends in the ministry had not enlisted his pen in the campaign for peace which was still going forward; it was Arbuthnot who was now shouldering the responsibility of moulding public opinion, and had already published four of the five pamphlets known collectively as *The History of John Bull*.² Swift no longer regarded peace as a contingency but as a fact assured, and accordingly his interest in propaganda had cooled; it was the authentic history of the whole series of events leading up to the peace which he was now desirous of writing, and he flattered himself that he alone combined a full knowledge of the facts and the historian's qualifications — it is not surprising that he erred regarding the extent to which he had been admitted to the secrets of the ministry nor that, with his belief in the adequacy of common sense, he never questioned his fitness to write history. No task to which he set his hand during these four years seemed half so important or claimed so much time and care as the voluntarily undertaken *History of the Four Last Years of the Queen*, which he regarded as his most substantial contribution to political letters and a work in every way fitted to vindicate the ministry and insure the triumph of peace. His superiors, however, took quite a different view, finding so much inflammatory matter in this historical account that they hastened to suppress it to Swift's everlasting disgust.

Through the last months of 1712 and into 1713 Swift was absorbed in the ill-fated *Four Last Years of the Queen*. But when he perceived that his work only occasioned alarm in those to whom he submitted it for judgment, he dropped it and turned his attention in goodly earnest to the rewards now long over-due him.³ (Through 1712 he had continued to issue political verses, and during the summer he had written several prose pamphlets. But with the arrival of the new year he ceased, after publishing two articles in the *Examiner* (16 January 1713 and 2 February) and *Mr. Collins's Discourse of Freethinking*, to argue the tory cause in print.) Regarding his own preferment, Swift had been on tenter-hooks since the beginning of 1712. At that time the deaneries of Wells, Ely, and Lichfield had all been vacant, and as early as February he had applied to Oxford for Wells. By March, despite the fact that no action had been taken, Archbishop King was writing as though Swift had the deanery in his pocket, and Stella and Dingley were equally certain. '. . . I am not Dean of Wells, nor know any thing of being so,' Swift replied peevishly (*The Journal to Stella,* 21 March 1712); but the rumour in Ireland was not to be headed off, and the lords justices went so far as to nominate a successor to Laracor. Oxford, meanwhile, did nothing to confirm or to crush the report, and month by month Swift's irritation and uneasiness increased. It was not until mid-April 1713 that matters came to a head. On the thirteenth of this month Swift saw the warrants for the three deaneries, and his worst fears were confirmed — not one of them was for him. Enraged as he had every right to be, he at once took the step which he might have taken long before had his pride not held him back, and demanded either that the ministry now reward him for his services or dismiss him for good and all. His action produced immediate effect: the warrants for the deaneries were held up; Erasmus Lewis rushed about in great agitation; Oxford and Ormond, the lord-lieutenant, went into hurried conference. Had only the deaneries been vacant it would not have been such a tangled situation, but there were in addition a canonry at Windsor to be filled and the two Irish bishoprics of Raphoe and Dromore. The first plan now proposed called for the raising of Stearne, the dean of St. Patrick's, to the see of Dromore, and Swift's appointment to the deanery thus vacated; but Ormond, ready otherwise to confer St. Patrick's on Swift, boggled at Stearne's being made a bishop, and for ten days Swift was suspended between proposals and counter-proposals. At one moment, with Ormond yielding, his preferment to St. Patrick's seemed assured; at

the next his friends were scoffing at an Irish deanery and
backing him for the canonry at Windsor, which would at
least keep him in England.   On 23 April it was finally
determined : Stearne should have Dromore, Swift the deanery.   The year before when just this arrangement had been
suggested as one which he could bring off Swift had regarded
it with contempt; now he accepted it with something like
a sigh of relief, for although he could never reconcile himself to exile in Ireland, he knew at last the full strength of
his enemies.

We shall never know all who worked against Swift nor
exactly how they moved behind the scenes.   The clearest
contemporary account is that given in Swift's verses entitled
The Author upon Himself, where the archbishops of York
and Canterbury,— Tenison and Sharpe,— the duchess of
Somerset, and the queen are all named as inimical to his
preferment in England.   One surmises that his authorship
of *A Tale of a Tub,* his libel upon the duchess of Somerset,
and his venomous partisanship, which from 1710 on had
elicited increasingly strident attacks upon his character, had
built up a damning case against him.   It has remained for
a historian of the present day to show how the man whom
Swift trusted and honoured above all others consistently
sacrificed him in the interests of mean jobbery — Oxford was
careful to reserve the first preferments for clerics who had
served the private fortunes of the Harley family.[4]

On 1 June Swift left London to proceed to Dublin for
his installation.   The preceding month had brought him no
joy.   The congratulatory letters from Ireland had been
coolly formal.   Archbishop King, for instance, had gone out
of his way to devise some particularly feline manner of
taking the new dean down, and had written at length about
the projected spire for St. Patrick's, to be built of brick
and to rise a hundred and twenty feet above the steeple,
which was one hundred and twenty feet high and twenty-one
feet in the clear; if Swift would inform himself of the mysteries of steeples before he left England, he could supervise
this great work at the Cathedral and give 'the people there

an advantageous notion of [him]'—this to the man concerned with England's weightiest problems! But it was
Steele's attack upon him which had filled Swift's cup of
bitterness to overflowing. Angered by a slighting reference in the *Examiner* to Lord Nottingham's daughter, Steele
had replied in the *Guardian* by insinuating that the ob-
jectionable article was of Swift's authorship and had gone
on to reflect harshly upon his former friend. On 13 May
Swift addressed to Addison a letter in which he disclaimed
the imputed authorship and remonstrated against Steele's
uncharitable conduct. Addison refused to be drawn into
the dispute, merely turning the letter over to Steele, who
composed a reply in which almost every sentence was a dag-
ger thrust. Three more letters passed between the two—
Swift's first directly to Steele, Steele's second reply, and
Swift's closing rejoinder. Swift would have done well to
let the matter rest here. But he had been touched to the
quick; he was resolved to crush Steele at the first opportunity.

Swift was installed dean on Sunday 13 June; on the
twenty-fifth he left for Laracor. Shortly he was receiving
letters from Erasmus Lewis urging his speedy return to
England—Oxford and Bolingbroke were quarrelling again;
only Swift could calm the troubled waters. Early in September Swift reached London.

To all appearances the dean of St. Patrick's, moving with
easy familiarity among the great ones of the court, was now
a mighty dignitary, and in certain respects appearances told
the truth. For the first and only time, Swift's hands now
rested upon the control levers. In matters affecting the
church in Ireland, no other man's word counted for more:
he had at his call Sir Constantine Phipps, lord chancellor
of Ireland; he was instrumental in the promotion of Lindsay to the primacy; he laid down the law to Archbishop
King in the grand style. In Dublin there was even talk of
his advancement to a bishopric. Bishop Kennett's well-
known and unflattering description of Swift exhibiting himself in full glory among the throng waiting in the queen's

antechamber dates from this period, and for all its maliciousness one can believe that it reflects the overbearing manner assumed by Swift in his brief moment of power.

But behind his make-up Swift's countenance bore a different expression. In his verses in imitation of Horace's *Quinque dies* it is the sense of defeat that is expressed — if he seemed all unction when addressed by his new title, inwardly he writhed at those words which spelt exile. As for Oxford and Bolingbroke, whose quarrels had brought him back from Ireland, each day seemed to bring them nearer to the breaking-point. There was nowhere a ray of hope: his own case was irremediable; his friends would not see the grinning death's-head behind them.

For the last time Swift engaged in the war of pamphlets. Steele, recently elected to parliament from Stockbridge, undertook to censure the ministry in a pamphlet entitled *The Importance of Dunkirk Considered* (22 September). Here was the opening for which Swift had been waiting since his altercation with Steele. At the end of October appeared *The Importance of the Guardian Considered,* as fierce a personal attack as ever came from Swift's dreaded pen. Once again — and for the last time under a tory ministry — the great journalist was to strike at Steele and the whigs: in January 1714 Steele, in *The Crisis,* redoubled his cries against the tories, and the following month, on the opening of parliament, Swift published *The Public Spirit of the Whigs.* Though for a time it looked as though Swift might fall before the fury of the house of lords, who voted his pamphlet 'a false, malicious, and factious libel' because of its attack upon the Scotch peers, issued an order for the attachment of publisher and printer, and offered a reward of £300 for the discovery of the author,— ostensibly unknown, — in the end it was the author of *The Crisis* who was made to pay, by expulsion from the commons, for journalistic indiscretion.

After his parting salvo, Swift stood by for three months, hoping against all hope that the ministry would heed the danger signals now displayed in every quarter, compose their differences, and fix upon a plan of vigorous and united ac-

tion. But by June he knew that all was lost. His usefulness
at an end and unable to bear the daily sight of a political party in its death-throes, he left London and sought
retirement in his friend John Geree's rectory of Letcombe
Bassett in Berkshire. The letters which poured in from
London brought grim confirmation of all his fears. So exactly did events unfold in accordance with his predictions,
that suspense was replaced by that poignant irony felt by a
spectator who knows the outcome of the tragedy which he is
witnessing. In such a mood Swift paused to examine himself as the flood closed about him, executing in the verses
in imitation of Horace's *Hoc erat* and in the metrical composition entitled *The Author upon Himself* two notable
self-portrayals. Then his mind moved back over the events
of the great years now drawing to a close, to the fierce en-
gagements, to the victories, to all the gains that might have
been secured, to the tragic passions within the ministry that
had limited their achievements and were now bringing ruin
upon the party. With the stern emotional repression which
is so easily mistaken for coldness, Swift now recorded his
thoughts upon all these matters, reviewing the history of the
tory ministry, searching out its weaknesses and errors, and
tracing the course that might have led into safe waters.
Some Free Thoughts upon the Present State of Affairs and
*Some Considerations upon the Consequences hoped and
feared from the Death of the Queen* were written at Letcombe; *Memoirs relating to that Change which happened
in the Queen's Ministry in the year 1710* is dated October
1714, but was perhaps begun at the Berkshire rectory;[5]
while *An Enquiry into the Behaviour of the Queen's last
Ministry,* on which Swift was at work as late as 1721,[6] goes
back at least in spirit to the last days of the ministry.

In the *Free Thoughts* Swift was compelled to reflect upon
Oxford's administration. But if the historian's judgment
was harsh, the loyalty of Swift the friend was unshaken, and
on 3 July he wrote Oxford a kind of apology for what he
had been compelled to set down in the *Free Thoughts*:
'. . . in your public capacity you have often angered me to
the heart, but, as a private man, never once.' But the true

test of Swift's loyalty came when, some days later, Oxford was removed from office. Unhesitatingly Swift laid himself at the other's service, offering to cancel his own plans if Oxford desired his attendance.

The queen died on 1 August. Oxford would not detain him. Swift was free, now, to retire to exile in Ireland. Presumably he left Letcombe on Monday 16 August, but of the circumstances of his return to Dublin nothing is recorded.

The queen's death was the long-awaited signal for the *auto-da-fé* to begin, a signal which the whigs received with proper manifestations of joy. But if Oxford, Bolingbroke, and others might be forced to answer with their lives for their conduct while in office, no one save a few enemies in Dublin seriously believed that the dean of St. Patrick's had been implicated in any malfeasance. He was guilty only of journalistic exploits, and his punishment was to be immersion in Grub-Street filth. Of the countless satires upon him which now poured from the press, one may cite the *Hue and Cry after Dean Swift* (1714) and *Dr. Swift's Real Diary* (1715), both of which were afterwards gathered up by Dean Smedley and reprinted along with satiric matter of a later date in *Gulliveriana* (1728). But Swift was already in too great misery to be much affected by Grub-Street malice or the derisive cries with which the whigs greeted him upon his return to Dublin. His moral reserves had been drained dry; finding himself in exile at last, he had not the strength to tear himself loose from the rack of self-pity. The tortures which he suffered are indicated only too clearly in the verses *In Sickness,* written in October.

4

To record Swift's activities under the tory ministry is one thing, to weigh his conduct quite another. A recent estimate of Swift the tory champion has produced the charge that by the violence of his pen he hurried his party towards Jacobitism.[7] Now, some distinction must be made between Swift's motives and the unforeseen consequences of his acts. Thus, if Swift's immoderate political verses and pamphlets did in fact exert a ponderable pressure in the direction of Jacobitism — and this would seem debatable — no critic or historian has ever questioned his perfect ignorance of the intrigue between his friends and the pretender; had he believed that there was an iota of truth in the accusations constantly made by the whigs he would instantly have severed all bonds with the tories.

A more serious charge which can be brought against the great tory propagandist is that of intemperance. To what extent, it is fair to ask, did passion carry him beyond clear principles? Before this question can be answered, it is apparent that the principles by which he professed to be guided throughout these clamorous years must be uncovered. For these one does not have to search long — one need only turn to his letters and the *Journal,* to his controversial prose, and to his historical writings to find them set forth time and again, always with clarity, always with convincing earnestness. Nor were they improvisations of the moment, but convictions deriving straight from his central body of ideas. If he argued these convictions with an immoderation which yet stuns us, that, in part at least, is because the journalist like the moralist was a genius whose art clothed the idea with overwhelming intensity. If his political tone cannot be wholly explained in this manner, the extent to which he gave utterance to passions aroused only by blind partisanship is exceedingly difficult to determine.

We have previously followed Swift's mind through the period from 1699 to 1710, when it was engaged with the problems relating to church and state; we have observed how it articulated the political principles of the Revolution, how it defined the church as an institution validated by the assent of reasonable men, how it came more and more to insist upon government which would guarantee in both political and religious matters the rational will of the majority. His conversion to the tory party was as much as anything a conversion, long delayed, to the church party. But as already pointed out, his intention was not to lend his power to the setting-up of a domineering church-state. And whatever the political creed of the rank and file of the tories,

Swift himself sought to purge the party of its old absolutism
and in its place to inject his own theories of freedom in
accord with human experience and universal reason.
Clearly his desertion of the whigs had in it an element of
self-seeking, but it was so preponderantly a response to intellectual conviction that he must be acquitted of the accusation of baseness.

Once a tory, Swift gave enthusiastic assent to what he believed was the great purpose of all the operations of the
ministry.   War he hated, not for its horrors but for its stupidity, nowhere more clearly reflected than in the professional soldier, whom of all men he most contemned.   The
war then in progress he hated for further reasons : because it
had been carried on by the whigs, because it had glorified
the duke of Marlborough, because it had been financed by
the monied men of the City, because it had carried England
out of her domestic sphere into European affairs.   Almost
from the hour of his arrival in London he joined in the cry
for peace.   'It is affirmed by the Tories,' he wrote on 9
September 1710 to Archbishop King, 'that the great motive
of these changes was the absolute necessity of a peace, which
they thought the Whigs were for perpetually delaying.'   A
month later he wrote, again to the archbishop, that the ruin
of the whigs was due not only to personal causes but to their
stubbornness in prolonging the war : 'In short, [people] apprehended the whole party to be entirely against a peace for
some time, until they were rivetted too fast to be broke, as
they otherwise expected, if the war should conclude too soon.'
As journalist, it was on the necessity of peace that he dwelt
with all his consummate emphasis.   '. . . if,' he wrote in his
opening number in the *Examiner,* 'if the war continues some
years longer, a landed man will be little better than a farmer
at a rack rent, to the army, and to the public funds.'   He
went on to give a rapid sketch of the rise, after the Revolution, of a new set of whigs who, 'in order to fasten wealthy
people to the new government,' had proposed the expedient
of a funded national debt ; the war, financed in this manner, had created a new class of monied men, whose interests
were inimical to those of the landed men — the backbone of

England — and who had every reason to desire a prolongation of the war.   A like theme served him in the opening pages of *The Conduct of the Allies*: after the Revolution, England entered into a foreign war and began to borrow millions upon funds of interest:

And this pernicious counsel closed very well with the posture of affairs at that time: For, a set of upstarts, who had little or no part in the Revolution, but valued themselves by their noise and pretended zeal when the work was over, were got into credit at court, by the merit of becoming undertakers and projectors of loans and funds: These, finding that the gentlemen of estates were not willing to come into their measures, fell upon those new schemes of raising money, in order to create a monied interest, that might in time vie with the landed, and of which they hoped to be at the head.

Regarding the ministry, Swift's ideas were just as clear. Oxford's ministry stood (1) for peace, (2) for the protection of the church against all her enemies from rank Socinians to indifferent whigs.   Such a double purpose was enough for him; so long as there was no malfeasance, what need of speculating on every intention and motive? '. . . I follow those who, I think, are most for preserving the Church and State, without examining whether they do so from a principle of virtue or of interest' (To Archbishop King, 31 December 1713).   It was, furthermore, a ministry representing less the interests of a party than the interests of the entire kingdom; its opponents, the whigs, were but a faction thrown together by the force of common and selfish interests (*A Letter of Advice to the Members of the October Club*).   Swift's most remarkable statement of his belief that the ministry was truly national in character occurs in the closing pages of *An Enquiry into the Behaviour of the Queen's last Ministry*:

. . . I am not so weak as to think one ministry more virtuous than another, unless by chance, or by extraordinary prudence and virtue of the prince; which last, taking mankind in the lump, and adding the great counterbalance of royal education, is a very rare accident; and, where it happens, is even then of little use, when factions are violent.   But it so falls out, that, among contending parties in England, the general interest of church and state is more the private interest of one side than the other; so that, whoever professeth to act upcn a principle of observing the laws of his country, may have a safe rule to follow, by discovering whose particular advantage it chiefly is, that the constitution should be preserved entire in all its parts. For there cannot, properly speaking, be above two parties in such a government as ours; and one side will find themselves obliged to take in all the subaltern denominations of those who dislike the present establishment, in order to make themselves a balance against the other; and such a party, composed of mixed bodies, although they differ widely in the several fundamentals of religion and government, and all of them from the true public interest; yet, whenever their leaders are taken into power, under an ignorant, unactive, or ill-designing prince, will probably, by the assistance of time or force, become the majority, unless they be prevented by a steadiness, which there is little reason to hope, or by some revolution, which there is much more reason to fear.

Just as he had always regarded the dissenters, whatever their numbers, as a faction which threatened the rule of reason in matters religious, so he came to look upon the whig party as the enemy of that political philosophy maintained by all enlightened men. In both religion and government, those who denied *his* principles he saw only as dangerous scoundrels — the dissenters actuated by enthusiasm, the whigs by guileful self-interest. It was at this point, if anywhere, that Swift crossed the line separating reasoned conviction from blind prejudice. But to whatever degree his intellectual pride committed him to causes which the future was to disown, his persecuting temper had behind it a theory of human freedom which is the essence of rational democracy. If he was a stern repressor of his enemies, he was at the same time a champion of liberty.

Peace and the interests of the church were to be secured by a ministry above party. How this ministry should have proceeded was to Swift as plain as a pike-staff. In May 1711, when the split between Oxford and St. John was apparent to all who were close to the ministry, and factions were forming within the ranks of the party, Swift described to Peterborough the three different tory camps:

. . . I think it plain that there are among the Tories three different interests: one, of those, I mean the Ministry, who agree with your Lordship and me, in a steady management for pursuing the true interests of the nation ; another is, that of warmer heads, as the October Club and their adherents without doors : and a third is, I fear, of those who . . . would sound a parley, and who would make fair weather in case of a change ; and some of these last are not inconsiderable.

Though he loved Oxford as he never did St. John, he became increasingly impatient with the lord treasurer's 'mysterious and procrastinating leadership' ; it was Oxford who seemed to be deflecting from the interests of the ministry ; his refusal to turn all enemies out of office was beginning to mark him as one of those who would sound a parley and make fair weather.   Though Swift looked askance at the October Club, he never ceased to urge severe measures, and to the end he regarded Oxford's mildness as a grave defect ; but before the great crisis of December 1711 he had come to the conviction that the queen was forcing upon Oxford a policy of moderation the full responsibility for which the lord treasurer was compelled to accept silently.   Looking back upon the conduct of the ministry from his retreat at Letcombe, Swift saw the errors with a clearness that bred both sorrow and anger.   The art of government is shrouded in no cloud of mystery: 'God hath given the bulk of mankind a capacity to understand reason when it is fairly offered ; and by reason they would easily be governed, if it were left to their choice.'   Politicians who follow devious ways out of a love of intrigue do so at great peril.   That the tory ministry has faced the greatest distress and been very near the brink of ruin is owing less to the address of their enemies than to their own failures.   Their 'reserved mysterious way of acting' was often imputed 'to some hidden design, which every man conjectured to be the very thing he was most afraid of.'   'But,' Swift continues,

the effects of this mystical manner of proceeding did not end here : For, the late dissentions between the great men at court . . . are said to have arisen from the same fountain ; while on one side [i.e., Oxford's] very great reserve, and certainly very great resentment on the other [Bolingbroke's] . . . have inflamed animosities to such a height, as to make all reconcilement impracticable.   Supposing this to be true, it may serve for a great

lesson of humiliation to mankind, to behold the habits and passions of men otherwise highly accomplished, triumphing over interest, friendship, honour, and their own personal safety, as well
as that of their country. . .   (*Some Free Thoughts upon the
Present State of Affairs.*)

Reviewing Swift's conduct during the tory supremacy, one
cannot but come to the conclusion that never has vociferous
propagandist had a clearer consciousness of underlying principles, a keener perception of desired ends.

5

SWIFT'S life in London during the Oxford ministry was not
confined, as the foregoing descriptions might suggest, to politics and journalism.   His friends and acquaintances were
many, and in their society he passed a great deal of time.
Previously, as one of the Addisonian circle, he had given
evidence of his rare social endowments.   The tory group
who moved close to the ministry now accepted him uncon-
ditionally.   For all the strange fascination which he exercised over women, Swift was a man's man, richly endowed
with the qualities in greatest esteem in the urban and mas-
culine civilization which flowered under Queen Anne.   He
combined wit and humour, conviviality, social perceptions,
invigorating common sense, and loyalty.   Had it not been
for the curse of his Irish background, he might well have
attained undisputed rule over the Augustans.   But if others
forgot that he was in England not by right but on sufferance,
Swift never did, and in the end his banishment to St. Patrick's confirmed what he had known all along — London
could always dispense with an Irish lion.

Upon his return to London in the autumn of 1710, Swift,
as we have already seen, resumed his old place among the
whig men of letters, consorting with Addison, Steele, and
Congreve as in the old days, and contributing prose and
verse to the *Tatler*.   Could Swift have had his way, his
change of political allegiance would not have altered his relations with the group who had been the first to recognize
his genius; his deep sense of loyalty to those to whom he

felt bound by ties of friendship led him to the naïve belief that political differences could be sunk. Congreve, indeed, was willing enough to forget partisanship; Addison could not condone political defection, but he was ready to hide his disapproval behind a chilly reticence; it was Steele who made of Swift's renunciation of the whigs a personal affront — and thus prepared the way for the regrettable feud which three years later broke out between the two.

Bolingbroke, Oxford, and the latter's agent, Erasmus Lewis, were the earliest of Swift's new friends. As he gained prominence as a journalist, his acquaintance with the leading tories of the day was rapidly extended. The men and women who now entered his life were noted faithfully in the *Journal;* many of them Swift regarded as mere acquaintances, but on a surprisingly large number he bestowed the full warmth of friendship. Of these latter, Prior and Arbuthnot stand out. Swift may have met Prior on some previous sojourn in London, but of this there is no evidence; so far as is known, it was at Harley's that he was first introduced to this poet now in the diplomatic service. They were suited to each other, having a great deal more than politics in common. Soon Swift's verses were showing less of Addison's influence and correspondingly more of Prior's. They collaborated more than once in political verse, though it is impossible to identify their joint productions with any certainty — *The Fable of the Widow and her Cat* (January 1712) is possibly one of them. But collaboration was not necessary for something of Prior's familiar style to be passed on to Swift, whose verse was of a narrow register but susceptible of surprising modulation within its limits.

Of all the men whom Swift counted among his friends, there is none whose character shines out of the past more brightly than John Arbuthnot's. He was not only a distinguished physician — in 1709 he had been made physician in ordinary to the queen — but a wit as well and in addition to all a highly versatile man of letters. But it was his personal qualities more than his talents which endeared him to his friends. He was a solid, hearty man, whose bluntness and robust honesty bespoke a mind in perfect health; he was never lacking in awareness, he was ever ready with understanding and sympathy. The deep love and admiration which Arbuthnot felt for Swift and which the latter returned in full measure would prove, in the absence of all else, that beneath Swift's genius, behind that countenance which filled his enemies with loathing and still repels the tender-minded, there lay moral qualities unsuspected by the world at large. It was these which Arbuthnot perceived. At the moment of Swift's departure from England in 1714 Arbuthnot wrote :

I am sure I never can forget you, till I meet with, what is impossible, another, whose conversation I can delight so much in as Dr. Swift's, and yet that is the smallest thing I ought to value you for. That hearty sincere friendship, that plain and open ingenuity in all your commerce, is what I am sure I never can find in another man.

Twelve years later, when Swift had revisited England for the first time since the fall of the tories and had again departed for Ireland, Arbuthnot wrote that the princess of Wales had remarked upon the dean's wit and good conversation ; 'I told her Royal Highness,' he went on, 'that was not what I valued you for, but for being a sincere honest man, and speaking truth when others were afraid to speak it.' Had Swift had an Arbuthnot by him throughout life he would have been in many ways a different man ; if nothing could have altered his essential genius, kindliness and penetrating understanding on the part of those with whom he was thrown would have driven back many of the neurotic shadows which overcast his mind, would have rendered him less prone to conceal his deeper nature behind an ironic front.

In the days of his greatness Swift delighted to serve his friends. Why is it necessary, as some have believed, to question his motives ? Whether he was actuated by a pleasurable sense of power or by simple good will or by both at once, the fact remains that he stood ready to assist whenever possible. For the whigs with whom he had coursed when the names of Partridge and Bickerstaff were household words he was for ever demanding clemency from the ministers. He was never too busy to assist those of his friends who came over from Ireland for a look about London and a whiff of the smoke that rolled from the battlefield of politics. He had his retainers, too, like William King the civilian and little Harrison, for whom he secured employments. No one who has read the *Journal* will forget Harrison. He was a young man of limited talent, we gather, who for some obscure reason had aroused the interest and pity of the great journalist. Swift set him up in a new *Tatler*, but it was at once apparent that, as an imitator of Steele, Harrison would never succeed. Swift then obtained for him the post of secretary to Loid Raby, ambassador extraordinary to The Hague, and a year later announced with pride to Stella that 'little Harrison whom I sent to Holld is now actually made Qu-s Secrty at te Hague. . .' But despite the high-sounding title, a queen's secretary was numbered among the more lowly of her majesty's servants; so slight in fact was his prestige that the government felt no compunction in forgetting that a salary was owing him. Poor Harrison returned to London with a dozen Holland shirts for his patron but not a farthing in his pocket, and within a fortnight he lay seriously ill. Swift carried him off to Knightsbridge, and then went the rounds of the ministers, obtaining thirty guineas from Bolingbroke and a treasury order for £100. Two days later (14 February 1713), accompanied by Parnell, he walked to Knightsbridge to visit the sick man:

. . . I had te 100 ll in my Pocket. I told Parnel I was afraid to knock at te door; my mind misgave me. I knockt, & his man in Tears told me his Master was dead an hour before. Think what Grief this [is?] to me; I went to his Mothr, & have been ordering things for his Funerall with as little Cost as possible, to morrow at ten at night. Ld Treasr was much concernd when I told him. I could not dine with Ld Tr nor any where, but got a bit of meat towards Evening. no loss ever grieved me so much. poor Creature.— Pray Gd Almighty bless poor [MD] — adieu —
I send this away to night and am sorry it must go while I am in so much Grief.

Swift's regular presence at Oxford's Saturday dinners has already been noted. It was during his absence from London in June 1711, while he was a guest of Lord Shelburne at

Wycombe, that the Society, now better known as the Brothers Club, was founded by Swift's tory friends to 'advance conversation and friendship, and to reward deserving persons with . . . interest and recommendation.' To this group, which numbered among others St. John, Ormond, Bathurst, Landsdowne, Masham, Arbuthnot, and Freind, Swift was at once admitted. It met on Thursdays, each member supplying the dinner in his turn. When Swift entertained, the Club gathered at a tavern, and great was the host's concern at the size of the bill — what for St. John or Ormond was an inconsiderable sum left a vicar's pocket a good deal lighter.

In historical perspective, however, Oxford's Saturday dinners and the Brothers Club assume a rather trivial appearance beside the famous Scriblerus Club,[8] which came into existence towards the close of 1713 or early in the following year.[9] The leading spirit, to judge by what the members wrote to one another, was Arbuthnot, with Swift, Parnell, Gay, and Pope enthusiastically abetting him, and others like the lord treasurer adding to the merriment on occasion. (During the earlier years of the tory ministry Swift and Pope seem not to have known one another. Until the appearance of *Windsor Forest* in the spring of 1713, it was assumed that Pope, as one of Addison's circle, stood aloof from the party in power, but his celebration of the peace in the concluding lines of his poem called him to the attention of the tories. When Swift returned to England in September 1713 he and Pope were already sworn friends, having probably met before the publication of *Windsor Forest*.[10] Doubtless it was through Pope that Swift became acquainted with Gay.) The Scriblerus Club considered politics quite beneath its notice; if there was conviviality, well and good, but it must be incidental to the great purpose which lay ahead. This was the joint composition of the *Memoirs of Martinus Scriblerus,* which in Pope's words was 'to have ridiculed all the false tastes in learning, under the character of a man of capacity enough, that had dipped into every art and science, but injudiciously in each.' This work was off to an auspicious start, only to be benighted, alas, when absolute dark-

ness fell at the queen's death. Yet something remained.
The first book of the *Memoirs* was given to the world in the
second volume of Pope's *Prose Works* (1741), and in the
preceding years scattered fragments had from time to time
been cast up on the shore — for example *Peri Bathous; or
the Art of Sinking in Poetry* (in the Pope and Swift *Miscellanies. The Last Volume,* which appeared 8 March
1728), in which Pope set the stage for the entrance in May
1728 of the first edition of the *Dunciad;* the *Virgilius Res-
tauratus,* given in the 1729 or 'authorized' edition of the
Dunciad, which edition was also adorned with prolegomena
and notes by the famous Martinus; and *An Essay of the
Learned Martinus Scriblerus concerning the Origine of
Sciences* (in the Pope and Swift *Miscellanies. The Third
Volume,* 1732).[11] But it is the *Memoirs of Martinus Scriblerus* which the reader of Swift will find of particular interest
by reason of the close relation between this amiable satire
and *Gulliver's Travels.* Precisely how the *Memoirs* was
composed we shall never know; but even if Arbuthnot's
hand was the principal shaping force — as there is every
reason to believe — there was undoubtedly constant collaboration on the part of the five Scriblerians. At some point
or other in the confabulations it was suggested, it would
seem, that Martin be sent out on voyages to strange lands,
and Swift took it upon himself to handle these incidents.
But he had not proceeded far when fate intervened, the
Club was broken up, and the composition of the *Memoirs*
was brought to an untimely end. The satiric fragments devised by Swift do not appear to have found a place in the
published *Memoirs.* Swift, however, kept them by him;
and when at length his creative energies returned to him,
some six or seven years after the queen's death, he took
out his old sketches and proceeded to build upon them the
magnificent work which was published in 1726 as *Gulliver's
Travels.* Herein, according to the best informed opinion
to-day, lies the real kinship between the *Memoirs* and *Gulliver's Travels.* This is a point worth emphasizing, because
the two works are seemingly joined by a closer link than
this, which turns out, however, to be no real link. The

Memoirs of Martinus Scriblerus was not printed until fifteen years after the publication of *Gulliver's Travels*. When the *Memoirs* appeared, it contained in the thirteenth chapter [12] a brief sketch of Martin's travels: Martin made four voyages, we are told, on the first of which he discovered the remains of the ancient Pygmaean Empire; on the second, the land of giants; on the third, a kingdom of philosophers governed by the mathematics; while on the last he met with adventures which reduced him to the utmost melancholy, 'proceeding almost to a disgust of his species.' It seems pretty clear that this entire sketch of Martin's travels was added by Pope shortly before he published the *Memoirs* in 1741, [13] in which case his motive is manifest and in no way discreditable: it was not that he was seeking to raise doubts concerning the originality of Swift's great satiric work, merely that he thought to enhance the *Memoirs* in the reader's eye by adding to Martin something of Gulliver's universal fame.

Lastly, something must be said of the enigmatic relations which at this time sprang up between Swift and Esther Vanhomrigh. [14] Esther's father, probably a native of Holland, had been a merchant in Dublin for some years before his death, which occurred late in 1703. In 1707 his widow, accompanied by her four children, of whom Hessy or Esther was the eldest (born in 1688, it is believed), established herself in London, and it was here that Swift, during his protracted sojourn in England which ended in 1709, came to know the family intimately. When he returned to Ireland in 1709 he received more than one letter from Esther.

In the autumn of 1710 he resumed his intercourse with the Vanhomrighs, and in December took lodgings in St. Albans Street only five doors away from them. He moved to Chelsea in the spring of 1711, but was at their house, where he kept his best wig and gown, twice daily, once on his arrival in town in the morning, when he dressed for the day's business, and again in the evening, when he changed back into his old wig and gown before setting out to walk the 5748 steps up Pall Mall, through the Park, out at Buckingham House, and so to Chelsea a little beyond the church.

By this time Esther was well on the way to becoming Vanessa. On her part, the assumption had already taken root that this fascinating clergyman, nearly twice her age, was somehow her special property ; on Swift's side there was amusement at her appropriative attitude, some sarcasm, and a good deal of cajolery. Yes, it was a dangerous game that they were playing, and we have been told repeatedly that Swift should have broken away while there was still time. It is curious how many episodes in his life lie at the mercy of the easy moralizer. Biographers and critics not in the habit of delivery *ex cathedra* pronouncements on the conduct of great men of letters have not hesitated to impose moral judgments of unyielding inflexibility on Swift ; whereas the questionable behaviour of another elicits civilized commentary, there is not a regrettable incident in Swift's life which has not been interpreted as an enormity and made the subject of an edifying sermon. Yet a modicum of imaginative sympathy should make us aware of the presence in Swift, as in all men, of subtle gradations of moral tone and colour. Why he lingered near Vanessa we do not know — nor, probably, did he.

In the summer of 1712 Swift was much at Windsor, and here the Vanhomrighs apparently paid him a visit — this, at least, is the latest interpretation of his cryptic letters to Vanessa from Windsor, into which it was once customary to read a sinister meaning. Vanessa's attitude was undoubtedly undergoing a profound change at this time, but whether either she or Swift as yet fully recognized its nature seems doubtful. It was not until the following year that the truth stood fully revealed, and a passionate woman faced, unabashed, the man she loved. In June 1713 Swift left to be installed dean. Vanessa's first two letters were restrained enough, but in her third and fourth she threw reticence aside. ' 'Tis unexpressible the concern I am in ever since I heard . . . that your head is so much out of order. . . I am impatient to the last degree to hear how you are. I hope I shall soon have you here.' She takes him to task for his cruel silence : 'If you are very happy it is ill-natured of you not to tell me so, except 'tis what is inconsistent with

mi[ne].' Was she thinking of Stella? To these importunate letters Swift replied but once (8 July). 'I told you
when I left England,' he wrote, 'I would endeavour to forget everything there, and would write as seldom as I could.'
They were carefully chosen words, intended to establish his
own position beyond the possibility of misconstruction : he
was not only immune to but repelled by these ardours of
romantic passion.

At no time does his conduct with regard to Vanessa lend
itself to assured interpretation, but it is after his return to
England in the autumn of 1713 that it takes on its air of
greatest mystery. The tone of the letters which passed between them makes it quite certain that the two protagonists
were not groping helplessly in the dark ; it is merely that
their letters communicate only fragmentary meaning to us
because the symbols are sometimes private ones, because
many incidents referred to are otherwise unknown to us,
and because the master-key — Swift's attitude — conforms to
no familiar pattern. So few unchallengeable facts appear,
that Swift's behaviour from the time of his apparently definitive letter of 8 July 1713 down to the moment ten years later
when Vanessa's death rang down the curtain on the final
scene of the drama can be regarded from almost any point
of view suggested by the observer's temperament. It may
be said, however, that most dispassionate inquirers are ready
to accept the letter of 8 July 1713 as proof of Swift's physical
coldness then and at all future times. If this be the correct interpretation, the emotions excited by Vanessa become
a problem of emotions in which the physical element had
been cauterized. That in one way or another Swift was profoundly stirred by her is apparent throughout. When he
returned to London as dean of St. Patrick's, it was not to
hold himself at a distance from Vanessa but to establish a
new association with her upon terms which he defined and
to which she apparently consented. They had entered upon
a compact, and it was this which he proceeded to celebrate
in *Cadenus and Vanessa,* written at Windsor in the autumn
of 1713, in which, as in his letters, he spoke in words fraught
with meaning for Vanessa but ambiguous to all others.

At Letcombe some months later, when he knew that the day of his exile was fast approaching, he could again have dismissed her as he had seemed to do a year before in Ireland, but by this time her mother was dead and she and her sister Mary were grievously set upon by creditors. It was impossible to desert her at such a time; '. . . if you want to borrow any money,' he wrote, 'I would have you send to Mr. Barber or Ben Tooke, which you please, and let them know it, and the sum, and that I will stand bound for it, and send them my bond' (8 July). Unfortunately he could not thus befriend Vanessa without falsely encouraging her, and this at the moment when he was seeking to terminate this friendship against his permanent withdrawal to Ireland. Vanessa was querulous when he refused to address her in his letters with the 'dear' which he commonly bestowed on Tooke the publisher and Barber the printer. Apparently she disregarded his admonitions and visited or tried to visit him in his retreat. And finally, she announced that she and her sister had determined, for financial reasons, to move to Ireland. Swift could only warn her that by such a plan she could not hope to prolong their old relations:

If you are in Ireland while I am there I shall see you very seldom. It is not a place for any freedom, but where ever[y]thing is known in a week and magnified a hundred degrees. These are rigorous laws that must be passed through; but it is probable we may meet in London in winter, or if not, leave all to Fate, that seldom cares to humour our inclinations. I say all this out of the perfect esteem and friendship I have for you. (12 August.)

But Vanessa was not to be balked, and before the year's close had taken up her residence at Celbridge, a few miles out of Dublin. Only tragedy lay in store for her, only bitterness for the man whom she pursued with such frenzy. But however their story is to be read—and no one interpretation can be pressed with anything like insistence—it fills us with a great compassion.

6

BUT more important than any of the experiences which grew out of his work for the tory ministry or his intercourse

with friends was the effect produced by the utter wreck of
the political cause which in the course of four years he had
come to load with his entire store of intellectual and moral
values.   The Restoration was no greater shock to Milton
than was the whigs' assumption of power to Swift.   Rational
freedom had gone down in defeat before the forces of darkness; the ministry's subtleties and mystical ways, prevailing
over blunt common sense, had played into the enemy's
hands; private passions had hastened the catastrophe — Great
Britain now lay at the mercy of a faction which in short
time would permanently corrupt the will and reason of the
people.   Some years later, at the end of *An Enquiry into
the Behaviour of the Queen's last Ministry,* Swift wrote as
follows:

. . . abuses in administration may last much longer than politicians seem to be aware of; especially where some bold steps are
made to corrupt the very fountain of power and legislature: In
which case, as it may happen in some states, the whole body of
the people are drawn in, by their own supposed consent, to be
their own enslavers; and, where will they find a thread to wind
themselves out of this labyrinth?   Or, will they not rather wish
to be governed by arbitrary power, after the manner of other nations?   For whoever considers the course of the Roman empire
after Cæsar's usurpation, the long continuance of the Turkish
government, or the destruction of the Gothic balance in most
kingdoms of Europe, will easily see how controllable that maxim
is, that, *res nolunt diu malè administrari:* Because, as corruptions
are more natural to mankind than perfections, so they are more
likely to have a longer continuance.   For the vices of men, considered as individuals, are exactly the same when they are
moulded into bodies; nor otherwise to be withheld in their effects, than by good fundamental laws; in which, when any great
breaches are made, the consequence will be the same as in the
life of a particular man, whose vices are seldom known to end
but with himself.

It was not only Swift. who saw in the events of 1714 a
cutting of all the dikes which held in check the perversities
of human nature.   Arbuthnot wrote: 'I have an opportunity calmly and philosophically to consider that treasure
of vileness and baseness, that I always believed to be in the
heart of man; and to behold them exert their insolence and

baseness; every new instance, instead of surprising and griev-
ing me, as it does some of my friends, really diverts me, and
in a manner improves my theory. . .'   (To Swift, 12 August
1714.)   To see nothing but ignoble surrender in the gen-
eralized pessimism which Swift, like Arbuthnot, now embraced, is not only to forget his passionate conviction that
the victory of the whigs was the triumph of every selfish interest in the nation, but is also to overlook his ideological
background.   Unquestionably the immediate cause of the
preponderance of pessimism in Swift's work after 1714 is the
shock which he suffered — and from which he never fully
recovered — when the tory party went down in defeat, but
it is scarcely necessary to press the point that the events of
the last four years of the queen merely substantiated a view
of life and of man to which Swift was committed by his intellectual heritage, his moral realism, and his fierce intensity
of apprehension.   In defeat he became again the great
artist, giving consummate expression to the moral pessimism
of the age into which he had been born.

CHAPTER II
NON-CONTROVERSIAL LETTERS

1

THE products of Swift's pen during the four last years of Queen Anne's reign may be classified under seven heads: (1) controversial verses, (2) controversial prose pamphlets, (3) controversial articles in the *Examiner*, (4) historical papers, (5) purely literary contributions to the *Tatler* of Steele and the *Tatler* of Harrison, (6) two pamphlets, *A Proposal for Correcting, Improving, and Ascertaining the English Tongue* and *Mr. Collins's Discourse of Freethinking*, the first strictly non-political and the second of only indirect political import, (7) non-controversial verses. The present chapter is concerned only with those of Swift's writings which fall under the last three of these heads. As for his controversial verse and prose, his contributions to the *Examiner*, and his historical essays, enough has been said in the preceding chapter to indicate their general nature and something of their peculiar qualities. In thus distinguishing between the compositions animated by political interest and the pieces not so animated, there is no implication that the former are less interesting or rest upon a necessarily lower level of accomplishment; *A Short Character of His Ex. The Earl of Wharton* and *The Conduct of the Allies*, to take two examples from the political category, are masterpieces in their way, more significant in respect of the author's art than many of his purely belletristic productions.

Swift's first publication after his return to London in September 1710 was a paper printed by Steele in No. 230 of the *Tatler* (28 September 1710). His subject, which he developed with a firmness of touch which did not preclude a certain urbane grace and much humour, was the parlous state to which the English tongue was being reduced by a number of current 'corruptions.' He calls to Isaac Bickerstaff's attention the 'deplorable ignorance that for some years hath reigned among our English writers, the great depravity of our taste, and the continual corruption of our style,' in illustration whereof he copies out a letter he has lately received from a person highly accomplished in the present polite way of writing.

'Sir,

'I *cou'dn't* get the things you sent for all *about Town.*— I *thôt to ha'* come down myself, and then *I'd ha' brôut'um ;* but I *han't don't,* and I believe I *can't do't,* that's *pozz.— Tom* begins to *g'imself airs* because *he's* going with the *plenipo's.—* 'Tis said, the *French* King will *bamboozl' us agen,* which *causes many speculations.* The *Jacks,* and others of that *kidney,* are very *uppish,* and *alert upon't,* as you may see by their *phizz's.— Will Hazzard* has got the *hipps,* having lost *to the tune of* five hundr'd pound, *thô* he understands play very well, *nobody better.* He has promis't me upon *rep,* to leave off play ; but you know 'tis a weakness *he's* too apt to *give into, thô* he has as much wit as any man, *nobody more.* He has lain *incog* ever since.— The *mobb's* very quiet with us now.— I believe you *thôt* I *banter'd* you in my last like a *country put.—* I *sha'nt* leave Town this month, *&c.'*

In this specimen of modern wit are to be observed four kinds of impropriety. These are, first, the 'breaks' at the end of every sentence, quite meaningless but now regarded as a great refinement. Next are to be noted the current abbreviations and elisions, altogether of the Gothic strain and showing 'a natural tendency towards relapsing into barbarity, which delights in monosyllables, and uniting of mute consonants.' The third impropriety lies in the use of words like *banter, bamboozle, country put,* and *kidney,* altogether the invention of 'pretty fellows,' and the fourth in the choice of phrases now 'worn to rags by servile imitators.' All of these false refinements are to be fought first by argument and fair means, but these failing, the purity of the English tongue can only be preserved by Mr. Bickerstaff's assuming the authority of censor and condemning each new barbarism in an annual *index expurgatorius.*

This short essay on linguistic propriety Swift followed up a year and a half later with his much more pretentious *Proposal for Correcting, Improving and Ascertaining the English Tongue* (dated 22 February 1712 but not printed till May). The *Proposal* is a work of some importance, not merely because it contains Swift's most dogmatic utterances regarding language, but because it also shows how logically his rigid linguistic theories followed from his controlling beliefs. His perpetual interest in the state of the English tongue and his unremitting efforts to impose on it a single and clearly defined standard, evidence more than a finical purist and a dictatorial man of letters. To him the manner of using language was an unfailing indication of a nation's taste; 'corruptions' meant not only a dangerous decay of taste but a general recession from the high level of civilization, and while it was true that the laws of God and nature had decreed that this civilization must some day fall in ruins, it was meanwhile the duty of every enlightened man to prevent the premature victory of barbarism. In advocating, as he did in the *Proposal,* the establishment of an English Academy to guard the purity of the language by codifying it for all time, he was expressing in the clearest way his negative philosophy of history — change can only be decay. Our language is extremely imperfect — thus begins the argument of the *Proposal;* its daily improvements are by no means in proportion to its daily corruptions; the pretenders to polish and refine it have chiefly multiplied abuses and absurdities; in many instances it offends against every part of grammar. Now, there is 'no absolute necessity why any language should be perpetually changing.' It was during the period from the beginning of Queen Elizabeth's reign down to the Rebellion of 1642 that the English tongue received most improvement, but since then, what with the enthusiastic jargon of the Commonwealth saints followed by the licentiousness which entered with the Revolution, the corruptions have outnumbered the refinements: new and unauthorized words are foisted upon us by impressive dunces; the practice of abbreviating words, introduced by Restoration poets, has gained credit; spelling is rendered ridiculous by the erroneous opinion that we ought to spell exactly as we speak; the affected use of the newest phrases coined in the coffee-houses and gaming ordinaries is made fashionable by the young men of the universities who have a horror of pedantry and wish to show by any means that

they know men and manners;—in a word, not being a very
polite nation, we have a tendency to lapse into the barbarity
of those northern nations from whom we are descended.
Following this analysis comes the Proposal. Let such persons as are generally regarded as best qualified assemble at
appointed times after the example of the French Academy.
Their first task will be to throw many improper words out
of the language, to correct many, and to restore a certain
number long since antiquated but useful on account of their
energy and sound.

But what I have most at heart, is, that some method should be
thought on for ascertaining and fixing our language for ever,
after such alterations are made in it as shall be thought requisite.
For I am of opinion, it is better a language should not be wholly
perfect, than that it should be perpetually changing; and we
must give over at one time, or at length infallibly change for the
worse. . .

We of the present, with our scientific attitude towards
linguistic phenomena and our knowledge that speech, ever
in flux, exhibits multitudinous differences from era to era
and from locality to locality, have revolted against the concept handed down by the prescriptive grammarians of the
eighteenth century that there is a single, abiding standard
of correct usage. This revolt was long overdue, at least in
the United States, where pious purists found eager audiences
for their ill-informed generalities and for years continued
to lay down with never a challenge arbitrary laws which
destroyed our sense of idiom, extracted the last grain of salt
from our speech, and denied the propriety of age-old expressions. Now that the revolt is by way of establishing its
purpose, we shall not listen to Swift's philological pronouncements seriously and we have no need to be disturbed
by them. Writing as he did before prescriptive grammarians became the adherents of a dogma which living
philosophy had ceased to nourish, he serves to remind us
that originally this eighteenth-century attitude towards language was part of an ordered system of beliefs.

To return to Swift's literary contributions to the periodi-
cals. He made his final appearance in Steele's *Tatler* on

2 December 1710 when, aided by Rowe and Prior, he ridiculed in a short letter to Isaac Bickerstaff the new term *Great Britain,* which was coming into use as a result of the Union; the writer of the letter complies with the new usage to the extent of calling a Scotchman a North-, an Englishman a South-Briton, and of referring to a North-British mist and North-British collops.

In the following year Swift established his protégé Harrison in a new *Tatler,* and is said to have contributed six essays between January and March to this languishing periodical. These essays — it is possible to question Swift's authorship of several of them — must have been dashed off in odd moments in the midst of far more urgent duties, for they are of marked inferiority. The best of them are the two numbers (6 and 15 March 1711) devoted respectively to good manners and to the shameful conduct often accorded men of real wit by those who consider themselves superior by virtue of wealth.

There remain for consideration the non-political verses of this period — having glanced at *Mr. Collins's Discourse of Freethinking* in a previous chapter, we need not take it up here. The prose pieces which we have just reviewed, though not devoid of all interest, add little to our knowledge of Swift and nothing to his stature as an artist. His contemporaneous verse, on the other hand, is of major importance, by reason both of its extraordinary quality and of Swift's intensely personal themes. *A Description of a City Shower,* the Imitations of Horace's *Quinque dies* and *Hoc erat, Cadenus and Vanessa,* and *The Author upon Himself,* if not great poetry, are at any rate masterly compositions in the eighteenth-century familiar style.

A Description of a City Shower, which appeared on 17 October 1710 in Steele's *Tatler,* is companion to the earlier *Description of the Morning,* and like it was designed to parody current fashion, in this instance the use of the Drydenic triplet and alexandrine. The approaching storm is first described, and then are depicted the town scenes as the downpour drives the passers-by to shelter.

To shops in crowds the daggled females fly,
Pretend to cheapen goods, but nothing buy.
The Templar spruce, while every spout's
                              abroach,
Stays till 'tis fair, yet seems to call a
                              coach.
The tuck'd-up sempstress walks with
                              hasty strides,
While streams run down her oil'd umbrella's
                              sides.
Here various kinds, by various fortunes led,
Commence acquaintance underneath a shed.
Triumphant Tories, and desponding Whigs,
Forget their feuds, and join to save their
                              wigs.
Box'd in a chair the beau impatient sits,
While spouts run clattering o'er the roof
                              by fits,
And ever and anon with frightful din
The leather sounds ; he trembles from within.

But this splendid bit of realism is almost eclipsed by the
closing paragraph, where parody rides to triumph on a mag-
niloquent triplet and alexandrine :

               Now from all parts the swelling kennels flow,
And bear their trophies with them as they go :
Filth of all hues and odour, seem to tell
What street they sail'd from, by their sight and smell.
They, as each torrent drives with rapid force,
From Smithfield to St. Pulchre's shape their course,
And in huge confluence join'd at Snowhill ridge,
Fall from the conduit prone to Holborn bridge.
Sweeping from butcher's stalls, dung, guts, and
                              blood,
Drown'd puppies, stinking sprats, all drench'd in
                              mud,
Dead cats, and turnip-tops, come tumbling
                              down the flood.

A Town Eclogue, which was printed in Harrison's *Tatler*
for 13 March 1711 over the initials L.B., W.H., J.S., S.T.,
describes the unsavory dealings of Corydon, of Lincoln's Inn,
with a ribbon-girl of the Royal Exchange. Written, like

so many similar pieces of that day, to cast ridicule upon the pastoral, it misses fire and achieves only dullness.

Swift's Imitation of Horace's *Quinque dies,* entitled *Part of the Seventh Epistle of the First Book of Horace Imitated: and Address'd to a Noble Peer,* was written after his return to London in September 1713. At that moment he was in no happy frame of mind, outward appearances to the contrary. The cordiality with which he had been greeted by Oxford and the others as he rejoined the ministerial circle as dean of St. Patrick's was in bitterly ironic contrast with their previous hesitancies over his preferment, and even now, when their protestations of friendship seemed to deny any past disloyalty to him, they were withholding the grant of £1000 from the privy purse to defray the expenses of his installation as dean. These were the matters and this was the mood which Swift recorded in his Imitation of Horace, which must rank as one of his notable compositions in verse both because of the skill with which he bends the original to his own purposes, the vigour and compression of his lines, and the half-humorous, half-bitter tone which he succeeds in striking. Harley, we are told, caught his first glimpse of Swift as the latter was cheapening old authors at a book-stall near Whitehall, and promptly dispatched Erasmus Lewis to invite the doctor to dinner. Here the author gives us a magnificent portrait of himself; he was, we learn,

> A clergyman of special note
> For shunning those of his own coat;
> Which made his brethren of the gown
> Take care betimes to run him down:
> No libertine, nor over nice,
> Addicted to no sort of vice;
> Went where he pleas'd, said what he thought;
> Not rich, but owed no man a groat;
> In state opinions à la mode,
> He hated Wharton like a toad;
> Had given the faction many a wound,
> And libell'd all the junto round;
> Kept company with men of wit,
> Who often father'd what he writ:
> His works were hawk'd in ev'ry street,
> But seldom rose above a sheet:

> Of late, indeed, the paper-stamp
> Did very much his genius cramp ;
> And, since he could not spend his fire,
> He now intended to retire.

Repelling Lewis's overtures, he shortly afterwards, however, swallows the bait which the minister dangles before him and becomes Harley's man. The latter, to carry on the jest, takes Swift down to Windsor.

> Swift much admires the place and air,
> And longs to be a Canon there ;
> In summer round the Park to ride,
> In winter — never to reside.
> A Canon ! — that's a place too mean :
> No, doctor, you shall be a Dean. . .

And a dean Swift becomes, but before he is allowed to loll in his seat with his chapter round him, what vexations he must pass through — patents, instalments, first-fruits, tenths, chapter-treats ! When he next stands at Harley's gate, behold him a thousand pounds in debt, dirty, pale, thin, dressed in a rusty gown and an old wig. Here, for Harley, is the cream of the jest : is the dean, he asks, so intent upon investing his wealth shrewdly that he thus neglects himself ?

>   'Truce, good my lord, I beg a truce,'
> The doctor in a passion cry'd,
> 'Your raillery is misapply'd ;
> Experience I have dearly bought ;
> You know I am not worth a groat :
> But you resolved to have your jest,
> And 'twas a folly to contest ;
> Then, since you now have done your worst,
> Pray leave me where you found me first.'

To Lord Harley, on his Marriage followed shortly after the Imitation. The occasion of these new verses was the marriage of Oxford's son to the daughter of the duke of Newcastle. Swift's celebration of the event was wholly voluntary, but that fact did not raise his lines above the pedestrian level.

Cadenus and Vanessa, regarded by some as the finest of Swift's metrical pieces, cannot be dated with certainty.

After its publication in 1726 Swift stated that he had written it at Windsor in 1712, but in view of the fact that he was not Decanus — whence the anagram Cadenus — until the following year, its composition is usually assigned to the latter months of 1713. Of this remarkable work, one thing can be said with absolute assurance — its subtle craftsmanship is the result of a concern far in excess of that evidenced in any of Swift's other metrical compositions. Whence this concern arose is a question that each must answer for himself, but there is no denying its presence : it is expressed in the involved design of the piece and in the elaborate care with which the enveloping story is handled; it is seen directly in the extraordinary passages in which the words of Cadenus and Vanessa are given and their thoughts analysed. Excitement does not describe it. It is rather a fascination by the theme, a determination to explore a situation, to define and sum up.

In *Cadenus and Vanessa* we have an interlude enacted by two human characters preceded and followed by a fable of Venus and the Court of Love. The parts are interwoven with too great skill : that is, the scene between Cadenus and Vanessa is given a dependence upon the mythological story which it need not have and which diverts attention from self-contained drama of unusual character. The interlude gets under way when Cupid, to avenge his mother, determines that Vanessa shall fall in love with her forty-four year old teacher. He shoots the arrow into her heart and then withdraws, leaving the two mortals to experience the consequences undisturbed by gods or men. Cadenus is unaware of the change which has now come over their relations; understanding nothing of love, he continues to regard his pupil with fatherly interest, and is disturbed only by Vanessa's distraction and her wandering thoughts. At length he concludes that his instruction has grown offensive to her and that the time has come for them to break off. When he speaks his mind, Vanessa has too great a scorn of feminine behaviour to give way to tears; instead, she declares her love in terms which Cadenus has unwittingly taught her :

> Had he employ'd his time so long
> To teach her what was right and wrong;
> Yet could such notions entertain
> That all his lectures were in vain?
> She own'd the wandering of her thoughts;
> But he must answer for her faults.
> She well remember'd to her cost,
> That all his lessons were not lost.
> Two maxims she could still produce,
> And sad experience taught their use;
> That virtue, pleased by being shown,
> Knows nothing which it dares not own;
> Can make us without fear disclose
> Our inmost secrets to our foes;
> That common forms were not design'd
> Directors to a noble mind.
> Now, said the nymph, to let you see
> My actions with your rules agree;
> That I can vulgar forms despise,
> And have no secrets to disguise;
> I knew, by what you said and writ,
> How dangerous things were men of wit;
> You caution'd me against their charms,
> But never gave me equal arms;
> Your lessons found the weakest part,
> Aim'd at the head, but reach'd the heart.

Here is the psychological climax of the interlude. The full shock has now been received by both characters; from this point on the drama centres in their reactions, in their efforts to reorganize themselves. The man and woman debate with each other, the man debates with himself, and from time to time the voice of public opinion is heard in a whisper. Shame, disappointment, guilt, surprise are Cadenus's first emotions; until the moment of her declaration he had never sensed her as a woman, aware only of her mind. Look at the situation from the world's point of view—how, if her passion is sincere, can he clear himself of the inevitable inferences? Speaking aloud for the first time since her startling disclosure, he seeks to misconstrue her meaning; she rallies well, he tells her, and from her serious air one might believe that she spoke not in jest but in earnest. Vanessa will not lose her advantage by pausing to disclaim histrionics, but follows up the attack by showing that her passion for him springs from the reason he has taught her and the love of learning, wit, and wisdom which he has implanted in her mind. There is silence while Cadenus dives into his own thoughts. She has, he acknowledges, scored a victory over him; her arguments cannot kindle love in him, but they show such command of reason that as tutor he can only capitulate to his aptest pupil. His emotions have now undergone a change, which he realizes immediately. Guilt and surprise have now given way to pride — to be preferred before a crowd of beaux! Fully aware at last of what he has felt from the first but has tried to conceal from himself, he must now justify this pride. Why, after all, should a brilliant girl of judicious taste not choose a man of his great merit? The wave of humorous self-contempt subsides, and he searches for an attitude which will express his feelings honestly. What is love? That compound of pleasure and pain where the hot and the cold, the sharp and the sweet are continually mingled he is incapable of experiencing. But friendship he can offer —

> A constant, rational delight,
> On virtue's basis fix'd to last. . .

He speaks and Vanessa hears him out, with an expression not described but which we may imagine as an enigmatic smile. The pupil, it seems, must now become tutor. Has he not taught her to despise all arguments in the lofty style, to contemn all sublime conceits? He has fairly abdicated the throne, and must now sit at her feet while she instructs him in matters of the heart.

> But what success Vanessa met,
> Is to the world a secret yet.
> Whether the nymph, to please her swain,
> Talks in a high romantic strain;
> Or whether he at last descends
> To act with less seraphic ends;
> Or to compound the business, whether
> They temper love and books together;
> Must never to mankind be told,
> Nor shall the conscious Muse unfold.

So˙ ends the interlude. To its full meaning only two people have held the key. But amid much which is uncertain one thing shows clearly — that quality of Swift's mind which held Vanessa fascinated and once caused her to write that no human creature was capable of guessing at his thoughts because never anyone living thought like him.

It was while in retirement at Letcombe in the weeks preceding the queen's death that Swift wrote both his Imitation of Horace's *Hoc erat — Imitation of Part of the Sixth Satire of the Second Book of Horace* — and the verses entitled *The Author upon Himself*. If the former is the finer achievement artistically, its matter, having to do with Swift at the height of his influence with the tory ministry, has nothing of the biographical value of the statements set forth in *The Author upon Himself*. In this latter piece Swift is dealing directly with the evil legend which has pursued him since his rise to prominence and with those powerful enemies who through delusion or out of revenge have sought his ruin. There is no reason for believing that the account which he gives here of the events which resulted in his exclusion from preferment in England and his banishment to St. Patrick's is not substantially accurate. His defence against the calumny and misrepresentation which he has suffered is peculiarly forcible, dwelling as it does on the single point that no man in holy orders can hope to escape detraction if he is a wit. He opens with a burst of indignation at the duchess of Somerset, Archbishop Sharpe, the queen, and the host of clergymen who have cried him up as an infidel:

> By an old — pursued,
> A crazy prelate, and a royal prude;
> By dull divines, who look with envious eyes
> On ev'ry genius that attempts to rise;
> And pausing o'er a pipe, with doubtful nod,
> Give hints, that poets ne'er believe in God.
> So clowns on scholars as on wizards look,
> And take a folio for a conj'ring book.
>   Swift had the sin of wit, no venial crime;
> Nay, 'twas affirm'd, he sometimes dealt in rhyme;
> Humour and mirth had place in all he writ;
> He reconcil'd divinity and wit:

16

> He moved and bow'd, and talk'd with too much
>   grace;
> Nor show'd the parson in his gait or face;
> Despised luxurious wines and costly meat;
> Yet still was at the tables of the great;
> Frequented lords; saw those that saw the queen;
> At Child's or Truby's, never once had been;
> Where town and country vicars flock in tribes,
> Secured by numbers from the laymen's gibes;
> And deal in vices of the graver sort,
> Tobacco, censure, coffee, pride, and port.

His entrance into politics is then described; his favour at the hands of Harley; his influence, great as a duke's.   With rapid strokes the high points of the campaign against him are sketched in: the earl of Nottingham and the whigs inflame the lords and commons against him; the archbishop of Canterbury is alarmed by *A Tale of a Tub*—'A dang'rous treatise writ against the spleen'—and sends Archbishop Sharpe to warn the queen against the author; the duchess of Somerset, infuriated by his reproaches, instils her venom into the royal ear; in revenge for *The Public Spirit of the Whigs* the duke of Argyle harries him and a price is set on his head.   Then, after a brief period of triumph, his withdrawal from the scene:

> By faction tired, with grief he waits awhile,
> His great contending friends to reconcile;
> Performs what friendship, justice, truth require:
> What could he more, but decently retire?

A few weeks after writing these verses he was in Ireland. The four tremendous years were but a dream, and he who never before had flinched shrank back in terror from the reality now brought to pass.

BOOK IV

1714 – 1726

BIOGRAPHICAL SYNOPSIS

1714-1726

Aug. 1714 :	Returned to Ireland and into seclusion at the deanery.
1716 :	According to gossip, married Stella in Bishop Ashe's garden at Clogher.
1718 :	Made the acquaintance of Sheridan and Delany.
1720 :	The awakening of the old powers : *The Progress of Poetry, The Progress of Beauty, A Letter of Advice to a Young Poet, A Letter to a Young Gentleman, lately enter'd into Holy Orders ; Gulliver's Travels* probably begun ; publication of the first Irish tract, *A Proposal for the Universal Use of Irish Manufacture.*
2 June, 1723 :	Vanessa died, Swift setting out on his journey through the south of Ireland directly thereafter.
1724 :	Swift's agitation through the *Drapier's Letters* against Wood's coinage.
26 Aug. 1725 :	Proclamation in Ireland of the withdrawal of Wood's coinage.
Latter part of 1725 :	*Gulliver's Travels* finished.
March-Aug. 1726 :	In England again, visiting old friends.
28 Oct. 1726 :	*Gulliver's Travels* published.

CHAPTER I

THE FIRST YEARS OF EXILE

1

THERE was not a whig in Dublin — now a city of exultant whigs — who did not feel a savage joy at the powerless state to which the once mighty champion of Oxford's ministry had now been reduced. But Swift was indifferent alike to the coldness of those who had formerly professed friendship and to the imprecations of his declared enemies; his thoughts were not in Dublin at all, but in England with Oxford and Bolingbroke and Arbuthnot. He was not without hope that the leaders of his party would, under George I, retain some measure of power in the new ministry. The rout of the tories shortly after the king's arrival in England ended that delusion, and it was then that he gave way to the utter discouragement which he expressed in the verses *In Sickness*, written in October.

His friends at this time were but a handful : Archdeacon Walls, Dr. Raymond of Trim, his vicar Worrall, and his curate Warburton. His ecclesiastical superior, Archbishop King of Dublin, had been none too cordial since Lindsay's appointment to the primacy; now, swept away by the partisanship of the hour, he looked upon Swift as someone poisonous and suspect, to be baited as a dean and kept under close watch as a citizen. 'You are to understand,' Swift wrote to Pope after almost a year's residence at the deanery,

that I live in the corner of a vast unfurnished house. My family consists of a steward, a groom, a helper in the stable, a footman, and an old maid, who are all at board wages, and when I do not dine abroad, or make an entertainment, which last is very rare, I eat a mutton-pie, and drink half a pint of wine. My amusements are defending my small dominions against the Archbishop, and endeavouring to reduce my rebellious choir. *Preditur haec inter misero lux.* (28 June 1715.)

A little more than half of life, said Machiavelli, is under the control of fate, a little less than half can be moulded by resolute will. The observation applies exactly to Swift's career in Ireland from 1714 on. So great were his recuperative powers, so indomitable his will to command the situation regardless of the overpowering advantage which fate appeared to hold, that at length he achieved a seemingly complete victory by bending to his own purpose every circumstance not ruled by forces unalterable by moral energy. But it was not in the course of a day or of a year that he regained his poise. The successive shocks occasioned by the ministerial disruption, by the queen's death, and by the destruction of the tories left him so broken in spirit that it was five years before he fully overcame his neurotic depression and again faced the world with an air of mastery. In the meantime, however, he had been emerging by degrees from retirement at the deanery; his circle of friends had been greatly enlarged, and their country residences offered welcome escape from Dublin. By 1718, though not yet wholly rehabilitated, he was once again a social man, enlivening with gaiety and wit every group into which he came.

One of the first of his new friends was Knightley Chetwode, a gentleman of unshaken tory sentiment, who possessed two country residences, one at Martry, a few miles to the north of Laracor, and the other — Woodbrooke — in the Queen's county. Then came the Grattans and the Rochforts. There were seven sons in the Grattan family : the eldest was Henry, grandfather of the Irish patriot; of the younger brothers Robert was in holy orders and at this time held a prebend in St. Patrick's. Their widowed mother lived at Belcamp, where Swift was a frequent visitor. He was likewise well known at Gaulstown, the residence of the Rochforts — ex-Chief Baron Robert Rochfort, his sons George and John, and George's wife. Others whom Swift came to number among his friends or with whom he renewed acquaintance were Peter Ludlow of Ardsallagh, Robert Cope of Loughgall, Bishop Ashe, and Bishop Stearne. Early in 1718 the names of Sheridan and Delany, henceforth associated with the dean's, were added to the list. The Reverend Thomas Sheridan, father of Swift's biographer and grandfather of the dramatist, was in 1718 a young but eminent

schoolmaster in Dublin. The Reverend Patrick Delany was
still a junior fellow of Trinity College, Dublin. And always,
of course, there were Stella and Mrs. Dingley. Swift's Irish
correspondence of this time revolves about these and less
intimate friends, while his personal verses are for the most
part *jeux d'esprit* growing out of social incidents.

During the months immediately following his return to
Ireland, when illness and depression lay heavy upon him and
he forbore all company save that of his closest friends, his
mind turned constantly to England. As he worked intermit-
tently at *An Enquiry into the Behaviour of the Queen's last
Ministry* the past lived again. Of present affairs in London
he had news in the letters which came from Bolingbroke,
Arbuthnot, and others. But correspondence with English
tories, however innocent such correspondence might be, involved a certain amount of danger, for the present agents
of the government regarded any communication between
persons associated with the late ministry as presumptive evidence of a plot to bring in the pretender. In June 1715 two
letters addressed to Swift, one by the duke of Ormond and
the other by John Barber, were seized by the authorities at
Dublin and transmitted to Archbishop King and the earl of
Kildare as acting lords justices. The archbishop was so over-
joyed that Swift had at last been delivered into his hands that
he overlooked the trivial nature of the messages and had the
letters forwarded immediately to the secretary of state in
charge of Irish affairs and to Sunderland, the lord-lieutenant.
There was even some talk of putting the dean in close con-
finement.

In the midst of such humiliations Swift learned that the
commons had voted the impeachment of Oxford, Bolingbroke, and Ormond. The latter two fled. Oxford alone
stayed to face his accusers, and on 9 July 1715 was committed
to the Tower to await trial. A year before, Swift had offered
to attend Oxford when the latter had been dismissed by the
queen; this offer he now renewed (19 July). In 1716 he
addressed to the former lord treasurer, who was still in the
Tower, an Imitation of Horace's Ode *Augustam amice
pauperiem,* and upon Oxford's release he expressed for a

third time his readiness to abandon all plans of his own were his presence desired by his friend (9 July 1717).

In 1716 Archbishop King's efforts to worry his enemy at St. Patrick's took a different form.   He now succeeded, working through Theophilus Bolton, later archbishop of Cashel, but now chancellor of St. Patrick's, in stirring up trouble within the chapter and heaping annoyances upon the dean. Swift turned to his friend Atterbury for advice.   'I am here at the head of three and twenty dignitaries and prebendaries,' he wrote to the bishop, 'whereof the major part, differing from me in principles, have taken a fancy to oppose me upon all occasions in the Chapter-house ; and a ringleader among them has presumed to debate my power of proposing, or my negative, though it is what the deans of this Cathedral have possessed for time immemorial, and what has never been once disputed' (24 March 1716).   Atterbury replied, not very helpfully, and Swift was left to devise his own method of combating the archbishop.

Happily, the relations between Swift and King were to undergo a gratifying change in the near future.   Before their enmity gave way to common purpose, however, the archbishop found yet another opportunity of striking at Swift.   His previous thrusts had been merely annoying ; this time he drew blood.   Towards the end of 1716 it was rumoured that Bolingbroke had secured a pardon and was returning to England.   With sly malice the archbishop, who happened to be in London at the moment, penned a long letter to Swift, at the very end of which he added these words : 'We have a strong report, that my Lord Bolingbroke will return here, and be pardoned ; certainly it must not be for nothing.   I hope he can tell no ill story of you' (22 November 1716).   To Swift this was an unendurable insult. At the seizure of his letters he had but shrugged his shoulders ; the incitement of his chapter against him he had accepted as a more or less legitimate act of war ; but this cruel implication, first, that his past was treasonable, and secondly, that one of his closest friends would be ignoble enough to turn informer cut him to the heart.   His riposte found its way through King's guard :

. . . I am surprised to think your Grace could talk, or act, or correspond with me for some years past, while you must needs believe me a most false and vile man; declaring to you on all occasions my abhorrence of the Pretender, and yet privately engaged with a Ministry to bring him in, and therefore warning me to look to myself, and prepare my defence against a false brother, coming over to discover such secrets as would hang me. (16 December 1716.)

In this year — 1716 — was enacted, if at all, that strange scene in the garden at Clogher, where gossip has it that Bishop Ashe united Swift and Stella in meaningless matrimony. Despite all that has been brought forward in proof of the marriage, it is significant that no one has ever suggested a really plausible motive for it. Both Swift and Stella lived with superb pride by the code of rational conduct. If they broke this code to participate in a secret ceremony that had no significance, the explanation must be sought not in the realm of reason but of nonsense.

It was in 1718, as has already been said, that Swift became acquainted with Sheridan and Delany. Both of these younger men were witty and overflowing with good spirits and undoubtedly had a great deal to do with the awakening about this time of the dean's long dormant energies. Soon Swift was engaging with great relish in a war of verse with a number of friends, headed by Sheridan and Delany, and his old intensity began to show itself in the bagatelle. His position in Dublin, furthermore, had undergone a marked change since the day of his unhappy arrival in 1714. Even Archbishop King had relented, and the renewed friendship between them was shortly to be sealed by Swift in his *Ode to Archbishop King*. This recession of the bitter partisanship which had previously overwhelmed Swift was the result of the new patriotism which was beginning to weld the English in Ireland into united opposition to England. Of this patriotic party Archbishop King was one of the most energetic leaders, and he was quick to recognize in the dean of St. Patrick's a passionate ally. Although Swift was not to fire his opening broadside at the English interest until 1720, when — probably in May — he published *A Proposal for the*

Universal Use of Irish Manufacture, we have it on Delany's authority that the 'subjects of which the *Proposal* treats had for a considerable time been the topic of Swift's conversation and even of his sermons.'

When the *Proposal* appeared, Swift was himself again, his energy and intensity as great as in the days of Oxford's ministry. This was at once reflected in his verses. While he did not cease to banter Sheridan in trifling rhymes, to exchange thrusts with Delany, or to address Stella and others in occasional pieces, he no longer confined his verses to subjects of immediate social interest. *The Progress of Poetry, The Progress of Beauty,* and *The Description of an Irish Feast* (all 1720), although they fail to rise to the level of many of his earlier metrical compositions, do indicate an unmistakable renewal of the artistic impulse. Turning to literary prose, he scored two brilliant triumphs in *A Letter of Advice to a Young Poet* and *A Letter to a Young Gentleman, lately enter'd into Holy Orders* (both 1720).

But it was in the avalanche of pamphlets and satiric verses which as an Irish patriot he now let loose that we recognize that crushing power of intellect and invective which had once made the author of the *Examiner* and *The Conduct of the Allies* such a dreaded antagonist. The tory cause existed now only in the minds of a few political outcasts, but the cause of human liberty as maintained by the English in Ireland against tyrannical legislation and a ruthless administrative policy had just begun to glow. With all his might Swift threw himself into the struggle, to achieve before he was through a far nobler victory than any he might have won for Oxford and the tories. The campaign opened with the appearance of a pamphlet which rang with a tone hitherto unheard in Ireland. The government promptly took action against the printer of *A Proposal for the Universal Use of Irish Manufacture,* and in so doing increased immeasurably the effectiveness of the dean's propaganda. Swift now pressed forward irresistibly, issuing tracts and satiric verses on the bursting of the South Sea bubble, on the proposed National Bank, and on general conditions in Ireland. For four years this went on. Then, in 1724, the Drapier made his first, dramatic appearance in print, and even Walpole and the English privy council, in the past serenely unaware of Ireland save as a colony to be bled white in the interests of England, took notice. The second and third *Drapier's Letters* followed. The climax came in October with the issuance — at the moment when the new lord-lieutenant, sent over to take command of the disturbance, was landing in Dublin — of *Letter No. IV*, better known as *A Letter to the Whole People of Ireland*. For the discovery of the author of this 'wicked and malicious pamphlet' a reward of £300 was offered, but though there was not a soul in the entire city ignorant of the fact that the Drapier was dean of St. Patrick's, not a person could be induced to lodge official information with the government. The battle to force the withdrawal of Wood's detested coinage was practically won.

Between the tory journalist and the Drapier there is one great difference. Whereas the man who supported Oxford and drove back the opponents of the peace had but passing concern for anything which did not pertain to events of the hour, the Irish patriot found time to contemplate the universal aspects of human nature. *Gulliver's Travels* was not published until 28 October 1726, but it seems that by 1720 Swift was at work upon it. At least it is certain that by April of the following year he had set forth upon his imaginary voyages (Letter to Charles Ford, 15 April 1721), and on 14 August 1725 he wrote to Ford that he had finished the satire. One is prone to think of *Gulliver's Travels* as the product of otherwise unoccupied years. As a matter of fact, it was written in the very midst of the campaign against the English interest.

Swift's correspondence during this period of agitation has little of the historical interest attaching to the letters of 1710-1714. In the days of tory supremacy there had been two people — Stella and Archbishop King — whose eagerness to know all that was taking place in London had called forth from Swift the liveliest of résumés. In the 1720's, on the

other hand, his correspondents in Ireland knew quite as
much as he of what passed in Dublin, while his friends
in England would only have been bored by regular reports
from the provinces.   Swift's letters of this time, therefore,
are principally taken up with personal matters.   Perhaps the
most interesting letter is that which he wrote to Pope on
10 January 1722.   It is in effect an *apologia pro vita sua,*
in which he not only justifies his political past but indicates
something of the future course which he feels compelled to
take.   He begins with his retirement to Berkshire and his
composition of *Some Free Thoughts upon the Present State
of Affairs,* touching rapidly upon the queen's death, his return to Ireland, and his subsequent life of seclusion.   He
mentions his recent discourse 'to persuade the wretched
people to wear their own manufactures instead of those from
England,' and describes the extraordinary efforts of the chief
justice to browbeat a jury into returning a verdict against
the printer of the tract.   Then he turns to his own defence,
mentioning first his persistent efforts while close to the tory
ministry to protect whigs like Addison, Congreve, Rowe, and
Steele, and coming at length to the principles which he professed 'in the time of her late glorious Majesty' and which
since then he has never contradicted 'by any action, writing,
or discourse.'   He has always declared himself against a
popish successor to the crown.   The principle of revolution
he has consistently held to mean 'that whenever those evils
which usually attend and follow a violent change of government, were not in probability so pernicious as the grievance
we suffer under a present power, then the public good will
justify such a revolution.'   At all times he has professed a
mortal antipathy against standing armies in time of peace.
The institution of annual parliaments he has always looked
upon as the foundation of liberty.   'I ever abominated that
scheme of politics, now about thirty years old, of setting up a
moneyed interest in opposition to the landed; for I conceived, there could not be a truer maxim in our government
than this, that the possessors of the soil are the best judges
of what is for the advantage of the kingdom.'   Lastly, he has

at all times opposed the suspension, even in times of emer-
gency, of those laws upon which the individual's liberty depends, for it is a practice which leads to the infamous
tyrannies of the dictator.

Much of this exposition of controlling principles is, it
must be realized, two-edged, for in defining the beliefs which
he had maintained in the reign of Queen Anne he was marshalling them against Walpole and the present whig régime
— thus, the suspension of the laws which insure liberty had
reference directly to the suspension of the Habeas Corpus
Act in Ireland in 1716 and indirectly to all of Walpole's
high-handed methods.   But it was the principle of the
landed interest before the moneyed which was to serve as
his favourite weapon against Hanoverian whiggism.   Like
Pope and Bolingbroke and Pulteney, who in a few years were
to take the field against the political philosophy which had
flourished since the queen's death, Swift saw in the domination of the whigs the unholy triumph of the commercial
spirit, the defeat of squirearchy, and the gradual destruction
of rational political liberty.

In 1723 Swift's private life was overcast by black clouds —
he and Vanessa had quarrelled and a few months later — on
2 June 1723 — Vanessa died.   What had taken place between
them remains a secret, nor is there any way of knowing what
emotions tore at Vanessa's heart or racked the man whom
she had pursued so desperately.   The gossips had many
circumstantial stories to relate, but Vanessa carried her history with her to the grave and Swift concealed whatever he
felt — hatred, compassion, or remorse — behind a bitter,
proud silence.

In the autumn of 1714 Vanessa, disregarding Swift's admonitions, had come over to Ireland with her younger sister
Mary and had taken up residence at Celbridge.   It was the
last thing that Swift desired, and apparently he laid down
at once the most stringent regulations governing visiting and
correspondence.   Of the letters which passed between them
from the autumn of 1714 down to May 1719 we have eight,[1]
and from these the only conclusion which can be drawn is

that Swift was doing everything in his power to hold her off. He was constantly pleading the fear of gossip, writing on one occasion as follows :

> This morning a woman who does business for me told me she heard I was in —— with one ——, naming you, and twenty particulars, that little master and I visited you, and that the Archbishop did so ; and that you had abundance of wit, etc. I ever feared the tattle of this nasty town, and told you so ; and that was the reason why I said to you long ago that I would see you seldom when you were in Ireland. And I must beg you to be easy if for some time I visit you seldomer, and not in so particular a manner. (? End of 1714.)

Their final years of correspondence are represented by twenty letters which have been preserved, the earliest to be assigned to 1719-1720, the last written by Swift on 7 and 8 August 1722. There is not such another sequence of letters in the English language. The emotions excited in the reader fall into no pattern, for in the scene at which he is allowed to gaze there is no shaping purpose, nor do the two characters have recourse to the illusion of order and justice. It is unrelieved, undisguised reality. When Vanessa's passion breaks out of all bounds Swift resorts to petty concessions. She may, he tells her, address him as Cad —, the dash to signify what cannot in safety be written in a letter. At the same time he counsels rational restraint and even recommends exercise. Then, some time after 8 August 1722, a definite break occurred between them. Highly coloured stories to account for this rupture were told by Swift's earlier biographers, according to whom Vanessa heard rumours of the marriage to Stella and wrote to Swift — some say to Stella — asking if the report were true. Swift thereupon rode out to Celbridge, strode into the room, and transfixing Vanessa with a deadly glance, threw the letter upon the table and departed in silence. This blow was too much for Vanessa ; she sank rapidly, revoked a will in Swift's favour, and died shortly afterwards. The only indisputable facts are these : Vanessa died on 2 June 1723; on 1 May she had made a will in which she disregarded Swift entirely, naming as her chief beneficiaries Berkeley, the future bishop, then dean of Dro-

more, and one Robert Marshall.   (There is every reason to
believe that Vanessa was striking at Swift through the terms
of this will, and that she furthermore directed Marshall to
publish at her death her correspondence with Swift and
Cadenus and Vanessa.)   On 11 May Swift was writing to
a friend that he intended to make a southern journey that
summer, and directly after Vanessa's death he set out with
every appearance of haste.   He did not return to Dublin
until the autumn, having in the meantime travelled as far
as Skull, in the extreme south-west of Ireland, returning by
way of Clonfert.   It would appear that well before Vanessa's
death Swift had sensed the approach of a storm and that he
wished Stella out of Dublin when it broke—in any case,
Stella and Mrs. Dingley were guests of Charles Ford at
Woodpark through the entire summer, probably from April.
This visit of Stella's was the occasion of two metrical pieces
by Swift, *Stella's Distress on the 3ᵈ fatal day of Octobʳ 1723,*
—this being the day of her return to Dublin,—and the lines
beginning, 'Don Carlos in a merry Spight.'²

The only aftermath of this tragedy was the publication,
doubtless by Marshall, of *Cadenus and Vanessa* in 1726,
when Swift was visiting his old friends in England.   Warned
that the verses were on the point of being made public, he
merely expressed indifference and took no steps to prevent
their circulation.   Not only was Swift unconscious of anything to his discredit in this composition, but we know that
of Vanessa's executors Berkeley was of the opinion that there
was nothing in the piece which reflected upon Swift and that
the letters cast discredit upon Vanessa alone.   If Swift spoke
out in his own defence, it was only in the verses *On Censure,*
the date of which—*ca.* 1727—suggests that they were written
apropos of the publication of *Cadenus and Vanessa* :

> Yet whence proceeds this weight we lay
> On what detracting people say !
> For let mankind discharge their tongues
> In venom, till they burst their lungs,
> Their utmost malice cannot make
> Your head, or tooth, or finger ache ;
> Nor spoil your shape, distort your face,
> Or put one feature out of place ;

> Nor will you find your fortune sink
> By what they speak or what they think ;
> Nor can ten hundred thousand lies
> Make you less virtuous, learn'd, or wise.
>   The most effectual way to balk
> Their malice, is — to let them talk.

In 1724 the pall which the closing episodes of the Vanessa affair had cast over Swift was thrown aside as the aroused Drapier took up arms against the English interest. The success of his campaign is to be measured not alone by its political results — the withdrawal of Wood's halfpence, and the emergence for the first time in Ireland's history of a common cause — but by the adoration in which the dean was henceforth held by a grateful people. He was now a national hero, his person sacred, his word law; his slightest act was recorded in popular chronicle, and endless myths — the despair of the biographer — attached themselves to his name. Lord Carteret, despatched to Ireland to quell the tumult which had broken lose in 1724, proclaimed the reward for information against the Drapier, but there his zeal as lord-lieutenant ended, and before many months had gone by he was entertaining Swift at Dublin Castle and Swift in turn was playing host to Lady Carteret. His credit with the lord-lieutenant Swift had no idea of using to his own advantage, but he did seek the advancement of his friends. Sheridan was one of those who profited, for in July 1725 he was presented by Lord Carteret to the living of Rincurran in the county of Cork, his institution taking place on 19 July. Shortly afterwards, however, a comic disaster blighted poor Sheridan's chances of further consideration from his majesty's government. He was still in Cork when the anniversary of George I's accession came round. By a series of fantastic coincidences it was Sunday, Sheridan was unexpectedly called upon to preach, and the only sermon which he had by him was on the text 'Sufficient unto the day is the evil thereof.' Not perceiving the incongruity of such a text on such a day, Sheridan began to preach, when from the congregation there arose a general murmur. The scandalous affair was of course reported up and down the country, and Richard Tighe is said to have ridden post haste from Cork to Dublin to lodge information with the lord-lieutenant, who was forced to forbid Sheridan's appearance at Dublin Castle.   Swift sent his friend to *Gulliver's Travels* for consolation :

It is indeed against common sense to think, that you should choose such a time, when you had received a favour from the Lord Lieutenant, and had reason to expect more, to discover your disloyalty in the pulpit.   But what will that avail ?   Therefore sit down and be quiet, and mind your business as you should do, and contract your friendships, and expect no more from man than such an animal is capable of, and you will every day find my description of Yahoos more resembling. (To Sheridan, 11 September 1725.)

But it is to be observed that while he prescribed resignation to the victim, Swift himself rose up in fury against the informer Tighe, whom he proceeded to castigate in satiric verse of unbounded virulence.

For several years Swift had been talking about revisiting his friends in England.   It was probably his desire to arrange for the publication of *Gulliver's Travels*, now finished, which finally determined him to make the journey. He crossed early in March 1726 and by the middle of the month was in London, taking lodgings 'in Bury Street, next door to the Royal Chair.'   Here Pope spent two days with him, and then Arbuthnot appeared, to take the dean a fortnight's 'course through the town with Lord Chesterfield, Mr. Pulteney, etc.'   Later there was a visit with Bolingbroke at Dawley, near Uxbridge, and then Swift took up his abode at Twickenham, where he was Pope's guest until his departure for Dublin in August.

What with conviviality, politics, and literature the time went quickly.   At this moment the court of the prince and princess of Wales was the sole rallying point for discontented spirits, and it was only to be expected that such a notorious rebel as the dean of St. Patrick's should pay his respects there.   It was doubtless for the purpose of enlisting support for the opposition that William Pulteney had descended upon Swift during the latter's first days in town.

But the Irish patriot proved a shy bird, and it was not until Princess Caroline had several times requested to see him that he presented himself, with the remark that having sent for a wild boy from Germany — this rarity, said to have been imported from a German forest, was then the talk of London — she doubtless had a curiosity to see a wild dean from Ireland. It was at this time that Swift also made the acquaintance of Mrs. Howard, afterwards countess of Suffolk, who was the prince of Wales's mistress and lady-in-waiting to the princess.

His reception by the princess of Wales attracted little attention. What caused wide comment was his conversations with Walpole. Early in April Swift and some of his friends dined with Sir Robert — at the latter's invitation, according to Swift. Later the dean requested a private interview, which took place on 27 April and was reported in detail in a letter sent by Swift to Lord Peterborough on the following day. The discussion, we learn from this letter, was confined to Irish affairs and was, from Swift's point of view, entirely unsatisfactory. Rumour said at once that Swift had offered to capitulate in return for preferment in England, but there seems no reason to doubt that his only purpose in approaching Walpole was to set forth the plight of Ireland. True enough, three months later Swift wrote to Sheridan of an offer of a settlement in England 'within twelve miles of London, and in the midst of my friends.' He added: 'But I am too old for new schemes, and especially such as would bridle me in my freedoms and liberalities.' It would seem, however, that such an offer came from a friend and the sacrifice of freedoms and liberalities referred to a surrender of his privileges as dean of St. Patrick's and not to his abjuration of political principles.

But when the wits foregathered politics could not hold first place, and when Gay put in an appearance the Muse trailed along. Swift's *Advice to the Grub-street Verse Writers*, his piece entitled *To Charles Mordaunt, Earl of Peterborough*, and several lesser compositions in verse seem to have been the direct outcome of this visit to England, while the pieces entitled *On Reading Dr. Young's Satire, A Love Poem from a Physician to His Mistress, On Censure,* and *The Furniture of a Woman's Mind* are to be referred either to this first visit or to the one made in 1727. Nor was his host at Twickenham idle, for the *Dunciad* was now taking form and it was either in 1726 or the following year, when Swift was again a guest at Pope's villa, that Pope revealed something of his satiric schemes. Also to be discussed was the joint *Miscellany* which Pope and Swift were projecting, the first two volumes of which were eventually published on 24 June 1727.

The most important business of all, however, Swift held back until the very last. It was only after he had left Twickenham and was spending a few final days in London with Gay that he set in motion the elaborate machinery which he and Pope had devised to insure the anonymous publication of *Gulliver's Travels.* Their plot owed something, doubtless, to Pope's innate love of the stratagem, and something to the desire of the entire group at Twickenham to heighten the fun of Gulliver's first appearance before the world, but it was chiefly a device on Swift's part to enable him to disclaim the authorship of the satire if there were need or else to repudiate a 'corrupt' text — both thoroughly dishonourable procedures, to our way of thinking, but at that time practices common enough. Thus it came about that Benjamin Motte, who now owned the publishing business of Swift's old friend Tooke, received a letter, dated 8 August 1726, from one Richard Sympson, who offered for sale a copy of the travels of his cousin, Mr. Lemuel Gulliver. 'I have shown them,' wrote Sympson, 'to several persons of great judgement and distinction, who are confident that they will sell very well; and, although some parts of this and the following volumes may be thought in one or two places to be a little satirical, yet it is agreed they will give no offence. . .' There followed an interchange of letters between Benjamin Motte and Richard Sympson, the upshot of which was that the manuscript was deposited with the publisher in a manner quite as mysteri-

ous as the correspondence. On the day of publication—
28 October—Swift had been in Ireland for something like
two months.

One further incident which occurred at the time of his
first sojourn among his friends in England must be mentioned—Stella's illness and the anguish which it caused
Swift. In a letter of 7 July he mentioned that Stella had
not been in good health, but his words showed nothing of
alarm. On the following day, in writing to Sheridan, he
again referred to Stella, this time expressing some apprehension. During the following week the reports from Ireland must have been progressively discouraging, for by
mid-July he was in the last degree of mental agony. Now,
Arbuthnot, Gay, and Pope knew little of Stella; to them
Swift could not reveal the torment which he suffered on
her account—to have done so would have amounted to a
kind of unfaithfulness, a gross divulgence of intimacies incomprehensible to outsiders. Only to a few friends in Ireland, as close to Stella as to himself, could he unburden
his heart. In three remarkable letters, to Worrall, to Stopford, and to Sheridan, he spoke of his admiration of Stella;
of their friendship, greater than love; and of his inability
to bear her death with philosophic resignation. All the
enormous sensitiveness of the man, concealed out of horror
of self-revelation or distorted into savage irony, is for once
given expression, and the tenderness all but stifled by the
circumstances of his life finds voice in the description of
this friendship. He is glad that he is in England, for he
'would not for the universe be present at such a trial of
seeing her depart.' To Worrall he wrote, 'I am of opinion
that there is not a greater folly than to contract too great
and intimate a friendship, which must always leave the
survivor miserable'; to Stopford, 'Dear Jim, pardon me, I
know not what I am saying; but believe me that violent
friendship is much more lasting, and as much engaging,
as violent love'; to Sheridan, 'I look upon this to be the
greatest event that can ever happen to me; but all my
preparations will not suffice to make me bear it like a
philosopher, nor altogether like a Christian. There hath

been the most intimate friendship between us from her childhood, and the greatest merit on her side, that ever was in one human creature toward another.   Nay, if I were now near her, I would not see her; I could not behave myself tolerably, and should redouble her sorrow.'

But Stella did not die in 1726.   At his return to Dublin Swift found her much recovered, although still 'very lean and low.'   The event which he feared so greatly was, however, less than two years away.

CHAPTER II

THE IRISH PATRIOT

1

SWIFT's career as an agitator in behalf of the Irish interest lends itself to widely differing interpretations. One view, still maintained by modern critics embodying the traditionally hostile attitude towards Swift, is that revenge was the sole cause of his outburst against the English administration. It would be false to deny that such self-interest was a powerful, perhaps the leading, incentive, nor does it seem that Swift himself ever imagined that his motives were purely disinterested.

Yet all who have been qualified to discuss Swift's place in eighteenth-century Ireland have freely admitted his great services as a patriot. Thus, however ignoble his actuating impulses may have been, the ends which he achieved cannot be judged solely in terms of motive. It has been pointed out repeatedly that the immediate results of his endeavours were slight and that even the withdrawal of Wood's coinage — open acknowledgment that the Drapier had worsted the government — brought about no real change on the part of the English administration towards Ireland; his great accomplishment lay rather in rousing Ireland from its lethargy, in proclaiming the principles of rational liberty, and in uniting the patriotic party against a blind, cruel policy. It must be remembered, however, that his point of view was that not merely of an Irish-born Englishman but of an Englishman of the established church and of the governing class: the spoliation of the native Irish he took for granted, catholicism he contemned, presbyterianism he hated and denounced. The injustices against which he made war were those imposed upon the aristocratic English in Ireland. And yet, had Swift never transcended this narrow spirit he would not have been held in reverence by generation after generation of Irishmen, and in *A Letter to the Whole People of Ireland* (the fourth

Drapier's Letter) one does find an awareness and a sympathy which cut quite through his inherited prejudices. But the truth is that even when his patriotism was limited by the interests of one class its chief elements were bitter realism and a hatred of injustice, and his overpowering expression thereof has lived on to deny the narrow dogmatisms that time and place imposed on his mind.

2

THE conditions which obtained in Ireland during the period of Swift's agitation — the third and fourth decades of the eighteenth century — were determined by the hideous events of the preceding century.[1] The wholesale confiscations of Irish land had not ended with the Ulster plantations under James I but had continued into the reign of Charles I, to be given a terrific impulse when Strafford was sent over as lord-deputy in 1632. Seven years later Strafford was recalled to England, and in 1641 the Rebellion in Ireland broke out. For years all was confusion. Then, in August 1649, Cromwell landed, and after slaughtering the enemy at Drogheda and later at Wexford imposed some kind of order by the Articles of Kilkenny (1652). When he withdrew to England he left Ireton to carry out his policy, which consisted in a settlement of transplanters, completed by 1659. No person who had taken part in the Rebellion could hope for mercy from the Cromwellian administration; he was condemned to death, or at the least he suffered the confiscation of his property. Thus were the catholic landowners dispossessed to make way for protestant transplanters. At the Restoration a great hope surged through those Irishmen who had suffered by the Cromwellian settlement, for they had always been distinguished by their loyalty to the Stuarts, and from Charles II they confidently expected deliverance from the wrongs imposed by the roundheads. A large measure of religious liberty was, indeed, forthcoming, but Charles II now found himself restricted in regard to the redistribution of Irish land for the reason that many of the persons who had worked

with greatest effect for his return were not old royalists
at all but men who once had sworn allegiance to Cromwell. Some effort was made, through the Act of Settlement and the Act of Explanation, to reinstate the catholic
landowners, but by and large the Cromwellian settlement was merely confirmed, with the result that whereas
before 1641 three-fourths of the cultivated land was in the
possession of catholics, after the Acts only one-fourth remained in their hands.

Yet despite their intense dissatisfaction with the Act of
Settlement and the Act of Explanation the native Irish fared
better through the twenty-five years following the Restoration than at any other time during the century, and Ireland
as a whole enjoyed an unprecedented prosperity. It was
the Revolution of 1688 which put an end to this comparatively happy period. The Irish royalists rallied to the Stuart
banner, James landed early in 1689, and peace and order
gave way to violence and confusion. Bent upon righting
the wrongs legalized by the Acts of Charles II, the natives
rose against the English settlers, great numbers of whom fled
across the Channel. The royalist ascendency was short lived,
however, for King William, arriving in June 1690, quickly
re-established the supremacy of English protestantism.

That William II had no desire to crush the Irish as Cromwell had crushed them was shown clearly enough in the
terms of the Treaty of Limerick (October 1691), by which the
catholics were to be accorded the same religious freedom
as they had enjoyed under Charles II and were to be left in
possession of their estates as held under the Act of Settlement.
But William's enlightened ideas were not shared by the
English in Ireland, who, having been threatened with utter
ruin during the catholic resurgence under James, were now
determined to break their enemies once and for all. The
Irish parliament — recently closed to catholics by an Act
passed in England (1691) obliging every member to abjure
the doctrine of transubstantiation — refused to confirm the
Treaty of Limerick, and instead set about constructing the
Penal Code. The purpose of this Code, as Lecky has said,
was to deprive catholics of all civil rights, to reduce them to

ignorance, to dissociate them as much as possible from the soil, and to create dissent within their homes. A catholic was forbidden to carry arms, he could hold no public office, he could not teach school, he could not practise law, he could not educate his children in a catholic seminary, he could not receive a legacy in land nor make a lease for longer than thirty-one years; if his wife became a protestant she was appropriately rewarded, but if he married a protestant there were heavy penalties; he could not sit in parliament, nor after 1727 vote in parliamentary elections. Though the Penal Code was extended under Anne and the first two Georges, it was of course impossible of strict enforcement even when protestant bitterness was at its height; the widening of the rift between English and Irish and the reduction of the native population to a state of hopelessness were its greatest evils.

Thus, the so-called Protestant Ascendancy, which extended from the time of the Revolution of 1688 down to the end of the eighteenth century, rested upon the refusal of the English in Ireland to treat with the natives on any such terms as those laid down in the Treaty of Kilkenny. But because these Englishmen were forced to rely upon his majesty's arms for protection against the hostile neighbors surrounding them, they were compelled to accept the legislative disabilities which a jealous government imposed upon the Irish parliament. The tradition of legislative dependence upon England went back to the time of Henry VII, when it was enacted (Poyning's Law) that no parliament in Ireland should be summoned without the king's knowledge and previous consent, and that no measures should be submitted to it until they had first received the approval of the king and council in England. After King William's victory in Ireland, when the parliament at Dublin was seeking every means of penalizing the catholics, it consented to waive its right to originate money bills in return for the privilege of dealing as it chose with the enemy. From that time on the parliament in Ireland assembled biennially to vote the revenues prescribed by the English government, whereupon it was prorogued before it could become contumelious. Finally, in 1720 the

English parliament passed an act asserting its absolute right to make laws binding on Ireland.

These legislative disabilities, however, were quite over-shadowed by the commercial restrictions. Up to the time of the Restoration, Irish industry had been allowed to go its own way, but with the rise of the commercial classes in England to political power any prosperity in Ireland came to be regarded as a menace to the welfare of English interests, a menace to be removed as quickly as possible by prohibitive legislation. The Navigation Acts, first promulgated in 1663 and strengthened in succeeding years, prohibited direct export and import between Ireland and the colonies. At first these worked no great hardship, since Ireland after the Cromwellian settlement had taken up trade in livestock and imported chiefly to England. But at length the English farmers took alarm and Acts were passed in 1665 and 1680 totally prohibiting the importation to England of Irish cattle, sheep, pigs, beef, pork, mutton, butter, and cheese.

The effect of these Acts of 1665 and 1680 was twofold. The Irish provision trade throve, and salt beef, tallow, and hides were exported with great profit. But it was the manufacture of wool which largely took the place of the prohibited trade in livestock. This meant enclosures of land on a great scale with the resultant hardships to the tenant farmers, who were sacrificed in order that cultivated land might be turned into the more profitable sheep-walks. As later events were to prove, the great increase of pasturage was full of economic dangers, but these went unseen as the manufacture of woollen goods became Ireland's chief industry and brought comparative prosperity — until the English woollen merchants stepped in. In 1698 and 1699 were passed those laws which by prohibiting absolutely the export of Irish woollens to any place but England and virtually prohibiting their export there struck the final blow needed to impoverish Ireland and to render it incapable of competing with any English interest.

A few words must be said about the established church in Ireland. Its membership was confined to a fraction of the protestant inhabitants, and to that fraction who were en-

dowed with the greater portion of all the land and who held
what little power remained to Irish-born Englishmen. In-
evitably the established church reflected the arrogance of
its communicants, most strikingly in matters pertaining not
to the catholics but to the dissenters. On the presbyterians
of Ulster it made relentless war, not because it was imbued
with high tory doctrine — the church in Ireland was predominantly whig — but because it felt, however unconsciously,
that these dissenters constituted the only really serious threat
to its supreme position. The Sacramental Test in Ireland,
for the retention of which Swift fought so fiercely, went back
to 1704, in which year a bill of the Irish parliament for the
suppression of catholics had been supplemented in the English privy council by a clause imposing a test on all holders
of civil or military office, to which clause the Irish parliament
had given its consent. The dissenters secured some relief
in 1719, when a Toleration Act was put through, but all of
Walpole's later efforts to secure a repeal of the Test were
repelled in the upper house in Ireland. Swift's intolerance
of the dissenters was fundamentally an emotional and intellectual conviction deriving from seventeenth-century writers,
but it was greatly strengthened by his long association with
the established church in Ireland.

It must not be thought, however, that the established
church enjoyed a position free of all discouragements. In
the first place, its wealth had been seriously diminished since
the Reformation by losses and encroachments. Again, its
tithes were gathered with difficulty, partly on account of the
poverty of the small farmers, partly by reason of the hostility
with which even landowners belonging to the established
church regarded this taxation. But the most severe
handicap under which it laboured was the one imposed, as
always, by the English interest, which reserved most of the
substantial preferments in Ireland for men sent over from
England. This policy, totally discouraging to Irish-born
Englishmen, sapped the vitality of Dublin University, the
natural training-ground for leaders in the church.

Turning from the established church to agrarian conditions, one comes to the heart of Ireland's misery. So long

as the woollen trade had been permitted to flourish, the increase of pasturage at the expense of tillage had brought about no calamitous consequences but instead a fairly general prosperity. When, however, the export of wool was prohibited, the vast enclosures became for the natives a sentence to dreadful peonage. In the face of the English legislation against the woollen industry, the land-owners persisted in retaining their sheep-walks and even enlarging them, and as a consequence the dearth of tillage was acute and land rents were enormously high. The miserable cottier who worked the soil and lived in his squalid cabin must pay dues to the priests, tithes to the alien clergy of the established church, and rack-rents to his landlord, usually a tenant holding a number of small farms on lease from some large landowner, who probably preferred to reside in Dublin or in England. Reduced by this system of absenteeism and tenant-farming to a condition that passes belief, the cottiers were still a degree better off than the thousands of ragged natives who begged from parish to parish.

SWIFT, of course, was not the first who raised his voice in protest. In 1698 William Molyneux had published *The Case of Ireland's Being Bound by Acts of Parliament in England stated,* wherein he denounced the legislative disabilities, maintaining that the Irish parliament had the right to legislate for Ireland. Another famous tract was *Some Considerations for the Promotion of Agriculture and Employing the Poor,* issued by Viscount Molesworth in 1723. The rise of the patriotic party subsequent to the queen's death and the leadership accorded it by Archbishop King have already been mentioned. But as this party grew in solidarity the English interest was correspondingly strengthened, for in 1724 Hugh Boulter succeeded to the Irish primacy and throughout his eighteen years' incumbency England's rigid and systematic control of Irish affairs, both secular and ecclesiastical, reached its height.

3

BEFORE taking up Swift's Irish tracts chronologically we shall do well to consider the scope of his analysis and his general conclusions. No one can read his many pamphlets called forth by Irish questions—they fill two volumes in Temple Scott's edition of the *Collected Prose Works*—and the pieces in verse similarly occasioned without amazement : his mere productivity is astonishing, but more so is the sustained energy pulsing through these writings. This is the man who is popularly believed to have lived at a distance from society, engrossed in misanthropic satire !

The first of his great Irish tracts was *A Proposal for the Universal Use of Irish Manufacture* (1720), a militant summary of the evils created by the laws passed against Irish manufacture and agriculture. When Swift turns to his fellow-countrymen, his flail descends first upon those landowners who continue to raise sheep in utter disregard of the restrictions upon the wool trade, then upon the country landlords who by the unmeasurable screwing and racking of their tenants 'have . . . reduced the miserable people to a worse condition than the peasants in France, or the vassals in Germany and Poland.' Everywhere in Ireland is proof that when a people are subjected to political slavery, they in turn become tyrants : 'Whoever travels this country, and observes the face of nature, or the faces, and habits, and dwellings of the natives, will hardly think himself in a land where either law, religion, or common humanity is professed.'

After the *Proposal*, his most cogent analyses of Irish conditions are to be found in *Maxims controlled* [i.e., *confuted*] *in Ireland* (1724?), *The Present Miserable State of Ireland* (second half 1726?), and *A Short View of the State of Ireland* (1728). Some of the revealing economic paradoxes which he takes up in the *Maxims* are these : whereas high prices are elsewhere the consequence of wealth and commerce, in Ireland they are the result of the greatest want ; the low interest rate in Ireland does not indicate a great plenty of money but instead the complete discouragement of trade so that there is no demand for loans ; the high purchase of lands in Ireland is not a sign of wealth but of not knowing how else to invest ready money; the increase of buildings in Dublin does not indicate a flourishing condition in the nation — merely the presence in the city of a great number of absentee landowners. In *The Present Miserable State of Ireland* he is concerned with the commercial restrictions, with the scarcity of money caused by the residence outside of Ireland of so many absentees, and with the exorbitant land rents. *A Short View of the State of Ireland,* in many ways the most effective of these major tracts, enumerates the causes of a nation's prosperity and proceeds to show why it is that these causes do not exist in Ireland or have been rendered inoperative. Swift sums up in these words:

. . . I would be glad to know by what secret method it is that we grow a rich and flourishing people, without liberty, trade, manufactures, inhabitants, money, or the privilege of coining; without industry, labour or improvement of lands, and with more than half of the rent and profits of the whole Kingdom, annually exported, for which we receive not a single farthing. . .

Then, assuming the ironic tone, he invites the worthy commissioners from England to make a tour of the kingdom; let them observe the fair face of nature, the prosperous farms, the beautiful country seats. 'But my heart,' he proceeds, abandoning irony with dramatic suddenness,

is too heavy to continue this journey longer, for it is manifest that whatever stranger took such a journey, would be apt to think himself travelling in Lapland or Ysland, rather than in a country so favoured by Nature as ours. . . The miserable dress, and diet, and dwelling of the people. The general desolation in most parts of the Kingdom. The old seats of the nobility and gentry all in ruins, and no new ones in their stead. The families of farmers who pay great rents, living in filth and nastiness upon butter-milk and potatoes, without a shoe or stocking to their feet, or a house so convenient as an English hog-sty to receive them. These indeed may be comfortable sights to the English spectator, who comes for a short time only to learn the language, and returns back to his own country, whither he finds all our wealth transmitted.

Nostrâ miseriâ magnus es.

The Dantesque note ocurs not infrequently in the Irish tracts. That it has gone undetected is probably to be explained by the greater frequency of Swiftian irony, which of course attained its most perfect expression in *A Modest Proposal* (1729).

Like all of his contemporaries in Ireland, Swift found monetary questions of absorbing interest, and in 1724, when Wood's halfpence occupied the thoughts of Irishmen to the exclusion of all else, he seized upon the technicalities of coinage as the means for inflaming the kingdom against the English ministry. But his concern with these matters extended to the entire banking system. When a National Bank for Ireland was proposed, Swift, scenting another wild 'project' like that of the South Sea Company, wrote numerous verses and several tracts (1720-1721) ridiculing it, and thus contributed to its defeat.

When the South Sea bubble burst in 1720-1721 Dublin was hard hit. Tradespeople suffered, but it was the plight of the weavers, of whom there were over six thousand in the city, that was most touching. Early in 1721 a performance of *Hamlet* was given for their benefit, the *Epilogue* to the play being written by the dean. It was also in 1721 that Swift seems to have begun a custom, carried on for many years, of lending money without interest to small tradesmen whom he thought to be deserving.

In the smaller tracts, that followed one another in a steady stream, Swift ranged from topic to topic. Now, as in *An Answer to a Paper, called 'A Memorial of the Poor Inhabitants . . . of Ireland'* (1729), he concentrated on the agrarian difficulties; again, as in *A Letter to the Archbishop of Dublin, concerning the Weavers* (1729), he gave his undivided attention to the problems peculiar to the woollen industry. Constantly he preached economic self-sufficiency, and to this end made repeated suggestions of the kind to be found in *An Answer to Several Letters sent me from Unknown Hands* (1729), where he outlined what we to-day should call programmes of road construction, bog reclamation, and reforestation.

Swift's sociological approach to the conditions staring

every resident in Ireland in the face is interesting to study.
With his perceptions and emotions determined by the seventeenth-century *Zeitgeist* he was untouched by philosophical humanitarianism, yet the misery which he beheld filled
him with rage and pity.   Again, as an ethical rigorist he
habitually attributed the evils suffered by man not to the
shortcomings of society but to the moral weaknesses of the individual, but he found it impossible steadfastly to maintain
that the beggars of Ireland were starving solely as a consequence of their own immorality.   Of these contradictions,
however, he was never even remotely aware.   Having shown
the economic causes of the general poverty in Ireland, he
would turn upon the beggars, charging them with full responsibility for their misery.   It is not a clash but a curious
interplay of forces, with austere ethical theory now in control and again a realism with eyes only for existing conditions.   Because Swift could not blot from his consciousness
a horrid sight, he was moved by a compassion foreign to
his formal thought.

Of pamphlets of a sociological nature three may be cited.
The earliest of these is *The Last Speech and Dying Words
of Ebenezer Elliston* (1722).   At this time the citizens of
Dublin were being preyed upon by gangs of ruffians who
prowled about the streets robbing the unwary.   One of
the most notorious of these criminals was Ebenezer Elliston,
and when he was at last apprehended, tried, and hanged,
Swift took occasion to issue a pretended dying confession
which should act as a deterrent upon all of Elliston's comrades.   Thanks to a verisimilitude reminiscent of Defoe,
Swift's deception passed unquestioned and was immediately
effective in reducing the number of crimes.   Elliston, resolved to 'die like a man the death of a dog,' is made to
deliver upon himself and his class a judgment of surpassing
severity :

This is a short picture of the life I have led ; which is more
miserable than that of the poorest labourer who works for four
pence a day ; and yet custom is so strong, that I am confident, if
I could make my escape at the foot of the gallows, I should be
following the same course this very evening.   So that upon the

whole, we ought to be looked upon as the common enemies of mankind; whose interest it is to root us out like wolves, and other mischievous vermin, against which no fair play is required.

The other tracts are *Considerations about Maintaining the Poor* (date of composition unknown) and *A Proposal for giving Badges to the Beggars* (1737). In both of these his impatience with the countless ineffectual schemes that have been proposed for dealing with the indigent lends unpleasant harshness to his voice, nor does his bitterness stop short of the wretched natives of whom he writes. His sole prescription is that beggars must be confined to and looked after by their native parishes; those originating in Dublin should be given distinctive badges in order that foreign beggars may be driven from the city. Thus, in the *Considerations* he writes as follows:

The prodigious number of beggars throughout this kingdom, in proportion to so small a number of people, is owing to many reasons: to the laziness of the natives; the want of work to employ them; the enormous rents paid by cottagers for their miserable cabins and potato-plots; their early marriages, without the least prospect of establishment; the ruin of agriculture, whereby such vast numbers are hindered from providing their own bread, and have no money to purchase it; the mortal damp upon all kinds of trade, and many other circumstances, too tedious or invidious to mention.

And to the same causes we owe the perpetual concourse of foreign beggars to this town, the country landlords giving all assistance, except money and victuals, to drive from their estates those miserable creatures they have undone.

But in the *Proposal* he dismisses all purely social causes, tracing the evils borne by the natives back to their own viciousness:

To say the truth, there is not a more undeserving vicious race of human kind than the bulk of those who are reduced to beggary, even in this beggarly country. For, as a great part of our publick miseries is originally owing to our own faults . . . so I am confident, that among the meaner people, nineteen in twenty of those who are reduced to a starving condition, did not become so by what lawyers call the work of GOD, either upon their bodies or goods; but merely from their own idleness, attended with all manner of vices, particularly drunkenness, thievery, and cheating.

As a succeeding paragraph shows, Swift brooded horribly upon the irresponsible marriages among the natives and the enormous birth-rate, their lack of foresight and restraint in these respects constituting in his mind their fundamental viciousness.   In a later age Swift undoubtedly would have taken a scientific attitude towards the control of population ; as it was, the problem both in its broad, sociological aspects and as it touched upon individual conduct remained something beyond solution, an evil that haunted him from youth to old age.

In 1733 Swift wrote an ironic little essay called *A Serious and Useful Scheme, to make an Hospital for Incurables, of Universal Benefit to all His Majesty's Subjects*.   It was the Digression concerning Madness over again, save that at sixty-five his pen had lost the incomparable touch which it had had when it inscribed *A Tale of a Tub*.   But even while he was treating of madness in this satiric vein, he was laying plans to found at his death a hospital for the insane. In March 1733 he mentioned to Pope his intention of settling his fortune to a public use, and in the following years he drew up the precise terms of his bequest.   After his death it was found that the £7000 which he had left was altogether insufficient, but parliament granted the additional funds necessary for the erection of St. Patrick's Hospital, popularly known as Swift's Hospital, which still stands to bear testimony to the dean's humanity.

4

WE may now turn to the history of Swift's public writings from 1714 through the period of agitation against Wood's coinage.   In the majority of cases he came forward as the patriot, exhorting Ireland to self-sufficiency, castigating the English administration with deadly invective.   But at all times — though most frequently in the years after 1726 — any rumour of a new attempt to repeal the Test roused him to instantaneous action against the dissenters.   Thus, one of the earliest of his compositions after his return from London — at least it was attributed to Swift after his death —

is the metrical piece entitled *The Fable of the Bitches* (1715), apropos of certain proceedings against the Test. He was likewise provoked to satire and denunciation by any action on the part of the Irish bishops which appeared to him to be taken in their own interests at the expense of the lower clergy. It was in 1723, in a tract entitled *Some Arguments against Enlarging the Power of Bishops in Letting of Leases,* that he first took up arms against his superiors in the church and was largely responsible for the defeat of certain bills which they had introduced in the lords.

If the ascription to Swift of *The Speech of The P[rovo]st of T[rinit]y C[olle]ge to his Royall Highness George Prince of Wales* is correct, it was in 1716, on the occasion of the prince of Wales's appointment as chancellor of Dublin University in place of the duke of Ormond, that the dean turned to political satire in verse for the first time since the death of the queen. But he was then in no mood for an earnest campaign against his enemies, and until 1720 he rarely broke silence. In that year, however, he leapt into action with the publication, about May, of *A Proposal for the Universal Use of Irish Manufacture.* This was at once declared a seditious pamphlet, Waters, the printer, was taken up, and a grand jury found a true bill against him. Swift retaliated upon the jury in *An Excellent New Song on a Seditious Pamphlet,* of which the following is a stanza:

> Whoever our trading with England would hinder,
>   To inflame both the nations do plainly conspire,
> Because Irish linen will soon turn to tinder,
>   And wool it is greasy, and quickly takes fire.
>   Therefore, I assure ye,
>   Our noble grand jury,
> When they saw the Dean's book, they were in a great fury;
> They would buy English silks for their wives and their
>   daughters,
> In spite of his deanship and journeyman Waters.

At his subsequent trial Waters was acquitted, but Lord Chief Justice Whitshed, ever afterwards an object of Swift's abuse, refused to accept the verdict, laid his hand on his heart and swore that the author of the pamphlet designed to bring in the pretender, and sent the jury back nine times until they were forced to bring in a special verdict by which the matter was left to the judge.   Eventually the lord-lieutenant granted a nolle prosequi.

Swift at once followed up his opening thrust, and in the ensuing year and a half issued a number of pieces in which he ridiculed the proposal to establish a National Bank in Ireland.   In 1722 and 1723 there was a noticeable thinning of the stream of verse and pamphlets relative to public questions, but this, as it proved, was a recession preceding the torrent of 1724.

If the fierce resentment aroused in Ireland by Wood's copper coinage needs no explanation, the masterly if unscrupulous manner whereby Swift played upon the resentment, heightening yet controlling it, is perfectly apparent.[2]   It was, of course, the denial to Ireland of rational political liberty which was in this instance the main cause of Swift's indignation, and this became clearer in each succeeding *Drapier's Letter*.   But it is an erroneous belief, though one which has often been expressed, that Swift perceived in Wood's copper money none of the dangers which he described so luridly and that he seized upon this new coinage merely to force the all-important issue between the Irish and English interests.   In England there was, of course, a government mint, as there was in Scotland under the Act of Union.   Ireland had repeatedly petitioned for a mint of its own, but the English authorities were not to be persuaded into abandoning the system whereby a patent to issue coins in Ireland for a certain number of years was sold to the highest English bidder.   In the days of Charles II this method had worked well enough, but James's arrival in Ireland had thrown the monetary system, like everything else, into confusion, the fiat money issued under royal authority undergoing immediate depreciation.   After the Revolution the coinage of money under patent from England was resumed, but the patentee overstocked the country with the result that his currency became undervalued.   Ireland knew what depreciated money meant.   To say that the Drapier did not exaggerate the actual dangers would be absurd, but dangers there nevertheless were, as every Irishman with a memory knew.

By 1720 it was agreed on all sides that something must be done about the Irish currency, for the insufficiency of coins in circulation and their heterogeneous character had become a daily annoyance. The Irish desired above all their own mint, but in the absence of that they felt that their greatest need was small silver coins. England, however, took the view that a large issue of copper halfpence and farthings would suffice, and accordingly issued a new patent to an English iron merchant named William Wood, who was granted the exclusive right to coin such copper money for fourteen years beginning in 1722.[3] It was stipulated that the coins were to be issued gradually over the fourteen-year period, that in all not more than 360 tons of copper were to be minted, and that the pieces were to be of good, pure, and merchantable copper, 30d. to the pound weight. Thus, 360 tons of copper, then worth about £60,000, were to be minted into coins having a value of £100,800. According to rumour, the patent had actually been issued to the king's mistress, the duchess of Kendall, who had sold it to Wood for a goodly sum. The fact that Ireland's wishes had never been consulted in this matter, the absurd disproportion — something like one to four — between the amount of the new copper coinage and the rest of the Irish currency, and the arrogance of Wood himself, who was soon talking of pouring his money down the throats of the people if they refused to accept it, combined to arouse an intense antagonism towards both the coinage and the English administration authorizing it.

Shortly after the patent was granted to Wood (12 July 1722), the commissioners of the revenue in Dublin protested to the authorities in England, but nothing came of this, and it was not long before the copper coins began to pour in. When the duke of Grafton, the lord-lieutenant, arrived in August 1723, he found that feeling was already running high. In September the Irish parliament met, and within a few weeks both houses adopted Addresses to the king wherein they called attention to the manifold dangers to ensue from an enforcement of the patent. It has appeared 'by Examinations taken in the most Solemn Manner,' read the Address of the commons, 'That, tho' the Terms [of this Patent] had been strictly Comply'd with, there would have been a Loss to this Nation of at least· 150 *per Cent.* by Means of the said Coinage, and a much Greater in the Manner the said *Half-Pence* have been Coined.' The Address framed by the lords was similar in tone and substance : 'We are most Humbly of Opinion, That the Diminution of Your MAJESTIES Revenue, the Ruin of our Trade and the Impoverishing of Your People, must unavoidably attend this Undertaking, and We beg leave to Observe to Your MAJESTY, That from the most exact Enquiries and Computations We have been able to make, it Appears to Us, That the Gain to 𝔚𝔦𝔩𝔩𝔦𝔞𝔪 𝔚𝔬𝔬𝔡 will be excessive, and the Loss to this Kingdom by Circulating this Base Coine greater than this poor Country is able to bear.' [4]

But still the powers in England could not or would not believe that the discontent in Ireland was anything more than a momentary display of petulant insubordination, and it was not until March 1724 that the English privy council became sufficiently impressed with the seriousness of the situation to order an inquiry into Wood's patent. Before this, however, the Drapier had sprung to life, for it was in February, when the possibility of compelling Walpole's ministry to take action still seemed quite beyond hope, that Swift composed the *First Letter* (ptd. probably early in March), addressed to the '*Tradesmen, Shop-Keepers, Farmers,* and *Common-People* in General, of the Kingdom of *IRELAND.*'

The mighty journalist who once had shaped public opinion for a tory minister was alive again, but never in the days of the queen had he commanded a style and voice comparable to what he now displayed. The opening paragraph of the *First Letter,* peremptory, hortative, establishes at once the tone which was to be sustained throughout the· long series of pamphlets and satiric verses :

What I intend now to say to you, is, next to your Duty to God, and the Care of your Salvation, of the greatest Concern to your selves, and your Children, your *Bread* and *Cloathing*, and every common Necessary of Life entirely depend upon it. Therefore I do most earnestly exhort you as *Men,* as *Christians,* as *Parents,* and as *Lovers of your Country,* to read this Paper with the utmost *Attention.* . .

In this opening *Letter* Swift's tactical genius is shown in the manner in which the vituperation is all directed at the person of William Wood — before united action against a general policy could be hoped for, it was necessary to arouse consuming hatred for a man of flesh and blood. Wood is *'a mean ordinary Man, a Hard-Ware Dealer,'* who has procured his patent by a wicked cheat; he is a blood-sucker, working underhand to force his halfpence upon a country which he designs to drain of its gold and silver; 'It would be very hard if all *Ireland* should be put into *One Scale,* and *this sorry Fellow WOODS into the other,* that Mr. *WOODS* should weigh down *this whole Kingdom. . .'* Did his majesty but know how Wood designed utterly to ruin the kingdom, he would immediately recall the patent 'and perhaps shew his Displeasure to SOME BODY OR OTHER. . .'

If any of the *Drapier's Letters* is unblushingly sophistical, it is this first one. Invective is not enough; there must be facts in overwhelming number, and these must be marshalled with an apparently irrefutable logic. The arguments converge on three points: (1) the halfpence will depreciate in value, (2) their number will be limitless, (3) they are so poorly minted that counterfeit coin will flood the kingdom. What may be looked for in the way of depreciation is illustrated with a homely example: 'if a *Hatter* sells a Dozen of *Hatts* for *Five Shillings* a-piece, which amounts to *Three Pounds,* and receives the Payment in Mr. WOODS's Coin, he really receives only the Value of *Five Shillings.'* But it is for the second point that the most fantastic arguments are reserved. To begin with, what assurance is there that Wood will stay within his patent, which limits the amount of copper to be minted to 360 tons? There is none; '. . . Mr. WOODS when he pleases may by Stealth send over *another* and *another Fourscore and Ten Thousand Pounds,* and buy *all our Goods for Eleven Parts in Twelve,* under the Value.' A link is here dropped from the chain of reasoning, but is easily supplied : before Wood has finished, the sole currency in Ireland will be his halfpence and farthings. From this, what follows? Let it be assumed that five of the copper halfpence weigh an ounce ; £100 in halfpence will then weigh 600 pounds avoirdupois, a 3 horse load ; a sum of £8,000 will therefore require 240 horses to draw it, £40,000 calling for 1,200 horses.

They say 'SQUIRE C—Y has *Sixteen Thousand Pounds a Year,* now if he sends for his *Rent* to Town, *as it is likely he does,* he must have Two *Hundred and Forty Horses* to bring up his *Half Years Rent,* and Two or Three great *Cellars* in his House for Stowage. But what the Bankers will do I cannot tell. For I am assured, that some great Bankers keep by them *Forty Thousand Pounds* in ready Cash to answer all Payments, which Sum, in Mr. WOODS's Money, would require Twelve Hundred Horses to carry it.

Was there ever such exuberant logic? The truth is that the first of the *Drapier's Letters* is, in its peculiar fashion, one of Swift's humorous masterpieces, and it is quite unbelievable that all of its readers missed its inspired lunacy — let the English parliament and privy council look to their laurels ! But if one will sound out the Drapier's reasoning, one will find that it is not utterly specious. The only assumption needed to bring it into relation to truth is that what had already happened in Ireland could happen again, and such an assumption did not seem far-fetched to any Irishman : other patentees had flooded the kingdom with their coins, other issues of currency had depreciated and been widely counterfeited. Wood's halfpence would never have fallen to the point at which £3 in copper coins would be worth but 5s. sterling, but there was every reason to suppose that there would be some depreciation ; similarly, no one would ever have required 1,200 horses to complete a business transaction, but it looked very much as though Ireland's currency would soon consist mainly of halfpence and farthings. The Drapier exaggerated unscrupulously, but for all that he had history with him.

Shortly after the publication of the first *Letter* there appeared a ballad — *Ireland's Warning, Being an Excellent New Song, upon Woods's Base Half-pence* — to the twenty-one stanzas of which some have believed that Swift contributed.[5] The following are the opening stanzas :

Ye people of Ireland, both country and city,
Come listen with patience, and hear out my ditty :
At this time I'll choose to be wiser than witty.
        Which nobody can deny.

The halfpence are coming, the nation's undoing,
There's an end of your ploughing, and baking, and brewing ;
In short, you must all go to wreck and to ruin.
        Which, &c.

Both high men and low men, and thick men and
          tall men,
And rich men and poor men, and free men and thrall
          men,
Will suffer ; and this man, and that man, and all
          men.
        Which, &c.

In this manner were the Drapier's earlier words now set to a lilting rhythm that fixed emotion beyond the possibility of change, and Wood, though he had yet to learn the truth, was beaten. The summer wore on. In London the committee of the council was now finishing its report, certain details of which leaked out with the result that on 1 August Dublin learned that the privy council would be advised to reduce the total amount of coinage from £100,800 to £40,000. Had such a concession been made a year earlier, before the Drapier had spoken, it would probably have been received in Dublin with joy unbounded; by August 1724, however, Ireland was not to be appeased with concessions but only with the absolute withdrawal of the Patent, as the Drapier's *Second Letter* (dated 4 August) straightway made clear.

The arrival of the official report some days later served to call forth the *Third Letter* (dated 25 August). Without

for an instant remitting his attack upon Wood, Swift now felt
safe in extending the issues to include the really fundamental ones of political liberty.　By what right did the privy
council in England decree how much of Wood's brass money
the people of Ireland should accept?　'Were not the People
of *Ireland* born as *Free* as those of *England?*' he thundered.

How have they forfeited their Freedom?　Is not their *Parliament* as fair a *Representative* of the *People* as that of *England?*
And hath not their Privy Council as great or a greater Share in
the Administration of Publick Affairs?　Are they not Subjects of
the same King?　Does not the same *Sun* shine on them?　And
have they not the same *God* for their Protector?　Am I a *Free-
Man* in *England,* and do I become a *Slave* in six Hours by cross-
ing the Channel?

The entire country was by this time in an uproar, and
Dublin seethed with excitement as petitions and declara-
tions against Wood followed one another in a steady stream.
On 8 September there was a huge demonstration, the citizens
marching through the street with an effigy of Wood — an
incident which called forth among other things *A Full and
True Account of the Solemn Procession to the Gallows, at
the Execution of William Wood, Esquire, and Hard-Ware-
Man,* which has been attributed to Swift, and the dean's
verses entitled *A Serious Poem upon William Wood, Brazier,
Tinker, Hard-Ware-Man, Coiner, Counterfeiter, Founder
and Esquire.*

　　Lord Carteret, who had succeeded to the lord-lieutenancy,
was on his way to the scene of trouble to match diplomacy
against the Drapier's pen.　He was given no time to or-
ganize his forces, however, for even as he landed (22 October)
his antagonist struck a double blow.　One of the new publications was the short *Epigram:*

> Carteret was welcomed to the shore
> First with the brazen cannon's roar;
> To meet him next the soldier comes,
> With brazen trumps and brazen drums;
> Approaching near the town he hears
> The brazen bells salute his ears:
> But when Wood's brass began to sound,
> Guns, trumpets, drums, and bells, were drown'd.

The second piece was *A Letter to the Whole People of Ireland.*

In this *Fourth Letter,* the greatest of the series, Swift was but raising to a higher level of intensity the political thesis which he had broached in the previous *Letter.* The meaning of *prerogative* is set forth, and this leads by degrees to that famous sentence which caught in a few words the logic and the emotions of the patriots : 'The Remedy is wholly in your own Hands, and therefore I have digressed a little in order to refresh and continue that *Spirit* so seasonably raised amongst you, and to let you see that by the Laws of GOD, of NATURE, of NATIONS, and of your own Country, you ARE and OUGHT to be as FREE a People as your Brethren in *England.*'

Action against the Drapier was the last step which Carteret had desired or intended to take, for he had set his heart upon a triumph to be achieved through skilful diplomacy, but confronted with the *Letter to the Whole People of Ireland* he was obliged to change his course and accordingly summoned a meeting of the Irish privy council, at which it was determined that Harding, the printer of the *Fourth Letter,* should be prosecuted by law and that a proclamation should be issued offering a reward of £300 for the discovery of the author of the 'wicked and malicious pamphlet.' Dublin's answer to the proclamation was to chant through the streets a verse from the first book of *Samuel :* 'And the people said unto Saul, shall *Jonathan* die, who hath wrought this great salvation in Israel? God forbid : as the Lord liveth there shall not one hair of his head fall to the ground; for he hath wrought with God this day : So the people rescued *Jonathan* that he died not.'

It was on 27 October that the privy council met. Apparently Swift was secretly informed by his friends of Lord Carteret's plans, for the *Letter to the Lord Chancellor Middleton* (ptd. for the first time as *Letter VI* in the fourth volume of Swift's *Works,* 1735), in which the dean virtually disclosed his authorship of the *Fourth Letter,* is dated 26 October. At the moment of composing his *Letter to the Lord Chancellor Middleton* Swift, it seems, convinced that

not even the lord-lieutenant would venture to proceed
against him, had determined to throw off his pseudonym
and stand forth as the champion of Ireland. But when
Swift's friends sounded out Carteret, the latter let it be
known that no man, not even the Drapier dean, was strong
enough thus to oppose the government. The result was
that Swift reconsidered his plan and suppressed the *Letter*.

On 7 November Harding, the printer, was taken into
custody and the Crown made ready to prosecute him. It
was at this juncture that Swift wrote his *Seasonable Advice*
(dated 11 November, distributed 14 November), addressed
to the members of the grand jury before whom Harding's
case would come and exhorting them not to present the
Drapier's *Fourth Letter* as seditious. (At about the same
time Swift seems also to have produced *To his Grace the
Arch-Bishop of Dublin, a Poem*, together with the verses
entitled *An Excellent New Song upon his Grace our good
Lord Archbishop of Dublin*, both of which pieces were
probably called forth by the knowledge that Archbishop
King, as a member of the privy council, had refused to sign
the proclamation against the Drapier. To this period may
also be assigned *Prometheus, a Poem*, the finest of Swift's
metrical denunciations of Wood, which concludes with these
ten summarizing couplets :

> Ye powers of Grub-Street, make me able
> Discreetly to apply this fable ;
> Say, who is to be understood
> By that old thief Prometheus ? — Wood.
> For Jove, it is not hard to guess him ;
> I mean his Majesty, God bless him.
> This thief and blacksmith was so bold,
> He strove to steal that chain of gold,
> Which links the subject to the king,
> And change it for a brazen string.
> But sure, if nothing else must pass
> Betwixt the king and us but brass,
> Although the chain will never crack,
> Yet our devotion may grow slack.
> But Jove will soon convert, I hope,
> This brazen chain into a rope ;

With which Prometheus shall be tied,
And high in air for ever ride;
Where, if we find his liver grows,
For want of vultures, we have crows.)

As matters turned out, the Crown never proceeded with
the prosecution of Harding, and when the grand jury assembled they were urged instead to make a presentment of
the *Seasonable Advice*.   Upon their refusal to do so (21
November) they were dismissed by Swift's old enemy, Lord
Chief Justice Whitshed, and a new jury was summoned.   It was
learned, however, that certain members of the first jury had
been ready to give in to the demands of the lord chief justice,
and these traitors to the cause of Ireland were at once gibbeted in *An Excellent New Song upon the Late Grand-Jury*,
a ballad by the Drapier.   On the last day of the Term (28
November) the second grand jury was given the opportunity
to make a presentment of the *Seasonal Advice*, but instead
of doing so they made a presentment of 'all such Persons as
have attempted, or shall endeavour by fraud or otherwise,
to Impose the said Half-pence upon Us'[6] — an act almost beyond question instigated directly by Swift.

The enemy was now in full retreat, but still the dean
showered them with squibs.   The satiric verses written during the closing weeks of the campaign include such pieces
as *Wood, an Insect; On Wood the Iron-monger; Will.
Wood's Petition to the People of Ireland, being an excellent
New Song*; and *A Simile, on our Want of Silver, and the
only Way to remedy it*.   But it was for the lord chief justice
that the full force of Swift's fury was reserved, as can be seen
from *Verses on the upright Judge* and *Whitshed's Motto on
his Coach*.   In December came the *Fifth Letter* (dated 14
December, appeared 31 December), addressed to the Right
Honourable the Lord Viscount Molesworth, in which the
Drapier defended himself against the charges based on the
Letter to the Whole People of Ireland.   He has been
accused of malice and wickedness against the public, of designs to sow sedition, of attempting to alienate the affections
of the people of Ireland from those of England.   In reality,

he has been moved only by a belief in the principles of
freedom and liberty.

Eight months later the English government issued a vaca-
tion of Wood's patent, and on 26 August 1725 the Irish
council met and proclaimed the joyful news.   Swift had been
at work that summer upon another *Letter — An Humble
Address to both Houses of Parliament* (ptd. as *Letter VII* in
the *Works,* 1735) — which was to have appeared at the opening of parliament ; but, upon learning of the cancellation
of the patent, Swift abandoned all idea of further publication.   When parliament met in the autumn, the lord-lieutenant called upon both houses to make suitable acknowledgment of his majesty's remarkable favour and condescension,
shown in the withdrawal of Wood's patent.   The commons
complied at once ; the lords only after a debate in which
Archbishop King, independent to the last, opposed this bending of the knee before the English powers.   If the verses
celebrating this final gesture of defiance on the part of the
patriots were written by Swift,— his authorship has been both
affirmed and questioned,[7]— *On Wisdom's Defeat in a
Learned Debate* may be said to have been the dean's parting
shot in the war against Wood's halfpence.

In the foregoing account no mention has been made of certain of Swift's satiric pieces in verse which, although not
without national implications, were directed at individuals
who for more or less personal reasons had aroused the dean's
ire.   The outstanding victims were Dean Jonathan Smedley,
Ambrose Philips, and Richard Tighe.   Smedley was Swift's
junior by but four years, and like the dean of St. Patrick's
had received his education at Trinity College, Dublin, had
taken holy orders, had held an obscure living in Ireland,
and had finally achieved a deanery.   That one Jonathan was
a whig and the other a tory does not fully account for the
intense hatred which they felt for each other, but the further
reasons for their enmity do not appear.   Smedley is said to
have been the author of the excoriating verses affixed to the
door of St. Patrick's Cathedral the day of Swift's installation ;
he was also the editor and partial author of *Gulliveriana*

(1728), perhaps the most scurrilous of the many attacks in print upon Swift. Early in 1724 Smedley, having been promoted from the deanery of Killala to that of Clogher by the duke of Grafton, then lord-lieutenant, was impelled to write the verses entitled *Dean Smedley's Petition to the Duke of Grafton,* in which he thanked the lord-lieutenant for the new deanery but went on to request 'some pretty cure' where in a 'parsonage-house with garden sweet' he might pass his last years in comfort. The *Petition* was too much for Swift, who promptly penned the ironical *Duke's Answer.* Later in the same year, after Smedley had issued a broadside against Swift for making war upon the English interest, Swift struck again, in *A Letter from D.S — t to D.S — y.*

Ambrose Philips, the poet whose *Pastorals* had won for him the soubriquet of Namby Pamby, had been numbered among Swift's friends in the days when they were both whigs and both of the Addisonian circle. Philips, however, had remained a whig; he had aroused Pope's ire; but, most serious of all, he had recently come over to Ireland in the train of Primate Boulter. These were more than sufficient reasons to cause Swift to fall upon him. Of the satiric verses with which Philips was showered by Irish writers, the pieces *On Rover* and *A Christmas Box for Namby Pamby* have by some been attributed to Swift.

Sheridan's unfortunate experience at Cork and the part played therein by Richard Tighe have already been taken up. As a result of this affair Swift conceived for Tighe an undying hatred, which he voiced in three satires included under the single title of *To The Honourable Mr. D. T.* (1725).

The foregoing group of satires is intrinsically of no great importance, but mentioned it must be for the reason that it indicates the course which Swift's satiric powers were to take altogether too frequently in the ensuing years. With *Gulliver's Travels* behind him Swift was to find in verse the chief vent for his genius. His metrical compositions, particularly those of the thirties, often rose to a high level, but too often his themes were not general but purely personal. The ageing Swift is not a pleasant figure. So absolute was the Drapier dean's sway in Ireland that he could brook no opposition, and those who in any way annoyed or angered him suffered a punishment similar to that which had been meted out to Smedley and Tighe.

CHAPTER III
OTHER VERSE AND PROSE

1

As the black mood which had descended upon Swift after the queen's death relaxed its numbing grip, the controversialist and the artist came to life at one and the same moment, and while the Drapier was arousing a nation by his *Letters* and verses, Lemuel Gulliver was making ready to delight the world with an account of his strange adventures. It was not mere coincidence that Swift's revival of interest in the political scene was accompanied by a renewal of his artistic impulses — it should be clear by this time that the energy which drove the man of action was not different from that which sustained the artist.

It was towards the end of his fifth year of exile in Ireland that Swift became active again. By 1720 he was beginning to write with something of the old abandonment; by 1724 he was working as he had done in the great years of 1711 and 1712. Of the writings produced within the period to which the present book is devoted *Gulliver's Travels* and the tracts and verses relating to Ireland are of course the major items. In addition to these there are, however, a number of pieces both in prose and in verse that bear the full imprint of Swift's genius, and it is with these miscellaneous compositions that the present chapter has to do.

2

WITHIN the period of which we are speaking there are only two prose compositions of a strictly non-controversial character, but they are both notable works. The earlier of these is *A Letter to a Young Gentleman, lately enter'd into Holy Orders* (dated 9 January 1720 ; ptd. 1721), which has already been studied ; the second is *A Letter of Advice to a Young Poet* (dated 1 December 1720 ; ptd. 1721) .

In this second *Letter* the reader will find little which he has not already encountered in the author's earlier writings : the attack on poetic enthusiasm and the ridicule of those who would achieve universal knowledge through the use of abstracts, summaries, and indexes carry one back to *A Tale of a Tub* and *The Mechanical Operation of the Spirit,* while the derisive treatment of irreligious wits and of writers in constant search of the eccentric calls to mind any number of earlier passages. Yet the *Letter to a Young Poet* is *sui generis.* Not only has it a peculiar importance by virtue of the fact that Swift nowhere else discoursed of poetry at such length, but it is also distinguished by the texture of its satire and irony, for it is a grave discourse, evenly modulated, but with crushing irony lurking in every phrase.

The opening paragraph is in itself a masterpiece of ironic statement. The writer, addressing a young man who has resolved to become a poet, expresses his satisfaction with the youth's choice of a profession, and goes on to praise poetry as that which not only advances its practitioners to fortune but is of great use to mankind and society :

. . . history, ancient or modern, cannot furnish you an instance of one person, eminent in any station, who was not in some measure versed in poetry, or at least a well-wisher to the professors of it. Neither would I despair to prove, if legally called thereto, that it is impossible to be a good soldier, divine, or lawyer, or even so much as an eminent bellman, or ballad-singer, without some taste of poetry, and a competent skill in versification. But I say the less of this, because the renowned Sir Philip Sidney has exhausted the subject before me, in his 'Defense of Poesie,' on which I shall make no other remark but this, that he argues there as if he really believed himself.

The remainder of the *Letter* consists chiefly of prescriptions to enhance the poet's assurance and skill. In the first place, those who look for favour from the Muse should rid themselves as quickly as possible of those early prejudices implanted by a Christian education, for the smallest quantity of religion 'will muddy and discompose the brightest poetical genius.' Again, since every man should work solely upon his own materials and produce 'only what he can find within himself,' the poet is under no necessity of becoming a good scholar or of troubling himself with philosophy, and if he must draw upon the ancients he can do so by means of abstracts, abridgments, summaries, and indexes.

Now, verse without rhyme is a body without a soul or a bell without a clapper, from which it follows that no aspiring poet should neglect to furnish himself with a goodly supply of rhymes. Let him also lay up a store of images and a variety of similes for all subjects. Frequent attendance at the coffee-houses and the playhouses is an indispensable part of his education. Under no conditions should he allow himself to be shaken in the modern notion 'that a poet must never write or discourse as the ordinary part of mankind do, but in number and verse, as an oracle. . .' He should always remember to dress badly while in company, to show his wit 'by cutting and slashing, and laying about him, and banging mankind,' and to publish his compositions with a show of great reluctance and only after a friend has been hired to raise a prolonged and insistent clamour for their appearance in print.

In his closing paragraphs the author weaves a new thread of irony into his discourse by offering a number of suggestions for the encouragement of poetry in Ireland, his main consideration being the great benefits to Irish trade which will follow from the rise of the poetic science. A Grub Street, a blind alley fitted up at the public charge as an apartment for the Muses, a playhouse, a corporation of poets — were Dublin to be supplied with these the entire kingdom would be advantaged.

For all its ironical indirection, the *Letter to a Young Poet* tells us a great deal about Swift's positive doctrines of poetry — more, in fact, than can be gathered from any one of his other compositions. If poetry is not inspired insight into Beauty and Truth, what is it? Swift's answer seems to be that it is the cultivated statement of the thoughts and perceptions shared by enlightened men of taste. That there is such a thing as artistic genius he was no more denying than was Sidney; his quarrel with the Sidneian school was rather over the meaning of artistic genius. Believing as he did that imagination is entirely the outgrowth of certain physical conditions, and believing furthermore that Beauty is a deception which obscures reality, Swift saw in the mysterious powers which some would confer on the poet only arrant nonsense. The genius was not a seer; he was one distinguished from his fellows by his greater intellectual capacity, by his keener wit, and by his extraordinary voice. As we have previously seen, Swift's uncompromisingly hostile view of the poetic imagination was something unique, and not, as many would have it, the characteristic attitude of his age. But despite his debasement of imagination, he was, by virtue of his own genius and exquisite taste, fully sensitive to the inexplicable qualities of great literature. His insistence that poetry must be civilized, that it must reach through to reality, and that its matter must be acceptable to men of sense in no way ruled out the artistry which only genius can come by.

3

SWIFT's miscellaneous verse of this time is fairly extensive, and may be arranged under the three heads of compositions of public interest, personal verses, and literary pieces.

The four metrical compositions of public interest of which we shall speak were all occasioned by events in England. Of these the earliest, attributed to Swift by Sir Walter Scott, is *A Wicked Treasonable Libel,* which was written about 1721 in response to the rumour that King George was on the point of securing a divorce in order to marry his mistress, the duchess of Kendal. The sentiments expressed in the *Libel* and the phrasing are thoroughly Swiftian, as the six opening lines will show:

> While the king and his ministers keep such a pother,
> And all about changing one whore for another,
> Think I to myself, what need all this strife,
> His majesty first had a whore of a wife,
> And surely the difference mounts to no more
> Than, now he has gotten a wife of a whore.

On 16 June 1722 the duke of Marlborough died. It is a pity that Swift, who in the *Examiner* had attacked the great

soldier so ignobly, was not magnanimous enough at least to
remain silent at his enemy's death.   But the satirist was alike
incapable of moderating his moral judgments or of concealing them behind the conventional reticences, and in *A
Satirical Elegy* he reiterated the charges which he had levelled
at Marlborough in the days of the queen, closing with six
powerful lines on the fall of Pride :

> Come hither, all ye empty things !
> Ye bubbles raised by breath of kings !
> Who float upon the tide of state ;
> Come hither, and behold your fate !
> Let Pride be taught by this rebuke,
> How very mean a thing's a duke ;
> From all his ill-got honours flung,
> Turn'd to that dirt from whence he sprung.

To this same year — 1722 — belong the verses *Upon the
Horrid Plot,* Swift's scoffing commentary on the government's
proceedings against his friend, Bishop Atterbury, recently
accused of implication in a plot to restore the pretender.

Finally, there is the *Verses on the Revival of the Order of
the Bath* (1725).   The last couplet of this short satirical
piece,

> And he who'll leap over a stick for the king,
> Is qualified best for a dog in a string,

anticipated the account in *Gulliver's Travels,* Book 1,
chapter iii, of the trial of dexterity which the Lilliputian
candidates for the coloured silken threads were forced to
undergo.

4

THE twelve-year period from late 1714 down to the close
of 1726 abounded in verses of a personal nature, of which
some, like those commemorating Stella's long visit to Woodpark during the summer of 1723, have already been referred
to, while others, like the innumerable sallies called forth in
the course of the metrical war which Swift kept up with
Sheridan and Delany, do not require critical comment.   Of

the personal verses of which we have not yet spoken, by all odds the most interesting are those addressed to Stella, and to them we shall confine ourselves.

It was Swift's habit, beginning in 1719, to celebrate Stella's birthday, which fell on 13 March, in verse. We have in all, seven of the birthday poems, the series coming to an end in 1727 and being broken in 1720 and 1726. If there is anywhere a key to the enigmatic relations between Swift and Stella, it lies in these extraordinary occasional pieces, which have sometimes been called love poems and again poems of friendship, but which in truth embody emotions too subtle and complicated to be accurately described in conventional terms. Insistently Swift dwells upon Stella's progressive physical deterioration, and in contrast upon her qualities of mind and character, which remain untouched by advancing years. In the verses for 1721 he wrote,

> Now this is Stella's case in fact,
> An angel's face a little crack'd.
> (Could poets or could painters fix
> How angels look at thirty-six :)
> This drew us in at first to find
> In such a form an angel's mind ;
> And every virtue now supplies
> The fainting rays of Stella's eyes.

A similar strain is found in the piece for 13 March 1725.

> No length of time can make you quit
> Honour and virtue, sense and wit ;
> Thus you may still be young to me,
> While I can better hear than see.
> O ne'er may Fortune show her spite,
> To make me deaf, and mend my sight !

Elsewhere, as in *To Stella visiting me in my Sickness,* which in 1720 took the place of a birthday poem, Swift dwelt upon her courage, for it appears that she scorned to affect feminine fears — we know that on one occasion when faced with physical danger she chose to stand her ground like a man. Here is an expression of Swift's true attitude towards women, which, despite certain passages in his works, was a noble and

generous one. Unlike the majority of the great satirists,
Swift did not look upon woman as a flagitious and inferior
being; properly, she was man's equal, contemptible only
when she assumed the conventionally feminine rôle and laid
reason aside for wiles and affected airs. When Swift browbeat the women of his acquaintance, it was to make them act
like the rational beings that he assumed they were. But he
had no need to browbeat Stella, who from the Moor Park
days had received the imprint of his own mind and whose
every word and action were worthy of her teacher. She was
altogether his, a woman of high courage, sense, and honour.
He bestowed on her paternal affection and pride, friendship,
and the tenderness that he felt for all who were close to him.

These emotions are nowhere more clearly expressed than
in *To Stella, Who Collected and Transcribed his Poems* (ca.
1721). Swift glories in the fact that theirs is a relationship
existing in defiance of all the laws of romance :

> Thou, Stella, wert no longer young,
> When first for thee my harp was strung,
> Without one word of Cupid's darts,
> Of killing eyes, or bleeding hearts ;
> With friendship and esteem possest,
> I ne'er admitted Love a guest.

There follow thirty-four couplets which in substance are as
remarkable as anything which Swift ever indited and should
be read with scrupulous care by everyone desiring to understand the basic pattern of Swift's mind and character. The
scrubby poet — we give Swift's sense rather than his words —
is deluded by a fleeting glimpse of some Chloe, Sylvia, Phillis,
or Iris into imagining the damsel to be a paragon of beauty,
and proceeds to translate his delusion into romantic verse.
But sooner or later comes the cruel awakening when he
discovers Chloe tippling with footmen, Sylvia an inmate of
Bridewell, Phillis mending her ragged smocks, or Iris dis-
figured by disease. It is only true poets who can look quite
through the false beauty at the surface to the inner reality.

> Now, should my praises owe their truth
> To beauty, dress, or paint, or youth,
> What stoics call without our power,

They could not be ensured an hour ;
'Twere grafting on an annual stock,
That must our expectation mock,
And, making one luxuriant shoot,
Die the next year for want of root :
Before I could my verses bring,
Perhaps you're quite another thing.
    So Mævius, when he drain'd his skull
To celebrate some suburb trull,
His similes in order set,
And every crambo he could get ;
Had gone through all the common-places
Worn out by wits, who rhyme on faces ;
Before he could his poem close,
The lovely nymph had lost her nose.
    Your virtues safely I commend ;
They on no accidents depend :
Let malice look with all her eyes,
She dares not say the poet lies.

Whatever else went into that series of nauseating compositions which in *A Lady's Dressing Room* attained the ultimate
degree of disgust, one element was moral realism.   It was
this same moral realism which controlled his feelings for
Stella.

Many are the writers who have represented Stella as a
woman cruelly used by an egoistic lover and deprived of
everything which she had a right to expect from one to
whom she had sworn loyalty and love.   This pity for Stella
is doubtless a sign of admirable chivalry on the part of Swift's
critics, but it speaks well neither for their sense of evidence
nor for their knowledge of the world.   What is there —
rumours aside — to show that Stella ever thought of Swift
as her lover or looked forward to marriage with him?   And
again, are we justified in assuming that she felt her life incomplete and longed for the joys of marriage rather than the
privileges which were hers as the dean's closest friend and
companion?   If we may judge by the verses which she wrote
for Swift's birthday in 1721, she accepted her position in a
spirit utterly free from self-pity and regret:

        St. Patrick's Dean, your country's pride,
    My early and my only guide,

Let me among the rest attend,
Your pupil and your humble friend,
To celebrate in female strains
The day that paid your mother's pains;
Descend to take that tribute due
In gratitude alone to you.
　　　　When men began to call me fair,
You interposed your timely care:
You early taught me to despise
The ogling of a coxcomb's eyes;
Show'd where my judgment was misplaced;
Refined my fancy and my taste.
　　　　Behold that beauty just decay'd,
Invoking art to nature's aid:
Forsook by her admiring train,
She spreads her tatter'd nets in vain;
Short was her part upon the stage;
Went smoothly on for half a page;
Her bloom was gone, she wanted art,
As the scene changed, to change her part;
She, whom no lover could resist,
Before the second act was hiss'd.
Such is the fate of female race
With no endowments but a face;
Before the thirtieth year of life,
A maid forlorn, or hated wife.
　　　　Stella to you, her tutor, owes
That she has ne'er resembled those:
Nor was a burden to mankind
With half her course of years behind.
You taught how I might youth prolong,
By knowing what was right and wrong;
How from my heart to bring supplies
Of lustre to my fading eyes;
How soon a beauteous mind repairs
The loss of changed or falling hairs;
How wit and virtue from within
Send out a smoothness o'er the skin:
Your lectures could my fancy fix,
And I can please at thirty-six.
The sight of Chloe at fifteen,
Coquetting, gives not me the spleen;
The idol now of every fool
Till time shall make their passions cool;
Then tumbling down Time's steepy hill,
While Stella holds her station still.

O ! turn your precepts into laws,
Redeem the women's ruin'd cause,
Retrieve lost empire to our sex,
That men may bow their rebel necks.
        Long be the day that gave you birth
Sacred to friendship, wit, and mirth ;
Late dying may you cast a shred
Of your rich mantle o'er my head ;
To bear with dignity my sorrow,
One day alone, then die to-morrow.

5

OF purely literary compositions in verse the years now under
consideration were not highly productive.   There is nothing
here to equal the metrical pieces written under Addison's
inspiration in 1708 and 1709 or the five or six great metrical
performances of the 1710-1714 period.   It was not, indeed,
until 1729 that Swift again reached his true level in non-
controversial verse, when, beginning with *The Journal of a
Modern Lady,* he proved repeatedly that he had lost not a
whit of his former power.

Phyllis, or the Progress of Love was written in 1716, and
as the reference in the closing lines shows, Swift was still
living in the glorious past, for the inn at Staines where
Phyllis and her husband are seen as landlord and hostess lay
on the road between London and Windsor and must have
been passed countless times by Swift as he made the journey
in Oxford's or Bolingbroke's company.   At the beginning of
the tale Phyllis is a perfect prude, blushing with simulated
modesty whenever a man looks at her.   At length a lucky
suitor wins her, but with the completion of all the arrange-
ments for the wedding Phyllis's modesty departs and that
very night she runs away with John the butler.   Their
money gone, Phyllis first pawns her trinkets and is at last
reduced to selling her virtue : —

        When food and raiment now grew scarce,
Fate put a period to the farce,
And with exact poetic justice ;
For John was landlord, Phyllis hostess ;

> They keep, at Stains, the Old Blue Boar,
> Are cat and dog, and rogue and whore.

The Progress of Poetry (1720) is in every way superior to the verses on Phyllis, and though completely outdistanced by the later piece *On Poetry — a Rhapsody*, is worthy to stand as an envoy to the *Letter to a Young Poet*. The well-fed goose does not cackle, but turned out to graze in the common she grows lank and spare and before long is flying over the parish, singing harmoniously as she wings her way. So the poet. Replete, he is good for nothing, but let him starve and his powers increase in proportion to his hunger:

> Now his exalted spirit loathes
> Encumbrances of food and clothes;
> And up he rises like a vapour,
> Supported high on wings of paper.
> He singing flies, and flying sings,
> While from below all Grub-Street rings.

The Progress of Beauty (1720) is one of the revolting compositions of the order of *The Lady's Dressing Room*. The disgust of which Swift was the master lies in every line that tells of Celia's appearance as she rises in the morning:

> The paint by perspiration cracks,
>   And falls in rivulets of sweat,
> On either side you see the tracks
>   While at her chin the conflu'nts meet.

That in such a description Swift was drawing to a certain degree upon actual experience and not entirely upon diseased imagination is shown in a very interesting way by a passage from *The Journal to Stella*: 'I was to see lady —, who is just up after lying-in; and the ugliest sight I have seen, pale, dead, old and yellow, for want of her paint. She has turned my stomach. But she will soon be painted, and a beauty again' (21 December 1711).

Little has thus far been said of Swift's rhythms. Small argument is needed to show that the author of *Mrs. Frances Harris's Petition* (1701), *The Place of the Damned* (1731), *Helter Skelter* (1731), and *Street Cries for Fruitwomen* (at-

tributed to Swift; undated) was endowed with a rhythmic
sense somewhat unusual in the age of couplets. *The Description of an Irish Feast* (1720), said to have been adapted
from an Irish song, is still further evidence that Swift's
quixotic mind sometimes beat to unconventional measures:

> The floor is all wet
> 　　With leaps and with jumps,
> While the water and sweat
> 　　Splish-splash in their pumps.
>
> Bless you late and early,
> 　　Laughlin O'Enagin!
> But, my hand, you dance rarely.
> 　　Margery Grinagin.

At odd moments during 1724 and '25 Swift diverted himself by writing a great number of *Riddles,* now of more
interest to the student of folk-lore than to the average reader
of verse. Swift's two visits to England in 1726 and '27 were
productive of a number of metrical pieces. The lines *On
Censure* have already been spoken of in connexion with
the events surrounding Vanessa's death. Of the other compositions, it will suffice to mention two, *A Love Poem from
a Physician to his Mistress* and *The Furniture of a Woman's
Mind.* The former is revoltingly scatological and were it
the first of its kind from the author's pen might lend a certain
plausibility to Delany's contention in the *Observations* that
the defilement of Swift's style was to some degree the result
of Pope's influence during the dean's sojourns at Twickenham. *The Furniture of a Woman's Mind,* on the other
hand, is quite free from disgusting imagery, is genuinely
humorous, and for all its weight of detail exhibits the fine
satiric touch:

> A set of phrases learn'd by rote;
> A passion for a scarlet coat;
> When at a play, to laugh or cry,
> Yet cannot tell the reason why;
> Never to hold her tongue a minute,
> While all she prates has nothing in it;
> Whole hours can with a coxcomb sit,
> And take his nonsense all for wit;

Her learning mounts to read a song,
But half the words pronouncing wrong ;
Has every repartee in store
She spoke ten thousand times before ;
Can ready compliments supply
On all occasions cut and dry ;
Such hatred to a parson's gown,
The sight would put her in a swoon ;
For conversation well endued,
She calls it witty to be rude ;
And, placing raillery in railing,
Will tell aloud your greatest failing ;
Nor make a scruple to expose
Your bandy leg, or crooked nose ;
Can at her morning tea run o'er
The scandal of the day before ;
Improving hourly in her skill,
To cheat and wrangle at quadrille.

But it is only when hung beside the portraits of Stella, the
model of her sex, that Swift's satiric representations of woman
can properly be understood.

BOOK V

GULLIVER'S TRAVELS

CHAPTER I

HISTORY AND BACKGROUND OF THE BOOK

1

THANKS to the work of three distinguished scholars of our own day, the history of the composition of *Gulliver's Travels* is no longer a matter of conjecture.[1] The various stages in the growth of Swift's great satire from its inception in 1714 to its publication on 28 October 1726 now stand fully revealed.

That *Gulliver's Travels* and the *Memoirs of Martinus Scriblerus* are more than distantly related we have previously seen. It will be remembered that in 1714 Swift, as one of the Scriblerians, was engaged upon fragments of a satiric nature dealing with Martin Scriblerus's supposed voyages to strange lands. Though these fragments have not survived, something of their contents can be told: it seems certain that two distinct voyages had taken shape, one to a land of pygmies, another to a kingdom of philosophers. Swift had not proceeded far, however, when the shadow of the approaching political disaster drove all thought of Martin from his mind and in a few weeks sent him into retirement at Letcombe.

When Swift returned to Dublin in the autumn of 1714 he apparently brought with him the manuscript of the two unfinished voyages, but not with any idea of completing what was to have been his contribution to the *Memoirs*. Broken in spirit, he had no heart for the *jeu d'esprit*. It is not, in fact, until 1721 that we find him again engaged upon these travels. His earliest reference to them occurs in a letter written on 15 April of this year to Charles Ford; 'I am now writing a History of my Travells,' Swift informed his friend, 'which will be a large Volume, and gives Account of Countryes hitherto unknown; but they go on slowly for want of Health and Humor.'[2]

When Swift set to work upon what was to become *Gulliver's Travels* he unquestionably had before him the manuscript of 1714, and in a sense he was but continuing the narrative which he had begun in the days of the queen.[3] Before his retirement to Letcombe he had completed, as we have just seen, certain portions of Martin's voyage to the land of the pygmies and of the voyage to the kingdom of the philosophers; these he now incorporated in the account of Gulliver, taking from the 1714 manuscript chapters i and ii and possibly other parts of the Voyage to Lilliput, and many passages of the Voyage to Laputa. Otherwise, *Gulliver's Travels* owes little to the earlier work: it is packed with commentary on political events subsequent to the queen's death; it is no longer a mere *jeu d'esprit* but a satire of unequalled scope and depth; and the hero has been transformed from a lubberly pedant into Lemuel Gulliver.

Before long some of Swift's friends in England had learned, probably through Ford, of the work in progress — 'I long to see your Travels,' wrote Bolingbroke in December 1721. In Ireland there seem to have been very few who had any knowledge of the projected satire, but at least Vanessa had been confided in, for a letter of hers to Swift written about June 1722 contains references to Gulliver's experiences in Brobdingnag.

Composition of the *Travels* went on slowly. In July 1722, while visiting his friend Robert Cope at Loughgall, Swift wrote to Ford complaining of the bad weather and confessing that instead of writing — he has, he says, almost forgotten how to hold a pen — he has been reading through 'abundance of Trash,'[4] which we learn from a letter to Vanessa consisted of books of history and travel. But by the beginning of 1724 he had finished the first draft of parts i, ii, and iv and was engaged upon part iii,— this we know from his letter to Ford of 19 January 1724, in which he wrote, 'I have left the Country of Horses, and am in the flying Island, where I shall not stay long, and my two last Journyes will be soon over,'[5] — and less than three months later he was telling Ford that with health, leisure, and humour he expected to finish his travels shortly (Letter of 2 April 1724).[6] But as spring wore on to summer the Wood affair swept everything else aside and Swift's energies were diverted entirely to the *Drapier's Letters*. As it turned out, it was not until the summer of 1725 that he completed his first draft.

THESE facts and what else is now known of the composition of *Gulliver's Travels* may be summarized as follows. Parts I and II were largely the work of 1721 and 1722; part IV was for the most part written in 1723; while the composition of part III extended from the early months of 1724 into the summer of 1725. Finally, the entire work was revised in 1725.

Swift began, then, with the voyage to the land of the pygmies, using for his first two chapters material composed in 1714. In 1714, it would appear, Swift had conceived this first voyage as primarily a diverting account of adventures experienced by a man of normal size in the midst of a race of tiny people; how brilliantly he had started to carry out this intention is shown by chapters i and ii of A Voyage to Lilliput, which will always cast their spell over the reader. But he had also intended to represent the pygmies as an ideally rational people, and in chapter vi — 'Of The Inhabitants Of Lilliput; Their Learning, Laws, and Customs. The Manner of Educating Their Children . . .'—their Utopian character, which stands in complete contradiction to the picture elsewhere given, was probably taken over from or was at least a reflection of the 1714 version.[7] The rest of the first voyage dates from 1721 and 1722, and with chapter iii the tone changes perceptibly : the narrative takes on a satiric edge and is studded with allusions to political events under George I. As a consequence of this break between the first two chapters and those following there is some inconsistency in Swift's symbols. The emperor of Lilliput is at the beginning a purely conventional monarch; Gulliver is Swift if anyone; while Bolgolam seems to represent the earl of Nottingham and his hatred for Gulliver to be an allusion to Nottingham's attack on Swift in the lords early in 1714. In the later chapters, however, the emperor becomes George I, Flimnap symbolizes Walpole, while

under Gulliver's adventures the political career of Bolingbroke is shadowed forth. By the time that we are well
into chapter iii, the Lilliputians, weighted with the trans-
gressions of the court of George I and the administration
of Walpole, have become a thoroughly contemptible people,
an impression greatly heightened by the account in chapter
iv of the squabbles between High and Low Heels and Big-
and Little-Endians and in chapter v of the emperor's in-
satiable desire for conquest. For this reason it is with
considerable surprise that we read in chapter vi of the admirable character of the Lilliputians' learning, laws, customs, and educational methods. Swift perceived this
inconsistency, and sought to correct it by inserting into
chapter vi the following passage:

In relating these and the following Laws, I would only be understood to mean the original Institutions, and not the most
scandalous Corruptions into which these People are fallen by the
degenerate Nature of Man. For as to that infamous Practice of
acquiring great Employments by dancing on the Ropes, or
Badges of Favour and Distinction by leaping over Sticks, and
creeping under them; the Reader is to observe, that they were
first introduced by the Grandfather of the Emperor now reign-
ing; and grew to the present Height, by the gradual Increase of
Party and Faction.[8]

But despite this explanation the Utopian characteristics attributed to the Lilliputians in chapter vi stand in sharp and
humorous contrast with their actual behaviour as elsewhere
depicted.

With the completion of the first draft of part I Swift took
up the second voyage and on the heels of that the fourth.
Neither the description of Brobdingnag nor of Houyhnhnm-
land had been anticipated in the 1714 manuscript; in parts
II and IV Swift was starting from scratch. Thus it is not
by chance that these two portions of *Gulliver's Travels* are
artistically the most impressive: because they were written
in a single stretch and sprang from an imagination undisturbed by recollections of past endeavours, each is marked
by a firm, logical contour of details and by a compelling
unity of mood. The satiric device which gives coher-

ence and oneness to the Voyage to Brobdingnag had
already been developed in the later chapters of part I,
where the minute stature of the Lilliputians came to stand
in direct relation to their contemptible moral nature. This
symbolization of moral nature through physical size is applied throughout part II, but with a different emphasis:
here it is the gigantic natives who are magnanimous, while
Gulliver, shrunk to pygmæan size, becomes the hapless rep-   G E
resentative of a pernicious race of little odious vermin, all
of whose social and political institutions reflect the corruption of European man. This contrast between the rational
and the irrational aspects of human nature, a contrast which
is seen emerging in the later chapters of part I and runs
strongly through all of part II, is the single theme of A Voyage to the Houyhnhnms, where as a result of satiric artistry
it is expressed in a manner which the world has thus far
found no way of neutralizing, least of all when it has resorted to frenzied abuse of the author.

Part III, the last to be written, stands upon much the same
footing as part I in that it incorporates material from the
Scriblerus manuscript. The Voyage to Laputa has nothing of the unity of the other Voyages, being made up of
four distinct incidents: the Flying Island, the Academy of
Projectors, satire on literary critics and historians, and the
description of the immortal Struldbrugs. The account of
the projectors had been written for the *Memoirs of Scriblerus*
and was now introduced as the second incident of part III,
although certain details were brought forward into the opening incident — that of the Flying Island. But that the main
portion of this first incident was written in the 1720's is
proved by the allegory attaching to the flying island of
Laputa and the subject kingdom of Balnibarbi, for under
these symbols Swift was setting forth England's tyrannical
treatment of Ireland; while the story of the rebellion (chapter iii), an almost undisguised allusion to the agitation
against Wood, could not have been written before 1724,
and since it contains a reference to the official announcement of the surrender of Wood's patent must have been
revised late in 1725.

In April 1725 Swift sought the seclusion of Sheridan's country place at Quilca. Here he worked through the summer, bringing the political allusions and allegory up to date and revising the entire satire. On 14 August 1725 he could write to Ford, 'I have finished my Travells, and I am now transcribing them; they are admirable Things, and will wonderfully mend the World.'[9]

Secretive up to this point, Swift now referred to the finished *Travels* without constraint, as in the letter to Sheridan in which he urged his unfortunate friend to face the disaster at Cork with stoicism and, by remembering the Yahoos, to 'expect no more from man than such an animal is capable of' (11 September). [To Pope he wrote two letters bearing upon the *Travels,* in the first of which (29 September 1725) occurs the famous statement that 'principally I hate and detest that animal called man, although I heartily love John, Peter, Thomas, and so forth,' and the equally well-known distinction — the informing idea of the Voyage to the Houyhnhnms — between man as *animal rationale* and merely *rationis capax.*]

FROM the moment when he took up his long-neglected manuscript in 1720 or 1721 Swift wrote with the idea of publication always in mind. Everyone knows that he desired to vex the world; what is sometimes forgotten is that he was also bent upon creating a work which should win universal acclaim. He had no thought of withholding his satire from the press, and upon its completion he looked about for some effective way of getting it before the public. The upshot was that Swift crossed to England in March 1726; spent the summer in the company of Pope, Arbuthnot, and others; and then, shortly before his departure for Ireland on 15 August, opened negotiations in the name of Richard Sympson with Motte the publisher. According to Pope, Motte received the *Travels* 'he knew not from whence, nor from whom, dropped at his house in the dark, from a hackney coach' (To Swift, [26] November 1726). Who the mysterious messenger in the hackney-coach was we do not know, but such facts as have come to light point strongly to Charles Ford.[10]

Gulliver's Travels was published by Benjamin Motte on 28 October 1726 in two octavo volumes.[11] Within a few weeks Motte issued two further octavo editions and in 1727 a fourth octavo edition, incorporating in the latter certain corrections furnished by Charles Ford. Now, it was not the original manuscript of Gulliver's Travels but a copy which had been dropped at Motte's house — to sustain the amusing intrigue and to insure the author of protection against any action which the satire might call forth from the powers in England it was necessary that the writing be in an unknown hand. But Swift preserved his original manuscript, and before the end of 1726 Ford, now in Dublin, was comparing it with Motte's first edition, in which he found many errors of the press as well as unauthorized alterations. The former he corrected in a list which he enclosed in a letter to Motte of 3 January 1727, and it was this list which Motte used in preparing the corrected edition — the fourth octavo — of 1727.

But the unauthorized alterations, of which Swift complained bitterly, still stood. Again it was Charles Ford who recorded the departures from the original manuscript, this time in an interleaved copy of the first Motte edition, now preserved in the Forster collection at South Kensington. Whether Ford ever submitted these larger corrections to Motte does not appear, but no use was made of them until Faulkner, the Dublin printer, undertook to publish a collected edition of the dean's works. Despite his statements to the contrary, Swift approved of Faulkner's plan and was eager above all to insure an edition of Gulliver's Travels which should set forth correctly the passages mangled by Motte. But the original manuscript was not to be found, and accordingly Swift wrote to Ford, requesting the interleaved copy containing the full corrections. Thus it came about that the edition of Gulliver's Travels published by Faulkner in 1735 was the first unmarred by Motte's temerarious alterations.

2

As ONE takes up the intellectual and literary background of *Gulliver's Travels* he should fix his mind upon an all-important fact, which he can only forget with disastrous critical results : there is no discontinuity between *Gulliver's Travels* and Swift's other works. The great prose satire presents nothing in the way of thought or mood which is not at least implicit in some earlier or later composition of his ; artistically it is inferior only to *A Tale of a Tub,* but this artistic excellence does not signify the presence of new elements. From start to finish *Gulliver's Travels* is an expression of Swift's controlling ideas.

In *genre,* the book is to be classed as an imaginary voyage. The extent to which Swift was influenced by the traditional characteristics of this *genre,* the extent to which he departed from these characteristics and worked in an original manner — these are matters of far more importance than his specific 'sources.'

Sir William Temple had been a great reader of travel accounts and had used the sociological information which they afforded to substantiate his philosophical theories. The library at Moor Park was therefore well stocked with books of travel, and we know that in 1697-1698 Swift read the *Voyage de Syam,* the *Voyage de Maroc,* and the *Histoire d'Æthiopie.* That Swift never lost his early acquired taste for such books is shown by the presence in his own library of the accounts of Purchas, Nieuhof, Le Blanc, Bernier, Dampier, and others, and also by his statement in a letter to Vanessa of July 1722 that he was reading 'I know not how many diverting books of history and travels.' [12]

In *Gulliver's Travels* Swift doubtless drew upon the authentic voyages for a great deal in the way of tone and for some concrete details, just as he lifted verbatim from Sturmy's *Mariner's Magazine* (1679) the account of the storm in the opening chapter of the Voyage to Brobdingnag.[13] But it was an imaginary voyage which he was writing, and it is to well-established characteristics of this literary type that much of *Gulliver's Travels* conforms.[14] From Lucian on, the imaginary voyage has been a vehicle for specific satire upon historians, scholars, courts, etc. How much satire of this sort — satire without an *arrière-pensée* — there is in *Gulliver's Travels* one does not perceive until he sets out to look for it. The imaginary voyage, however, has lent itself equally well to satire of a much higher order, in which man and society have been subjected to philosophic criticism. The age of discovery had presented to the European mind the sharp contrast between 'natural' man and society as found in the Americas and the sophisticated life of the Old World, and although it was some two centuries before the full implications were developed, Montaigne's agile mind had already seized upon the contrast and made of it the basis of a critique of European civilization. It was only natural that from this time forth the imaginary voyage should be used by writers eager to convict Europe of her sins by dwelling upon the supposedly ideal society brought to light in the new lands. There is something of this in *Gulliver's Travels,* particularly in part II, where we are made to scan European society through the eyes of the genial giants and to see it as it appeared to them — ridiculous, hateful.

But one cannot long study *Gulliver's Travels* in the light of the seventeenth-century imaginary voyages of the philosophic type without perceiving that the important thing is the manner in which Swift's satiric work does not conform to pattern. Since the differences which are disclosed illuminate as does nothing else the meaning of *Gulliver's Travels,* it will pay us to retrace our steps and consider once more the philosophic criticism contained in the imaginary voyage.

The age of discovery produced a wealth of authentic voyages and later a great many imaginary ones. What the explorers saw was determined to a certain extent by what they were ready to see; as for the writers of imaginary voyages, their depiction of life in the New World was largely controlled by pure theories. The sixteenth century inherited from the Middle Ages the legend of an Earthly Paradise, while in the Latin poets it read of a Golden Age.

Was it surprising that the men of the Renaissance, their imaginations afire with the tales brought home by the intrepid voyagers, cast eager eyes to the western continents to learn whether the Earthly Paradise and the Golden Age were perhaps more than myths? The earlier observers who studied the natives at first hand were torn between two conclusions, one that these people were of the order of beasts, the other that they were happier, more virtuous, and more reasonable than civilized men. The latter conclusion was to receive the assent first of the learned enthusiasts of the Renaissance, then of Christian missionaries, and at length of the eighteenth-century *philosophes*. This primitivism — the exaltation of 'natural' man and 'natural' society — is clearly enunciated in the *Essais* of Montaigne, where it becomes an instrument for attacking European civilization. By the end of the seventeenth century and the beginning of the eighteenth, the philosophic criticism of Europe — criticism which rests upon primitivistic theory and is 'rationalistic' in the sense that reason is brought into play against established dogmas — was full blown in the imaginary voyages. Take, for example, *La terre australe connue* (1676) by Gabriel Foigny: Foigny was a *libertin*, attacking Christianity in his description of austral peoples. In *L'histoire des Sévarambes* (1677-1679), Denis Vairasse d'Alais satirized the miracles of the Old and New Testament, and represented the religion of the *Sévarambes* as deism.

But in *Gulliver's Travels* there is no primitivism, no libertinism, no anti-Christian element. On the contrary, as a philosophic voyage it expresses the author's belief in the universality of reason, his ethical rigidity, his anti-rationalism and anti-intellectualism, and his theory of human Pride. The Houyhnhnm-Yahoo contrast is not one between man and animal,— though it does say, by way of *le mythe animal*, that beasts never degenerate to the level to which the human being is capable of falling,— nor again between an ideal people, the children of nature, and men corrupted by civilization, but between man governed by reason and man given over to his irrational instincts. The Houyhnhnms, we are told, are guided by nature, but the last thing that Swift

meant was by untutored impulse, the term *nature* being in
his vocabulary a synonym for *reason*.

A comparison of *Gulliver's Travels* with some outwardly
similar work representative of the libertine tradition will
emphasize the differences of which we have been speaking.
For instance, place *Gulliver's Travels* beside the Baron de
Lahontan's works, which have recently been cited by Professor Gilbert Chinard as influencing the composition of
the *Travels*.[15]   Lahontan, who had been in North America,
had published both voyages and memoirs.   In 1703 he issued at The Hague — published in English the year before
and revised by another hand in 1705 — his *Dialogues curieux
entre l'auteur et un sauvage de bon sens qui a voyagé.*
Lahontan's thorough-going intellectual libertinism is apparent in all of his writings, but above all in the *Dialogues
curieux,* which may be regarded as a summary of the case
which by that time had been built up against civilization and
Christianity by a long line of critics imbued with the idea
of natural man's superiority.   To the dogmas of Christianity
Lahontan opposes natural religion ; to the corruptions of
civilization, natural morality.   The savages are not without
religious consciousness, for nature has given them a perception of the divine; socially, they live in equality according
to nature; they are free from disease; they look upon the
arts and sciences of the Western World as a misfortune ; since
the animals are peaceful, they conclude that war is a curse
which man brings upon himself in attempting to live by
reason instead of by nature — 'la raison des hommes est le
plus grand instrument de leur malheur.'

Mr. Chinard has pointed out a number of similarities between Lahontan's writings and part IV of *Gulliver's Travels.*
Lahontan says that savages attribute the maladies of civilization to the use of salt; there is no salt in Houyhnhnm-land
and Gulliver comes to believe that its use is harmful.
The Houyhnhnms, like Lahontan's savages, believe that
Europeans wear clothes in order to hide their deformities.
Neither the horses nor the savages know how to lie, and both
attribute the complicated languages of civilization to the
desire to dissimulate.   When Gulliver describes the instru-

ments of war perfected in Europe the Houyhnhnms shudder
in horror precisely as Adario — Lahontan's 'sauvage de bon
sens' — had done on a like occasion.   There is also similarity
in the criticisms of European justice voiced by Lahontan and
Swift.⟩

But here the resemblances stop.   One must admit that
they are striking, yet it does not seem to follow — as Mr.
Chinard would have it — that Swift necessarily drew upon the
French writer.   Assuming, however, that he not only knew
Lahontan but used him, as perhaps he did, we are to observe
that he took over from the *libertin* not the barest shadow
of the latter's real meaning.   At every point Lahontan was
seeking to turn his reader away from civilization towards
unsophisticated nature, whereas Swift was never more unyielding in the austerity of his ethical prescriptions than
in A Voyage to the Houyhnhnms.   The nature which had
endowed the horses 'with a general disposition to all virtues'
was not that which had implanted deism in the savages; it
was the voice of reason given resonance by the civilized ages.⟩

AFTER all, Swift is the soundest expounder of the satiric
purpose behind *Gulliver's Travels,* and no criticism can
stand which does not take fully into account his statements
in his two letters written to Pope towards the end of 1725
(29 September and 26 November).

'...the chief end I propose to myself in all my labours is
to vex the world rather than divert it; and if I could compass
that design, without hurting my own person or fortune, I
would be the most indefatigable writer you have ever seen,
without reading.'   This from the earlier letter.   Quoted
often, they are words the precise meaning of which is lost
upon us unless we remember the universe of discourse in
which Swift and Pope moved.   How and why does one vex
the world?   To-day the only answer can be that one doesn't,
but the wits replied that man's Pride must be lashed and
lashed again and that satire is the proper flail.   Nor was it
right to accuse those who administered this chastisement
of misanthropy, for their perception of the flagitious side of
human nature derived from a reasoned philosophy, whereas

the misanthrope was one who out of revenge for his own
misadventures in the world spurned the entire race of mankind.

> . . . when you think of the world give it one lash the more at
> my request.   I have ever hated all nations, professions, and com-
> munities, and all my love is toward individuals : for instance, I
> hate the tribe of lawyers, but I love Counsellor Such-a-one, and
> Judge Such-a-one : so with physicians — I will not speak of my
> own trade — soldiers, English, Scotch, French, and the rest.   But
> principally I hate and detest that animal called man, although I
> heartily love John, Peter, Thomas, and so forth.   This is the sys-
> tem upon which I have governed myself many years, but do not
> tell, and so I shall go on till I have done with them.   I have got
> materials toward a treatise, proving the falsity of that definition
> *animal rationale,* and to show it would be only *rationis capax.*
> Upon this great foundation of misanthropy, though not in
> Timon's manner, the whole building of my Travels is erected ;
> and I never will have peace of mind till all honest men are of my
> opinion.

This long statement reaches its resolution in the words
'upon this great foundation of misanthropy, though not in
Timon's manner, the whole building of my Travels is erected,'
and to-day we should place misanthropy in inverted commas.
The sense is this : if it be 'misanthropy' to perceive that man,
endowed with reason, is yet dominated by his passions ; if it
be 'misanthropy' to hate man because the greater his bestiality the more insufferable his Pride, then I confess that I am
a 'misanthrope.'

Pope had written on 15 October that he had it in his head
to write 'a set of maxims in opposition to all Rochefoucauld's
principles.'   Swift replied on 26 November, asserting his unshaken admiration for La Rochefoucauld but first redefining
his own position as a commentator on man.   Again he seeks
to deflect the accusation of being a misanthrope :

> I desire you and all my friends will take a special care that my
> disaffection to the world may not be imputed to my age. . . . I tell
> you after all, that I do not hate mankind : it is *vous autres* who
> hate them, because you would have them reasonable animals, and
> are angry for being disappointed.   I have always rejected that
> definition, and made another of my own.   I am no more angry

with [Walpole] than I was with the kite that last week flew away
with one of my chickens ; and yet I was pleased when one of my
servants shot him two days after.   This I say, because you are so
hardy as to tell me of your intentions to write maxims in opposition to Rochefoucauld, who is my favourite, because I found my
whole character in him.

It is not true that Swift founded his whole character in the
French writer, but by this declaration he meant no more
than that like La Rochefoucauld he believed that man is
actuated not by the noble motives which he professes but
by sordid ones ; *Gulliver's Travels,* that is, had sprung not
from the disillusionment of old age but from a clear-headed
analysis of human nature.⌉

One cannot, of course, attribute the satiric effectiveness of
Gulliver's Travels solely to its underlying philosophy, for
as statement the work is altogether in excess of its intellectual
content.   Through artistry the idea is intensified, charged
with emotions, and thrust home in a manner that shocks the
nerves before it arouses the mind.   Nor is the book without
a kind of sensationalism, and in this lies its inferiority to
A Tale of a Tub.   The earlier satire is self-enclosed, its
mood being generated entirely from within.   *Gulliver's
Travels* has not this perfect integrity : its tone sometimes becomes forced as external emotions break through and assume
command.   This is to say that Swift's personal disappointments, his wretchedness in Ireland, the Vanessa incident, and
the bitterness which came from years of unflinching realistic
observation of the world all find expression in the satire.
Nevertheless, it is only through the informing ideas of *Gulliver's Travels* that one can hope to make his way into Swift's
meaning.

In recent years the intellectual and literary background of
the work has come to seem of much greater importance than
its specific sources.   Long before the scientific method extended its rule to the study of literature, it was realized that
Gulliver's Travels owed something to other works, and in
1820 Monck Mason, in his *History of St. Patrick's,* summarized what Orrery, Dunlop, Scott, and others had brought to
light on this point.   Mason gives Lucian, Rabelais, and

Cyrano de Bergerac as the writers whose influence is most apparent. It was not until German critics turned to Swift that the study of his literary sources took on professional earnestness. In 1888 Hönncher published the results of his investigation into the influence of Cyrano de Bergerac; in 1892 Borkowski attempted to show that Swift's indebtedness to other writers was so great that his originality lay open to question. In the ensuing years many scholars took up the hunt, but none with the intelligent pertinacity of Professor W. A. Eddy, whose *Gulliver's Travels; A Critical Study* (1923) will probably remain the definitive treatment of Swift's sources. It now appears that Cyrano de Bergerac's *Histoire comique de la lune* and *Histoire du soleil* are the two works on which Swift drew most extensively. After these come Lucian's *True History;* the sequel to the *True History* written by Lucian's French translator, d'Ablancourt; Rabelais's satire; the works of Tom Brown; and Berkeley's *Theory of Vision,* which may have given Swift the idea of relativity expressed in the contrasts between Lilliput and Brobdingnag. But the chief result of these modern investigations has been to throw Swift's originality into high relief. Borkowski's judgment has been completely reversed. *Gulliver's Travels* is now seen as an imaginative work of a high order, into which contributary streams flow only to lose their proper quality.

3

THE success of *Gulliver's Travels* was immediate and resounding. The group with whom Swift had passed the summer of 1726 and who had conspired with him to shroud the publication of his satire in mystery now kept their ears open, eager to send the author full reports of the judgments of the town. Arbuthnot wrote first, on 8 November; a few days later Gay and Pope, in a joint letter, sent further news. The book was in everyone's hands,— so Swift was told,— the conversation of the whole town, liked extremely, and generally attributed to him. According to Pope and Gay, it was being read 'from cabinet-council to the nursery' — the delight of children from the day of its publication.

Swift's grave versimilitude was highly relished, we gather, for stories were already being told of simple souls who had taken the book *au pied de la lettre*. Arbuthnot heard of a master of a ship who had declared 'that he was very well acquainted with Gulliver, but that the printer had mistaken, that he lived in Wapping, and not in Rotherhithe.' But it was Swift himself who had the most delicious story — of the Irish bishop who 'said that book was full of improbable lies, and for his part, he hardly believed a word of it.'

And since it was the age of wit, the readers of 1726 were not disposed to quarrel with the author for being a little satirical in one or two places, as Richard Sympson had put it. 'Gulliver is a happy man that at his age can write such a merry work,' wrote Arbuthnot. The princess of Wales, coming to the passage of the hobbling prince, laughed at the palpable hit. The duchess dowager of Marlborough was 'in raptures' — 'she says she can dream of nothing else since she read it.' Swift had not misjudged the temper of the times.

To be sure, there were dissenting voices. Lord Harcourt thought 'in some places the matter too far carried,' while others were of the opinion that the satire on general societies of men was too severe. Maids of honour and religious ladies protested, the first because Gulliver seemed to have a particular malice against them, the second because they deemed the author's designs impious and his work 'an insult on Providence depreciating the works of the Creator.' Bolingbroke was outspoken in his disapproval : it was 'a design of evil consequence to depreciate human nature.'

What Swift was probably most curious to learn was whether the town had detected his political references, for the satire abounded in them even after Motte had toned down a number of passages. Indeed, it was Swift's fear of the reprisals which these references might call forth from the government that had dictated the elaborate precautions in dealing with the publisher. But surprisingly enough, few readers perceived any but the most pointed allusions, the politicians agreeing to a man 'that it is free from particular reflections.' Erasmus Lewis was naturally on the look-out for *doubles entendres ;* he was reported as grumblingly searching for the key and 'daily refining' — Arbuthnot's way of telling Swift in a manner that would disclose no secrets to curious postal inspectors that Lewis was getting warm.   Pope and Gay had also met with people 'in search for particular applications in every leaf.'   Yet in spite of such curiosity and the keys that were duly published Swift's political allegory went undetected for the most part, and in *On the Death of Dr. Swift* he could refer to

> libels yet conceal'd from sight,
> Against the court to show his spite ;

adding

> Perhaps his travels, part the third ;
> A lie at every second word —

The acclamation accorded *Gulliver's Travels* upon its publication is in curious contrast with the abuse heaped upon it by its later readers.   Why enthusiastic approval turned to hatred is not easy to explain.   It is clear that Swift's character and all his writings suffered in the eighteenth century as a result of the disrepute which long attached to tory principles, and it is also clear that the softening of ethical doctrine and the rise of sentimentalism induced a certain amount of that horror which critics began to feel for *Gulliver's Travels,* particularly part IV.   But no historical factor or group of factors will altogether account for the extraordinary indignation excited by the great satire.   It would seem that some are born to admire Swift, others to abhor him.

Gulliver's Travels did not fare well at the hands of Swift's first biographers.   Orrery found in it 'a misanthropy that is intolerable.'   Delany considered the picture of the Yahoos too offensive to be copied.   Deane Swift alone justified it, maintaining that it was a denunciation of perverted reason, not a libel on mankind.   Of later eighteenth-century judgments that of William Godwin is unusual in that it is favourable, and interesting because it is perspicuous.

What is the tendency of Gulliver's Travels, particularly of that part which relates to the Houyhnhnmhns and Yahoos ?   It has frequently been affirmed to be, to inspire us with a loathing aversion to our species, and fill us with a frantic preference for the society of any class of animals, rather of men. A poet of our own day [William Hayley in *The Triumphs of Temper*], as a suitable remuneration for the production of such a work, has placed the author in hell, and consigned him to the eternal torment of devils. On the other hand it has been doubted whether, under the name of Houyhnmhns and Yahoos, Swift has done any thing more than exhibit two different descriptions of men, in their highest improvement and lowest degradation; and it has been affirmed that no book breathes more strongly a generous indignation against vice, and an ardent love of every thing that is excellent and honourable to the human heart.[16]

An inclusive survey of the critical assessments of *Gulliver's Travels* from the time of Swift's death down to the present would throw a great deal of light upon the formation of standard attitudes towards well-known works of art and the manner in which these attitudes are perpetuated. Until fairly recently it was unusual for the critic to approach *Gulliver's Travels* with an open and inquiring mind; his perceptions being patterned in advance, his chief thought was to express them with new vigour. Thus we have the late Augustine Birrell asking whether it is becoming to sit in the same room with the works of Swift. It is the great Victorian biographers who must be credited with first disarranging the critical pattern inherited from the eighteenth century and thus preparing the way for dispassionate and independent study of the satire. Yet it was not until 1917 that the conventional view of *Gulliver's Travels* was roundly challenged: in the Leslie Stephen Lecture for that year Sir Charles Whibley turned upon the sentimentalists who have condemned the celebrated satire as hateful and blasphemous, and went on to remark upon the singular misinterpretation of Swift's meaning. His later article on *Gulliver's Travels* in *Blackwood's Magazine*[17] is a forcible development of the point of view set forth in 1917. To-day the historical approach to Swift and his times has quite destroyed the violent emotions and prepossessions which formerly characterized so much of the criticism of *Gulliver's Travels,* and with a fuller understanding of the intellectual and literary background of the work has come a calmer appraisal of Swift's doctrines and art.

CHAPTER II

SOME CRITICAL NOTES ON *GULLIVER'S TRAVELS*

1

PART I of *Gulliver's Travels,* or A Voyage to Lilliput, was the work, as we have seen, of two different periods. Chapters i and ii and probably that part of chapter vi wherein Lilliput is treated as a Utopia were written in the early months of 1714 for the *Memoirs of Martinus Scriblerus;* the rest of the Voyage was not written before 1720-21 and was probably brought to something like its final form by the end of 1722. From chapter iii on the narrative bears clear marks of later composition in the form of numerous political allusions to events posterior to 1714.

The transformation of Martin's adventures in a land of pygmies into Gulliver's voyage to Lilliput must have called for extensive alterations in the earlier plan of the story in order to make room for new satiric matter. Yet in certain important respects Swift allowed himself to be controlled to the very end of part I by his original artistic intentions. This is shown by the fact that not only the framework of the whole Voyage but its distinctive tone derives from chapters i and ii. These opening pages of the narrative, by giving us a fleeting glimpse of a miniature world where everything is perfectly modelled to the scale of one inch to the foot, excite in us a child's delight and curiosity. The expectations thus aroused are not allowed to go unsatisfied in the ensuing chapters : the spirit of make-believe is perfectly sustained, the possibilities of the story are developed with unfailing resourcefulness, and the realistic details which soothe our sense of the fantastic are supplied with exhaustless ingenuity. The result is that the entire Voyage is suffused with humour, and this gives to the satiric passages a comical rather than a bitter air. Returning to his long-abandoned work, Swift was captivated, as it were, by his own early mood, and not until he had given it full play in A Voyage to Lilliput did

he allow his tone to become mordant. Of the four parts of
Gulliver's Travels, only part I can conceivably be called
charming.

It is apparent that from chapter iii on, one of Swift's purposes was to pack his narrative with sly allusions to the
English political scene.¹ The description of the rope-danc-
ing enforced upon the courtiers of Lilliput and sometimes
upon the chief ministers (chap. iii) is full of *doubles entendres,* as is the account of the two rival political parties
(chap. iv) and of the deadly enmity between Lilliput and
the neighbouring Empire of Blefuscu (chap. iv), while the
story of Gulliver's capture of the enemy's fleet and his subsequent ill treatment at the hands of his benefactors (chaps.
v and vii) is an extended allegory setting forth Bolingbroke's
political career. Now that these and other references to the
political life of the day have been disclosed by modern
scholarship, much of the reader's attention will henceforth
be diverted to this subsidiary political theme running
through A Voyage to Lilliput. Yet it would be a mistake to
see in Swift's frequent use of political allusion any great
satiric earnestness. It is not that he feared to speak out more
boldly but that he was still dominated by the artistic purposes
of the opening chapters which dictated a witty narrative
rather than a sustained satire. Swift had no desire to swoop
down upon his victims; he was content to exercise his ingenuity in portraying them under the guise of ridiculous
pygmies. The symbols which he uses in dealing with political matters have no high degree of consistency, they do not
overload the narrative, and they diminish in no way the
humour and the charm of the story.

More heavily underscored and more firmly knit than this
satire on individual political characters is the broader satiric
theme emerging from the representation of the Lilliputians
as morally contemptible. Now, in the two opening chapters
there is nothing contemptible about these little people; their
courage is remarkable and so is the skill with which they reduce the Man Mountain to submission. Perhaps they strike
us favourably because we, like Gulliver, have not yet lived
with them and learned their language. But it does not seem

that Swift's original intention was to portray them as despicable creatures; the flattering account of their customs and manners given in chapter vi suggests that he first conceived them as a Utopian people into whose kingdom a shipwrecked European traveller was to stray with amusing results.[2] If this is the case, it was only as he proceeded with the story that he perceived the satiric effect to be gained by a different treatment of the Lilliputians, who are shown in all their pettiness, involved in political jealousies and factions, at war with a neighbouring empire for reasons utterly preposterous, their emperor obsessed with the desire for conquest, Bolgolam consumed with jealousy for the giant who has taken the enemy's fleet single-handed, and Flimnap even suspecting his wife of immoral relations with Gulliver! Our *amour propre* is shrivelled up as we see our own passions trivialized in these ridiculous mannikins. Yet Swift does not press this satire to a savage conclusion. He allows the effect to remain predominantly humorous.

In addition to the charmingly fantastic quality of this Voyage, its element of political satire, and its reduction of human motives to the mean and contemptible passions displayed by diminutive beings, there is the Utopian theme developed in chapter vi, where the learning, laws, customs, and educational methods of the Lilliputians are set forth in ideal terms. Coming after Gulliver's realistic observations and none too happy experiences, this description is so incongruous as to call for explanation, and we are in fact told that only the original institutions of Lilliput are to be understood and 'not the most scandalous Corruptions into which these People are fallen by the degenerate Nature of Man.' Are we to read these words — and perhaps the entire Utopian sketch — as a sly dig at those writers given to creating impossibly ideal societies? Probably not. Swift had merely manoeuvred himself into an awkward position by embodying early material now standing in contradiction to his later representation of the Lilliputians, and was covering up faulty workmanship.

Lilliput's criminal code is a model of simplicity: if an accused man is acquitted, his informer is severely punished; 'They look upon Fraud as a greater Crime than Theft, and

therefore seldom fail to punish it with Death'; ingratitude
is also a capital crime; and rewards are provided for those
who have conspicuously obeyed the laws.   Their principles
of government are too good to be true — that is, they are precisely those which the English have never had the sense to
act upon.

In chusing Persons for all Employments, they have more Regard to good Morals than to great Abilities : For, since Government is necessary to Mankind, they believe that the common Size
of human Understandings, is fitted to some Station or other ; and
that Providence never intended to make the Management of publick Affairs a Mystery, to be comprehended only by a few Persons
of sublime Genius, of which there seldom are three born in an
Age : But, they suppose Truth, Justice, Temperance, and the
like, to be in every Man's Power ; the Practice of which Virtues,
assisted by Experience and a good Intention, would qualify any
Man for the Service of his Country, except where a Course of
Study is required.

Swift opens his discussion of the Lilliputian educational
system by observing that 'their Notions relating to the Duties
of Parents and Children differ extremely from ours,' and the
sub-acid flavour of this remark seasons what follows.   Since
men and women are joined together like other animals by
motives of concupiscence and since their affection for their
offspring proceeds from the same natural principle, the Lilliputians reason that a child is under no obligation to its
parents for bringing it into the world and that, furthermore,
'Parents are the last of all others to be trusted with the Education of their own Children.'   (If there is an unpleasant
undertone here,— evidence not of an aversion to children so
much as an unhealthy refusal to accept the physical terms
of life,— we ought not to miss the ironic accent, not uncommon in the reproaches levelled by perfectly humane bache-
lors at troublesome brats and over-fond parents.)   Public
nurseries are maintained in every town and to these all children except those of cottagers and labourers must be sent
and at a very early age.   Their parents may visit them
but twice a year and then for not more than an hour, and
although they may kiss their children at meeting and parting,

a professor stands by to see that they do not whisper to them 'or use any fondling Expressions, or bring any Presents of Toys, Sweet-meats, and the like.' There are different nurseries for the various social classes, and boys and girls are always sent to separate schools. However, the education given to girls is in almost all respects the same as that for boys, and thus 'the young Ladies there are as much ashamed of being Cowards and Fools, as the Men; and despise all personal Ornaments beyond Decency and Cleanliness.' In these matters they are guided by the maxim 'that among People of Quality, a Wife should be always a reasonable and agreeable Companion, because she cannot always be young.' The meaner families, besides being assessed the usual fee for the education of their children, are obliged to contribute a share of each month's income towards a portion for the child, For the *Lilliputians* think nothing can be more unjust, than that People, in Subservience to their own Appetites, should bring Children into the World, and leave the Burthen of supporting them on the Publick.' The children of cottagers and labourers, whose business is only to till and cultivate the soil, are not educated in the public nurseries, though the old and diseased among them are cared for in hospitals with the result that begging is unknown in Lilliput.

In the final pages of the narrative Gulliver returns to civilization and we experience with him the strange sensation of readjusting our sense of proportion to the normal world. But it should be noted that the contrast which is felt is purely and simply a physical one and altogether amusing.

2

A VOYAGE TO BROBDINGNAG, or at least the first draft of it, was probably completed in 1722 or 1723. Unlike the first Voyage it consisted wholly of fresh material and was written at one time, and as a consequence has a greater degree of artistic unity. In scheme it derives from part 1, Gulliver merely being turned from a giant into a pygmy, and the natives from pygmies into giants. In thus reversing the proportions of the first Voyage, Swift was, as a matter of fact,

doing a highly original thing, for although previous writers
of imaginary voyages had depicted both giants and pygmies
none had sensed the possibilities of a fully developed contrast between the two.   In tone, however, A Voyage to
Brobdingnag owes little to part 1: though many of its effects
are again the result of a lively ingenuity, we are conveyed
into an incongruous world rather than an entertaining one,
while the satire is no longer lambent but keen of edge and
weighted with a consistent purpose.

The idea of relativity was very much in Swift's mind as
he passed from Lilliput into Brobdingnag.   Finding himself among giants, Gulliver perceives instantly that they stand
in relation to him as he has stood in relation to the Lilliputians, whereupon his thoughts take a philosophical turn:

> I reflected what a Mortification it must prove to me to appear
> as inconsiderable in this Nation, as one single *Lilliputian* would
> be among us. . . Undoubtedly Philosophers are in the Right
> when they tell us, that nothing is great or little otherwise than by
> Comparison: It might have pleased Fortune to let the *Lilli-
> putians* find some Nation, where the People were as diminutive
> with respect to them, as they were to me.   And who knows but
> that even this prodigious Race of Mortals might be equally over-
> matched in some distant Part of the World, whereof we have yet
> no Discovery?

A Voyage to Brobdingnag is really a development of the
idea of relativity along two different lines and with contrary
effects.

In one direction, purely physical contrasts are explored
and we are soon made to realize that the human body, when
viewed through a microscope as in effect it is by Gulliver,
is utterly disgusting.   Swift does not build up to this conclusion but pushes it home with characteristic brutality from
the very start, giving in chapter i a revolting description of
a Brobdingnagian nurse's monstrous breast:

> It stood prominent six Foot, and could not be less than sixteen
> in Circumference.   The Nipple was about half the Bigness of
> my Head, and the Hue both of that and the Dug so varified with
> Spots, Pimples and Freckles, that nothing could appear more
> nauseous: For I had a near Sight of her, she sitting down, the

more conveniently to give Suck, and I standing on the Table. This made me reflect upon the fair Skins of our *English* Ladies, who appear so beautiful to us, only because they are of our own Size, and their Defects not to be seen but through a magnifying Glass, where we find by Experiment that the smoothest and whitest Skins look rough and coarse, and ill coloured.

Gulliver's encounters with rats (chap. i) and flies (chap. iii) and his terrifying experience with the monkey (chap. v) are all told so as to produce the maximum effect of disgust. The incident of Gulliver among the maids of honour (chap. v) stands upon a slightly different footing, for added to the disgust is a kind of illegitimate pleasure in the repellent. The description of the beggars (chap. iv) is a masterly etching, each line proclaiming the artist's savage imagination.

In another direction the idea of relativity is extended into the moral realm, and it is to be noticed that here Swift works with canny deliberation, withholding for several chapters the full significance of the contrasts which are being revealed. In fact, we are given a false scent to start with, for Gulliver, considering his hapless situation in this land of giants, asks, '. . . as human Creatures are observed to be more Savage and cruel in Proportion to their Bulk; what could I expect but to be a Morsel in the Mouth of the first among these enormous Barbarians who should happen to seize me?' And for a time, indeed, it looks as though Gulliver would perish at the hands of his captors, not by being eaten alive by them but by being worked to death by the greedy farmer who shows him for profit. It is only after he is purchased by the queen and taken to court that he begins to see the Brobdingnagians as they really are, an amiable and virtuous people. At this point, however, Gulliver's education — or the reader's — is still incomplete, for it is not until he begins to boast to his majesty of European institutions that the full truth comes out at last. When Gulliver has finished describing English politics, the king picks him up and strokes him gently, asking laughingly whether he is a whig or a tory: 'Then turning to his first Minister, who waited behind him with a white Staff, near as tall as the Main-mast of the Royal *Sovereign;* he observed, how contemptible a Thing was human Grandeur, which could be mimicked by such diminutive Insects as I' (chap. iii). 'Diminutive insects,' 'little odious vermin'—such, in comparison with the Brobdingnagians, do the people of Europe henceforth appear. The heart of the second Voyage lies in chapters vi and vii, where this moral relativity becomes the basis of an extended satire on western civilization.

In the earlier of these chapters we have Gulliver again in a boastful mood as, in compliance with the royal request, he sets forth the state of Europe in five audiences with the king. But in the sixth audience it is the king who talks. Marshalling his evidence from the notes which he has taken down during Gulliver's disquisitions, he finds Europe guilty of ignorance, idleness, and vice; its laws perverted, confounded, and eluded by underhand means; its original institution of government destroyed by corruptions; its governing classes and its clergy selected with no reference to virtue, integrity, and wisdom. Into his closing sentence he packs all the indignation which poor Gulliver's lectures have aroused in him: '. . . by what I have gathered from your own Relation, and the Answers I have with much Pains wringed and extorted from you; I cannot but conclude the Bulk of your Natives, to be the most pernicious Race of little odious Vermin that Nature ever suffered to crawl upon the Surface of the Earth.'

By this time Gulliver is so nettled by Brobdingnagian contempt that all their words of wisdom serve only to heighten his pride in his own species; from now on, in order to keep up his self-esteem, he takes the most condescending attitude towards this exemplary people. When the king rejects with every sign of horror and anger his proposal to introduce European methods of warfare into Brobdingnag, Gulliver exclaims,

A Strange Effect of *narrow Principles* and *short Views!* that a Prince possessed of every Quality which procures Veneration, Love and Esteem . . . should from a *nice unnecessary Scruple,* whereof in *Europe* we can have no Conception, let slip an Opportunity put into his Hands, that would have made him absolute Master of the Lives, the Liberties, and the Fortunes of his People. (Chap. vii.)

In a similarly contemptuous strain Gulliver then outlines their political ideas, their learning, their legal methods, and their taste in books. In all of these the Brobdingnagians show their dislike of over-refined speculations, their forthright, practical natures, and their strong moral sense. Of their learning, for instance, Gulliver has this to say : it is

very defective ; consisting only in Morality, History, Poetry and Mathematicks ; wherein they must be allowed to excel. But, the last of these is wholly applied to what may be useful in Life ; to the Improvement of Agriculture and all mechanical Arts ; so that among us it would be little esteemed. And as to Ideas, Entities, Abstractions and Transcendentals, I could never drive the least Conception into their Heads.

This second Voyage ends even more amusingly than the first. From the time that Gulliver is discovered floating in his box, to his return to his house in Redriff we are treated to one diverting incident after another. Whether it is that he is called upon to make a peculiarly difficult readjustment of perceptions or whether, as compensation for months of mortification, he now imagines himself an awe-inspiring giant, his fellow-beings all seem most contemptible little creatures, and as he rides home to Redriff he thinks himself in Lilliput once more and calls out to everyone he meets to stand out of the way. This heightening of the effect over that given in the closing pages of the previous Voyage foreshadows the remarkable ending of part IV, but it is still an effect arising almost entirely out of mere physical contrast.

3

In comparison with the rest of *Gulliver's Travels* A Voyage to Laputa, Balnibarbi, Luggnagg, Glubbdubdrib, and Japan is of marked inferiority ; this was the judgment of the first readers of the satire and it has never been reversed. The reasons for this inferiority are not far to seek. Part III was the last section of the book to be written, its composition extending from 1724 down to the latter months of 1725 ; when he came to it, Swift had already finished part IV, which is the intellectual and emotional climax of the satire ; a let-down was inevitable. Furthermore, Swift had worked out no unifying scheme for this voyage; he was in a mood of artistic relaxation, content to make of this portion of the work a catch-all for satiric fragments for which no place had been found in the other three parts. The satire on the projectors he took over from his Martinus Scriblerus papers, while into his account of the Flying Island he wove several passages full of allusions to England's policy towards Ireland and the Irish demonstrations against Wood's coinage — the strongest of these passages, which is to be found in Ford's interleaved copy, was never printed by either Motte or Faulkner. As a consequence of lax planning, A Voyage to Laputa falls into four loosely formed parts: the story of the Flying Island; the satirical sketch of Balnibarbi and of the Grand Academy of Lagado; the account of Gulliver's experiences in Glubbdubdrib, a satire on literary critics and historians; and the description of the revolting immortals of Luggnagg, the Struldbrugs. Nor is there any witty fillip at the end of the Voyage, where Gulliver's return to civilization gives rise to no humorous or stinging contrasts.

Satire on the misuse of the intellect, satire on the desire for long life, and satirical allusions to the Anglo-Irish situation — these are the basic themes into which part III may be resolved. What strikes one about Swift's treatment of intellectual abuses is that by being all-inclusive it misses fire; though many of the passages are in themselves wonderfully mordant, and though the central ideas behind the satire are perfectly apparent, the attack is delivered over too wide a front to fall anywhere with crushing effect. In Laputa the ridicule is directed at mathematics and music; in Balnibarbi at all kinds of projects; in the city of Lagado — the seat of the Grand Academy — at scientific experimentation and 'projectors in speculative learning'; in Glubbdubdrib at textual critics and historians. There are many specific references: in the passage on mathematicians Swift was, among other things, paying his respects to Sir Isaac Newton, who had assayed Wood's halfpence for the English privy council and had reported that the coins were up to specification; the Laputans' love of music is a hit at Italian opera, then the craze in London; the projects of Glubbdubdrib suggested instantly the South Sea Company; in the Grand Academy of Lagado the Royal Society is clearly depicted. The satire has, to be sure, a general drift, which gives it central meaning. The projectors are deficient in common sense, the mathematicians and scientists are lost in impractical speculations, the critics are pedants without taste, the modern historians are ignorant rogues — each of these classes exemplifies either corrupt taste or over-refined speculation, which are but two modes of corrupt judgment. Throughout this section of the satire Swift's anti-intellectualism finds constant expression, and it was never put more happily than in the imaginary conversation between Aristotle and the two moderns, Descartes and Gassendi (chap. viii). When the latter have explained their systems, Aristotle makes a few observations :

This great Philosopher freely acknowledged his own Mistakes in Natural Philosophy, because he proceeded in many things upon Conjecture, as all Men must do ; and he found, that *Gassendi*, who had made the Doctrine of *Epicurus* as palatable as he could, and the *Vortices* of *Descartes*, were equally exploded. He predicted the same Fate to *Attraction*, whereof the present Learned are such zealous Asserters. He said, that new Systems of Nature were but new Fashions, which would vary in every Age ; and even those who pretend to demonstrate them from Mathematical Principles, would flourish but a short Period of Time, and be out of Vogue when that was determined.

The strange things that have happened in our own day to the Newtonian system — to which Swift is referring — are not likely to drive us back to the anti-intellectual position ; they have, however, opened our minds to the fact, perfectly apparent to Swift, that 'new Systems of Nature [are] but new Fashions, which . . . vary in every Age.'

Chapter x, devoted to the description of the immortal Struldbrugs, is by all odds the most effective portion of the third Voyage, being the only part free from that diffusion which elsewhere lowers the voltage of the satire to a point of relative harmlessness. Life, Swift said repeatedly, is in itself undesirable, and though the wise man will bear it

with fortitude, his reason tells him that it were better had he
not been born.   Hence inordinate desire for life seemed to
Swift but a gross passion issuing from the depths of irrationality, and like all such manifestations was to be seared
away with the caustics of reason and moral realism.   Let the
lover all afire for Celia spend an hour exploring the secrets
of her dressing-room ; let the man who prays for a long life
gaze for a while upon the toothless, hairless, tasteless, disease-
ridden Struldbrugs.   Whatever else we may think of Swift's
revolting picture, we cannot attribute it to a psychopathic
state of mind brought on by his own advancing years, for as
a young man just past his twenties he was already of Juvenal's mind regarding old age, as the *Resolutions* of 1699
show.   In the Struldbrugs he was merely bringing to its most
forcible expression a theme which had always held a peculiar
fascination for him.

The political satire, most of it having reference to recent
occurrences in Ireland, is to be found chiefly in chapter iii,
in connexion with the methods used by the king of the
Flying Island to reduce to obedience his subjects living beneath him in Balnibarbi.   (There are, to be sure, other
references to Ireland in other parts of the Voyage, particularly in chapter iv, where the discredited Balnibarbian lord,
Munodi, is very likely Lord Midleton, and where the dismal
prospects in the city of Lagado and the neighbouring
country-side call to mind the state of Dublin and Ireland.)
When a revolt threatens in any part of the kingdom, the
Island is immediately flown to that quarter and brought to
rest at some distance above the town where the disturbance
centres.   Deprived of rain and sunlight, the rebels usually
submit in short order, and if they will not yield in the face
of these reprisals the Island can be dropped upon them with
a universal destruction both of houses and men.   The latter
measure, however, is seldom resorted to by the king and his
ministers.   For one thing, their estates lie all below, an
easy prey to a people driven to the last extremities of rage
and hatred ; and again, though the bottom of the Island is
adamant two hundred yards thick, it could easily be cracked
by too severe a shock.   At this point Gulliver tells of an

incident which took place about three years before his arrival in the kingdom.   The citizens of Lindalino, the second city in the realm, had often complained of royal oppressions, and shortly after one of his majesty's periodic visits to them they rose up, shut the gates of the city, seized the governor, and erected four large towers, fixing at the top of each a great loadstone.   It was eight months before the king was perfectly apprised of the rebellion.   He immediately ordered the Island to be moved to a position directly above the city, but in the course of a few days it became apparent that the Lindalinians were not to be broken by being deprived of sun and rain.   It was necessary to crush them. As the Island was being lowered it was observed, however, that its descent was much speedier than usual, and this led to the discovery of the four great loadstones, whose attraction was judged to be powerful enough to make the Island uncontrollable on closer approach.   'This Incident broke entirely the King's Measures and (to dwell no longer on other Circumstances) he was forced to give the Town their own Conditions.'   Thus did Swift allegorize Ireland's triumphant war against the halfpence.   This incident was omitted from all editions of *Gulliver's Travels* appearing before 1896, Aitken being the first editor to give it, taking it from Ford's interleaved copy of Motte's first edition.[3]

4

THE great Voyage which brings *Gulliver's Travels* to an end was written directly after the second Voyage, the first draft being finished by January 1724.   What above all distinguishes part IV from the three preceding parts is its rigorous artistic unity, which produces a cumulative effect of the greatest power.   Fantastic realism is again employed,— indeed, it is the satirical mode of the entire Voyage,—but behind it is a terrible logic to be found nowhere in the first Voyage and only fleetingly in the second.   The satiric intention presiding over A Voyage to the Houyhnhnms can be summed up in a single phrase : an assault upon man's Pride by way of *le mythe animal*.   Unless this is borne in mind

the dominant tone of the piece will not be caught nor will
the minor and sometimes contrasting tones.　Thus, the total
effect of the last Voyage is anything but a humorous one,
and yet there are many passages in which humour is the
principal ingredient.　Take, for instance, the lecture delivered by Gulliver's master on man's physical inferiority:
man's nails are of no use either to his fore or hinder feet;
his fore feet are not feet at all, since he never walks on
them; going only on his hinder feet, if these slip he must
invariably fall;

He then began to find fault with other Parts of my Body; the
Flatness of my Face, the Prominence of my Nose, my Eyes placed
directly in Front, so that I could not look on either Side without
turning my Head: That I was not able to feed my self, without
lifting one of my fore Feet to my Mouth: And therefore Nature
had placed those Joints to answer that Necessity.　He knew not
what could be the Use of those several Clefts and Divisions in
my Feet behind; that these were too soft to bear the Hardness
and Sharpness of Stones without a Covering made from the Skin
of some other Brute; that my whole Body wanted a Fence against
Heat and Cold, which I was forced to put on and off every Day
with Tediousness and Trouble. (Chap. iv.)

Certain critics have declared this to be an unforgivable
libel on the Human Form Divine, but the modern reader
has no right to laugh so long as he himself reads the passage as downright satire.　There are few flagitious aspects
of man's nature which are not dwelt upon at some point
or other in this Voyage, and at the end Pride has been left
without a single prop, yet in the course of his grim demonstrations the satirist sometimes winks at us.

A Voyage to the Houyhnhnms is a series of skilfully interwoven variations on two themes, one proclaiming the bestiality of man while under the control of the irrational, the
other descriptive of the life of reason.　There can be no
doubt as to which of these is the more effectively developed.
Through the Yahoos, a perfect symbol for the communication of disgust, moral degradation is made emotionally repulsive.　The life of reason, on the other hand, is given
merely an intellectual statement, for though we understand
the admirable Houyhnhnms we are not moved by them, and

this not because horses are an inappropriate symbol but because ideal civilization as conceived by Swift is an emotionless thing. That the two themes are not treated with equal artistic success is shown by the fact that part IV has so often been taken to mean one thing only — namely, that man is all Yahoo. The bestiality of man must of course be heavily underscored if the attack on Pride is to find its mark, but it was not Swift's intention to allow this negative theme to smother the positive one descriptive of the life of reason.

The equivalence between irrational man and the Yahoo is established with great skill. Gulliver has scarcely been put ashore by his mutinous crew and has not yet met with any of the noble Houyhnhnms when he is set upon by some forty of the most loathsome creatures he has ever seen. Describing them at length, he remarks, 'I never beheld in all my Travels so disagreeable an Animal, or one against which I naturally conceived so strong an Antipathy,' but in this first encounter he perceives nothing of their resemblance to himself. It is only after he has been led home by a Houyhnhnm, who takes him into the courtyard and compares him with one of the Yahoos tied up there, that he grasps their similarity to men, observing with horror and astonishment a perfect human figure in this abominable animal. The physical resemblance having been established, the moral similarity is built up by degrees as Gulliver comes to appreciate the impassive virtues of his noble masters and thereby to despise himself and his race. But the physical resemblance and the disgust which it occasions are never allowed to slumber in the reader's consciousness, incident after incident — one of the most striking being the bathing scene in chapter viii — inciting the emotions afresh.

Back of all this is an indictment of man and society perhaps as comprehensive and detailed as was ever penned by a satirist. It begins in chapter iv with Gulliver's description of his crew — there is no kind of immorality with which they are not familiar, drinking, whoring, gaming, treason, murder, theft, poisoning, robbery, perjury, forgery, counterfeiting, rape, sodomy, desertion — and continues through chapter vi. War as it is waged in Europe is described, together with the

motives of bellicose princes and ministers and the weapons
used at sea and in the field. At this point Gulliver's master
can contain himself no longer:

> . . . although he hated the *Yahoos* of this Country, yet he no
> more blamed them for. their odious Qualities, than he did a
> *Gnnayh* (a Bird of Prey) for its Cruelty, or a sharp Stone for
> cutting his Hoof. But, when a Creature pretending to Reason,
> could be capable of such Enormities, he dreaded lest the Corrup-
> tion of that Faculty might be worse than Brutality itself. He
> seemed therefore confident, that instead of Reason, we were only
> possessed of some Quality fitted to increase our natural Vices ; as
> the Reflection from a troubled Stream returns the Image of an
> ill-shapen Body, not only *larger,* but more *distorted.* (Chap. v.)

From war Gulliver passes on to the absurdities and injustices of the law, to the inequalities between rich and poor,
to the social and economic evils resulting from luxury and
intemperance, to the diseases common in Europe, and ends
by glancing at physicians, ministers of state, and the nobility
(chap. vi). The anti-rational view of man, upon which
this entire indictment rests, is emphasized in chapter vii,
where Gulliver's master, now fully informed concerning
Europeans, enlarges upon their similarity to the Yahoos;
'. . . he looked upon us,' Gulliver writes,

> as a Sort of Animals to whose Share, by what Accident he could
> not conjecture, some small Pittance of *Reason* had fallen, where-
> of we made no other Use than by its Assistance to aggravate our
> *natural* Corruptions, and to acquire new ones which Nature had
> not given us. That, we disarmed our selves of the few Abilities
> she had bestowed ; had been very successful in multiplying our
> original Wants, and seemed to spend our whole Lives in vain
> Endeavours to supply them by our own Inventions.

Of the five remaining chapters, viii and ix are given over
to the development of the second theme, a statement of the
principles of rational conduct. It is not, of course, the first
appearance of this theme, which is introduced the moment
the Houyhnhnms enter the story and from then on is interwoven with the satire on bestiality — the gravity, common
sense, cleanliness, and truthfulness of the horses serving as
a foil for the loathsomeness of Yahoos and corrupt men.
But not until the first theme has been fully and dramatically

treated is the ideology of the Houyhnhnms set forth at length and their society portrayed.

The Houyhnhnms 'thought, Nature and Reason were sufficient Guides for a reasonable Animal . . . in shewing us what we ought to do, and what to avoid' (chap. v). They are, in this respect, perfect children of the Enlightenment, grounding their intellectual life upon the law of the universality of reason. The question will at once arise whether they always mean by *nature* the same thing as *reason,* or whether at times they think of *nature* as something purer than civilization and standing in opposition to it.   Once or twice, indeed, they speak like noble and uncorrupted children of nature, as when they express surprise on discovering the secret of Gulliver's clothes, declaring that they are unable to understand 'why Nature should teach us to conceal what Nature had given' since they themselves are not ashamed of any parts of their bodies (chap. iii). But at such moments they are off centre.   Actually, they are not horrified by European society because it is too civilized but because it is not civilized at all.   Their prescription is not that man should revert to a primitive state — which to them suggests the Yahoos — but that he should begin to live by reason.   To them life according to nature means this life of reason.

Their grand maxim, 'to cultivate *Reason,* and to be wholly governed by it,' leads immediately to an intense anti-intellectualism.   They believe, that is, that there are certain truths which strike the mind with immediate conviction, and that beyond these truths nothing can be known with certainty.   Thus they fix rigorous limits to every kind of speculation, which must become vain and useless the moment it begins to deal with matters other than those presented by the general sense.' . . . Controversies, Wranglings, Disputes, and Positiveness in false or dubious Propositions,' we are told by Gulliver,

are Evils unknown among the *Houyhnhnms.*   In the like Manner when I used to explain to [my master] our several Systems of *Natural Philosophy,* he would laugh that a Creature pretending to *Reason,* should value itself upon the Knowledge of other Peoples Conjectures, and in Things, where that Knowledge, if it were certain, could be of no Use. Wherein he agreed entirely with the Sentiments of *Socrates,* as *Plato* delivers them . . . (Chap. viii.)

On the side of behaviour and social conduct their thorough-going adherence to the dicta of reason — here we have to do with that 'rationalism' out of which Swift's rigid ethical theories arose — renders them almost passionless creatures. Unperturbed by any violent emotions, they regard one another with serene good will but never with what properly can be called affection, even their own offspring failing to excite in them any different feeling from that which they have for all colts and foals. They marry in accordance with eugenic principles and practise birth-control through restraint. Their young they educate with great care — 'Temperance, *Industry, Exercise* and *Cleanliness,* are the Lessons equally enjoyed to the young ones of both Sexes. And my Master thought it monstrous in us to give the Females a different Kind of Education from the Males. . .' Every fourth year a representative council of the whole nation is assembled, which draws up a national plan — regulating, among other things, the population — for the ensuing quadrennium. (Chap. viii.)

Since the Houyhnhnms are without letters, their knowledge is wholly traditional. Subject to no diseases, they have no need of physicians. Of astronomy they know only enough to enable them to calculate the year by sun and moon. Their poetry is of superlative excellence by reason of the justness of the similes, the minuteness and exactness of the descriptions, and the matter — 'Their Verses . . . usually contain either some exalted Notions of Friendship and Benevolence, or the Praises of those who were Victors in Races, and other bodily Exercises.' In the presence of death they maintain their habitual composure, facing it themselves with perfect resignation and accepting the loss of friends and relatives without a tinge of grief. (Chap. ix.)

Chapters x, xi, and xii together make up the long and cunningly wrought conclusion of the Voyage. It has already been pointed out that the contrasts experienced by Gulliver

on his return to civilization from Lilliput and Brobdingnag
are almost solely of the physical order.   Not so the contrasts
which assail him when, banished by decree from Houyhnhnm-land, he is forced back to human society.   Well before his ostracism he has come to a full realization of his
own physical and moral repulsiveness; he is a Yahoo, his
family, his friends, his countrymen, the entire human race
are Yahoos, and when he sees his reflection in water he
turns away with horror and detestation.   His own desire is
to live his life out among the horses, his noble masters.

I enjoyed perfect Health of Body, and Tranquility of Mind;
I did not feel the Treachery or Inconstancy of a Friend, nor the
Injuries of a secret or open Enemy.   I had no Occasion of brib-
ing, flattering or pimping, to procure the Favour of any great
Man, or of his Minion.   I wanted no Fence against Fraud or
Oppression: Here was neither Physician to destroy my Body,
nor Lawyer to ruin my Fortune: No Informer to watch my
Words and Actions, or forge Accusations against me for Hire:
Here were no Gibers, Censurers, Backbiters, Pick-pockets, High-
waymen, House-breakers, Attorneys, Bawds, Buffons, Gamesters,
Politicians, Wits, Spleneticks, tedious Talkers, Controvertists,
Ravishers, Murderers, Robbers, Virtuoso's; no Leaders or Fol-
lowers of Party and Faction; no Encouragers to Vice, by Seduce-
ment or Examples: No Dungeon, Axes, Gibbets, Whipping posts,
or Pillories; No cheating Shop-keepers or Mechanicks: No
Pride, Vanity or Affectation: No Fops, Bullies, Drunkards, strol-
ling Whores, or Poxes: No ranting, lewd, expensive Wives: No
stupid, proud Pedants: No importunate, over-bearing, quarrelsome, noisy, roaring, empty, conceited, swearing Companions:
No Scoundrels raised from the Dust upon the Merit of their
Vices; or Nobility thrown into it on account of their Virtues:
No Lords, Fidlers, Judges or Dancing-Masters. (Chap. x.)

When he is told that he may no longer dwell among the
Houyhnhnms he has already foreseen the mental tortures
which he must endure upon a return to his native land.

From the moment when Gulliver, about to put to sea,
prostrates himself before his Master and reverently kisses his
hoof, to the end of the story Swift's inventiveness in devising
incidents which will convey his hero's disgust for his kind
has no parallel in satiric literature, though it is a question
whether it does not finally degenerate into sensationalism.

The final chapter (xii) is a kind of coda.   First comes a

diatribe against those Europeans who sail to new lands, there
to plunder and enslave the natives.⟩ Montaigne had protested against this cruelty to uncivilized peoples, as had many
later writers, so that Swift was here taking a well-established
line. ⟨The last paragraphs canalize all the satiric energy
generated in the preceding pages of the Voyage and direct
it against the <u>Pride of man</u> :

My Reconcilement to the *Yahoo*-kind in general might not be
so difficult, if they would be content with those Vices and Follies
only which Nature hath entitled them to.   I am not in the least
provoked at the Sight of a Lawyer, a Pick-pocket, a Colonel, a
Fool, a Lord, a Gamester, a Politician, a Whoremunger, a
Physician, an Evidence, a Suborner, an Attorney, a Traytor, or
the like : This is all according to the due Course of Things : But,
when I behold a Lump of Deformity, and Diseases both in Body
and Mind, smitten with *Pride*, it immediately breaks all the
Measures of my Patience ; neither shall I be ever able to comprehend how such an Animal and such a Vice could tally together. ⟨

5

⟨ONE result, certainly, of an analytical study of *Gulliver's
Travels* is the perception that each of its four parts has its
peculiar mood, tone, and effect.   Part I is an ingenious fairy-
tale, delightful even when it stings, as it often does.   As
narrative part II is but a sequel to the first Voyage, depending
for interest upon similarly fantastic situations.   But as narrative it counts for little ; it is efficient, keen satire.   Part III
is an *omnium gatherum,* interesting in places by reason of
the political allusions, rising in one chapter to a high level
of satiric intensity, but frequently dull and, taken as a whole,
markedly ineffective.   Part IV is in spirit and execution
closest to part II, but distinguished from it by a purpose altogether relentless and an execution which is ruthless.

Such, however, is the effect of part IV upon most readers
that the impression of the book as a whole which they carry
away is really only the impression left by A Voyage to the
Houyhnhnms, and this is evidence, not of artistic success,
but of a certain lack thereof.   Indeed, *Gulliver's Travels*
reveals several artistic defects.   For one of these Swift cannot be wholly blamed.   So much of his meaning depends

upon the feelings evoked in 1726 by the term *Pride* that with the comparative neutralization of this word there has come a great loss of satiric effectiveness. Every non-contemporary work of art suffers, it is true, from our inability to come to it precisely in the spirit of those for whom it was immediately executed, but if one will consider how triumphantly the concept of enthusiasm still comes to life in *A Tale of a Tub* he will sense something of artistic ineptitude in *Gulliver's Travels*. Again, the work is overloaded with satiric material, and anything that is thereby gained in intellectual force is more than offset by the loss in deftness. But the greatest weakness — this has already been touched upon — is peculiar to the fourth part, and, with a slight shift in point of view, is to be seen as the very source of the tremendous effectiveness of this Voyage. One refers to the sensationalism into which Swift falls while developing the theme of bestiality, a sensationalism which diverts attention from the concurrent statement of the life of reason and comes perilously close to breaking down the perceptions and judgments enforced in this latter statement.

Another way of presenting the same case is this: parts I and II are, each in its way, almost perfect; had part III been omitted entirely and part IV been toned down and brought into closer accord with the second Voyage, *Gulliver's Travels* would have been a finer work of art. In any event, however, it must have remained inferior to *A Tale of a Tub*, for its matter could not give rise to that intellectually rigorous form and meaning which make Swift's early satire an incomparably brilliant achievement. In *Gulliver's Travels* there is, of course, a range quite beyond the younger author of the *Tale*, the range which comes only with years and experience. In Swift's case, however, this greater range was not accompanied by that deepening of insight which with so many great writers more than compensates for the technically looser performances of their later years. It is not that Swift's moral perceptions were becoming less acute but that by no possibility could they have been more acute than they had always been. Swift came to maturity at one leap. From then on it was a matter of artistic statement.

BOOK VI

1727 – 1745

BIOGRAPHICAL SYNOPSIS

1727-1745

April-Sept.
  1727 :
In England for the last time.

26 Jan. 1728 :
Death of Stella.

17 Aug. 1742 :
Swift found of unsound mind and memory, incapable of taking care of his person or fortune.

19 Oct. 1745 :
Death of Swift.

CHAPTER I

THE LATTER YEARS OF EXILE

1

At the beginning of 1727 Swift had already entered upon his sixtieth year. The forces which finally wrecked his body and mind had been long at work sapping his constitution, and from 1729 on, their presence can be detected clearly: the disease from which he had suffered for so many years — its symptoms the oft-mentioned 'giddiness and deafness' — was tightening its hold upon him, and in addition there was the natural, progressive decay accompanying old age. Yet so great was his resistance, so indomitable his physical and intellectual energy, that an astonishingly long period was to elapse before he finally yielded to these disintegrating forces — by the close of his seventy-first year (1738) his energy, it is clear, had been broken down, but not until 1742 was he declared of unsound mind. Nothing is farther from the truth than the idea commonly entertained regarding Swift's latter years of activity. He was still the great artist, producing verse and prose of undiminished brilliance and intensity, and he remained an imperious public figure. Many anecdotes illustrating his outrageous lack of self-control were later to be told by the men and women who had known him during the decade or so preceding his collapse, but these stories are to be severely discounted as obvious adornments of the Swift legend. Domineering he had always been, and it is easy to understand how in later life, long accustomed to the reverence of an entire kingdom, he found it impossible to brook the slightest check. But if the aging dean was a formidable and sometimes an unbearable person, we have only to turn to his works of this period to convince ourselves that his genius remained unimpaired until disease finally overcame him.

The sombre tone of Swift's latter years was the result, not of incipient insanity, but of the circumstances of his life.

Stella was dead; his friends in England were dropping off
one by one; the glorious years of the queen were only a
memory — a crueller memory with each passing year; in Ireland conditions had never been worse.   And he, Jonathan
Swift, who from youth had brooded with fascinated horror
upon the indignities of old age, now felt these indignities
creeping upon him.   It was unspeakably terrible, this watching oneself being turned into a Struldbrug, but watch one
would up to the moment of oblivion.   There was to be no
turning away, there were to be no anodynes.

2

In 1727 Swift made his last journey to England.   He crossed
early in April, was at Oxford by the eighteenth, and by the
twenty-second was with Pope at Twickenham.   For the next
six months he was among his old friends, but he was ill much
of the time and travelled little, remaining at Pope's during
the greater part of his stay.   He was revisiting England for
a number of reasons.   It was improbable that he would ever
again make the journey — he had come, as it were, to take
farewell of Pope, Gay, Arbuthnot, Bolingbroke, and the rest.
Then too he was now proposing to write the memoirs of the
first earl of Oxford and he desired to secure materials from
the present earl, the son of the tory minister.   Furthermore,
he had half made up his mind to proceed from England to
France in search of health.   But it was literature and after
that politics which presented the most urgent claims.

During his visit to England in the previous year he and
Pope had concerted their joint *Miscellanies,* the first two
volumes of which had gone through the press after Swift's
return to Ireland.   But they had not yet been issued, nor
had a preface been composed.   Not long after Swift's arrival
at Twickenham in 1727, the two authors sat down to write
this preface, which is dated 27 May.   Before the end of June,
Volumes I and II of the *Miscellanies* made their appearance.
(The 'Last Volume' was issued in March of the ensuing
year.   In 1732 came a fourth volume, designated as Volume III.)   But it is doubtful whether Swift was as interested

in these *Miscellanies* as in his friend's great satiric poem, which was taking shape during these summer months. In his verses *To Mr. Pope while he was writing the Dunciad* the dean demanded that his own part in the composition of that masterpiece be duly acknowledged, maintaining that unless he had been deaf and unfit for conversation Pope would not have written a line.

So far as politics were concerned, Swift had begun to manifest interest in the anti-Walpole patriots, headed by Pulteney, and in their political organ, the *Craftsman,* which had been appearing since December 1726 and to which Bolingbroke, assuming the name of the 'Occasional Writer,' was now contributing a series of letters. Any movement which promised to annoy Walpole, let alone check him, appealed to Swift, and there was always the chance that Ireland might profit if the chief minister were harried with effective malice. Once again Swift turned to political writing, drafting *A Letter to the Writer of the Occasional Paper.* But he could not warm to his subject, and his *Letter,* with which Bolingbroke was but indifferently pleased, was never finished and was not published for many years.

Yet despite the half-hearted way in which he fell in with the journalistic schemes of Pulteney and Bolingbroke, his letters to Ireland show that he was following political developments with something of his old interest. Things were in a 'strange situation,' he wrote to Sheridan; there was 'a firm settled resolution to assault the present administration, and break it if possible'; Walpole was exceedingly peevish; 'I am in high displeasure with him and his partisans,' but 'I have at last seen the Princess twice this week. . .' (13 May.) The scene was altogether changed when, on 15 June, news arrived in London that King George had died on his way to Hanover. Swift's commentary, which took the form of the verses entitled *A Pastoral Dialogue,* was indirect, being concerned with Mrs. Masham rather than the late king. He was in London and on the point of setting out for France when certain of his friends dissuaded him from leaving England at this critical moment. Bolingbroke foresaw — or at least pretended to foresee — the ruin of Walpole and the rise of the tories to effective influence; Swift must by no means cross to France — 'the opportunity for quitting Ireland for England is, I believe, fairly before you' (Bolingbroke to Swift, 17 June). Swift turned to Mrs. Masham for advice, and she too urged him to remain. So confidently did his friends talk of the political changes about to take place that for some days he entertained a faint hope that at long last his exile in Ireland might be ended honourably. On 24 June he wrote to Sheridan thus :

The talk is now for a moderating scheme, wherein nobody shall be used the worse or better for being called Whig or Tory, and the King hath received both with great equality, showing civilities to several who are openly known to be the latter. . . We have now done with repining. if we shall be used well, and not baited as formerly ; we all agree in it, and if things do not mend it is not our faults — we have made our offers, if otherwise, we are as we were.

But Swift and his tory comrades were not to feed themselves on these false hopes for long. Before the end of June parliament reassembled, and it was soon apparent that Walpole was as firmly in the saddle as ever. Swift vented his ire in the verses entitled *A Character of Sir Robert Walpole*, said to have been written for Mrs. Masham. His friends tried to draw him into new schemes for undermining the whigs, but Swift was through with England and her politics. As he pondered over the events of June, the feeling that grew upon him was resentment at those who had given him false hopes by urging him to abandon his journey to France. Mrs. Masham, indeed, he never forgave, and three years later he was chiding her for having 'acted too much like a courtier' when she advised against his leaving London.

Swift's last weeks in England were anything but happy ones. He was ill, all hope of a deliverance from Ireland was at an end, and Stella was again sinking. As in the previous year so now the discouraging reports concerning Stella which he received from Sheridan filled him with anguish, and again he hid his feelings from those at Twickenham ; only in his letters to Ireland did he permit himself any expression of his emotions.

On Monday 18 September Swift set out from London. As he pushed north towards Chester he knew that in all probability he had looked for the last time upon the scene of his great triumphs and was not again to rejoin his English friends.   Characteristically, he repressed all sentiment, dwelling instead upon the miseries of the journey and magnifying each *contretemps* a thousandfold.   At Holyhead he was detained almost a week by adverse winds, and as he fumed and fretted in the wretched inn he kept track of his thoughts in what has come to be known as *The Holyhead Journal*.

> I never was in hast before
> To reach that slavish hatefull shore.
> Before, I always found the wind
> To me was most malicious kind,
> But now the danger of a friend,
> On whom my fears and hopes depend,
> Absent from whom all Clymes are curst,
> With whom I'm happy in the worst,
> With rage impatient makes me wait
> A passage to the land I hate.

He arrived in Dublin to find Stella still alive. Pope, who had learned of her illness from Sheridan, ventured now to refer to it and to the distress which it had occasioned Swift at Twickenham.   He did so with the utmost delicacy: 'To your bad health I fear there was added some disagreeable news from Ireland which might occasion your so sudden departure' (2 October).   On his part, Swift now brought himself to say farewell to Pope as he had not dared to do when leaving him:

You are the best and kindest friend in the world. . . I have often wished that God Almighty would be so easy to the weakness of mankind, as to let old friends be acquainted in another state; and if I were to write an Utopia for heaven, that would be one of my schemes.   This wildness you must allow for, because I am giddy and deaf. (12 October.)

3

Shortly before leaving on his last journey to England Swift had celebrated Stella's birthday — it was to prove her last — in verses marked by unusual tenderness. He made no attempt to conceal what they both knew was fast approaching; instead, he turned with her to consider what lay behind them:

> Although we now can form no more
> Long schemes of life, as heretofore;
> Yet you, while time is running fast,
> Can look with joy on what is past.

During the final weeks of 1727 he was awaiting Stella's death, in what mood can be seen from a letter of consolation which he wrote to a woman who had just lost her daughter: 'Self-love, as it is the motive to all our actions, so it is the sole cause of our grief. The dear person you lament is by no means an object of pity, either in a moral or religious sense' (To Mrs. Moore, 7 December 1727). He had no fear of death; when it approached others he did not shrink back at the realization of his own mortality. It was the loss of friendship that sickened him, and he hated himself for what he regarded as the impurity of his grief. The thoughtless observer can easily mistake this attitude, but as Stella followed the words of those prayers which Swift wrote for her in her illness we may be sure that she at least was not deceived:

Lessen, O Lord, we beseech Thee, her bodily pains, or give her a double strength of mind to support them. And if Thou wilt soon take her to Thyself, turn our thoughts rather upon that felicity, which we hope she shall enjoy, than upon that unspeakable loss we shall endure. Let her memory be ever dear unto us; and the example of her many virtues, as far as human infirmity will admit, our constant imitation. Accept, O Lord, these prayers poured from the very bottom of our hearts, in Thy mercy, and for the merits of our blessed Saviour. Amen.

Stella died on Sunday 28 January 1728 about six o'clock at night. Swift, who was entertaining friends at the deanery, received word by messenger some two hours later, but it was not until his guests had left at eleven o'clock that he could be alone with his thoughts. Instinctively he reached for pen and paper and began to write. On Tuesday night Stella was buried in the Cathedral. Swift, too ill to attend, turned once more to his journal, which he had headed *On the Death of Mrs. Johnson;* 'It is now nine at night,' he wrote, 'and I am removed into another apartment, that I may not see the light in the church, which is just over against the window of my bed-chamber.'

4

FOR some eleven years after Stella's death — until the close of 1738, that is — Swift continued to play an active part in the world. But it was only the sheer energy of his mind that sustained him and kept despair at bay. To Bolingbroke he wrote in 1729: 'I never wake without finding life a more insignificant thing than it was the day before. . . But my greatest misery is recollecting the scene of twenty years past, and then all on a sudden dropping into the present. . .' A year later, addressing the same correspondent, he found those unforgettable words to describe his closing years — unless delivered from Ireland he would, he said, die there 'like a poisoned rat in a hole' (21 March 1730).

So long as his friends in England lived, he did not feel entirely cut off from the past. With Lady Betty Germain he often corresponded. About 1732 Charles Ford took up permanent residence in London, and between him and Swift there passed many letters. Gay died at the close of 1732, and until within less than a month of his death he was addressing the liveliest and most affectionate of communications to his banished friend. Arbuthnot lived on till 1735. The doctor and the dean did not flood each other with letters but when they did write their words bespoke deep feeling. 'I am going out of this troublesome world; and you, among the rest of my friends, shall have my last prayers, and good wishes' — such was Arbuthnot's final message. They had been such a glorious company, these Queen Anne wits! Now that death was stalking them, the past lived anew for them and made their parting the more difficult.

Bolingbroke, who survived until 1751, remained in touch with the dean for many years after the latter's final visit to England. He was associated in Swift's mind as was no other living person with the stirring years of the tory ministry; a letter from him banished for a space the hideous reality of

the present and awoke memories of better days. For this
reason Swift clung to him, and once in a moment of wildness
went so far as to propose that Bolingbroke and Pope should
come over to Ireland and take up permanent residence at
the deanery. Bolingbroke was still determined that a suitable living should be found for Swift in England, and in
1732 he broached a plan whereby an exchange might be
effected between the rector of Burghfield, in Berkshire, and
the dean of St. Patrick's. It was doubtless an impracticable
scheme, but Swift was not displeased by his friend's efforts.
After 1734 their correspondence fell off, though letters passed
between them as late as 1738.

But it was Pope who occupied the foremost place in Swift's
thoughts during these latter years, and their correspondence
ended only with the dean's loss of memory in 1740.   It were
unreasonable to question Pope's motives in keeping up this
long association with one who had stepped out of the English
scene ; as for Swift's responsiveness to Pope, it is not to be
impugned by the most obdurate cynic.   Let it be granted
that Pope, with the future in mind, was seeking to link their
names together ; the fact remains that here were two men
who found happiness in each other and succeeded, through
mutual affection and good will, in maintaining an unbroken
friendship.   True, it has been held that Pope twice betrayed
this friendship, once in the matter of the publication in 1732
of the fourth volume — designated as Volume III — of the *Miscellanies,* and a second time in connexion with the publication of the Swift-Pope correspondence, but to-day one hesi-
tates to write Pope down a villain without first reviewing the
evidence against him with great care.   After the appearance
of the *Miscellanies,* Volume III, in October 1732 Swift expressed to Motte his dissatisfaction with Pope's editing.   But
Pope has been condemned not so much for these imputed
editorial faults as for his dealings with the London publishers
Gilliver, Motte, and Bowyer, all of whom were drawn into
this affair of the *Miscellanies,* Volume III.   Pope, it has been
suggested, had begun by deliberately playing Motte off against
Gilliver with a view to enhanced profits for himself, whereupon the dean, his suspicions aroused, sought to circumvent

Pope by means of a rival volume to be published by Bowyer. The entire incident is so confused and so much of the correspondence pertaining to it has disappeared, that it is impossible to tell precisely what did happen, but it is clear that if anyone dealt disingenuously with the publishers it was Swift rather than Pope, nor is there an atom of evidence to show that Pope was motivated by greed for profits.

The second incident wherein Pope has been accused of disloyalty to Swift has been presented as an elaborate plot on Pope's part to gain control of his correspondence to Swift and to insure its publication but in such a way that Swift rather than he would appear to be the one responsible for its having fallen into the printer's hands.   Under this interpretation, the facts are fitted into place in the following manner :   In 1735 Curll had published certain letters of Pope.   Whether or no Pope had himself engineered the business, he made of Curll's act an excuse for putting forth two years later, as though in self-defence, an authorized version of the same letters.   Curll's volumes also permitted him to approach Swift regarding the disposition of whatever of their correspondence was then in the dean's possession.   Swift's reply was disconcerting: 'You need not fear any consequence in the commerce that has so long passed between us; although I never destroyed one of your letters.   But my executors are men of honour and virtue, who have strict orders in my will to burn every letter left behind me' (3 September 1735). It was the villain Curll who came to Pope's rescue, by publishing in 1736 a letter of Bolingbroke's and one of Pope's to Swift,— how Curll obtained the copies has seemed clear enough to those convinced of Pope's habitual double-dealing, — and Pope was enabled to speak more to the point.   This time Swift seems to have fallen in with his friend's designs, for it appears that in 1737 he entrusted to Lord Orrery, who was then setting out for England, all the letters from Pope in his possession.   The next developments were highly involved, but the upshot was that in 1740 there came into Swift's hands a volume printed in England and containing the correspondence between Pope, Gay, Bolingbroke, and himself.   Swift made the volume over to Faulkner, the Dublin printer. Pope protested, then took the attitude that Faulkner had proceeded too far to be stopped. With the letters assured of publication in Dublin, the way was opened for an 'authorized' edition of the correspondence. When it appeared in London in 1741, this 'authorized' version contained a prefatory note stating that the letters as now published were 'copied from an impression sent from Dublin, and said to have been printed by the Dean's direction,' an impression 'which was begun without our author's [Pope's] knowledge, and continued without his consent.'

Put in this way, it makes an ugly story, and it becomes yet uglier if one holds to the view that during the final and crucial stages of the plot Swift's mind was so far impaired that he was a helpless instrument in Pope's hands. But until all the facts in the case have been more carefully studied it would be well to suspend judgment. Is it beyond possibility that Swift understood and co-operated in Pope's scheme to publish their correspondence?

5

Swift's latter years were not unmarked by social intercourse with friends in Ireland. He was often at Belcamp, the residence of the Grattans. The Grange, near Dublin, made attractive by the presence of Lady Acheson's mother, was another of his favourite resorts. He paid a long visit to Sheridan when the latter was master of the free school in Cavan. Delany, now married, entertained on a grand scale at his villa Delville, in a northern suburb of Dublin, and in these festivities the dean often joined. From time to time he repaired to Howth Castle, not far distant from the city, where Lord and Lady Howth were always happy to receive him. But the place of foremost association with the elderly Swift was Market Hill, now known as Gosford Castle, near Armagh. Here lived Sir Arthur and Lady Acheson, Sir Arthur a stout tory and hence bearable, his wife too charming and clever to need political convictions to attract her guest. Swift showed his complete approval of Lady Acheson by sponging unmercifully on Sir Arthur. In 1728 he settled

down for six months at Market Hill, and he spent the summer there in 1729 and again in 1730. Most of his personal
verses written during these latter years were incited either by
Sheridan or the Achesons. *A Pastoral Dialogue* (1728), *The
Grand Question Debated* (1729), and *A Panegyric on the
Dean* (1730) are among the best of these verses and all three
pieces concern affairs or people at Market Hill.

Sheridan remained almost till his death Swift's closest
friend in Ireland, for ever deluging the deanery with pun-
ning Anglo-Latin missives, which were answered in kind. A
breach between the two occurred shortly before Sheridan's
death on 10 October 1738,— precisely what happened is not
very clear,— but when Swift penned later that year *The
Character of Doctor Sheridan*, which was one of the last
things he ever wrote, he bore no grudge.

After Stella's death a number of new faces began to appear
in the circle at the deanery. The most prominent of these
new comers was Swift's future biographer, John Boyle, fifth
earl of Orrery, the son of Charles Boyle of the Epistles of
Phalaris. Lord Orrery came to Ireland for the first time in
1731, making Swift's acquaintance shortly after his arrival.
From the first he stood in high favour with the dean, who
later wrote to Pope that 'next to yourself I love no man
so well.' Orrery has suffered in the eyes of posterity as
the author of *Remarks on the Life and Writings of Dr.
Jonathan Swift*, but the lamentable appearance which he
makes in his own pages is the result of an uncritical mind,
amusing self-esteem, and an utter unawareness of Swift's true
greatness, not of any ill-will or meanness. He meant no
harm to Swift's memory; while the dean lived he attended
him faithfully, chivalrously.

Then there were the three citizens' wives: Mrs. Grierson,
scholar and poet; Mrs. Sican, a woman of sound literary
judgment; and Mrs. Barber, 'our chief poetess,' who enjoyed
Swift's particular favour. Whenever Mrs. Barber crossed to
England, she went armed with introductions from the dean;
when she published verse, it was the dean who solicited sub-
scriptions from the great. On one occasion she was forced
to pay dearly for her association with Swift. She had re-

turned to Dublin in 1732, but the following year saw her
again in London, where she arrived bearing certain verses
of Swift's which were to be conveyed to the printer in all
secrecy. Mrs. Barber passed them on to Pilkington, who
in turn arranged for their publication. Before the end of
the year London was reading *An Epistle to a Lady who
desired the Author to make Verses on Her in the Heroic
Style* and *On Poetry — a Rhapsody*, which despite their innocuous titles were loaded with political satire amounting,
in the eyes of all good whigs, to lese-majesty. The government stepped in and Wilford the publisher, Gilliver the
printer and bookseller, Pilkington, Motte, and Mrs. Barber
were taken into custody. The first three were soon released,
but Motte and Mrs. Barber lay in prison for a year. When,
some years later, Swift learned that Mrs. Barber was in distressing circumstances he sent her the manuscript of *Polite
Conversation* to publish for her own profit.

There were, lastly, the Pilkingtons,— the Reverend Matthew and his wife, Lætitia,— who had been introduced to
Swift after Stella's death. By 1732 Pilkington was in London being used by Swift as a secret agent in the matter of
the *Miscellanies,* Volume III. Later that year Swift prevailed
on John Barber, his printer in the days of the queen and
now the newly elected lord mayor of London, to make
Pilkington his chaplain. When in the following year
Lætitia, accompanying Mrs. Barber, arrived in London she
found Matthew enamoured of an actress and not disposed
to desert a mistress for a wife. Poor Lætitia returned to
Dublin alone, where she was promptly scorned by the good
citizens, who were now attributing the misfortunes of those
implicated in the publication of the *Epistle* and the *Rhapsody*
solely to the treachery of the lord mayor's chaplain. It was
apparent, however, that Swift did not believe Pilkington to
be an informer, for he received Lætitia on her return and
later Matthew himself, when the latter finally consented to
rejoin his wife. But within a few years of their reunion
they became the centre of scandal, Matthew secured a divorce
on the ground of adultery, and Swift disowned both of them.
Lætitia found her way to London, where she eked out a

precarious existence, composing in the last years of her life her *Memoirs* (I and II, 1748; III, ptd. posthumously, 1754), in the pages of which the elderly dean of St. Patrick's is sketched so vividly.

When one considers those who gained admittance to Swift during his last years of activity, one begins to appreciate the part which Stella had once played. Orrery might have passed muster, but we may be sure that in her quiet and altogether effective way she would have seen that people like the Pilkingtons did not visit the deancry a second time.

CHAPTER II

THE WRITER AND THE PUBLIC FIGURE: LAST PHASE

1

FOR almost ten years after Stella's death Swift remained a commanding public figure, able through pamphlet or satiric verses to modify the course of the Irish parliament, to call down the wrath of the kingdom upon his own enemies, and to flutter the English dove-cotes. The man who as journalist and agitator had swayed opinion for over a quarter of a century did not close his mind to public affairs until disease and old age claimed him, and until that time he retained almost to the full his genius for timely utterance. In this final period of the dean's activity some will mark the great patriot, to the end a champion of justice; others will see the psychopathic artist or again the egoist ready to overwhelm with satiric abuse anyone presumptuous enough to cross him. All must agree, however, that he displayed a power of mind and will that for a man in the sixties, deserted by fortune and threatened by physical and mental decay, is utterly amazing.

But behind the indomitable public figure one soon discerns the lonely old man, increasingly conscious that he has outlived the world, and retiring more and more into himself. Stella's death had interposed a great gulf between him and the world. Men and women he saw as from a distance, creatures in vague masks moving aimlessly; events were dull echoes out of the past — only one's own thoughts had the vividness of reality. While engaged in controversy Swift forced a pseudo-actuality upon the world of affairs, but when the desire for artistic statement was uppermost he put an end to such make-believe and plunged into his own mind for the truth that had ceased to appear in external trivialities. Prose he still wrote, but it was in verse that he spoke most naturally and effectively, his self-centredness giving to

his metrical compositions of this final period a magnificent
intensity.

2

ON 11 May 1728 appeared the first number of the *Intelligencer*, a weekly publication — it ran to nineteen numbers —
issued by Sheridan and Swift as a medium both for the discussion of Irish problems and for the excoriation of their
personal enemies.   Swift was soon using its columns for the
infliction of further punishment upon Richard Tighe, whose
betrayal of Sheridan seemed more dastardly as the years
passed.   In a June number appeared *A Dialogue between
Mad Mullinix and Timothy*, wherein Tighe is represented
as setting himself up as the government's sole guardian in
Ireland :

> The public safety, I foresee,
> Henceforth depends alone on me. . .

In July came *Tim and the Fables*, shorter but more diabolical
than the *Dialogue*.   Four additional satires against Tighe,
not published in the *Intelligencer*, were recovered after
Swift's death.

As long as he remained capable of consistent thought,
Swift could not for a single moment blot out from his consciousness the appalling conditions in Ireland, and long
after Wood's halfpence had ceased to be an issue he continued to put forth pamphlets devoted to the economic and
social problems of the kingdom.   The years 1728 and 1729
were filled with these writings, his increased activity in this
respect being caused by the unparalleled poverty and misery
which at this time extended over the entire land.   'As to
this country,' Swift wrote to Pope in August 1729,

> there have been three terrible years' dearth of corn, and every
> place strewed with beggars. . . Imagine a nation the two thirds
> of whose revenues are spent out of it, and who are not permitted
> to trade with the other third, and where the pride of women
> will not suffer them to wear their own manufactures, even where
> they excel what come from abroad.   This is the true state of
> Ireland in a very few words.   These evils operate more every

day, and the kingdom is absolutely undone, as I have been telling often in print these ten years past.

It was the hopelessness of the situation that infuriated him — in England, the cruel, calculating selfishness of those classes who feared Ireland as a commercial competitor; at home, stupidity, indifference, perversity. At some moment of dramatic tension, like that created by Wood in 1724, it was possible to play upon the emotions. But of what avail were emotions against the radical evils which had been allowed to operate for so many years that they were now taken for granted? Reason and reason alone could save the Irish, and though his counsel went unheeded he would not cease to apply rational analysis to the nation's ills. In March 1728 he wrote, by way of rejoinder to one Sir John Browne, *An Answer to a Paper, called 'A Memorial of the Poor Inhabitants, Tradesmen, and Labourers of the Kingdom of Ireland.'* It is a short but wonderfully concise pamphlet, setting forth 'the steps by which we arrived at this hopeful situation.' Another, and better known summary of the causes of the widespread distress is *A Short View of the State of Ireland,* which also appeared in 1728. In the following year Swift turned his attention to the plight of the weavers, issuing among other things *A Letter to the Archbishop of Dublin, concerning the Weavers* and *A Proposal that all the Ladies and Women of Ireland should appear constantly in Irish Manufactures.* In all of these writings Swift was keeping his emotions under control, for his object was not to kindle passions but to point out the course given by reason. There came a moment, however, when he could contain himself no longer, and it was then that he composed *A Modest Proposal for preventing the Children of Poor People from being a Burthen to their Parents or Country, and for making them Beneficial to the Publick* (1729). This immortal piece is not only the greatest of Swift's Irish tracts; it is also the best introduction to his satiric art, so clearly do irony and *le mythe animal* appear as calculated devices and at the same time peculiar modes of Swift's intellectual and emotional energy.

The year 1730 was marked by the appearance of a new

adversary, whom Swift proceeded to gibbet as formerly he had gibbeted Dean Smedley and Richard Tighe. Delany, the recipient of several preferments from Lord Carteret, had ventured to ask for more in an *Epistle* in verse addressed to the lord-lieutenant. Swift was amused by his friend's unconcealed ambitions and answered the *Epistle* with *An Epistle upon an Epistle,* which contained lines directed against Smedley but which was otherwise innocuous. However, in February 1730 Swift followed up his first verses with others, entitled *A Libel on D—D—And a Certain Great Lord,* and these were provocative in the highest degree, dwelling as they did upon the shabby treatment accorded wits like Congreve, Steele, and Gay by the politicians, and proceeding to a castigation of Walpole. The Irish parliament, which was then in session, fell upon the *Libel* and talked of a violent prosecution of the author and the printers. Swift waited until the session had come to an end, whereupon he turned on Lord Allen, who had led the attack against him, and in two satires—*Traulus. The First Part,* and *Traulus. The Second Part*—sank his fangs into this new assailant. The fury of the dean's onslaught can be judged from the following lines, which occur in the second piece:

> Traulus, of amphibious breed,
> Motley fruit of mongrel seed;
> By the dam from lordlings sprung,
> By the sire exhaled from dung:
> Think on every vice in both,
> Look on him, and see their growth.

In 1731 Swift was twice moved to satiric commentary on political events in England. On 1 June of this year occurred the incident which he was prompt to make the subject of the verses entitled *On Mr. Pulteney's being put out of the Council.* The more striking piece, composed several months earlier, is the *Epistle to Mr. Gay,* a forthright attack upon Walpole ending with this anecdote and moral:

> I knew a brazen minister of state,
> Who bore for twice ten years the public hate.
> In every mouth the question most in vogue
> Was, when will they turn out this odious rogue?

A juncture happen'd in his highest pride :
While he went robbing on, his master died.
We thought there now remain'd no room to doubt ;
The work is done, the minister must out.
The court invited more than one or two :
Will you, Sir Spencer? or will you, or you?
But not a soul his office durst accept ;
The subtle knave had all the plunder swept :
And, such was then the temper of the times,
He owed his preservation to his crimes.
The candidates observed his dirty paws ;
Nor found it difficult to guess the cause :
But, when they smelt such foul corruptions round him,
Away they fled, and left him as they found him.
　　Thus, when a greedy sloven once has thrown
His snot into the mess, 'tis all his own.

Not long after the sallies just referred to, Swift found
within the affairs of the Irish church occasion for new controversy. In the parliamentary session of 1731-1732 there
were introduced two bills — a Bill of Residence and a Bill
of Division — which the dean of St. Patrick's chose to believe
were selfish measures devised by the bishops to subject and
plunder country incumbents. Had Swift been a bishop
— such is the inevitable question — would he have been so
quick to scent a plot against the humble clergy? Unquestionably he would not have been. However, if we must
moralize this answer, we might remember that a valid champion is not necessarily one whose motives are immaculate.
Swift let drive at the bishops in two pamphlets, *On the Bill
for the Clergy's residing on their Livings* and *Considerations
upon two Bills,* and when the bills were thrown out early
in 1732 he celebrated the defeat of his ecclesiastical superiors
by inditing *An Excellent New Poem on the Bishops,* in
which he declared,

　　Our bishops, puft up with wealth and with pride,
　　To hell on the backs of the clergy would ride.

Scarcely had this storm blown over when one of much
greater magnitude gathered in the distance. This time it
was the dissenters who were the source of the disturbance.
By 1732 it was plain to everyone in Ireland that at the first

opportune moment a concerted assault was to be launched against the Test; the church was already in a state of alarm and girding itself for battle. Since *A Letter concerning the Sacramental Test* (1709) and *A Letter to a Member of Parliament, in Ireland* (subsequent to December 1709) Swift had written nothing in prose which bore directly upon dissent and the Test. Now, however, he began to issue a series of pamphlets designed to defeat the dissenters' schemes in advance of any open move on their part in the Irish parliament. Because Swift was but one of many writers at this time belabouring the presbyterians there is still some doubt as to his exact contributions to this war of words and as to the dates of the tracts ascribed to him, but Temple Scott's list is probably not too far off: *The Advantages proposed by Repealing the Sacramental Test* (1732 ?); *Queries relating to the Sacramental Test* (1732); *The Presbyterians' Plea of Merit* (1732 ?); *A Narrative of the Several Attempts for a Repeal of the Sacramental Test* (1733 ?; the ascription to Swift is now questioned[1]); *Some Few Thoughts concerning the Repeal of the Test* (1733 ?); *Reasons Humbly Offered for Repealing the Sacramental Test* (1733); *Ten Reasons for Repealing the Test Act* (1733 ?). When parliament met in October 1733 it soon became evident that the house of commons stood solidly against a repeal of the Test. This did not mean, however, that the members were ready to strengthen the established church; representing as they did the larger landowners, they were eager to support any legislation designed to restrict the taxing power of the church, and they proceeded during the latter weeks of 1733 to take up with enthusiasm a bill relating to tithes from flax and hemp which, had it passed, would have reduced the incomes of many of the clergy. Though Swift would not have been affected,— his lands did not lie in the northern, flax-growing counties,— it was not in him to maintain silence at a moment when numbers of his fellows were threatened with heavy financial loss. He sought to lay his views before the house and at the same time addressed the public in a pamphlet entitled *Some Reasons against the Bill for Settling the Tithe of Hemp, Flax, &c.* The proposed legislation was

finally dropped, but out of the affair came the notorious encounter — of words only, as it turned out — between the dean
of St. Patrick's and Serjeant Bettesworth, member of parliament and vociferous supporter of the bill.   For his recent
conduct in the house Bettesworth soon found himself in the
company of Smedley, Tighe, and Lord Allen ; he protested,
he raged, but the more fiercely he struggled against his tor-
mentor the less his chance of escape.   Swift's first petard
exploded in the closing days of December.   During the
autumn just passed, while the Test was being debated with
such feeling, the dissenters had often been heard to use the
terms 'brother protestants' and 'fellow Christians' in reference to the members of the established church.   These terms
Swift now turned to satiric use in his verses *On the Words
Brother Protestants and Fellow Christians*.   In times of
stress, we are told, natural distinctions are forgotten, the
superior generously consorting with those beneath them.
But once things have taken this turn it always happens that
many of inferior rank begin to give themselves airs.   Thus
the corn-cutter calls the great physician brother doctor ; thus
the curate, writing to the dean, subscribes himself 'Your
loving brother'; and

> Thus at the bar the booby Bettesworth,
> Though half a crown o'er pays his sweat's worth ;
> Who knows in law nor text nor margent,
> Calls Singleton his brother sergeant.

That his name rhymed with *sweat's worth* had apparently
never occurred to the Serjeant, who straightway threatened
to cut off the dean's ears and actually went in search of
him armed with a sharp knife and accompanied by a footman and several thugs.   He found Swift at Worrall's house,
where there ensued a scene which was shortly to be a topic
of conversation even in London drawing-rooms.   '. . . I
found the chief weight of [Bettesworth's] argument lay,' Swift
wrote to the duke of Dorset,

upon two words that rhymed to his name, which he knew could
come from none but me. He . . . told me, that since I would
not own the verses, and that since he could not get satisfaction

by any course of law, he would get it by his pen, and show the world what a man I was.

When he began to grow over-warm and eloquent, I called in the gentleman of the house, from the room adjoining, and the Serjeant, going on with less turbulence, went away. (January 1734.)

Whether Bettesworth had any real intention of assaulting Swift seems highly doubtful, but his threat was taken seriously; all patriotic Irishmen rose to defend their idol, and the inhabitants of the Liberty of St. Patrick's passed a solemn Resolution to defend the life and limbs of the dean against Bettesworth 'and all his ruffians and murderers.' In the meantime Swift followed up his advantage, riddling his luckless opponent with such verses as those in *An Epigram*, in *The Yahoo's Overthrow*, and in *On the Archbishop of Cashel and Bettesworth*.

For a booby like Bettesworth any sort of jingling rhymes would do. But that Swift had not taken leave of his great satiric Muse, England was at that moment quite aware, for by 31 December 1733 there had appeared in London both the *Epistle to a Lady* and *On Poetry — a Rhapsody*, the publication of which was shortly to involve so many persons in difficulties. These two pieces are of unequal merit; for although the *Epistle* is in no way a failure, the *Rhapsody* rises to a level of satiric power and intensity seldom attained even by Swift. The former composition — its full title is *An Epistle to a Lady who desired the Author to make Verses on Her in the Heroic Style* — takes the form of a dialogue, in the course of which the author explains his inability to treat the lady in the heroic manner, which is not his natural vein. From this point he wanders, as though by chance, into the region of politics:

> I, as all the parish knows,
> Hardly can be grave in prose:
> Still to lash, and lashing smile,
> Ill befits a lofty style.
> From the planet of my birth
> I encounter vice with mirth.
> Wicked ministers of state
> I can easier scorn than hate;

And I find it answers right :
Scorn torments them more than spight.
All the vices of a court
Do but serve to make me sport.
Were I in some foreign realm,
Which all vices overwhelm ;
Should a monkey wear a crown,
Must I tremble at his frown ?
Could I not, through all his ermine,
'Spy the strutting chattering vermin ;
Safely write a smart lampoon,
To expose the brisk baboon ?
　　　　When my Muse officious ventures
On the nation's representers :
Teaching by what golden rules
Into knaves they turn their fools ;
How the helm is ruled by Walpole,
At whose oars, like slaves, they all pull ;
Let the vessel split on shelves ;
With the freight enrich themselves :
Safe within my little wherry,
All their madness makes me merry :
Like the waterman of Thames,
I row by, and call them names ;
Like the ever-laughing sage,
In a jest I spend my rage :
(Though it must be understood,
I would hang them if I could ;)
If I can but fill my niche,
I attempt no higher pitch. . .

But beside its companion piece, the *Epistle* seems a tame
performance. *On Poetry—a Rhapsody* is one of Swift's
longer metrical compositions, but so wonderfully sustained
is the irony, of such high voltage is the satire, that the level
of intensity, instead of declining as the piece continues, rises
steadily from couplet to couplet. The opening passages are
concerned with Pride : why, since it is clear that there have
never been more than three genuine poets produced in a
single age, does every fool aspire to literary fame ?

What reason can there be assign'd
For this perverseness in the mind ?
Brutes find out where their talents lie :
A bear will not attempt to fly ;

> A founder'd horse will oft debate,
> Before he tries a five-barr'd gate;
> A dog by instinct turns aside,
> Who sees the ditch too deep and wide.
> But man we find the only creature
> Who, led by Folly, combats Nature;
> Who, when she loudly cries, Forbear,
> With obstinacy fixes there;
> And, where his genius least inclines,
> Absurdly bends his whole designs.

There follow hundreds of lines of advice to the would-be poet — lines in which the ironic tone never once cracks.   At length the satirist approaches a new topic: the indignity and shame of prostituting the Muse by flattering kings, of whom — abroad — not one can be found that is not polluted with every vice.   Nothing in Byron's *Vision of Judgment* surpasses the rhetorical period to which we are now treated. Only in England will the poet find a king truly worthy of celebration:

> Fair Britain, in thy monarch blest,
> Whose virtues bear the strictest test;
> Whom never faction could bespatter,
> Nor minister nor poet flatter;
> What justice in rewarding merit!
> What magnanimity of spirit!
> What lineaments divine we trace
> Through all his figure, mien, and face!
> Though peace with olive binds his hands,
> Confess'd the conquering hero stands.
> Hydaspes, Indus, and the Ganges,
> Dread from his hand impending changes.
> From him the Tartar and Chinese,
> Short by the knees, entreat for peace.
> The consort of his throne and bed,
> A perfect goddess born and bred,
> Appointed, sovereign judge to sit
> On learning, eloquence, and wit.
> Our eldest hope, divine Iülus,
> (Late, very late, O may he rule us!)
> What early manhood has he shown,
> Before his downy beard was grown,
> Then think, what wonders will be done
> By going on as he begun,

An heir for Britain to secure
As long as sun and moon endure.

By this time our poet has gathered such momentum that he
must perforce include in his song the rest of the royal family
and after them the 'great vicegerent of the king,' England's
chief minister ; he threatens, in fact, to go on for ever when
a *caetera desiderantur* puts an untimely end to his praises.

During the two years that followed, only minor outbreaks
on Swift's part are recorded, but in 1736 there occurred an
eruption of unparalleled fury, occasioned by the conduct
of the Irish house of commons. In a recent pamphlet — *A
New Proposal for the Better Regulation and Improvement
of Quadrille* — written by Bishop Hort but revised by Swift
there was found to be an uncomplimentary reference to
Bettesworth, still a member of parliament. The commons
at once took action against the printers of the *Proposal* and
thereby evoked the dean's wrath, which found immediate
expression in satiric verses (*On a Printer being sent to New-
gate ; On Noisy Tom,* and other pieces). But this was only
a preliminary incident. In March, shortly before proroga-
tion, parliament once more gave ear to the plaints of the
landowners, who were now clamouring against the tithes on
pasturage,— tithes of agistment was the term,— and the house
of commons, by resolution, showed its sympathy for the
graziers. It was then that Swift wrote *The Legion Club,* the
most terrible of all his philippics. Let the parliament house
be razed, let the members of the house of commons be confined like madmen !

> Could I from the building's top
> Hear the rattling thunder drop,
> While the devil upon the roof
> (If the devil be thunder proof)
> Should with poker fiery red
> Crack the stones, and melt the lead ;
> Drive them down on every skull,
> When the den of thieves is full ;
> Quite destroy that harpies' nest ;
> How might then our isle be blest !
> For divines allow, that God
> Sometimes makes the devil his rod ;

And the gospel will inform us,
He can punish sins enormous.
    Yet should Swift endow the schools,
For his lunatics and fools,
With a rood or two of land,
I allow the pile may stand.
You perhaps will ask me, Why so?
But it is with this proviso:
Since the house is like to last,
Let the royal grant be pass'd,
That the club have right to dwell
Each within his proper cell,
With a passage left to creep in
And a hole above for peeping.

The Legion Club is the last of the great satires.   Thereafter there is little to record, save that in 1737, when the standard of gold was lowered by government proclamation, Ireland's champion once more spoke forth in verse (*Ay and No* and the ballad 'Patrick astore, what news upon the town?').   But the light was failing; soon there would be only darkness.

3

OF the prose compositions of the dean's latter years *A Modest Proposal* is far and away the greatest.   Something must be said, however, of a number of pieces in the non-controversial manner, two of which are masterpieces of humour.

The earliest of the prose writings of which we shall here take account is *A Letter to a Very Young Lady on her Marriage,* published in 1727 in Volume II of the joint *Miscellanies.*   What young lady Swift had in mind — opinions differ on this point — really does not matter since the proffered advice was intended to be of universal applicability.   It may safely be said that no one who has not studied this *Letter* is qualified to hold any sort of opinion concerning the episodes in Swift's life involving Vanessa and Stella.   Here, in all its apparent harshness, is the belligerently anti-romantic attitude: man and wife may become friends in time, but it is impossible for them to remain lovers.   It is not the cynic who is speaking but the clear-eyed realist, and though it is

regrettable that this man of reason remained for ever anæsthetized to so much that is valid in normal emotional experience, a genuine soundness and health shows forth in his
detestation of sentimentality. Nor is he an anti-feminist.
If the conditions springing out of marriage fill him with
loathing it is for the reason that they bear so unjustly upon
the woman, who must surrender her rightful place in civilized society. Your parents, Swift writes to the lady addressed in the *Letter*, have bred you well, 'but they failed,
as it is generally the case, in too much neglecting to cultivate
your mind; without which it is impossible to acquire or
preserve the friendship and esteem of a wise man, who soon
grows weary of acting the lover and treating his wife like
a mistress, but wants a reasonable companion, and a true
friend through every stage of life.' He proceeds to offer her
much specific advice: do not lay off at once your modest
behaviour of a virgin; do not display affection to your husband in public; do not take the advice of your female
friends. Your chief duty is to gain and preserve the friendship and esteem of your husband:

You have but a very few years to be young and handsome in
the eyes of the world; and as few months to be so in the eyes
of a husband, who is not a fool; for I hope you do not still
dream of charms and raptures, which marriage ever did, and
ever will, put a sudden end to. Besides yours was a match of
prudence and common good liking, without any mixture of
that ridiculous passion which has no being but in play-books
and romances.

In a short and unfinished piece entitled *Of the Education
of Ladies* (date of composition unknown; ptd. 1765) the
tone is ironic but the views expressed are fundamentally the
same as those set forth in the *Letter*. And here may be
mentioned *An Essay on Modern Education*, which came
out in 1728 as the ninth number of the *Intelligencer*. As
his use of the word *modern* is enough to indicate, Swift can
find nothing good to say of current ideas of education:

. . . the very maxims set up to direct modern education are
enough to destroy all the seeds of knowledge, honour, wisdom,

and virtue among us. The current opinion prevails, that the study of Greek and Latin is loss of time; that public schools, by mingling the sons of noblemen with those of the vulgar, engage the former in bad company; that whipping breaks the spirits of lads well born; that universities make young men pedants; that to dance, fence, speak French, and know how to behave yourself among great persons of both sexes, comprehends the whole duty of a gentleman.

But beside this querulous passage, consider the following:

There is one circumstance in a learned education, which ought to have much weight, even with those who have no learning at all. The books read at school and college are full of incitements to virtue, and discouragements from vice, drawn from the wisest reasons, the strongest motives, and the most influencing examples. Thus young minds are filled early with an inclination to good, and an abhorrence of evil, both which increase in them, according to the advances they make in literature. . .

There are, finally, *A Complete Collection of Genteel and Ingenious Conversation* — usually referred to as *Polite Conversation* — and the *Directions to Servants*. It was in August 1731 that Swift wrote to Gay that he had retired to the country 'for the public good.' He had, he went on, two great works in hand,

one to reduce the whole politeness, wit, humour, and style of England into a short system for the use of all persons of quality, and particularly the maids of honour; the other is of almost equal importance, I may call it the Whole Duty of Servants, in about twenty several stations, from the steward and waiting-woman down to the scullion and pantry-boy.

Both works, it is believed, had their inception early in the century,— *Polite Conversation,* Swift told Pope, was begun about 1704 (Letter of 12 June 1732),— and there is obvious kinship between them and *Mrs. Frances Harris's Petition.* But Lord Berkeley's chaplain, for all his diabolical insight into the manners of both the drawing-room and the servants' quarters, did not have it in him to pursue his subject with the relentlessness understood so well by the dean. *Directions to Servants,* which remained unfinished, was first published in 1745; *Polite Conversation* was completed by 1737,

in which year Swift sent it to his friend, Mrs. Barber, who
published it in England in 1738.   They are superb pieces,
both of them, compounded of the purest Swiftian humour,
the secret of which died with the dean of St. Patrick's.

4

WITH a few notable exceptions, the pieces in verse and prose
which have been referred to in the three previous sections
are less interesting intrinsically than as evidence of the remarkable way in which Swift's powers held up.   Such is not
the case with respect to the purely literary verses of the last
period.   *The Journal of a Modern Lady*, the *Verses on the
Death of Dr. Swift*, *The Beasts' Confession*, *The Place of
the Damned*, and *The Day of Judgment* are among the
greatest of Swift's metrical compositions.   As has been said,
it was in verse that Swift spoke most naturally and effectively during his latter years.

The Journal of a Modern Lady, which was completed
early in 1729, sets forth in the familiar style and with all the
peculiar intensity which Swift brought to this manner, the
'annals of a female day.'   By noon my lady is awake and
pondering over her last night's misfortunes at quadrille ; at
four she goes to dinner, during which she disgusts everyone
present except her booby husband with her airs and stale
wit ; evening comes and with it tea, female friends, and
scandal :

> Now voices over voices rise,
> While each to be the loudest vies :
> They contradict, affirm, dispute,
> No single tongue one moment mute ;
> All mad to speak, and none to hearken,
> They set the very lap-dog barking ;
> Their chattering makes a louder din
> Than fishwives o'er a cup of gin ;
> Not schoolboys at a barring out
> Raised ever such incessant rout ;
> The jumbling particles of matter
> In chaos made not such a clatter ;
> Far less the rabble roar and rail,
> When drunk with sour election ale.

> Nor do they trust their tongues alone,
> But speak a language of their own ;
> Can read a nod, a shrug, a look,
> Far better than a printed book ;
> Convey a libel in a frown,
> And wink a reputation down ;
> Or by the tossing of the fan,
> Describe the lady and the man.

With the disbanding of this club my lady is left all alone, an easy prey to the spleen, but her vapours and hysteric fits vanish promptly with the appearance of her gaming friends. The table, cards, and counters are straightway set and play begins, lasting far through the night until the watchman calls, 'Past four o'clock.'

> Now all in haste they huddle on
> Their hoods, their cloaks, and get them gone ;
> But, first, the winner must invite
> The company to-morrow night.
> Unlucky madam, left in tears,
> (Who now again quadrille forswears,)
> With empty purse, and aching head,
> Steals to her sleeping spouse to bed.

Probably the strangest of all Swift's metrical compositions is *Death and Daphne,* written about 1730 for Mrs. Pilkington : the curiously dry description of Death has the proper macabre note, while the conceit from which it derives point is in quality almost 'metaphysical.'   Worried by the decrease in 'the burial article,' Pluto summons a council at which he decrees that Death must marry and get a numerous breed —

> Young deathlings, who, by practice made
> Proficient in their father's trade,
> With colonies might stock around
> His large dominions under ground.

Death goes to London, fits himself out like a beau,— the description should be read,— and with his mind running on his match seeks out Daphne, whose fame has reached his ears.   Behold the vanity of woman !   So far from drawing back in terror, Daphne hastens to complete the conquest which her beauty has begun.

> What pride a female heart inflames?
> How endless are ambition's aims:
> Cease, haughty nymph; the Fates decree
> Death must not be a spouse for thee;
> For, when by chance the meagre shade
> Upon thy hand his finger laid,
> Thy hand as dry and cold as lead,
> His matrimonial spirit fled;
> He felt about his heart a damp,
> That quite extinguish'd Cupid's lamp:
> Away the frighted spectre scuds,
> And leaves my lady in the suds.

In 1730 and 1731 there came from Swift's pen four noxious compositions, *The Lady's Dressing Room, A Beautiful Young Nymph going to Bed, Strephon and Chloe,* and *Cassinus and Peter.* The problems peculiar to these verses have been discussed elsewhere and need not be gone into a second time. From scatology one turns with relief to the capital verses entitled *Helter Skelter, or The Hue and Cry after the Attorneys going to ride the Circuit,* which exhibits Swift's complete mastery of vigorous rhythm:

> Now the active young attorneys
> Briskly travel on their journeys,
> Looking big as any giants,
> On the horses of their clients;
> Like so many little Marses
> With their tilters at their a — s,
> Brazen-hilted, lately burnish'd,
> And with harness-buckles furnish'd,
> And with whips and spurs so neat,
> And with jockey-coats complete,
> And with boots so very greasy,
> And with saddles eke so easy,
> And with bridles fine and gay,
> Bridles borrow'd for a day,
> Bridles destined far to roam,
> Ah! never, never to come home.

So far as the production of verse is concerned, the year 1731 proved to be one of the greatest in Swift's life, for it was then that the *Verses on the Death of Dr. Swift, The*

Place of the Damned, and *The Day of Judgment* saw the light, while *The Beasts' Confession* followed in 1732. These four pieces, together with *On Poetry — a Rhapsody* and *The Legion Club* display the great artist in his final phase. The *Verses on the Death of Dr. Swift* are dated November 1731. Most often quoted are the splendid lines describing how the news of his death is received by his women friends as they sit at cards,—'The Dean is dead : (and what is trumps?)',— but undoubtedly the most remarkable passages are those containing the author's estimate of himself. The following are the concluding lines of the piece :

> 'Perhaps I may allow the Dean,
> Had too much satire in his vein ;
> And seem'd determined not to starve it,
> Because no age could more deserve it.
> Yet malice never was his aim ;
> He lash'd the vice, but spared the name ;
> No individual could resent,
> Where thousands equally were meant ;
> His satire points at no defect,
> But what all mortals may correct ;
> For he abhorr'd that senseless tribe
> Who call it humour when they gibe :
> He spared a hump, or crooked nose,
> Whose owners set not up for beaux.
> True genuine dulness moved his pity,
> Unless it offer'd to be witty.
> Those who their ignorance confest,
> He ne'er offended with a jest ;
> But laugh'd to hear an idiot quote
> A verse from Horace learn'd by rote.
>   Vice, if it e'er can be abash'd,
> Must be or ridiculed or lash'd.
> If you resent it, who's to blame?
> He neither knew you nor your name.
> Should vice expect to 'scape rebuke,
> Because its owner is a duke?
>   'He knew an hundred pleasant stories,
> With all the turns of Whigs and Tories :
> Was cheerful to his dying day ;
> And friends would let him have his way.
>   'He gave the little wealth he had
> To build a house for fools and mad ;

And show'd by one satiric touch,
No nation wanted it so much.
That kingdom he hath left his debtor,
I wish it soon may have a better.'
And, since you dread no farther lashes
Methinks you may forgive his ashes.

The Beasts' Confession to the Priest, cited elsewhere
as a forcible and unadorned statement of *le mythe animal*
and the theme of Pride, is excellent as intellectual presenta-
tion but as artistic expression it suffers from too close definition.   Yet in *The Place of the Damned* and *The Day of
Judgment* lies proof that Swift could still match the idea
and the emotion in incandescent verse.   Many are of the
opinion that *The Day of Judgment* is his greatest metrical
composition.   It is, in any case, the perfect expression of
his closing period :

> With a whirl of thought oppress'd,
> I sunk from reverie to rest.
> An horrid vision seized my head ;
> I saw the graves give up their dead !
> Jove, arm'd with terrors, burst the skies,
> And thunder roars and lightning flies !
> Amaz'd, confus'd, its fate unknown,
> The world stands trembling at his throne !
> While each pale sinner hung his head,
> Jove, nodding, shook the heavens, and said :
> 'Offending race of human kind,
> By nature, reason, *learning*, blind ;
> You who, through frailty, stepp'd aside ;
> And you, who never fell — *through pride :*
> You who in different sects were shamm'd,
> And come to see each other damn'd ;
> (So some folk told you, but they knew
> No more of Jove's designs than you ;)
> — The world's mad business now is o'er,
> And I resent these pranks no more.
> — I to such blockheads set my wit !
> I damn such fools ! — Go, go, you're *bit.*'

EPILOGUE

'. . . I DESIRE you will look upon me as a man worn with years, and sunk by public as well as personal vexations. I have entirely lost my memory, uncapable of conversation by a cruel deafness, which has lasted almost a year, and I despair of any cure.' Thus Swift to Pope in August 1738. He was sinking rapidly under the weight of manifold afflictions and he knew it. He knew also that before death came he must pass through twilight into darkness, but until the last light went out he would assert, alone and in silence, his own individual existence as something different from the shadows striving to obliterate it. Death he did not fear; it was the loss of moral consciousness preceding death that he revolted against.

It was on 12 August 1742, in answer to a petition by two of his friends, that a commission *de lunatico inquirendo* was issued.[1] On 17 August the commissioners found him of unsound mind and memory, not capable of taking care of his person or fortune. Guardians were accordingly appointed and his person was entrusted to the care of the Reverend John Lyon. But behind the imbecile countenance, twisted by a stroke of palsy, a mind still glimmered. Swift's last recorded words are those mentioned by Deane Swift in a letter to Lord Orrery of 4 April 1744: 'This puts me in mind of what he said about five days ago. He endeavoured several times to speak to his servant — now and then he calls him by his name — at last, not finding words to express what he would be at, after some uneasiness, he said, "I am a fool."' The will of iron and the superb pride still triumphed over the shadows.

Swift died 19 October 1745, being then in his seventy-eighth year. He was buried on the night of the twenty-second in St. Patrick's Cathedral, not far from Stella.

If Swift is not the greatest of the Augustans, he is beyond question the most compelling. It is in respect of the man himself that judgments must differ most sharply, but whether

one regards his character with sympathy or with detestation
one will always feel the strange fascination of his personality.
As an artist, Swift's greatness is indisputable.   Partly, this
greatness lies in the incomparable matching of substance and
voice.   Its chief source, however, is not craftsmanship but
the moral realism through which all of Swift's terrific intellectual intensity found expression.   It is not as you think —
look !

A SELECTIVE BIBLIOGRAPHY OF SWIFT

A SELECTIVE BIBLIOGRAPHY OF SWIFT

In this bibliography are given only such items as the author has seen and taken into account.

A. Editions

The Prose works of Jonathan Swift. Ed. Temple Scott. London, 1897-1908. 12 vols. ('Bohn's standard library.')

A Tale of a tub, to which is added the Battle of the books and the Mechanical operation of the spirit. Ed. A. C. Guthkelch and D. Nichol Smith. Oxford, 1920.

The Drapier's letters to the people of Ireland. Ed. Herbert Davis. Oxford, 1935.

Swift : Gulliver's travels and selected writings in prose and verse. Ed. John Hayward. New York, 1934. [The text of *Gulliver's travels* given here is based upon Faulkner's 1735 edition, now recognized as the first authentic edition of the satire.]

The Poems of Jonathan Swift. Ed. W. E. Browning. London, 1910. 2 vols. ('Bohn's standard library.')

The Correspondence of Jonathan Swift. Ed. F. Elrington Ball. London, 1910-1914. 6 vols.

Journal to Stella. Newly deciphered and edited by J. K. Moorhead. New York and London, [1925]. ('Everyman's library.')

Vanessa and her correspondence with Jonathan Swift. Ed. A. M. Freeman. London, 1921.

The Letters of Jonathan Swift to Charles Ford. Ed. D. Nichol Smith. Oxford, 1935.

B. Contemporary Items

(In chronological order)

King, William. *Some remarks on the Tale of a tub. . . By the author of the Journey to London.* London, 1704.

Wotton, William. *Reflections upon ancient and modern learning. To which is now added a Defence thereof, in answer to the objections of Sir. W. Temple, and others. With Observations upon the Tale of a tub. . . Third edition corrected.* London, 1705.

A Complete key to the Tale of a tub ; with some account of the authors, the occasion and design of writing it, and Mr. Wotton's Remarks examin'd. London, 1710.

Dennis, John. 'To the Examiner. Upon his wise paper of the tenth of January, 1710/1.' In his *Original letters, familiar, moral and critical* (London, 1721), I, 296-302.

[? Smedley, Hugh.] *An Hue and cry after Dr. S—t.* . . London, 1714.

Essays divine, moral, and political. . . *By the author of the Tale of a tub, sometime the writer of the Examiner, and the original inventor of the Band-box-plot.* . . London, 1714.

Dr. S—'s real diary. . . London, 1715.

A Letter from a clergyman to his friend, with an account of the travels of Capt. Lemuel Gulliver. . . London, 1726.

Smedley, Hugh. *Gulliveriana: or, a fourth volume of Miscellanies. Being a sequel to the three volumes, published by Pope and Swift.* . . London, 1728.

Some memoirs of the amours and intrigues of a certain Irish Dean. . . *The third edition.* London, 1730.

C. Standard Biographies

(In chronological order)

Orrery, John Boyle, 5th earl of. *Remarks on the life and writings of Dr. Jonathan Swift.* London, 1752 [ptd. 1751].

Delany, Patrick. *Observations upon Lord Orrery's Remarks on the life and writings of Dr. Jonathan Swift.* London, 1754.

Swift, Deane. *An essay upon the life, writings, and character, of Dr. Jonathan Swift.* London, 1755.

Sheridan, Thomas. 'The life of Doctor Swift.' In *The Works of* . . . *J. Swift* . . . *arranged* . . . *with notes by T. Sheridan* (17 vols.; London, 1784), vol. 1.

Berkeley, George Monck. *Literary relics, containing original letters from.* . . *To which is prefixed, an inquiry into the life of Dean Swift.* London, 1789.

Scott, Sir Walter. 'A life of the author.' In *The Works of J. Swift* (19 vols.; Edinburgh, 1814. 2nd ed., 19 vols.; Edinburgh, 1824), vol. 1.

Mason, William Monck. A biographical study of Swift. In his *History and antiquities of the collegiate and Cathedral Church of St. Patrick* (Dublin, 1820), pp. 225-444.

Forster, John. *The life of Jonathan Swift*, vol. 1 [no more published]. London, 1875.

Craik, Henry. *The life of Jonathan Swift.* London, 1882. 2nd ed., London, 1894. 2 vols.

Stephen, Leslie. *Swift.* London, 1882. ('English men of letters.')

Collins, John Churton. *Jonathan Swift; a biographical and critical study.* London, 1893.

Van Doren, Carl. *Swift.* New York, 1930.

Gwynn, Stephen. *The life and friendships of Dean Swift.* New York, 1933.

D. Books, articles, correspondence, etc., devoted to Swift or containing references to him.

(In chronological order)

Spence, Joseph. *Anecdotes, observations, and characters of books and men. Collected from the conversation of Mr. Pope, and other eminent persons of his time.* London, 1820.

Pilkington, Lætitia. *Memoirs of Mrs. L. Pilkington.* Dublin printed, London reprinted, 1748-1754. 3 vols.

Delany, Mary, Mrs. *The Autobiography and correspondence of Mary Granville, Mrs. Delany. . .* London, 1861. 3 vols. Second series, London, 1862. 3 vols. [Mary Granville, who married Dr. Delany in 1743, met Swift during a visit to Ireland which extended from Sept. 1731 to April 1733. Her references to Swift are scattered through these six volumes.]

Warburton, William, bishop of Gloucester. Letter to Bishop Hurd, 18 Nov. 1751. Given as Letter xxxvi in *Letters from a late eminent prelate (W.W.) to one of his friends [Bishop Hurd]*, Kidderminster, 1808. [Concerns the relations between Lord Orrery and Swift.]

A review of Lord Orrery's *Remarks. Monthly review*, v (1751), 407-24, 475-87.

Richardson, Samuel. Letter to Lady Bradshaigh, 22 April 1752. In *The Correspondence of Samuel Richardson* (London, 1804), vi, 170-76. [Concerns Swift's relations with Temple.]

Shiels, Robert. 'The Revd. Dr. Jonathan Swift.' In Cibber's *The lives of the poets of Great Britain and Ireland to the time of Dean Swift* (London, 1753), v, 73-100.

A review of Delany's *Observations upon Lord Orrery's Remarks. Monthly review*, xi (1754), 56-77.

Amory, Thomas. *Memoirs of several ladies of Great Britain: interspersed with literary reflections. . .* [n.p.], 1755. [The passage concerning Swift is given by Pons, *Swift: les années de jeunesse et le 'Conte du tonneau'* (Strasbourg and London, 1925), p. 33 n.]

Hawkesworth, John. 'An account of the life of the Rev. Jonathan Swift, D.D., Dean of St. Patrick's, Dublin.' In *The Works of J. S. . . . with some account of the author's life, and notes . . . by J. Hawkesworth*, vol. 1 (London, 1755).

S., C.M.P.G.N.S.T.N. *Gentleman's magazine*, Nov. 1757, pp. 487-91. [An article, the purport of which is that Swift and Stella were half-brother and -sister, both natural children of Sir William Temple.]

Dilworth, W. H. *The life of . . . Jonathan Swift.* London, 1758.

Beattie, James. *Essays: on poetry and music as they affect the*

25

mind. Edinburgh, 1776. [Contains critical remarks on *Gulliver's travels.*]

Swift, Deane. Letter to John Nichols, 7 June 1778. In Nichols, *Illustrations of the literary history of the eighteenth century,* v (London, 1828), 380-85. [Deane Swift inquires who the author was of the article in the *Gentleman's magazine* for Nov. 1757, and goes on to show that Swift's mother could not have had an intrigue with Sir William Temple.]

A review of *A supplement to Dr. Swift's Works,* vol. II, 1779. *Monthly review,* LXI (1779), 356-65.

Johnson, Samuel. 'Swift.' In his *Lives of the English poets,* London, 1781.

Warton, Joseph. *Essay on the genius and writings of Pope,* vol. II. London, 1782. [Wharton quotes James Harris, *Philological inquiries* (London, 1781), on the subject of misanthropy in *Gulliver's travels.*]

Blair, Hugh. 'Critical examination of the style in a passage of Dean Swift's writings.' In his *Lectures on rhetoric and belles lettres* (Dublin, 1783), II, 138-64.

Percy, Thomas, bishop of Dromore. Letter to John Nichols, 25 March 1789. In Nichols, *Illustrations of the literary history of the eighteenth century,* VIII (London, 1858), 78-80. [In 1786 and 1787 there had been several references in the *Gentleman's magazine* to the rape said to have been committed by Swift at Kilroot. Bishop Percy investigated this story, and in this letter to Nichols reports that he can find no substantiation for it.]

Godwin, William. *The enquirer. Reflections on education, manners, and literature.* London, 1797. [Contains a discussion of *Gulliver's travels.*]

Swiftiana. London, 1804. 2 vols.

Barrett, John. *An essay on the earlier part of the life of Swift.* London, 1808.

Craufurd, Quintin. *Essai historique sur le Docteur Swift. . .* Paris, 1808.

Dunlop, John. *History of fiction.* Edinburgh, 1814. 3 vols. [Contains a comparison between *Robinson Crusoe* and *Gulliver's travels.*]

Jeffrey, Francis. A review of Sir Walter Scott's edition of *The Works of Jonathan Swift. Edinburgh review,* XXVII (1816), 1-58.

Berwick, Edward. *A defence of Dr. Jonathan Swift, dean of St. Patrick's, Dublin; in answer to certain observations passed on his life and writings, in the fifty-third number of the Edinburgh review.* London, 1819.

Allot, Richard, dean of Raphoe. Letter to Sir Walter Scott, 2 Feb. 1826. In *The Private letter-books of Sir Walter Scott,*

ed. Wilfred Partington (London, 1930), pp. 329-31. [In support of the story concerning Swift's alleged misconduct at Kilroot.]

Macaulay, Thomas Babington. A review of Courtenay's *Memoirs . . . of Temple*, 2 vols., London, 1836. *Edinburgh review*, LXVIII (1838), 113-87.

Wilde, Sir William R. W. *The closing years of Dean Swift's
life.* . . Dublin, 1849. 2nd ed. enlarged, Dublin, 1849.

Thackeray, W. M. 'Swift.' In his *English humorists of the
eighteenth century*, London, 1853.

Prévost-Paradol, Lucien. *Jonathan Swift, sa vie et ses œuvres.*
Paris, 1856.

Taine, Hippolyte Adolphe. 'Jonathan Swift.' In his *Histoire
de la littérature anglaise* (Paris, 1863-64), IV, chap. v.

Dilke, Sir Charles Wentworth. 'Swift, &c.' In his *Papers of a
critic* (London, 1875), I, 361-82.

'Swift.' *Blackwood's magazine*, CXIX (1876), 527-44.

Legg, J. Wickham. 'Swift's giddy fits.' *Academy*, 25 June
1881, p. 475.

Bucknill, J. C. 'Dean Swift's disease.' *Brain*, IV (1882), 493-506.

Hay, James. *Swift : the mystery of his life and love.* London,
1891.

Moriarty, Gerald P. *Dean Swift and his writings.* London,
1893.

Simon, Paul Max. *Swift ; étude psychologique et littéraire.* . .
Paris, 1893.

Birrell, Augustine. 'Dean Swift.' In his *Essays about men,
women, and books*, London, 1894.

King, Richard Ashe. *Swift in Ireland.* London, 1895. ('New
Irish library.')

Leslie, Alexander von W. 'Was Swift married to Stella ?' *An-
glia*, XVIII (1896), 1-55.

Skelton, Sir John. 'An apology for the Dean.' In his *Summers
and winters at Balmawhapple : a second series of The table-
talk of Shirley* (Edinburgh and London, 1896), II, 217-54.

Bailey, John Cann. 'Swift.' In his *Studies in some famous letters*, London, 1899.

Paul, Herbert. 'The prince of journalists.' In his *Men and
letters*, London and New York, 1901.

Bernard, J. H., dean of St. Patrick's. 'Dean Swift in Dublin.'
Blackwood's magazine, CLXXX (1906), 676-93.

Cordelet, Henriette. *Swift.* Paris, 1907. ('Cahiers de la Quin-
zaine.')

The Battle of the books. . . Ed. A. Guthkelch. London, 1908.
('The King's classics.')

Frye, Prosser Hall. 'Jonathan Swift.' In his *Literary reviews
and criticisms*, New York and London, 1908.

Rolleston, T. W. 'Two makers of modern Ireland.' *Fortnightly review*, XCI (1909), 1100-1116.

Lane-Poole, Stanley. 'The alleged marriage of Swift and Stella.' *Fortnightly review*, XCIII (1910), 319-32.

Smith, Sophie S. *Dean Swift*. London, 1910.

Jacobson, Arthur C. 'Literary genius and manic-depressive insanity with special reference to the alleged case of Dean Swift.' *Scientific American supplement*, 4 Jan. 1913, p. 2.

Dargan, H. M. 'The nature of allegory as used by Swift.' *SP*, XIII (1916), 159-79.

Thomas, Joseph M. 'Swift and the Stamp Act of 1712.' *PMLA*, XXXI (1916), 247-63.

Thompson, Elbert N. S. 'Tom Brown and eighteenth-century satirists.' *MLN*, XXXII (1917), 90-94.

Whibley, Charles. *Jonathan Swift*. Cambridge, 1917. (Leslie Stephen lecture, delivered 26 May 1917.)

Firth, C. H. 'The political significance of "Gulliver's travels."' *Proceedings of the British Academy, 1919-20*, pp. 237-59. (Read 10 Dec. 1919.)

Elder, Lucius W. 'The pride of the Yahoos.' *MLN*, XXXV (1920), 206-11.

Jones, R. F. 'The background of the *Battle of the books*.' *Washington University studies*, vol. VII, Humanistic series (1920), pp. 99-162.

Eddy, W. A. 'A source for *Gulliver's travels*.' *MLN*, XXXVI (1921), 419-22.

—— 'A source for Gulliver's first Voyage.' *MLN*, XXXVII (1922), 353-55.

—— 'Rabelais,— a source for *Gulliver's travels*.' *MLN*, XXXVII (1922), 416-18.

—— *Gulliver's travels; a critical study*. Princeton, 1923.

Goulding, Sybil. *Swift en France; essai sur la fortune et l'influence de Swift en France au XVIIIᵉ siècle, suivi d'un aperçu sur la fortune de Swift en France au cours du XIXᵉ siècle*. Paris, 1924.

Legouis, Pierre. 'Marwell et Swift: note sur un passage du *Conte du tonneau*.' *RAA*, I (1924), 240-42.

Secord, A. W. A review of W. A. Eddy's *Gulliver's travels; a critical study*. *JEGP*, XXIII (1924), 460-72.

The History of John Bull for the first time faithfully re-issued from the original pamphlets, 1712, together with an investigation into its composition, publication and authorship. . . Ed. Herman Teerink. Amsterdam, 1925.

Darnall, F. M. 'Traditional notions about Jonathan Swift.' *English journal*, XIV (1925), 514-21.

Gückel, W. and E. Günther. *D. Defoes und J. Swifts Belesenheit und literarische Kritik*. Leipzig, 1925.

James, M. R. 'Swift's copy of Dampier.' *TLS*, 26 Feb. 1925, p. 138.

Phillips, Mabel (Mrs. William Clyde DeVane). *Jonathan Swift's relations to science.* 1925. (Unpublished doctoral dissertation, deposited in the Yale University library.)

Pons, Émile. *Swift : les années de jeunesse et le 'Conte du tonneau.'* Strasbourg and London, 1925.

'Swift's Journal to Stella.' *TLS*, 24 Sept. 1925, pp. 605-6.

Gulliver's travels. The text of the first edition edited with an introduction by Harold Williams. London, 1926.

Baker, Harry T. 'Jonathan Swift.' *Sewanee review*, xxxiv (1926), 1-11.

Bradley, L. J. H. 'Swift's "Directions to servants."' *TLS*, 11 Feb. 1926, p. 99.

Digeon, Amélien. ' "Gulliver" et La Bruyère.' *RAA*, iii (1926), 245-47.

Eddy, W. A. *'The Anatomist dissected,—* by Lemuel Gulliver.' *MLN*, xli (1926), 330-31.

Firth, C. H. 'Dean Swift and ecclesiastical preferment.' *RES*, ii (1926), 1-17.

——'A story from *Gulliver's travels.'* *RES*, ii (1926), 340-41.

Wedel, T. O. 'On the philosophical background of *Gulliver's travels.'* *SP*, xxiii (1926), 434-50.

Whibley, Charles. *'Gulliver's travels.' Blackwood's magazine,* ccxx (1926), 549-60.

Williams, Harold. 'The canon of Swift : a late addition.' *RES*, ii (1926), 322-28.

——'The Motte editions of *Gulliver's travels.' Library*, 4th series, vi (1926), 229-63.

——'Swift's "Tale of a tub."' *TLS*, 30 Sept. 1926, p. 654.

'Gulliver's travels (October 28, 1726).' *TLS*, 28 Oct. 1926, pp. 729-30.

Gulliver's travels (extraits). . . Ed. Émile Pons. Paris. [1927]. ('Libraire Hachette.')

Firth, C. H. 'The canon of Swift.' *RES*, iii (1927), 73-4.

Hearsey, Marguerite. 'New light on the evidence for Swift's marriage.' *PMLA*, xlii (1927), 157-61.

Hubbard, Lucius L. *Notes on the Adventures and surprizing deliverances of James Dubourdieu and his wife. A source for Gulliver's travels. Also the Adventures of Alexander Vendchurch [London, 1719].* [Ann Arbor, Michigan], 1927.

Hutchins, Harry Clinton. A review of Williams's ed. of *Gulliver's travels,* London, 1926. *RES*, iii (1927), 466-73.

Pons, Émile. A review of Teerink's ed. of *The History of John Bull,* Amsterdam, 1925. *RAA*, iv (1927), 354-56.

White, Newport B. 'Bibliography of Dean Swift.' *TLS*, 9 June 1927, p. 408.

Williams, Harold. 'The canon of Swift.' *RES*, III (1927), 212-14.

—— 'A misplaced paragraph in "Gulliver's travels." ' *TLS*, 28 July 1927, p. 520.

'A misplaced paragraph in "Gulliver's travels." ' *TLS*, 30 June 1927, p. 460.

Miscellaneous poems by Jonathan Swift. Ed. R. Ellis Roberts. London, 1928.

Bennett, R. E. 'A note on the Cyrano-Swift criticism.' *MLN*, XLIII (1928), 96-7.

Dark, Sidney. 'Jonathan Swift.' In his *Five deans*. London, 1928.

Harrison, G. B. 'Jonathan Swift.' In *The social and political ideas of some English thinkers of the Augustan age, A.D. 1650-1750*, ed. F. J. C. Hearnshaw, London, 1928.

Leslie, Shane. *The skull of Swift; an extempore exhumation.* Indianapolis, Indiana, 1928.

Moore, John B. 'The rôle of Gulliver.' *MP*, xxv (1928), 469-80.

Ball, F. Elrington. *Swift's verse; an essay.* London, 1929.

Eddy, W. A. '*Gulliver's travels* and *Le théâtre italien*.' *MLN*, XLIV (1929), 356-61.

Read, Herbert E. 'Swift.' In *The sense of glory; essays in criticism*, Cambridge, 1929.

Rovillain, Eugene E. 'Jonathan Swift's *A Voyage to Lilliput* and *The Thousand and one quarters of an hour, Tartarian tales* of Thomas Simon Gueulette.' *MLN*, XLIV (1929), 362-64.

Williams, Harold. ' "Gulliver's travels": further notes.' *Library*, 4th series, IX (1929), 187-96.

—— 'A sentence of "Gulliver's travels" in Swift's hand.' *TLS*, 10 Jan. 1929, p. 28.

'The poems of Swift.' *TLS*, 4 July 1929, pp. 521-22.

Case, Arthur E. 'Philips or Carey?' *TLS*, 22 May 1930, p. 434.

Eddy, W. A. 'Ned Ward and "Lilliput." ' *N & Q*, CLVIII (1930), 148-9.

Leslie, Shane. 'Swift's handwriting.' *TLS*, 24 July 1930, p. 611.

Mayo, Thomas F. 'The authorship of *The History of John Bull*.' *PMLA*, XLV (1930), 274-82.

Rice, J. A., Jr. 'A letter from Stella.' *TLS*, 29 May 1930, p. 457.

Segar, Mary G. 'Philips or Carey?' *TLS*, 3 April 1930, p. 298.

—— 'Philips or Carey?' *TLS*, 24 April 1930, p. 352.

Williams, Harold. 'Stella's handwriting.' *TLS*, 5 June 1930, p. 478.

—— 'A Hue and cry after Dismal.' *RES*, VI (1930), 195-96.

Wood, Frederick T. 'Phillips or Carey?' *TLS*, 27 Feb. 1930, p. 166.
—— 'Philips or Carey?' *TLS*, 10 April 1930, p. 318.
—— 'Philips or Carey?' *TLS*, 8 May 1930, p. 394.
Darnall, F. M. 'Swift's religion.' *JEGP*, xxx (1931), 379-82.
Davis, Herbert. 'Swift's view of poetry.' In *Studies in English, by members of University College, Toronto* (Toronto, 1931), pp. 9-58.
Eddy, W. A. 'Tom Brown and Partridge the astrologer.' *MP*, xxviii (1931), 163-68.
Esdaile, Katharine A. 'The Fairy feast.' *TLS*, 12 Feb. 1931, p. 116.
S 'Notes on Swift.' *N & Q*, clx (1931), 350.
—— 'Swift and the Royal Society's *Philosophical transactions.*' *N & Q*, clxi (1931), 194.
Van Doorn, C. *An investigation into the character of Jonathan Swift.* Amsterdam, 1931.
Webster, C. M. 'The Yahoo's overthrow.' *TLS*, 14 May 1931, p. 390.
—— 'Temple, Casaubon, and Swift.' *N & Q*, clx (1931), 405.
—— 'Swift and the Royal Society's *Philosophical transactions.*' *N & Q*, clxi (1931), 99-100.
Williams, Harold. 'Mully of Mountown.' *TLS*, 19 Feb. 1931, p. 135.
Satires and personal writings, by Jonathan Swift. Ed. W. A. Eddy. London and New York, 1932.
Babcock, R. W. 'Swift's conversion to the tory party.' In *Essays and studies in English and Comparative Literature by members of the English department of the University of Michigan* (Ann Arbor, 1932), pp. 133-49.
Birss, John H. 'A volume from Swift's library.' *N & Q*, clxiii (1932), 404.
Darnall, F. M. 'Swift's belief in immortality.' *MLN*, xlvii (1932), 448-51.
Eddy, W. A. 'The wits *vs.* John Partridge, astrologer.' *SP*, xxix (1932), 29-40.
Frantz, R. W. 'Swift's Yahoos and the voyagers.' *MP*, xxix (1932), 49-57.
Nock, S. A. 'Not a Yahoo.' *Saturday review of literature*, 16 July 1932, p. 846.
—— 'Gulliver and Yahoos.' *Saturday review of literature*, 17 Sept. 1932, p. 113.
Webster, C. M. 'The puritan's ears in *A Tale of a tub.*' *MLN*, xlvii (1932), 96-7.
—— 'Notes on the Yahoos.' *MLN*, xlvii (1932), 451-54.
—— 'Swift's *Tale of a tub* compared with earlier satires of the puritans.' *PMLA*, xlvii (1932), 171-78.

—— 'Tom Brown and "The Tale of a tub."' *TLS*, 18 Feb. 1932, p. 112.

—— 'Swift and the English and Irish Theatre.' *N & Q*, CLXIII (1932), 452-54.

Williams, Harold. *Dean Swift's library.* Cambridge, 1932.

Gulliver's travels, a Tale of a tub, Battle of the books, etc. Ed. W. A. Eddy. New York, 1933.

Allen, Robert J. *The clubs of Augustan London.* Cambridge, Massachusetts, 1933.

Beattie, Lester M. 'The authorship of *The Quidnuncki's.*' *MP*, XXX (1933), 317-20.

Birss, J. H. 'A volume from Swift's library.' *N & Q*, CLXIV (1933), 334.

Dobell, Percy J. *A catalogue of works by Dr. Jonathan Swift, together with contemporary works relating to or illustrative of the life and works of the dean of Saint Patrick's, Dublin.* London [1933?]. (P. J. & A. E. Dobell's Catalogue no. 105.)

Gregory, Alyse. 'Stella, Vanessa, and Swift.' *Nineteenth century*, CXIII (1933), 755-64.

Gulick, Sidney L., Jr. 'Jonathan Swift's "The Day of judgement."' *PMLA*, XLVIII (1933), 850-55.

Taylor, William D. *Jonathan Swift, a critical essay.* London, 1933.

Webster, C. M. 'A possible source for *A Tale of a tub.*' *MLN*, XLVIII (1933), 251-53.

—— 'Swift and some earlier satires of puritan enthusiasm.' *PMLA*, XLVIII (1933), 1141-53.

Birss, John H. 'A volume from Swift's library.' *N & Q*, CLXVI (1934), 295.

Bonner, William H. *Captain William Dampier, buccaneer-author.* Stanford University, California, [1934].

Gold, Maxwell B. 'Swift's admission to Mrs. Whiteway confirmed.' *PMLA*, XLIX (1934), 964-65.

—— 'The Brennan affidavit.' *TLS*, 17 May 1934, p. 360.

Heidenhain, Adolf. *Über den Menschenhass. Eine pathographische Untersuchung über Jonathan Swift.* Stuttgart, 1934.

Higgins, T. F. 'Swiftiana.' *TLS*, 30 Aug. 1934, p. 589.

—— 'More Swiftiana.' *TLS*, 13 Dec. 1934, p. 895.

Kirkpatrick, T. Percy C. 'Faulkner's edition of Swift.' *TLS*, 12 April 1934, p. 262.

Morrison, Felix. 'A note on *The Battle of the books.*' *PQ*, XIII (1934), 16-20.

Rossi, Mario M., and Joseph M. Hone. *Swift; or, the egoist.* London, 1934.

Webster, C. M. 'Washington Irving as imitator of Swift.' *N & Q*, CLXVI (1934), 295.

Williams, Harold. 'The Brennan affidavit.' *TLS*, 24 May 1934, p. 376.

Yeats, W. B. 'The words upon the window-pane.' In his *Wheels and butterflies*, London, 1934.

Allhusen, E. L. 'A Swift epitaph?' *TLS*, 2 May 1935, p. 288.

Beattie, Lester M. *John Arbuthnot, mathematician and satirist.* Cambridge, Massachusetts, 1935.

Boyce, Benjamin. 'Predecessors of "The Tale of a tub."' *N & Q*, CLXVIII (1935), 110-11.

Korn, Max Armin. *Die Weltanschauung Jonathan Swifts.* Jena, 1935.

Leslie, Shane. *The script of Jonathan Swift and other essays.* Philadelphia, 1935.

McCain, John Walter, Jr. 'Swift and Heywood.' *N & Q*, CLXVIII (1935), 236-38.

McCue, G. S. 'A seventeenth-century Gulliver.' *MLN*, L (1935), 32-34.

Reimers, Hans. *Jonathan Swift : Gedanken und Schriften über Religion und Kirche.* Hamburg, 1935.

Rockwell, Frederick S. 'A probable source for "Gulliver's travels."' *N & Q*, CLXIX (1935), 131-33.

Webster, C. M. 'The satiric background of the attack on the puritans in Swift's *A Tale of a tub*.' *PMLA*, L (1935), 210-23.

Williams, Harold. 'A Swift epitaph?' *TLS*, 9 May 1935, p. 301.

—— 'The Drapier's Letters.' *TLS*, 6 June 1935, p. 364.

'New light on Swift.' *TLS*, 10 Jan. 1935, pp. 13-14.

Jones, Richard F. *Ancients and moderns. A study of the background of the Battle of the books.* Saint Louis, Missouri, 1936. ('Washington University studies' (new series), Language and Literature, No. 6.)

Secord, A. W. '*Gulliver* and Dampier.' *MLN*, LI (1936), 159.

Webster, C. M. 'A source for Swift's *A Meditation upon a broom-stick.*' *MLN*, LI (1936), 160.

ADDITIONAL BIBLIOGRAPHY

(A selective list of items which have appeared between
1937 and mid-1952)

A. Editions

The Poems of Jonathan Swift. Ed. Sir Harold Williams. Oxford,
1937. 3 vols.
The Prose works of Jonathan Swift. Ed. Herbert Davis. Oxford,
1937- (in progress). By mid-1952 the following vols. had
appeared : I, II, III, VI, VII, IX, X, XI. ('The Shakespeare Head
edition.')
Journal to Stella. Ed. Sir Harold Williams. Oxford, 1948. 2 vols.

B. Biographies, monographs, articles, etc., devoted to Swift or containing references to him.

(In chronological order)

Gold, Maxwell B. *Swift's marriage to Stella.* Cambridge,
Massachusetts, 1937.
Newman, Bertram. *Jonathan Swift.* London, 1937.
Nicolson, Marjorie, and Mohler, Nora M. 'The scientific back-
ground of Swift's *Voyage to Laputa.*' *Annals of Science*, II (1937),
299-334.
—— 'Swift's "Flying island" in the *Voyage to Laputa.*' *Annals of
Science*, II (1937), 405-30.
Sitwell, Edith. *I live under a black sun. A novel.* London, 1937.
Jackson, Robert Wyse. *Jonathan Swift, dean and pastor.* London,
1939.
Knight, G. Wilson. 'Swift and the symbolism of irony.' In his
The burning oracle. Studies in the poetry of action. London, 1939.
Berwick, Donald M. *The reputation of Jonathan Swift, 1781-1882.*
Philadelphia, 1941.
Clubb, Merrel, D. 'The criticism of Gulliver's "Voyage to the
Houyhnhnms," 1726-1914.' In *Stanford studies in language and
literature, 1941* (Stanford University, California, 1941), pp.
203-32.
Potter, George Reuben. 'Swift and natural science.' *PQ*, xx
(1941), 97-118.
Ross, John F. 'The final comedy of Lemuel Gulliver.' In *Studies
in the comic* (University of California publications in English,
vol. VIII, no. 2, 1941), pp. 175-96.
—— *Swift and Defoe : a study in relationship.* Berkeley and Los
Angeles, California, 1941.

378

Davis, Herbert. *Stella : a gentlewoman of the eighteenth century.*
New York, 1942.

Landa, Louis A. 'A modest proposal and populousness.' *MP*,
XL (1942), 161-70.

Davis, Herbert. 'The canon of Swift.' In *English Institute
Annual, 1942* (New York, 1943), pp. 119-36.

—— 'Swift and the pedants.' *Oriel Review*, I (1943), 129-44.

Landa, Louis A. 'Swift's economic views and mercantilism.' *A
Journal of English Literary History*, X (1943), 310-35.

Wittkowsky, George. 'Swift's *Modest proposal :* the biography of
an early Georgian pamphlet.' *Journal of the History of Ideas*,
IV (1943), 75-104.

Case, Arthur E. *Four essays on 'Gulliver's travels.'* Princeton,
1945.

Davis, Herbert. 'The conciseness of Swift.' In *Essays on the
eighteenth century presented to David Nichol Smith* (Oxford, 1945),
pp. 15-32.

Jackson, R. Wyse. *Swift and his circle : a book of essays.* Dublin,
1945.

Kliger, Samuel. 'The unity of "Gulliver's travels." ' *Modern
Language Quarterly*, VI (1945), 401-15.

Landa, Louis A., and Tobin, James Edward. *Jonathan Swift : a
list of critical studies published from 1895 to 1945.* New York,
1945.

Landa, Louis A. 'Jonathan Swift and charity.' *JEGP*, XLIV
(1945), 337-50.

—— 'Swift, the mysteries, and deism.' In *Studies in English,
Department of English, the University of Texas, 1944* (Austin,
Texas, 1945), pp. 239-56.

Rowse, A. S. 'Jonathan Swift.' In his *The English spirit ; essays
in history and literature*, London, 1946.

Ackworth, Bernard. *Swift.* London, 1947.

Davis, Herbert. *The satires of Jonathan Swift.* New York, 1947.

Fink, Z. S. 'Political theory in *Gulliver's travels.*' *A Journal of
English Literary History*, XIV (1947), 151-61.

Quintana, Ricardo. 'Situational satire : a commentary on the
method of Swift.' *University of Toronto Quarterly*, XVII (1948),
130-36.

Beckett, J. C. 'Swift as an ecclesiastical statesman.' In *Essays
in British and Irish history in honor of James Eaddie Todd*
(London, 1949), pp. 135-52.

Clifford, James L. 'Swift's *Mechanical Operation Of The Spirit.*'
In *Pope and his contemporaries : essays presented to George
Sherburn* (Oxford, 1949), pp. 135-46.

Hardy, Evelyn. *The conjured spirit—Swift.* London, 1949.

Stone, Edward. 'Swift and the horses : misanthropy or comedy ?'
Modern Language Quarterly, X (1949), 367-76.

Trevelyan, G. M. 'Jonathan Swift.' In his *An autobiography and other essays* (London, 1949), pp. 206-10.

Williams, Sir Harold. 'Swift's early biographers.' In *Pope and his contemporaries : essays presented to George Sherburn* (Oxford, 1949), pp. 114-28.

Memoirs of the extraordinary life, works, and discoveries of Martinus Scriblerus. Ed. Charles Kerby-Miller. New Haven, Connecticut, 1950.

Johnson, Maurice. *The sin of wit : Jonathan Swift as a poet.* Syracuse, New York, 1950.

Leyburn, Ellen D. 'Certain problems of allegorical satire in *Gulliver's travels.*' *Huntington Library Quarterly*, XIII (1950), 161-89.

Orwell, George. 'Politics vs. literature : an examination of *"Gulliver's travels."* ' In his *Shooting an elephant, and other essays.* London, 1950.

Starkman, Miriam Kosh. *Swift's satire on learning in 'A Tale of a tub.'* Princeton, 1950.

Tuveson, Ernest. 'Swift and the world-makers.' *Journal of the History of Ideas*, XI (1950), 54-74.

Elliott, Robert C. 'Swift's *Tale of a tub :* an essay in problems of structure.' *PMLA*, LXVI (1951), 441-55.

Leyburn, Ellen D. 'Swift's view of the Dutch.' *PMLA*, LXVI (1951), 734-45.

Kelling, H. D. 'Some significant names in *Gulliver's travels.*' *SP*, XLVIII (1951), 761-78.

Williams, Kathleen M. 'Gulliver's voyage to the Houyhnhnms.' *A Journal of English Literary History*, XVIII (1951), 275-86.

The Art of sinking in poetry. Ed. by Edna Leake Steeves. New York, 1952.

Davis, Herbert. 'Some free Thoughts of a Tory Dean.' *Virginia Quarterly Review*, XXVIII (1952), 258-72.

Ehrenpreis, Irvin. 'Swift's history of England.' *JEGP*, LI (1952), 177-85.

—— 'Swift on liberty.' *Journal of the History of Ideas*, XIII (1952), 131-46.

Elliott, Robert C. 'Gulliver as literary artist.' *A Journal of English Literary History*, XXIX (1952), 49-63.

BOOK I

CHAPTER I

On Swift's career at Trinity College, Dublin, see the following : John Forster, *The life of Jonathan Swift* (London, 1875), chap. ii ; Émile Pons, *Swift : les années de jeunesse et le 'Conte du tonneau'* (Strasbourg and London, 1925), pp. 122-35 ; and F. Elrington Ball, *Swift's verse ; an essay* (London, 1929), chap i.

1 Pope to Spence, *Spence's Anecdotes*, ed. John Underhill (London, [n.d.]), p. 87.

2 Swift's earliest authentic portrait — the one by Jervas and now in the Bodleian Library — dates from 1709-10. See Falkiner's essay on the portraits of Swift in *The Prose works of Jonathan Swift*, ed. Temple Scott (12 vols. : London, 1897-1908), XI, 3-56.

3 See Forster, *Swift*, chap. ii ; and Ball, *Swift's verse*, pp. 9-10.

4 See Ball, *Swift's verse*, pp. 10-11.

5 It should, however, be added that there were in Dublin at this time a number of well-informed men who were eager to advance the new science, and in 1683 the Dublin Philosophical Society was founded for the purpose of advancing the work of the Royal Society in London. Trinity College, so far from looking with disfavour upon the Society, supplied it with some of its most active members, among whom we find St. George Ashe, Swift's college tutor. But despite this enthusiasm for the new science among the men of Trinity College, the academic regimen which Swift knew remained what it had been when laid down by Laud in 1637. In chapter ii of her unpublished doctoral dissertation on *Jonathan Swift's relations to science* (1925), deposited in the Yale University library, Mabel Phillips (Mrs. William Clyde DeVane) gives an admirable account of the Dublin Philosophical Society and its connexions with Trinity College. I am greatly indebted to Mrs. DeVane for having furnished me with a copy of her dissertation, upon which this note is based.

6 Swift's *Ode to Temple* was long accepted as having been written, as stated in the title, at Moor Park in June 1689. To bring Swift's presence at Moor Park in June 1689 into accord with statements in the *Fragment of autobiography* it has been said that Swift joined Temple at Moor Park, accompanied Sir William back to Sheen later in 1689, and thereafter returned with him to Moor Park — see F. Elrington Ball, *The Correspondence of Jonathan Swift* (6 vols. ; London, 1910-14), III, 414n. But the *Ode to Temple* is now assigned to 1692 (Ball, *Swift's verse*, p. 22), and it seems safe to assume that Swift joined Temple at Sheen and was with him there until the Temples returned to Moor Park at the end of 1689 — 'we return'd at ye end of yᵗ year [1689] with him & his . . . Famely to More Parke' wrote Lady Giffard in her *Life of Sir William Temple* (given by G. C. Moore Smith in his edition of *The Early essays and romances of Sir William Temple*, Oxford, 1930).

7 *Fragment of autobiography, Prose Works*, XI, 377.

8 On the dating of these early metrical pieces, see Ball, *Swift's verse*, chap. ii. The *Ode to Sancroft* as well as the *Ode to Temple* was formerly dated 1689 ; Ball treats them both as of 1692, to which year they seem obviously to belong.

CHAPTER II

All those familiar with Miss Clara Marburg's study of Temple's thought — *Sir William Temple, a seventeenth century 'libertin'* (New Haven, Connecticut, 1932) — will appreciate how deeply I am indebted to her. For biographical data I have drawn to a certain extent upon Thomas P. Courtenay, *Memoirs of the life, works, and correspondence of Sir William Temple* (2 vols.; London, 1836). Temple's essays I quote from *The Works of Sir William Temple* (4 vols.; London, 1814).

M. Emile Pons — in his *Swift* — has treated Swift's residence at Moor Park in great detail, and though in many particulars I do not follow him, I have found his work of great assistance.

---

1 Lady Giffard's *Character* as given in *The Early essays and romances of Sir William Temple*, ed. G. C. Moore Smith, pp. 27-31.

2 '[Temple] was, *par excellence*, the man of taste.' Throughout Swift's writings there are constant references to 'taste' and 'men of taste.' By the former term Swift meant the attitude and instincts resulting from good sense, cultivation, and sound education ; and since Swift was dominated by the concept of uniformitarianism (see Book I, chap. iv of the present study), he believed that this attitude and these instincts were the same in all men of taste. It should be understood that wherever in the course of my study I use the word 'taste' I am using it in Swift's sense. There were other doctrines of taste. Temple, for instance — whose ideas regarding taste I do not discuss — took a point of view somewhat different from Swift's — see J. E. Spingarn's 'Introduction' (§ 9 : 'School of taste') in his edition of the *Critical essays of the seventeenth century* (3 vols.; Oxford, 1908-09) ; and Marburg, *Sir William Temple*, chap. iii.

3 See Marburg, *Sir William Temple*.

4 On Swift's toryism, see above all Keith Feiling, *A history of the tory party, 1640-1714* (Oxford, 1924), pp. 479 ff.

5 Culled from Thackeray's lecture on Swift in *Lectures on the English humorists of the eighteenth century*, *Works* (London, 1910-11), XI, 135, 137, 140-41.

6 Richardson to Lady Bradshaigh, 22 April 1752, *The Correspondence of Samuel Richardson* (6 vols.; London, 1804), VI, 170-76.

7 See Pons, *Swift*, pp. 146-47, 192-93.

8 The duchess of Somerset to Lady Giffard, 7-26 June 1709, *Martha, Lady Giffard, her life and correspondence*, ed. Julia G. Longe (London, 1911), p. 248. Miss Longe's book I have been unable to consult ; I am indebted to my friend Mr. Edward D. Holst for the quotation which I use.

9 It should be said that Pons seems inclined to believe, on the existing evidence, that Stella was Sir William's daughter (see his *Swift*, pp. 147-48n.). And Mr. Shane Leslie has recently written as though Stella's illegitimacy were beyond doubt — see his *Script of Jonathan Swift* (Philadelphia, 1935), p. 4. The last thing which the present writer desires to do is to become bellicose and querulous — as did Craik, for instance — when he finds himself in conflict with other writers over these and similar mysteries. My position, which I maintain tenaciously but without passion, is that none of the evidence *thus far adduced* to prove that Temple was Stella's father would stand in a court of law ; and that, since there can be an astonishing amount of smoke without any fire, one is unjustified in taking rumour for fact.

10 Evans's letter was first given by J. H. Bernard, then dean of St. Patrick's, in 'Dean Swift in Dublin,' *Blackwood's magazine*, CLXXX (1906), 676-93.

11 See Sir Walter Scott, 'A life of the author,' in *The Works of Jonathan Swift* (Boston, Massachusetts, 1883), I, 219-22, 221-22n.

CHAPTER III

The most thorough-going analysis of Swift's early verse is to be found in Pons, *Swift*. See also Ball, *Swift's verse*, chap. ii.

1 As previously noted (see note 8, chap. i), both the *Ode to Sancroft* and the *Ode to Temple* were formerly regarded as compositions of 1689. In treating them as of 1692 I follow Ball, *Swift's verse*, chap. ii.

2 Swift was by no means the only one who was taken in by the *Athenian Mercury*, for Dunton was careful to conceal the identity of himself and his colleagues, at the same time throwing out clever hints concerning the erudite membership of 'the Athenian Society,' under whose direction the *Athenian Mercury* was purported to be issued. In 1693 this deception was furthered — with Dunton's assistance — by Gildon's *History of the Athenian Society, for the resolving all nice and curious questions. By a gentleman, who got secret intelligence of their whole proceedings.* For an account of Dunton and his Society — upon which account I draw — see Robert J. Allen, *The clubs of Augustan London* (Cambridge, Massachusetts, 1933), pp. 188-92.

3 Every reader of the *Ode to Sancroft* must have been struck by the scientific imagery of this piece, particularly noticeable in the second stanza. In *Jonathan Swift's relations to science* Mabel Phillips (DeVane) has shown (pp. 121-22) that many of these images are to be found in the pages of the *Athenian Mercury*, though 'the parallel is never so exact as to make it clear that the *Athenian Mercury* was Swift's only source.'

4 Quoted from Ball, *Swift's verse*, p. 40.

CHAPTER IV

1 On the characteristic rationalism of the Enlightenment, see A. O. Lovejoy, 'The parallel of deism and classicism,' *MP*, XXIX (1932), 281-99. This article, upon which I draw so extensively throughout § 2 of this chapter, should be read by everyone interested in the ideas of the period.

2 On the neo-Stoicism of the Renaissance see the following : Léontine Zanta, *La renaissance du stoïcisme au XVIᵉ siècle* (Paris, 1914) ; J. B. Sabrié, *De l'humanisme au rationalisme : Pierre Charron (1541-1603) l'homme, l'œuvre, l'influence* (Paris, 1913) ; Henri Busson, *Les sources et le développement du rationalisme dans la littérature française de la renaissance* (Paris, 1922).

3 See George S. Brett, *A history of psychology* (3 vols. ; London, 1912-21), VOL. I; and Murray W. Bundy, *The theory of imagination in classical and mediæval thought (University of Illinois studies in language and literature,* XII, 1927, nos. 2-3).

4 Concerning the relation between sentimentalism and neo-Stoicism, see Miss Rae Blanchard's 'Introduction' in her edition of Steele's *Christian hero* (London, 1932). On Swift and sentimentalism, see T. O. Wedel, 'On the philosophical background of *Gulliver's travels,*' *SP*, XXIII (1926), 434-50, an interesting and suggestive article, though the central point — that Swift was consciously in revolt against the ethical point of view of sentimentalism — would seem to be overdone.

5 See Professor R. S. Crane's review of Bosker's *Literary criticism in the age of Johnson,* 'English literature, 1660-1800 ; a current bibliography,' *PQ*, X (1931), 177-78. Professor Crane points out that normally in neo-classical æsthetics as well as in ethics 'reason' did not mean the 'unimpassioned reason' of the Stoics but had reference rather to the general sentiments of men.

6 See the following : Murray W. Bundy, ' "Invention" and "imagina-

tion" in the Renaissance,' *JEGP*, xxix (1930), 535-45 ; J. E. Spingarn, 'Introduction,' *Critical essays of the seventeenth century* ; René Bray, *La formation
de la doctrine classique en France* (Paris, 1927). Cf. also Ruth L. Anderson,
Elizabethan psychology and Shakespeare's plays (University of Iowa studies,
humanistic series iii, 1927, no. 4).

7 See M. W. Bundy, *The theory of imagination.*

8 Cf. M. W. Bundy, 'Bacon's true opinion of poetry,' *SP*, xxvii (1930), 244-
64. In my statement of Bacon's views I draw directly from George Williamson, 'The Restoration revolt against enthusiasm,' *SP*, xxx (1933), 571-603.

9 *Answer to Davenant's Preface to Gondibert.*

10 'Dedication' of *The Rival ladies.*

11 See Herbert Davis, 'Swift's view of poetry,' *Studies in English, by members of University College, Toronto* (Toronto, 1931), pp. 9-58.

12 Throughout this paragraph I have drawn directly for substance and quotations from George Williamson, *SP*, xxx (1933), 571-603.

13 On the trend towards simplicity in prose style, see J. E. Spingarn, 'Introduction' (§ iv), in his *Critical Essays of the seventeenth century.* Cf. also
R. F. Jones, 'Science and English prose style in the third quarter of the
seventeenth century,' *PMLA*, xlv (1930), 977-1009 : 'The attack on pulpit eloquence in the Restoration : an episode in the development of the neo-classical
standard for prose,' *JEGP*, xxx (1931), 188-217 ; and 'Science and language in
England of the mid-seventeenth century,' *JEGP*, xxxi (1932), 315-31. For
further light on the development of sixteenth- and seventeenth-century prose,
see Professor Morris W. Croll's three articles : ' "Attic prose" in the seventeenth century,' *SP*, xviii (1921), 79-128 ; 'Attic prose : Lipsius, Montaigne,
Bacon,' *Schelling anniversary papers* (New York, 1923), pp. 117-50 ;
and 'The baroque style in prose,' *Studies in English philosophy. A miscellany in honour of Frederick Klaeber* (Minneapolis, 1929), pp. 427-56.

14 See the following articles by Mr. C. M. Webster : 'Swift's *Tale of a tub*
compared with earlier satires of the puritans,' *PMLA*, xlvii (1932), 171-78 ;
'Swift and some earlier satires of puritan enthusiasm,' *PMLA*, xlviii (1933),
1141-53 ; and 'The satiric background of the attack on the puritans in
Swift's *A Tale of a tub*,' *PMLA*, l (1935), 210-23.

15 On anti-rationalism see F. B. Kaye's 'Introduction' in his edition of
Mandeville's *The Fable of the bees* (Oxford, 1924) ; and Miss Blanchard's
'Introduction' in her edition of *The Christian hero.*

16 See Lucius W. Elder, 'The pride of the Yahoos,' *MLN*, xxxv (1920),
206-11 ; and, occasioned by the foregoing, Professor A. O. Lovejoy's article,
' "Pride" in eighteenth-century thought,' *MLN*, xxxvi (1921), 31-7.

17 On Swift's religion see F. M. Darnall, 'Swift's religion,' *JEGP*, xxx (1931),
379-82 ; and Darnall, 'Swift's belief in immortality,' *MLN*, xlvii (1932),
448-51. See also Hans Reimers, *Jonathan Swift : Gedanken und Schriften
über Religion und Kirche* (Hamburg, 1935).

CHAPTER V

All quotations from *The Battle, A Tale,* and *The Mechanical
operation* are from the edition of A. C. Guthkelch and D. Nichol
Smith (Oxford, 1920).

For a modern study of these satires there are three indispensable works : Guthkelch's 'Introduction' in his edition of *The
Battle of the books* (London, 1908) ; the 'Introduction' and historical and explanatory notes by Smith and Guthkelch in their
edition of *A Tale* and *The Battle ;* and Pons's critical study of the
satires in his *Swift.*

1 Dr. Charles Davenant to his son; given by Smith and Guthkelch, *A Tale of a tub,* pp. xii-xiii.

2 See Smith and Guthkelch, *A Tale of a tub,* p. xii.

3 See Johnson, 'Swift,' in his *Lives of the poets.*

4 Atterbury to Harley, 1704, *Hist. MSS. Com., Portland,* IV, 155.

5 Given by Stephen Gwynn, *The life and friendships of Dean Swift* (New York, 1933), p. 84.

6 By Smith and Guthkelch, *A Tale of a tub.*

7 By Smith and Guthkelch, *A Tale of a tub,* and by Pons, *Swift.*

8 On the ancient and modern controversy, the standard book was for many years Rigault's *Histoire de la querelle des anciens et des modernes* (Paris, 1856). This has been superseded by Hubert Gillot, *La querelle des anciens et des modernes en France de la Défense et illustration de la langue française aux Parallèles des anciens et des modernes* (Paris, 1914). See also J. B. Bury, *The idea of progress* (London, 1924).

9 See André Hallays, *Les Perrault* (Paris, 1926).

10 See A. Laborde-Milaà, *Fontenelle* (Paris, 1905); and Louis Maigron, *Fontenelle, l'homme, l'œuvre, l'influence* (Paris, 1906).

11 See R. F. Jones, 'The background of the *Battle of the books,' Washington University studies,* vol. VII, Humanistic series (1920), pp. 99-162. See also, by the same author, *Ancients and moderns. A study of the background of the Battle of the Books* (Washington University, St. Louis, Missouri, 1936), an expanded treatment of much of the material dealt with in the article of 1920.

12 See J. E. Spingarn's notes in his edition of Sir William Temple's *Essays on ancient and modern learning and on poetry* (Oxford, 1909).

13 The best account is by A. Guthkelch in his 'Introduction' in his edition of *The Battle.*

14 See Smith and Guthkelch, 'Introduction,' *A Tale of a tub;* and Pons, *Swift.* In what follows, my treatment of *A Tale* is often at odds with that given by M. Pons, but my indebtedness to his brilliant criticism is very great.

BOOK II

CHAPTER I

1 For the historical background, I have relied chiefly upon the following: Frederick W. Wyon, *History of Great Britain during the reign of Queen Anne* (2 vols.; London, 1876); G. M. Trevelyan, *England under the Stuarts* (New York, 1933); Trevelyan, *England under Queen Anne* (3 vols.; London and New York, 1930-34).

For the political background I have drawn upon the following: J. M. Robertson, *An introduction to English politics* (New York, 1900); *The social and political ideas of some great thinkers of the sixteenth and seventeenth centuries,* ed. F. J. C. Hearnshaw (London, 1926); *The social and political ideas of some English thinkers of the Augustan age, A.D. 1650-1750,* ed. F. J. C. Hearnshaw (London, 1928); and Keith Feiling, *A history of the tory party, 1640-1714* (Oxford, 1924).

2 See C. H. Firth, 'Dean Swift and ecclesiastical preferment,' *RES,* II (1926), 1-17.

CHAPTER II

In my discussion of the problems relating to church and state my indebtedness to Keith Feiling, *A history of the tory party,* is very great. I have also drawn upon Trevelyan, *England under the Stuarts,* and *England under Queen Anne.* I have consulted both *The social and political ideas... of the sixteenth and seventeenth centuries* and *The social and political ideas... of the Augustan age.*

On Swift's religion, see the following : F. M. Darnall, 'Swift's religion,' *JEGP,* xxx (1931), 379-82 ; 'Swift's belief in immortality,' *MLN,* xlvii (1932) , 448-51 ; and Hans Reimers, *Jonathan Swift : Gedanken und Schriften über Religion und Kirche* (Hamburg, 1935).

CHAPTER III

1 Regarding the chronology of Swift's metrical compositions of this period I have followed Ball, *Swift's verse.*

2 Thomas Birch, *The life of the Honourable R. Boyle* (1744), pp. 147-48.

3 It was the evils exhibited by nature that largely concerned the writers of eighteenth-century theodicies. On this entire subject, see A. O. Lovejoy, 'Optimism and romanticism,' *PMLA,* xlii (1927), 921-45.

4 I refer to Professor W. A. Eddy's recent studies of the Partridge affair : 'Tom Brown and Partridge the astrologer,' *MP,* xxviii (1931), 163-68 ; and 'The wits *vs.* John Partridge, astrologer,' *SP,* xxix (1932), 29-40. See also Eddy's note, 'Ned Ward and "Lilliput,"' *N & Q,* clviii (1930), 148-9. My account is merely a résumé of that given by Professor Eddy.

5 A bibliographical problem arises in connexion with *The Infallible astrologer.* On the relations between this work and *A Comical view of the transactions that will happen in the cities of London and Westminster* see Eddy, *N & Q,* clviii (1930), 148-49.

6 Mabel Phillips (DeVane) has discovered in the Yale University library in a collection of papers belonging to Thomas Hearne an anonymous and undated pamphlet entitled *A Further proof demonstrating the verity of heliocentrick directions in nativities,* which she tentatively ascribes to one George Parker and which she dates about 1706. This pamphlet, Mrs. DeVane shows, 'is in many ways an exact forerunner of Swift's attack upon Partridge' (*Jonathan Swift's relations to science,* pp. 254 ff.).

7 No one has ever challenged Swift's authorship of *A Description of the morning,* nor of the paper on style which appeared in No. 230 of the *Tatler* (Thursday 28 Sept. 1710), but the question whether any of the *Tatlers* between No. 9 and No. 230 contain material from Swift's pen is a matter of long-standing debate. In *Prose Works,* vol. ix. Temple Scott assigns nine *Tatlers* to Swift (Nos. 32, 35, 59, 65, 66, 67, 68, 70, 71) ; previously Sir Walter Scott had assigned Nos. 74 and 81 to Swift. But all of these ascriptions have been questioned either by Craik — *Life of Swift* (2 vols. ; London, 1894), i, 255n.— or by Ball in the *Correspondence,* i, 161n. Ball, after casting doubt on all previous ascriptions, would give Nos. 16, 21 and 31 to Swift (*Correspondence,* i, 166n.). With this problem of the Swift canon resting in hopeless confusion at the present, I have avoided it entirely by discussing only the *Description of the morning* and, in Book iii, Swift's unquestioned contributions to Nos. 230, 238, and 258 of the *Tatler.*

BOOK III

CHAPTER I

1 For the historical background I have used, principally, the following : Wyon, *History of Great Britain during the reign of Queen Anne ;* Trevelyan,

England under Queen Anne; and Feiling, *A history of the tory party, 1640-1714.*

2 In his edition of *The History of John Bull* (Amsterdam, 1925), Dr. Herman Teerink argues for Swift's authorship, but this contention has not been generally accepted — see Pons's review of Teerink's edition, *RAA,* IV (1927), 354-56 ; and Thomas F. Mayo, 'The authorship of *The History of John Bull,' PMLA,* XLV (1930), 274-82. The fullest and most recent discussion of the matter is given by Professor Lester M. Beattie in his study *John Arbuthnot, mathematician and satirist* (Cambridge, Massachusetts, 1935). Professor Beattie does not deny that in all probability Swift added touches to Arbuthnot's work ; and he is willing to grant that the preface to the fifth pamphlet, which in 1727 became the preface to the entire *History,* may have been of Swift's composing ; but with irresistible logic he shows that the body of the satire is to be attributed solely to Arbuthnot.

3 My discussion derives from C. H. Firth, 'Dean Swift and ecclesiastical preferment,' *RES,* II (1926), 1-17.

4 Firth, *ibid.*

5 Professor D. Nichol Smith — in *The Letters of Swift to Ford* (Oxford, 1935), p. xxxii — refers to the *Memoirs* as Swift's first work on returning to Dublin.

6 Professor D. Nichol Smith (*The Letters of Swift to Ford,* p. xxxii) has brought to light the fact that Swift was at work on *An Enquiry* as late as 1721.

7 See Trevelyan, *The age of Queen Anne,* III, 98-100.

8 Concerning the activities and publications of the Scriblerus Club, see the following : George A. Aitken, *The life and works of John Arbuthnot* (Oxford, 1892) ; Robert J. Allen, *The clubs of Augustan London* (Cambridge, Massachusetts, 1933) ; George Sherburn, *The early career of Alexander Pope* (Oxford, 1934) ; and Lester M. Beattie, *John Arbuthnot, mathematician and satirist.*

9 On the date of the first meetings of the Scriblerus Club, cf. Allen, *The clubs of Augustan London,* p. 263.

10 See Sherburn, *The early career of Pope,* pp. 71-72.

11 I mention only about half of the scattered Scriblerian fragments. It is very difficult to tell which of the numerous pieces fathered upon Martinus originated in the days of the Club's activities and which were composed at later dates by one or another of the members. The Scriblerian canon is discussed at length by both Allen, *The clubs of Augustan London,* pp. 260-83, and Beattie, *John Arbuthnot,* chs. iii and iv ; see also Sherburn, *The early career of Pope,* pp. 80-82. One of the most troublesome pieces is the *Memoirs of the life of Scriblerus* (London, 1723), which W. A. Eddy has attributed to Swift and reprinted in *Satires and personal writings, by Jonathan Swift* (London and New York, 1932) ; but the attribution to Swift is highly questionable — see Allen, *The clubs of Augustan London,* p. 273 ; Sherburn, *The early career of Pope,* pp. 273-75 ; and Beattie, *John Arbuthnot,* p. 263.

12 Chap. XVI in the 1741 edition of the *Memoirs;* in modern editions (Aitken's, for instance) this is given as chap. xiii. See Beattie, *John Arbuthnot,* p. 273, n. 1.

13 See Beattie, *ibid.,* p. 273, n. 4.

14 All the letters between Swift and Vanessa I quote from *Vanessa and her correspondence with Jonathan Swift,* ed. A. Martin Freeman (London, 1921) ; and in my account of the Swift-Vanessa episodes I am usually following that given by Mr. Freeman.

BOOK IV
CHAPTER I

¹ All references are to *Vanessa and her correspondence*, ed. A. Martin Freeman ; and it is from this edition that I quote.

² These two pieces, previously garbled into one, have only recently been given correctly by Professor Smith (*The Letters of Swift to Ford*, pp. 197-202).

CHAPTER II

¹ For Irish history my chief reliance has been upon the following : W. E. A. Lecky, *A history of Ireland in the eighteenth century* (5 vols.; London, 1919) ; Robert Dunlop, *Ireland from the earliest times to the present day* ([London], 1922) ; and Stephen Gwynn, *The history of Ireland* (New York, 1923).

² In this paragraph I am basing my statements chiefly upon the historical material presented by Temple Scott in his edition of the *Drapier's letters* (*Prose Works*, vol. VI).

³ From this point on, I draw directly upon the authoritative account of the war against Wood's halfpence given by Professor Herbert Davis in his recent edition of *The Drapier's letters to the people of Ireland* (Oxford, 1935). All quotations from the *Drapier's letters* are from this edition.

⁴ The Addresses are given by Davis, *ibid.*, pp. 193-95, whence I quote them.

⁵ Davis (*ibid.*, p. 374) finds it difficult to believe that Swift had anything to do with these verses.

⁶ Quoted from Davis, *The Drapier's letters*, p. 95.

⁷ According to Ball (*Swift's verse*, p. 193), Swift probably wrote or inspired these verses ; Davis (*Drapier's letters*, p. lxvi) thinks them the work not of Swift but of one of his group.

BOOK V
CHAPTER I

¹ 'The work of three distinguished scholars.' I am referring to the following : C. H. Firth, 'The political significance of "Gulliver's travels," ' *Proceedings of the British Academy, 1919-20*, pp. 237-259 ; Harold Williams, 'Introduction,' in his edition of the first edition of *G. T.* (London, 1926) ; and D. Nichol Smith, 'Introduction,' in his edition of *The Letters of Swift to Ford* (Oxford, 1935).

² Quoted from *The Letters of Swift to Ford*, ed. D. Nichol Smith, p. 92.

³ Almost all of my statements concerning the MS. of 1714 and its relation to *G. T.* as we know it I take over from Firth, *Proceedings of the British Academy, 1919-20*, pp. 237-59.

⁴ Quoted from *The Letters of Swift to Ford*, p. 97.

⁵ Quoted from *The Letters of Swift to Ford*, p. 101.

⁶ *The Letters of Swift to Ford*, p. 108.

⁷ Here I differ from Firth (*Proceedings of the British Academy, 1919-20*, pp. 237-59), who does not believe that chapter vi of the first voyage had a place in the 1714 MS.

⁸ All quotations from *Gulliver's travels* are from the edition of Mr. John Hayward (London, 1934), who gives the text of Faulkner's 1735 edition, now regarded as the authoritative one.

⁹ Quoted from *The Letters of Swift to Ford*, p. 122.

¹⁰ See D. Nichol Smith, *The Letters of Swift to Ford*, pp. xx-xxi.

¹¹ At this point I am drawing upon the following : Harold Williams, 'The Motte editions of "Gulliver's travels," ' *Library*, 4th series, VI (1926), 229-63 ;

Williams, 'Introduction,' in his edition of *G. T.*; Williams, ' "*Gulliver's travels*": further notes,' *Library*, 4th series, IX (1929), 187-96 ; and D. Nichol Smith, *The Letters of Swift to Ford*, pp. xliii-xliv.

¹² See Harold Williams, *Dean Swift's library* (Cambridge, 1932) ; and R. W. Frantz, 'Swift's Yahoos and the voyagers,' *MP*, XXIX (1932), 49-57.

¹³ On Swift's indebtedness to the authentic voyages see the following : A. W. Secord, review of W. A. Eddy's *Gulliver's travels ; a critical study*, *JEGP*, XXIII (1924), 460-62 ; R. W. Frantz, *MP*, XXIX (1932), 49-57 ; W. B. Bonner, *Captain William Dampier, buccaneer-author* (Stanford University, California, 1934), chap. ix ; and A. W. Secord, '*Gulliver* and Dampier,' *MLN*, LI (1936), 159.

¹⁴ On the imaginary voyage and its significance in European thought see the following : Gilbert Chinard, *L'exotisme américain dans la littérature française au XVI⁰ siècle* (Paris, 1911) ; Chinard, *L'Amérique et le rêve exotique dans la littérature française au XVII⁰ et au XVIII⁰ siècle* (Paris, 1913) ; Geoffroy Atkinson, *The extraordinary voyage in French literature before 1700* (New York, 1920) ; Atkinson, *The extraordinary voyage in French literature from 1700 to 1720* (Paris, 1922) ; Atkinson, *Les relations de voyages du XVII⁰ siècle et l'évolution des idées* (Paris, [1924]) ; and Louis Armand de Lom d'Arce, baron de Lahontan, *Dialogues curieux entre l'auteur et un sauvage de bon sens qui a voyagé*, ed. Gilbert Chinard (Baltimore, Maryland, 1931).

On the subject of Swift and the imaginary voyage see Pons's introductory remarks and notes in his edition of *G. T.* (Paris, [1927]) ; and W. A. Eddy, *Gulliver's travels ; a critical study* (Princeton, 1923).

¹⁵ In his edition of the *Dialogues curieux*.

¹⁶ Godwin, *The enquirer. Reflections on education, manners, and literature* (Philadelphia, 1797), p. 107. I have Prof. Alan McKillop of The Rice Institute, Houston, Texas, to thank for calling this passage to my attention.

¹⁷ Charles Whibley, '*Gulliver's travels*,' *Blackwood's magazine*, CCXX (1926), 549-60.

CHAPTER II

¹ Concerning these allusions, see C. H. Firth, 'The political significance of "Gulliver's travels," ' *Proceedings of the British Academy, 1919-20*, pp. 237-59.

² See note 7, Book v, chapter i.

³ It is given by Hayward in his edition of *G. T.*, pp. 833-34.

BOOK VI

CHAPTER II

¹ See D. Nichol Smith, *The Letters of Swift to Ford*, p. 161n.

EPILOGUE

¹ Needless to say, only the physician has a right to venture an opinion concerning the nature of Swift's disabilities, or to discuss the question whether or no the dean's last years were passed in 'insanity'. Sir William Wilde — in *The closing years of Dean Swift's life* (Dublin, 1849 ; 2nd ed. enlarged, Dublin, 1849) — was the first to approach these problems in anything like a modern, scientific way. The article by J. C. Bucknill ('Dean Swift's disease') which appeared in *Brain* in January 1882, pp. 493-506, has superseded Wilde's statement of the case and is the sanest discussion to date. Most recent writers upon Swift have been guided by Bucknill's diagnosis, and it is this which is reflected in my Epilogue.

INDEX

Accomplishment of the First of Mr. Bickerstaff's Predictions, The, 164, 166.

Acheson, Lady, wife of Sir Arthur, her mother, 340.

Acheson, Sir Arthur, 340.

Addison, Joseph, 67, 116, 123, 183, 193, 202-203, 236; Swift's letter to, 127; and Swift's verse, 162.

Advantages proposed by Repealing the Sacramental Test, The, 349.

Advice to the Grub-street Verse Writers, 242.

Æsop, *Fables*, 79-80.

Aitken, George A., his edition of *G.T.*, 319.

Allen, Joshua, 2nd Viscount, 350; Swift's attacks on, 347.

Anne, queen of England, 225; Swift urged to send her his *Proposal for the Advancement of Religion*, 123; and Swift's preferment, 192.

Answer to a Paper, called 'A Memorial of the Poor Inhabitants, Tradesmen, and Labourers of the Kingdom of Ireland, An,' 255, 346.

Answer to Several Letters sent me from Unknown Hands, An, 255.

Apollo Outwitted, 116, 163.

Apology for A Tale of a Tub, 86-87, 153, 168-170.

Arbuthnot, John, 36, 206, 244, 332; *The History of John Bull*, 180, 190; Swift's friendship with, 203-204; Swift-Arbuthnot correspondence, 212-213, 231, 303, 304, 305, 337.

Argument against Abolishing Christianity, An, 123, 130, 144, *145-146*, 147, 186.

Argyle, John, 2nd duke of, 226.

Aristotle, 59.

Ashe, Dillon, 115.

Ashe, St. George, afterwards bishop of Clogher, 115, 230.

Athenian Society, 33; *History of the Athenian Society*, 35.

Atterbury, Dr. Francis, later bishop of Rochester and dean of Westminster, 277; his remarks on *A Tale of a Tub*, 75; Swift's letter to, 232.

Author upon Himself, The, 192, 195, 218, 225-226.

Ay and No, 355.

Bacon, Francis, 63.

Barber, John, Swift's printer, 231, 242.

Barber, Mrs., the Dublin poetess, 341-342.

Battle of the Books, The, 9, 15, 20, 49, 57, 58, 75-76, *76-85*, 86, 94, 103, 153, 159.

Baucis and Philemon, 114, 116, 152, *158*, *162-163*.

Beast's Confession to the Priest, The, 71, 358, 361, 362.

Beautiful Young Nymph going to Bed, A, 65, 360.

Bentley, Richard, 93; his rôle in the ancient and modern controversy, 76ff.; *Dissertation upon the Epistles of Phalaris*, 80; *Dissertation*, 2nd ed., 80-81.

Bergerac, Cyrano de, his *Histoire comique de la lune* a source for *G.T.*, 303 ; his *Histoire du soleil* a source for *G.T.*, 303.

Berkeley, Charles, 2nd earl of, lord justice in Ireland, 106ff., 115, 123; Swift's squibs on, 153-154; Swift to accompany him to Vienna, 125.

Berkeley, countess of, wife of Charles, and Swift's *A Meditation upon a Broomstick*, 156.

Berkeley, George, afterwards bishop of Cloyne, 238; his *Theory of Vision* a source for *G.T.*, 303.

Bernier, 296.

Bettesworth, Serjeant Richard, Swift's altercation with, 349-351.

Bickerstaff papers, Swift's satiric attacks on John Partridge, 152, 162, 164.

Birrell, Augustine, 306.

Bolingbroke, Henry St. John, Viscount, 67, 237, 332, 333-334, 338; Swift's friendship with, 203; and Harley's Saturday dinners, 185; preparing Swift for *The Conduct of the Allies*, 187; and the *Craftsman*, 333; representation of in *G.T.*, 292, 308; his disapproval of *G.T.*, 304;

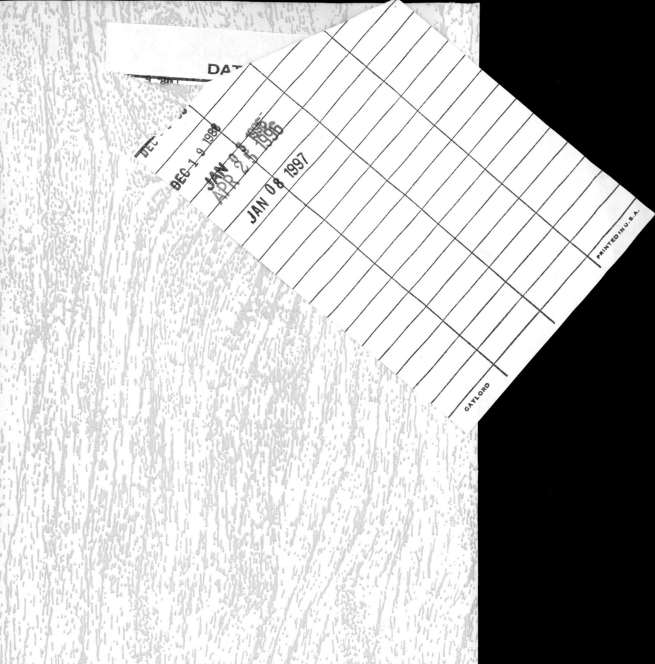